Uri Geller

Magician
or Mystic?

Also by Jonathan Margolis

Cleese Encounters
The Big Yin
Lenny Henry
Bernard Manning
Michael Palin

Uri Geller

Magician or Mystic?

JONATHAN
MARGOLIS

Welcome Rain Publishers
New York

URI GELLER: MAGICIAN OR MYSTIC?
First Welcome Rain edition 1999
All rights reserved.
Printed in the United States of America.

First published in Great Britain in 1998 by Orion Media
An imprint of Orion Books Ltd
Orion House, 5 Upper Saint Martin's Lane
London WC2H 9EA

Copyright © Jonathan Margolis 1998
Additional material for this edition Copyright © Jonathan Margolis 1999

Direct any inquiries to Welcome Rain Publishers
LLC, 532 Laguardia Place, Box 473, New York, NY 10012.

Library of Congress Cataloging-in-Publication Data
Margolis, Jonathan.
Uri Geller : magician or mystic? / Jonathan Margolis.
p.   cm.
Includes index.
ISBN 1–56649–025–1 (hardcover)
1. Geller, Uri, 1946–   . 2. Psychics Biography.
3. Magicians Biography I. Title
BF1283.G4M37   1999
133.8'092—dc21
[B]   99–36494
                                       CIP

Manufactured in the United States of America by BLAZE I.P.I.

First Edition: August 1999
1   3   5   7   9   10   8   6   4   2

In Memory of John Knopp

Acknowledgments

As well as to the Geller family and my own, my thanks are due to: Gabrielle Morris, John Knopp, Prof. Marcello Truzzi, James "The Amazing" Randi, Mike Hutchinson, Prof. John Hasted, Prof. Zvi Bentwich, Roni Schachnaey, Guy Bavli, Russell Targ, Dr. Hal Puthoff, Col. John Alexander, Paul McKenna, Dr. Friedbert Karger, Prof. Arthur Ellison, Tony Edwards, Prof. Brian Josephson, Prof. Yitzhak Kelson, David Berglas, Marvin Berglas, Lt. Commdr. Eldon Byrd, Matthew Manning, Ian Rowland, Dr. David Morehouse, David Blaine, Richard Winelander, Ruth Liebesman, Sen. Claiborne and Nuala Pell, Byron and Maria Janis, Bob and Candace Williamson, Charles Panati, David Dimbleby, Hazel Orme, Clare Kidd, Nigel Reynolds, Carl Palmer, Eamonn McCabe, Sabine Durrant, Neville Hodgkinson, Francine Cohen, Jack Houck, Ardash Melemendjian, Bob Brooks, Sam Volner, Uri Goldstein, Rebecca Hoffberger, Zev Pressman, Gary Sinclair, Suzanne Taylor, Peter Sterling, Guy Lyon Playfair, Miron Givon, Michael Rossman, Charles S. Kosczka, David Doubilet, Dr. Marc Seifer, Dr. Edgar Mitchell, Avi Seton, Miki Peled, Yasha Katz, Meir Gitlis, David Eppel, Ygal Goren, Prof. Amnon Rubinstein MK, Yechiel Teitelbaum, Eytan Shomron, Nurit Melamed, Ruth Hefer, John Randall, Capt. Gideon Peleg, Capt. Dov Yarom, Leah Peleg, Shoshana Korn, Rabbi Shmuley Boteach, David Robertson, Joy Philippou, Prof. Edward Grant, Ben Robinson, The Rev. Roger Crosthwaite, Yael Azulay, Louise Bourner, Simon Vyle, Liz Davis, Eileen Fairweather, Dr. Graham Wagstaff, Nick Jones, Robert and Sallie Stamp, Susan Wallace, Deborah Collinson, Chris Matthews, Judith Christie, Dave Donnelly, Vivienne Schuster, Jane Wood, Selina Walker, Bryony Coleman, and staff at the Bodleian Library, Oxford, the British Library Science Division, and the New York Public Library.

JONATHAN MARGOLIS

London, July 1998

Contents

Uri Geller

Magician
or Mystic?

Chapter 1

Greedy For Hidden Things?

"I believe this process. I believe that you actually broke the fork here and now."

Professor John Taylor, particle physicist and professor of mathematics at King's College, London, on BBC TV's *Dimbleby Talk-In*, with Uri Geller in 1973.

....

Twenty-five years ago, an acquaintance, now an international banker, was a student at the London School of Economics. He remembers going into a philosophy tutorial one November morning with three or four others to find that the tutor, a specialist in epistemology—the theory of knowledge—had scribbled a curious statement on the blackboard. It read: "Homo Sapiens . . . Homo Geller." The tutor explained that he had happened to watch Uri Geller perform on a BBC television show the previous Friday night and had been profoundly struck, as he thought about it over the weekend, by the evolutionary implications of this excitable, good-looking young Israeli, with his apparent abilities to bend metal with the power of his mind, to stop and start watches and to read other people's thoughts.

Geller had just arrived in Britain from the United States, where he had been a media sensation, and was now taking Europe by storm. In America, he had been the subject of major pieces in *Time* and *Newsweek*, of a cautiously approving editorial in the *New York Times*—and an "exposure" in *Popular Photography*, which managed with trick photography to replicate an ability Geller claimed: that he could be photographed through a camera lens cap. In Europe, now, he was the cover story in *Paris Match*, *Der Spiegel* and *Oggi* and hundreds of other magazines. In Britain, everyone was talking about him, and the newspapers were referring daily in front-page stories to Gellermania as the successor to Beatlemania. He featured on a huge scale in everything from the most popular tabloids to the weighty *Observer*, which made him its magazine cover story. Even the usually sober *New Scientist* ran a cover story on him, sixteen pages long, that culminated in the verdict that he was simply a good magician. The very next day, an article in *Nature* validated some of his paranormal powers.

The LSE epistemology tutorial on that November Monday morning had a sense of unusual purpose, of urgency, even. This man Geller was not some intellectual abstraction or a figure from ancient mythology. He was twenty-six and in town, hopping from broadcast studio to newspaper interview to physicist's laboratory. The media hype and public excitement was approaching the heights you might expect if a friendly Martian had landed.

Public hysteria was one thing, but a philosophy don at one of the world's most important universities and his high-flying young students had to look at Geller's claims in a cool, dispassionate manner. *If* the phenomena he demonstrated were genuine and not a series of sophisticated conjuror's stunts, then his emergence, it was agreed, was a deeply significant development for mankind. Were there other human beings like him, the tutorial group wondered. What would happen if two beings of Geller's power were to mate? Would this mean that those of us without such a mental capacity would soon be slaves to superhumans?

Uri Geller became a controversial figure worldwide, hailed by many serious scientists as a psychic superstar, and courted by celebrities, politicians and heads of state. He submitted to exhaustive laboratory experiments by physicists all over the world, some of whose results were intriguing. Other scientists denounced him as a fraud, having picked methodological holes in the same experiments. A number of professional stage magicians were outraged; they, after all, made their living by faking "paranormal" phenomena—a skill that convinced them that such miracles did not happen. No upstart was going to tell experts in creating illusion that they might have lived their professional lives under one.

Geller worked himself to the point of illness in achieving his childhood ambition, which was not so much to be a globally renowned miracle worker as to be rich and have endless beautiful girls running after him. As one of his closest friends in New York, the classical pianist Byron Janis, confides today: "He didn't want to be a psychic, he wanted to be a friggin' rock star." He certainly became one of the most famous people in the world, even if at times, his psychic career seemed to be verging on farce. In 1975, on a live NBC *Tonight* show with Johnny Carson, he failed for twenty-two minutes to make anything remotely paranormal happen. Carson is an amateur magician, who took professional advice on how he might best destabilize Geller and catch him out cheating. Whether he succeeded at disproving Geller was a matter of hot debate, and continues to be nearly twenty-five years later. The encounter left Geller depressed and embarrassed—even if for many people, his failure reinforced their belief in him: their perception was that real psychics are easily upset by aggressively doubting Thomases; mere magicians *always* succeed with their tricks. With characteristic optimism, and to the annoyance of his enemies, Geller overcame this setback and carried on in the US, performing, convincing people of his powers and being sought out as a friend and guru by his fellow celebrities. John Lennon would meet him for coffee; Salvador Dali had him to stay as a guest. Geller even appeared again on the *Tonight* show with rather more success—although without Carson in the chair.

In 1984, after a short period living on the slopes of Mount Fuji in Japan in an attempt to find an inner peace he felt he lacked in New York, Geller was still restless, and moved with his young family to England, where today he lives in a large house with elegant grounds by the river Thames. Here, he quietly cultivates rather mysterious business activities, which appear to be of a psychic nature but which he does not talk about openly. They are anything but imaginary, however: they provide his family with an enviable helicopters-and-five-star-hotels lifestyle—and himself with the financial security to pursue charitable interests, as well as novelwriting and the occasional small-scale public performance, just for fun.

So what *was* the Geller phenomenon all about? Could there have been something in it, beneath all the fun and hype, the showbiz and the commercialism? If Geller was genuine, his telepathy and psychokinesis challenged our most fundamental ideas about the laws of nature, as well as much of our understanding of brain function. If he was more than an illusionist, and science was unable to explain his abilities, then reason and science would begin to be regarded as illusory. It was no wonder that conservative scientists were at one with conjurors in their dismissal of Geller. Yet in the thirty years since he emerged, little has become of the new vision he seemed to offer of the human mind's unknown capabilities. He became less a figure of awe, and more a tolerated eccentric, loved by the tabloids for a ready quote, but to whom the label "Dubious" is more or less permanently attached in the mind of the intelligentsia.

The Uri Geller story is complex and, at times, baffling. The filmmaker Ken

Russell, who recently made a rather peculiar movie, *Mindbender*, based on Geller's life, summed up the enigma of his subject. Was Geller genuine, he was asked. "Only God knows," Russell replied, "and he's not telling."

What we do know is that Geller is driven by the longing to be regarded as more than a charismatic man who can bend cutlery by psychic means. A vegetarian, an exercise fanatic and self-appointed world-peace campaigner, he somehow lives an ascetic life even within the luxurious surroundings he has bought, and seems determined to fight his brash image. He will travel across the country on a Sunday to open a Scout fête, and happily bend a few spoons for those who crowd round him, even though he says it is an exhausting process. He wants to become a kind of ambassador for the paranormal; his message is that *everyone* has paranormal powers, not just him. He sees himself increasingly as an enabling power, and is constantly on the lookout for young Uri Gellers to carry this message beyond his lifetime until, he hopes, it is universally accepted.

Asked how he explains his powers, Geller is bashful. Perhaps he is just kidding when he says they might spring from some errant UFO commander's idea of a joke: "Perhaps they thought they'd give some ordinary guy these abilities just to see how the rest of the human race coped with it." He claims that he does not really understand his powers, and that he is scared to use them to what he thinks might be their fullest extent.

What follows is partly a biography of Geller, partly a journalistic investigation, and partly an account of my own wary journey of discovery into regions I had never previously visited, mysterious underworlds inhabited by paranormalists, psychic researchers, magicians—and scientists.

Most people find they have a more succinct—not to mention a more judicious—view of puzzling matters after sleeping on them for a night or two. In the case of most of Uri Geller's supporters and detractors, who have been known to swap places, the fact that Geller is still very much around after nearly thirty years has given them plenty of time to cogitate, assess, reassess and sleep on their final verdict. They have been afforded the luxury of as much hindsight as anyone could wish for. What *do* those who put their necks and reputations on the line for Uri Geller twenty-five years ago think in retrospect of him and his powers? What was done that was not revealed at the time? And what new research has been conducted on Geller?

Readers are entitled, of course, to know from what position I started my voyage round Uri Geller. The answer is: considerable skepticism. I was the last writer I would have expected to spend two years researching a book on the man. I am proud of having written a debunking piece on UFO's for *Time* magazine, have been delighted to be dismissive in print of such people as fortune-tellers and, when once visiting what was supposed to be the most haunted house in Britain, I was so convinced that the cause of the "mysterious" poltergeist effects was the non-paranormal mischief of a recessive-looking Uncle Fester character closeted upstairs that I refused to write the article I had gone to research. Also, to the great detriment of the family finances, I declined thirteen years ago to embark on a book that would follow up an article I had written for a British newspaper on how rabbis in Israel were using computers to discover mysterious hidden messages in the Hebrew of the Torah, the Five Books of Moses. After writing the article I became convinced that the theory behind the rabbis' work was fatally flawed, and dropped the research, despite being asked repeatedly by publishers to investigate further. A decade later, Michael Drosnin of the *Washington Post* developed the "hidden messages" theory into a worldwide bestseller, *The Bible Code*, which has earned him millions. I still think the theory is fallacious. Perhaps I'm wrong, but I hope I make the point that I think I have a decently jaundiced eye.

When I started researching Uri Geller two years ago, it was at a time of something approaching a worldwide paranormal orgy. *The X-Files* was an international cult, the UFO film *Independence Day* was the big summer hit, and a John Travolta movie, *Phenomenon*, with strong elements of Uri Geller in it, was also taking millions at the box office. Alternative-medicine pages were appearing in serious newspapers, while factual-style TV shows on the paranormal, such as the BBC's *Out Of This World*, were achieving huge ratings. It was almost as if, with the approaching end of the millennium, perhaps, in mind, there was mass popular dissatisfaction with the limits that science and technology impose on what is considered possible.

To a journalist and author who specializes in writing on the wackier, more bizarre side of current trends and events, as well as on comedy and—from a strictly bemused viewpoint—technology, this fascination with the unexplained seemed itself inexplicable. Was it not a perverse turn in mass thinking that what was once magical had become mundane, that while miracles such as medicine, computers, communications and cheap world travel were being taken for granted, we were all desperately seeking new magic, new mysteries? I recognized that the media and publishing were slightly culpable in this, and always had been since long before the mid-1990s supernatural boom and *The X-Files*. I had been impressed by a sentence the seventeenth-century London physician William Gilbert used in a book on magnetism, the spoon-bending of its day—some believed in this strange power, others were deeply skeptical. The problem was that although magnetism was clearly *something*—maybe sorcery, maybe a real physical force—people credited the mysterious, invisible energy with the most unlikely qualities. Its ability to remove the power of sorcery from women, put demons to flight, reconcile married couples, cure gout and make one "acceptable and in favor with princes" were just a few. As Gilbert complained: "With such idle tales and trumpery do plebeian philosophers delight themselves and satiate readers greedy for hidden things."

While accepting that science can be a little stubborn, and that it is marred by a regrettable tendency to brand some mavericks within its ranks as "heretical"—a strange word indeed for scientists to use—I have to say that until June 1996 the paranormal boom had left me unmoved. Indeed, outside the mental exclusion zones we all erect for ourselves—the odd superstition, the occasional trivial feeling that some coincidences are a little too strange to put down to chance alone—I was a devout rationalist. Scoffing at the paranormal seemed perfectly respectable.

Trying to establish the real story of Uri Geller has been an arduous, although continually fascinating, excursion. I have taken 22 flights, driven 11,000 miles on three continents, read (and often reread) 44 books, had 75 interviews with Geller's friends and enemies, spent countless hours in libraries in London, Oxford and New York searching for obscure, forgotten articles with some light to shed on my subject. I've met some intriguing and often delightful people along the way, from Geller's nemesis, the impish Canadian magician and ultra-rationalist James Randi, to John Alexander, a retired United States Special Forces colonel, who studied the paranormal as a non-lethal military weapon and believes strongly in Geller, to elderly Hungarian-Jewish ladies in Israel, who knew Geller as a spoon-bending toddler.

I have also spent days interviewing Geller, mostly while traipsing along the banks of the Thames in all weathers as he walks his dogs. These several-mile hikes, almost always in rain and thick mud, helped me to develop a real liking for him. I am pretty sure, however, that he has not paranormally warped my objectivity, or seduced me into relying on his version of events if there were other people to ask. And I am confident that the evidence I have unearthed from third parties, much of it never before revealed, will seriously challenge the preconceptions of both skeptics and believers.

Journalists are apt to be drawn, by heretical thought, lateral views, and evidence that goes against the grain, to challenge received wisdom: it is our duty to swim against the tide. A 1974 poll by the London *Daily Mail* recorded that

95 percent of the newspaper's readers believed that Uri Geller had psychic powers, yet I think that received wisdom in the late 1990s is that Geller is interesting, but a bit of a joker, and possibly a charlatan.

Because I believe that many intelligent people have come to doubt that Geller is "real," I admit that I found it more noteworthy, both journalistically and intellectually, when unexpected voices turned out to support him rather than when the predictable ones denigrated him. Similarly, when some of his less plausible-sounding stories were surprisingly backed up by independent witnesses, I felt a frisson of excitement (I have to say I would feel the same if I discovered Saddam Hussein was a fan of *Monty Python's Flying Circus*, or that Professor Richard Dawkins was training for the priesthood). But there is a more important point here: the kernel of the anti-Geller argument is a perfect example of the revered principle of Occam's Razor, which proposes that, all things being equal, the simplest explanation of anything is the most likely one: in other words, the heavyweight skeptics say, Geller cheats. It's a simple message, devastating if true, yet there is a limit to the number of times it can be restated. The opposite argument, that he is genuine, is bound to be more interesting, even if it were ultimately wrong.

There are more sides to the Geller story than the question of whether he is "real." For example, his position as a cultural icon is fascinating. Coming to live in England was a successful move for him and his family in all but one respect: regardless of where people lie on the skepticism–belief axis, there is a perception problem of him in Britain, which has held back many people, but particularly the middle-class intelligentsia, from taking him seriously. It is among such people that modesty, understatement and a subtle sense of irony are most admired. Even his best friends confess that while Uri Geller has many admirable qualities, he is not an exemplar of any of these. His style, consequently, tends either not to be appreciated or is found funny.

It has to be said that, unlike in the USA, Israelis are a rarity in the UK. Whether people in Britain identify Geller as Israeli or not, his direct, typically Sabra style is perceived as a little over-the-top: if Uri Geller thinks he is good at something, he has no problem in telling the world so. This is fine in the US and in Israel, where Geller is still a hugely respected favorite son, but the American maxim, "If it's true, it ain't braggin," tends not to apply in the UK, where you are not supposed to brag even if something *is* true. And Geller is not afraid of the over-ostentatious gesture, which also can cause the British to blanche a little. It would be fair to assume that Uri Geller is one of the few novelists who saw no credibility problem in the summer of 1997 in arriving at the Hay-on-Wye literary festival, that most quirky and bookish of annual British arts events, by private helicopter.

In many senses, Geller has never quite "got" Britain in the instinctive way he understood America, and this frequently makes him appear to the reticent British as his own worst PR man, psychic powers or no. That he is a typically extrovert showbusiness personality as well as being a typical Israeli just about ensures that in Cool Britannia he is often judged, on stylistic grounds alone, as distinctly uncool.

But OK, as everyone demands of me these days. You've explained where you are coming *from*, now tell us, where did you finish up? What was *your* verdict on Uri Geller? Is he real? Is he a liar? Can he still bend spoons? Is he as earnest as he seems, or does he have a funny side? Did all your clocks stop?

For two years, friends and colleagues have been listening to my travellers' tales and quizzing me on my developing personal theories as to the truth about the world's greatest living parapsychological exponent. "Interesting," they say, some believing I have given him too much credit, others angry that I have been too hard on him. "But in the end," they ask, "did you come to any conclusions?"

After two years of hearing it from all sides, I think I can safely say that, yes, I did.

Chapter 2

Into the Light

"I did that."

Uri Geller aged six, after making the watch of a schoolfriend, Mordechai, advance by an hour

....

Perhaps the story begins in Budapest, Hungary, in the 1920s, where a strikingly handsome young man called Tibor Geller was always told as he grew up that, although his family was devoutly Jewish and his grandfather was a prominent rabbi, there was gypsy blood somewhere way back in the Geller line. A corny old family myth, perhaps, and not uncommon in Hungary, but one that, later in his life, Tibor would often ponder in a different place and different circumstances, and wonder if it just *might* explain some things about his unusual son Uri.

Or maybe the real start of the mystery can be explained only by Uri himself, because he alone was there when it happened—and immediately we have our first problem in unravelling the enigma of Uri Geller. Family tales of Romany blood sound unlikely enough, but Uri's account of the genesis of his story invites skepticism from the first word. For one thing, it is the account of a child of four or five years old—not that Uri has changed his strange story in nearly fifty years. For another thing, everyone who recalls little Uri remembers a child with a famously fertile imagination although, significantly, not a child who lied. To put it at its baldest, Uri Geller is semi-convinced that he had a contact experience with extraterrestrial aliens in the middle of the day in a crowded quarter of Tel Aviv, Palestine, in a shady, walled garden, which then existed on a spot now occupied by a modern, eight-storey branch of the Hapoalim Bank.

There is characteristic bravery in his sticking for half a century to this clearly profound memory of what we have to assume was *something*, even if it was not quite a close encounter with a UFO. It has probably done this most image-conscious of men no favors, won him no friends, made him no fans or adherents, but he continues to insist that it happened. "Joan of Arc" recollections, as they are known, from childhood, early visions of a flash of light, are quite common among people who go on to have highly unusual lives with a touch of destiny about them. The memories seem similar. According to legend, in around 1425, when she was thirteen, Joan sat down under a tree when she was tired from playing, only to feel her world fade away as a globe of light came down beside her and adult voices she later identified as those of Saints Catherine, Margaret and Michael began to speak to her about how she would lead France against the invading English armies. In the 1970s one of the best reputed American "remote viewers"—as the US Army refers to psychics—was a Vietnam veteran from Florida called Joe McMoneagle. McMoneagle's Joan of Arc moment came in an orange grove one night in 1957 when he, too, was tired and "floated off." He was told by some speaking light source that he would be a strong soldier one day, who would go off to fight a war but come back unharmed.

Speaking as a fifty-two-year-old multimillionaire with powerful friends all over the world, Uri Geller makes no apologies for his account of the apparent event. It occurred in the shady garden of an old Arabic house opposite the Gellers' flat, which was at 13 Betzalel Yaffe, on the corner of the busy Yehuda Halevi Boulevard. In the late 1940s, as now, this was a noisy, vibrant downtown area, packed with characteristic Tel Aviv apartment blocks of four or five floors, alongside shops, offices and schools. Everywhere there were motorcycles, hooting, people shouting and arguing, dogs barking, children laughing, old ladies scuttling, and delicious lunch-time cooking smells coming from every apartment. The buildings, like the cooking and the faces on the streets, were a kaleidoscopic mix of Eastern and European, modern and ancient. Every few meters there was another dark doorway, with a glimpse of a still darker interior. For such a built-up district, though, Nature put up an impressive show: tiny patches of intense greenery, palm trees and flowers, some growing wild, but others assiduously cultivated, squeezed somehow between the buildings and defied the burning heat of the day. The gardens that Uri describes were mysterious, squirrelled-away places, secretive little holes that were almost impossibly tranquil in such a frenetic setting. "The garden had a rough iron fence, all rusty, and inside it was wild, with bushes and trees and flowers and grass," he recalls. "It looked like no one had taken care of it for ten years. The day before this strange thing happened, when I was four or five, I had slid through a gap in the fence and found a rusty rifle. It was one of the happiest days of my year. It was real and menacing-looking, and of course when I took it out I tried to hit it against the floor to see whether there was a bullet in the barrel. Just then a police car passed by. They stopped when they saw this little boy playing with a real rifle, and confiscated it.

"The next day, late in the afternoon, I thought I would find another one, and that's when it all happened. I went back to the garden and I suddenly heard kittens crying. My first reaction was to find them. I was very small, so going into the tall grass was like a jungle. The next thing I remember, I felt something above me and I looked up and saw a ball of light and heard an intense, high-pitched sound. It wasn't the sun, it was something more massive, almost like a plane, but nearer to me, above me. It was just hanging there. Then after some moments—I don't remember how long—something struck me. It was either a beam or a ray of light; it really hit my forehead and knocked me back into the grass. It was exactly like that scene in the John Travolta film, *Phenomenon*. I don't know how long I lay there but I got scared. I ran home and told my mother. Maybe I'd stayed there for another minute, not thinking, not wondering, not understanding. At that age, anything and everything is possible for a child. To me, it didn't look like some kind of phenomenon or a paranormal occurrence or a UFO. It just happened. But because it was a bit threatening, because it knocked me down, I tried to tell this to my mother, and obviously she thought I was making it up. And that was the end of that. It never ever happened again."

A short time after this, something else, slightly more earthly happened to Uri, to which there is a still living terrestrial witness in the form of his mother, Margaret. And, as this story concerns a Jewish mother and her only son, it involves soup, of course.

"We were sitting down to lunch in the kitchen eating mushroom soup, or possibly chicken, I don't quite remember," says Margaret Geller, who is now eighty-five and speaks only Hungarian and Hebrew. "All of a sudden I noticed that the spoon in his hand was bending. I didn't know what happened. I thought he might have bent it on purpose as a joke, to make me laugh. And then he said he didn't do anything and, that the spoon got bent by itself. I just wondered. But I always had the feeling that he was not like other children. He very much liked, how shall I put this?, to be independent and to boss around the other children, his friends. He was always the same, just like now."

Uri's account of the soupspoon affair accords, in its essentials, with his mother's. He recalls dipping some white bread in the soup, and then placing the spoon in his left hand—he is left-handed—and taking a few sips unhindered by any form of paranormal activity. His mother was standing, in the style of every Jewish mother in history, by the stove. But then, as Uri was lifting the spoon to his mouth, its bowl spontaneously bent downwards, depositing hot soup in his lap, then fell off, leaving him holding the handle. He remembers calling "Look what's happened," to his mother. She replied, as any flustered mother would, "Well, it must be a loose spoon or something."

"I knew that was silly," Uri says now. "You don't get 'loose spoons.'"

Uri Geller had been born in a small hospital in Tel Aviv at two in the morning on 20 December 1946, under the clownish sign of Sagittarius. The birth was entirely normal other than in one significant and disturbing respect: Margaret Geller had previously been pregnant eight times, and on each occasion had an abortion because Tibor, who did not seem to believe in contraceptives, also did not want children. Uri did not find out about his mother's multiple abortions until he was nearly forty, and when she quietly slipped it into the middle of an unrelated conversation. As an adult who believed firmly in life after death and reincarnation it was as great a shock to Uri as it might have been to discover he was adopted: he had always felt that he had some kind of guardian angel, and when he learned that he might have had eight brothers and sisters, he wondered whether perhaps he had more than one invisible protector. On quizzing his mother he discovered that when she became pregnant with him, she had found the strength and determination to stand up to Tibor, which brought Uri into existence.

Tibor Geller seems to have accepted his fate as a father: in Geller family photos Uri's father looks happy and content holding him at his circumcision, visibly proud of his first and only child. Uri was named after a young man who would have been his cousin, but who was killed in a trolley-bus accident in Budapest.

Uri maintains today that he is not angry with his parents about the abortions. He feels that if they had not happened, and his mother had already had several children when she became pregnant with him, it is most likely that *he* would have been aborted. Also it was a turbulent and unstable time in Palestine: even in the late 1940s, Uri was effectively a war baby, born and brought up in a violent society, with an understanding of the emotional chaos that war engenders.

Tibor and Margaret had married in the grandest synagogue in Budapest in 1938. Unlike Tibor's, Margaret's family was not religious. She had been born in Berlin, of Viennese parents; her family name was Freud, and if the Hungarian Gellers had gypsies to provide the exotica in their genetic makeup, the Freuds could point out proudly that Margaret's grandfather was Solomon Freud, a nephew of the great Sigmund. The Budapest Freuds owned a moderately prosperous furniture and kitchenware business. Much of Tibor and Margaret's courtship was spent rowing on Lake Balaton, outside Budapest in narrow racing sculls. Inevitably they capsized from time to time, and once Margaret's leg was trapped in the boat. It was only by swimming underneath it that Tibor was able to rescue her before she drowned.

Almost as soon as they were married, the Gellers fled from the imminent Nazi terror. Tibor made his way into Romania in November 1938, and talked his way on to a ship bound for Palestine. It took four months to get there and three attempts to land, under fire from British patrol vessels, before he made it to the shore in March 1939. Twenty refugees on the ship had been killed by gunfire during the long journey. Margaret had an easier emigration: she escaped Hungary through Yugoslavia, and caught a ship there for Palestine.

Once in Palestine, the Gellers were surrounded by the vicious three-cornered attrition between British, Jews and Arabs, and their life was typical of that of thousands of early Israeli settlers. Tibor took the Hebrew name Yitzhak and found work selling lollipops from a cart on the beach at Tel Aviv. After the Second World War, he worked as a taxi driver, running the gauntlet of flying bullets on the strife-torn road from the city to the airport at Lydda in a big old Chevrolet paid for—as most things were in the Geller household—by Margaret's work as a seamstress.

Soon Tibor discovered that his destiny was as a man of action, and shortly after the outbreak of the War, he joined the British Army. He fought in the Jewish Brigade with the Eighth Army under Montgomery. In 1941, his tank unit was surrounded by Rommel's troops for several weeks at Tobruk, and he was posted to Libya twice before the end of the war. Perhaps it is unfair to Tibor Geller to say that he loved warfare, but it was unquestionably his calling, and there was all too much of it waiting to be waged in the postwar Middle East. He joined the Haganah, the Jewish underground militia, which later became the Israeli Army, and spent most of his time away from Margaret. She passed her time at work gossiping with Hungarian friends in Tel Aviv's strikingly middle-European coffeehouses, and playing cards.

The sporadic street fighting and sniping in Tel Aviv did not stop because there was a new baby in the tiny flat up three flights of cool stone stairs on Betzalel Yaffe. Even today the stairway of the apartment block has bullet scars in its light blue walls. Uri has worked out that his first memory dates from 1947, when he was about six months old. "Our place was just a one-room apartment with a tiny kitchen for an entrance, a big living room and, behind a curtain, a bed which folded out of the wall, which my mother had to build for me. Across the road from the apartment was the railroad station for trains to Jerusalem, and close to that was a British post, like a police station. I'll never know why but a British soldier shot two bullets into our window. I was under that living-room window in my pram, where my mother had put me. I remember the two shots, and I remember glass falling almost in slow motion. My mother had put a little teddy bear next to me in the pram, and somehow it rolled over my face and it saved me. Maybe I would have been cut up, perhaps even killed."

With both his parents out for much of the time, Uri had much freedom as a little boy, although when his father was at home he exerted strict, militaristic discipline over his son. "I remember that when I got out of bed, if my shoe was half an inch misplaced he would immediately tell me to correct that." It was a demanding regime but, then, Tibor was rarely around. A neighbor nominally looked after Uri when his mother was out or working, but he was a streetwise urchin—and, by his own admission, a little strange.

Shortly after he had seen the flash of light in the Arabic garden, Uri remembers digging out the British bullet heads from where they had sunk into the opposite wall in his bedroom. One was squashed up, having hit masonry, but the other had penetrated only wood, and was still shiny and round enough to spark his imagination. "I used to go down the tiny little garden under the house, which was about three meters square and covered with grass and flowers, and I would pretend that the little bullet head was a rocket, and that this was a jungle. I would pretend that the rocket was taking off and then landing on another planet. I don't know where I got these ideas from, as I was only four or five. We had no TV or radio. I don't think we even had comics in Israel then."

He developed a space fixation, almost, he speculates today, "as if something was implanted in my mind" during his Joan of Arc experience. He had started to draw detailed space pictures, with astronauts sitting in rockets surrounded by controls and screens. "A street away was a junkyard of huge old water tanks, and there, too, I used to fantasize. I used to crawl into one, which was covered with big rivets, and pretend I was in some kind of capsule and was floating in space. My favorite childhood dream—and many people have it—was that I flapped my hands and I could fly."

By Uri's account two or three other strange phenomena began to crowd into his little world, aside from the alarming tendency of spoons and forks to bend occasionally when he touched them. That happened frequently enough for his parents to become accustomed to it—their minds were so full of wartime worries about survival that they seem to have discounted its significance as a scientific oddity. The first post-spoon-bending phenomenon to affect Uri made him a playground sensation at the kindergarten he attended around the corner on Achad Ha'am Street. He liked being the center of attention and his curious ability at will to affect watches and clocks in odd ways was the best way to achieve it—far more reliable than the fickle, unpredictable business of bending cutlery.

His facility with timepieces, he maintains, appeared as spontaneously as his spoon-bending. Shortly after he started school, Tibor bought his son a watch, of which he was, naturally, very proud. Uri was bored by school almost immediately, and the watch acted somehow as a barometer of his *ennui*. One day, he recalls looking at it and seeing that the class was over. But a glance at the wall clock showed there was still half an hour to go. Disappointed, he set it back thirty minutes and forgot about it—until the same thing started to happen day after day. There is, of course, every possibility that nothing more was happening than a little boy turning his watch forward consciously or otherwise in an attempt to will time forward. If this was so, Uri was prepared nevertheless to take matters further. He told his mother about it. The link between misbehaving watches and delinquent spoons was far from obvious, so she suggested there might be something wrong with the watch. In response, it contrived to spin four or five hours ahead at a jump. Suspecting that this was a prank, Margaret asked Uri to leave the watch at home. For weeks, under her gaze, it behaved quite normally. He began to wear it to school again. Still fascinated by the watch and convinced he hadn't deluded himself, he got into the habit of taking it off and leaving it on his desk, in the hope of catching it running fast. The day he succeeded, he shouted out in class, "Look at this watch!" and immediately wished he hadn't, because everyone laughed at him. He does not remember whether it was still racing ahead when he held it up, but the incident served as an early lesson that people would not simply accept his word, and would not necessarily believe what they saw in front of them. Back at home, he decided there was nothing more to it than that he had a weird watch, and he resolved not to wear it again. His mother said she would buy him a better one and, a few months later, she did.

Uri says he was relieved at having a regular, working watch this time, which did not do odd, unpredictable things and told the correct time. Then, one day, the bell rang for the end of playtime and he looked at his watch. He saw that the hands had bent, first upwards, so they hit the glass, then sideways. Convinced, now, that this was the spoon thing in another guise, his instant reaction was to keep it secret. When he got home, his father had arrived on one of his visits and asked sharply, "Did you open this watch?" Uri swore that he had not, and Margaret told Tibor about the peculiar things that had happened with the first watch.

Uri recalls Tibor and Margaret giving each other one of those despairing looks by which parents communicate a shared feeling of hopelessness about an errant child. Tibor had suggested that Uri see a psychiatrist immediately after he started vandalizing, as Tibor saw it, the hard-up family's cutlery; now that the child had taken to ruining expensive watches too, he was all the more convinced that this should happen. He was angry about Uri's mangled watch, but Margaret argued that whatever Uri was displaying seemed like a talent to her, so the visit to a psychiatrist never took place. But Uri was not given another watch for more than a year. (He gave up wearing them in his twenties, he says, when he no longer trusted them to tell the right time.)

The incident in the garden, the spoons, the intense space fantasies, the watches and even the humiliation of being laughed at in class had convinced Uri, even at this early stage in his life, that he was special, possibly even on some mission at the behest of a dimly perceived superior power. "It was real, it was vivid in my mind. I know to this day it was not childhood fantasy," he insists. Life continued, however, and much of it was mundane but happy. "I can remember two houses away from us was a tiny back-room condom factory and we used to get into the back garden, where they would throw out defective condoms. We used to blow them up as balloons. I think we knew what they were. I kissed a girl for the first time just behind that little garden. I was about seven."

A few weeks after the showdown with his parents over the second broken watch, Uri was eating school lunch when his friend, Mordechai, suddenly looked down at his watch and exclaimed that it had just moved ahead an hour. Prepared to risk all since he now had an independent witness with his own watch, Uri uttered a fateful statement: "I did that." Mordechai argued that he couldn't have done—the watch had never left his wrist. Uri asked him to take it in his hand, then he says, he looked at it and shouted, "Move." He made it jump two or tree times, and by the end of the lunch break, a crowd of excited boys was proclaiming that Uri Geller could perform the most wonderful trick with a watch. Of course, Uri would like to have explained that, as far as he was concerned, it wasn't a trick but something simpler. Wisely, he did not.

The incident rocketed Uri in his peers' estimation. Yechiel Teitelbaum, who was in his class and now runs a Tel Aviv cosmetics marketing company employing three hundred people, confirms this: "He was always different from other kids, very strange. He did a lot of things not every child can do, things beyond understanding; he left the impression of someone amazing, very sharp, very strong, very, very popular. He was always the leader, even in the kindergarten. We were together from four or five years old. He was always doing incredible things in the playground with wrist watches. I also remember there were stories about him stopping the big classroom clock, but in my memory it was the big clock in the teachers' room that Uri stopped. I don't remember him bending metal, but what left the biggest impression on me was something different. It was Uri's *telepathia*—how he would tell me exact things I was thinking about."

Telepathy with people and, Uri claims, with dogs and cats, was another paranormal aptitude with which he had been born, or had learned to simulate by trickery. From toddlerhood he was apparently famed in the apartment building for being able to feed the ferocious local feral cats down by the dustbins behind the pharmacy that occupied the bottom of the block. They would purr and eat out of his hand. The human telepathy manifested first for Mrs. Geller—as it did for Yechiel at kindergarten—with Uri's uncanny knack of saying what she had been going to say just before she said it. She learned to shrug it off: "She was accustomed to the idea of me being unusual," Uri says. He had premonitions, too, that went down in family history as accurate. One apparently came to him on a visit to the zoo during which he felt uneasy and asked to leave. A few minutes after he and Margaret had left, mother and son maintain, a lion escaped and terrorized the visitors.

Soon afterward, having a telepathic young son began to have *really* practical uses. Uri was in the habit of waiting up for Margaret to come home from her card evenings so that he could say goodnight. Practically every time, she noted, he seemed able to tell her how well she had done, and precisely how much she had won or lost. They began to develop a system by which Uri's talents, whatever they were, might be harnessed to help her. And with this early childhood intervention in his mother's card games, we come upon the first major problem in unscrambling the Uri Geller story. One of the principal difficulties the study of parapsychology has faced since the early twentieth century is "mixed mediumship." Or, to put it at its most basic, the fact that some promising psychic subjects will cheat at the same time as showing every sign of being genuinely psychic. Mixed mediumship was a paradox noted by the anthropologist Knud Rasmussen in the 1920s, when he interviewed an Eskimo shaman called Najagneq—who, incidentally, claimed to have gained his powers after being struck by a ball of fire. Najagneq admitted to the Dane that he used some sleight-of-hand conjuring tricks as an aid to persuading people to believe in him, and thereby to assist their recovery from illness. Rasmussen asked if any "real" powers were involved. Najagneq replied, "Yes, there is a power that we call Sila, one that cannot be explained in so many words."

The concept that paranormal powers and deliberate illusionism sometimes coexist in the same person, and might even, in rare cases, be different ends of the same stick, is a blessing for those who wish to debunk the paranormal. Their argument, and superficially it is not a bad one, is that if an alleged psychic *ever* cheats, *ever* tinkers with the effects he produces, be it to please an audience, an experimenter or his mum, then everything he does or ever has done and claimed as being paranormal is instantly nullified.

Yet in reality, the desire to enhance with a spot of deception what one can do by legitimate methods is common in many fields. In the 1986 World Cup finals, Diego Maradona of Argentina, the greatest midfield soccer player of all time, knocked England out with a goal he knowingly scored illegally, using his right hand to push the ball into the net; although this incident is used as an example of the Argentinian's tricky nature, it is rarely employed as an argument that Maradona was incapable of playing football legitimately. In Uri Geller's case, there is substantial evidence, as we will see in his subsequent career, that like Maradona he has the ability to do amazing things without needing to cheat. Yet from early childhood, the nature of what he found he could achieve, in that it was close to what conjurors do by trickery, exposed him to the *knowledge* of methods of cheating. Sometimes, it is safe to assume, he discovered ways of deceiving audiences; other times, even today, magician friends, of whom he has dozens, will tell him of their methods. In an ideal world, perhaps, Uri would somehow *unknow* such secrets but, for all practical purposes, he is stuck with them.

When he was four or five, it is a little unlikely that Uri was being tutored by magicians, and he had both the scope and the motivation to work out methods of augmenting his natural talents. Helping his mother financially was an overriding consideration for him, a priority of which he has never lost sight; like most people who have been poor, he remains keenly aware of money and financial security. Therefore he developed a method of assisting his mother at cards, which was a perfect example of mixed mediumship. "I had a system to tell her telepathically if someone was holding a joker," Uri admits. "But I didn't tell her telepathically, I would sit next to her and knock her knee. It's called kibitzing, when someone is playing cards and you sit next to them and you can see what they hold in their hand. Obviously, as an observer I was not allowed to see what the others were holding because I was with my mother. But I would look at the person she was sitting opposite. She—they were all women—would have a full hand of cards and I would just know by looking at the back of the cards whether she had a joker or two jokers, and would tell my mother. They played for money, and that helped her income. I also helped her by telling her not to play cards on certain evenings because she would lose."

Uri's powers, as he saw them, could apparently be used for his own benefit too. For a child used to wanting material possessions and not getting them—when he was younger, he had coveted an expensive model Jeep he saw in a toy shop—Uri developed the perfect gift: "I discovered that I could use a visualization technique to achieve certain things. For example, I love dogs and I just wanted a dog, and I would visualize and fantasize about a puppy in my mind, daydreaming. I will never forget the day when my father woke me up in the middle of the night and said, 'Uri, go to the balcony and look what I bought you.' And I went out, and there in a little box was a puppy. It was almost like I had a personal Aladdin lamp in my mind, that I would wish or rub and it would make my wishes come true. The puppy was a little Arabic mongrel, light brown and white. I called him Tzuki, to sound like the Hungarian for candy. Sadly, a car killed him when I was six or seven, and it was my fault in a way. I had him on a leash I had made, and it just broke and he ran on to the road and was killed in front of me. It was very traumatic. Both my mother and I cried all day. I only realized then how much I love animals. A few weeks later, my father bought me another dog, and I called him Tzuki as well."

Uri seemed to choose which of his curious abilities he would reveal to different people. He happily fooled around with their watches, but never boasted to his friends that he believed he could "magic up" a puppy—even with his imagination, he realized that this wish-fulfilment thing he had *could* be coincidental. It is not unusual, after all, for a father to buy a dog for his son. The one thing Uri never discussed or attempted to perform in the school playground was the bizarre spoon phenomenon, even though it was happening as often as once a week, and was seemingly coming under his control. Bending spoons was still unreliable for him, and to attempt it and fail would be to risk losing the considerable status he had gained with his apparent power over watch movements. But the spoon-bending had begun to extend beyond the confines of 13 Betzalel Yaffe. Margaret's main pastime was drinking coffee and eating cake with her girlfriends. Uri would often go along with her, but when he did alarming things happened. He would be quietly eating a piece of cake when spoons on the café table would curl up. The waiters would whisk them away, not wanting to give the impression that the café used bent spoons—or, indeed, attracted naughty little boys as customers. Margaret would try to explain to her friends and the staff that such things sometimes happened when Uri was around, but the feeling prevailed, albeit unspoken, that the handsome Geller child was merely mischievous and he felt awkward as he could not explain what was going on.

One of Margaret's Hungarian card-playing cronies was a younger woman, Shoshana Korn, who at that time was working in a hotel in Tel Aviv. The two met and became friends when Margaret—Manci to her friends—was pregnant with Uri. Shoshana, or Juji, as she is known, became Uri's godmother. "We were in a café on the corner of Pinsker and Allenby one day when Uri started to play with the spoons," Juji recalls. "He was five or six, and bent four or five coffee spoons double. I said, 'Manci, I hope you have plenty of money to pay the café owner.' Fortunately, the owner was amused. I said, 'Uri, you're going to ruin your mother.' He said, in Hebrew, that it just came to his head how to do this, but his mother wouldn't let him do it in the house. All the other people were amazed. And as well as being able to do these incredible things, Uri was very smart, too. He'd stop clocks and watches, but then he'd always start them again. Another friend of ours, Anush, said to Manci, 'You know, one day you won't have to work all night because he's going to make a lot of money.' Uri used to spend a lot of time with Anush and her husband, Miklos. I remember her saying you had to hide everything made of metal from Uri, because he'd bend it. Miklos was a handbag maker, and he would sometimes get very angry with Uri because he would bend his tools and the clasps he used. But then he'd say, 'I don't know what to do with this Uri. He's a genius.'"

In spite of the drawbacks of feeling different from other children because of the troubling powers he seemed to possess, and of sensing that people regarded him as mischievous and naughty (while more often they saw him as an investment), Uri regards this part of his childhood as happy: he was an only child, bright, good-looking, reasonably indulged, if not spoiled. His life, though, was at a turning point. Psychic or not, Uri probably realized that things were going wrong long before his father actually left, and was perhaps a less happy little boy than he appeared. Perhaps all the strange phenomena were poltergeist effects, which are said to affect unhappy children in particular—perhaps they still are poltergeist-based, for much about Uri Geller even as an adult suggests a damaged teenager still affected by Tibor Geller's abandonment of him, still torn between adoring and idealizing the man for his strength and despairing of him for his weaknesses. Few middle-aged men can speak with such power about coming not merely from a broken home, but a *ruined* home.

With the heady background of constant war and the rumblings of the founding of the State of Israel, it is, perhaps, hardly surprising that the suave and charming Tank Corps Sergeant Major Geller was unfaithful to Margaret as well as negligent in other areas of family duty. "Uri's father was very, very handsome, but liked to fool around," reflects Juji Korn. "He didn't work too hard, and whatever he made, he didn't give them. That's why Manci had to stay up all night sewing aprons on her machine."

Uri knew his father was seeing other women, partly because Tibor made the time-honored and eternally puzzling philanderer's error of trying to engineer meetings between his child and his favorite illicit lover. Perhaps he was trying to legitimize the liaison by seeking Uri's approval of her. He even arranged for one of his women to come round to their home to meet him. When she got to the apartment-block lobby, instead of walking up and knocking on the door, she whistled up the stairs for him. The significance of this in Israeli terms cannot be underestimated; it is a tradition in Israel that family members and intimates—but not mere acquaintances—have a special whistle for one another to say, "I'm home," "I'm over here," or whatever. Margaret and Uri, for example, had their own agreed whistling routine. Because she could not quite see Uri playing outside from the balcony of the Geller apartment, she whistled down three floors a few bars of the "Toreador" tune, which he would return. Even as a child, then, Uri knew what was happening when a strange woman whistled for his father, and he tried to make a noise so that his mother would not hear her. He was only too aware of how hurt Margaret would be. On another occasion, Tibor was with Uri and had to use a call-box. Uri had never spoken on a telephone before, and was excited when his father let him hold the receiver and speak into it. When he understood that he was talking to one of Tibor's girlfriends, he says, he became tongue-tied and felt bad about it. It soon got to the point where Uri preferred his father not to come home on leave because he saw the sadness Tibor caused Margaret. The signs of their coming divorce were obvious.

"He took me once to a coffee shop called Roval on Dizengoff Street, and he looked so meticulous and handsome in his uniform and black beret with a tank on it and the decorations," Uri recalls. "I remember walking in behind him and being in the doorway, and everyone eating and chatting, and the clanging of the cutlery on the plates and the spoons stirring coffee. And as my father entered the shop in front of me, there was a silence. Everyone froze. I could see it; all the women just stopped, because mostly women would go to have cakes and coffee. They stopped drinking and stopped eating cake and just looked at him. He had that kind of presence, and looked like a movie star. It was a fatal combination."

After the divorce Tibor eventually remarried, a woman called Eva, with whom he stayed and whom Uri respects. He does not blame her for the break-up of his parents' marriage: for that, he holds responsible his father—"I blame him totally," Uri says—and another woman called Tamar. "That was the woman who actually tarnished and ruined my mother's life. There were others, many others, but it was Tamar who chased my father. She was obsessively in love with him and she managed to destroy the marriage."

From time to time Uri and his mother still discuss the breakup. "My mother revealed something really touching when she was well into her eighties. She said, 'You know, Uri, I really now understand why your father wasn't attracted to me. I was always heavy. I was never thin, I was never attractive. I was very beautiful, I was gorgeous, I had a beautiful face and beautiful hair, but there were women around with great bodies.'

"It was so sad to hear my mother saying that. After sixty years, she realizes. She sees all these TV shows like *Oprah*, and all the debates about fat and thin, and how society dictates certain ideas about how men see women. And she finally understands, practically forgives him. She hated my dad, and she tried to incite me against him, and what he did to her. She never went into detail but I knew everything. And, sadly, she went on to have really bad luck with the second man in her life. Her second husband died. He had had a first heart attack, but he actually had the heart attack which he died of making love to my mother. No wonder she never got married after that, and abstained from sex and never wanted to hear about men again. It was a double whammy on her. First my father cheating on her because she'd put on a few pounds, and then finally finding someone in her life and he dies on her."

The disintegration of the Gellers' marriage ended Uri's days as a Tel Aviv street kid. After a short time in which she struggled as head of a one-parent family, Margaret no longer had the strength or the resources to be a full-time worker and a mother.

Although he recognized that the marriage had become pointless, Uri had not taken the breakup passively. On occasion, especially when Tibor raised the question of sending Uri to see a psychiatrist over the strange happenings, he would ask why his parents didn't see the psychiatrist instead.

Even before the couple formally split up Uri's behavior at school had begun to deteriorate in distinctly non-paranormal ways. One day, his teacher asked the class to bring in from home a Torah scroll, a miniature copy of the holy Jewish *Sefer Torah*, which many households in Israel own. The Gellers, who were not religious, did not have one, so Uri went to school empty-handed. He was immediately jealous of the other children, all of whom seemed to have a beautiful scroll. At recess, the children were told to put their scrolls in their desks. During the break, Uri sneaked into the classroom and stole an expensive white-covered scroll. It was hardly the crime of the century but Uri watched terrified from the balcony of his apartment as the teacher knocked on the front door of the block that afternoon. In a panic, as she walked up the stairs, he tore the scroll to shreds and threw the pieces down the lavatory. It was obvious that he was the only suspect, and to make matters worse, his father was at home that day. He never forgot the way Tibor looked when he learned that Uri had stolen a Torah, and then destroyed it. "My father was never mean or vicious, but he whipped me that day. He took me into the bathroom, tied me up and really whipped me."

Things got worse for Uri. There was a girl in his class called Naomi, whom he secretly loved and with whom he went to the cinema to watch Tarzan movies; she refused to speak to him any more. The other children ostracized him too. He spent hours alone with just Tzuki for comfort, so was pleased when he was told that new arrangements had been made for him. It was decided that the safest, most stable home for Uri would be in the country, on a kibbutz, a communal farm, called Hatzor, far to the south of Tel Aviv near Ashdod. It specialized in taking in children from broken homes in the big city. Here, for a small fee, but in reality for purely philanthropic reasons, they were lovingly looked after within a settled, nuclear family, where perhaps they would start to mend psychologically, and maybe even develop a taste for the simple, healthy country lifestyle. There was even a Hungarian-Jewish family, the Shomrons, who were ready and delighted to take in Uri. Just before he was ten, in 1956, Uri was packed off to the country.

Kibbutz Hatzor was beautiful and quiet, a Garden of Eden in comparison with the ferment of the streets of downtown Tel Aviv. But Uri hated it. He missed home, missed his dog, and hated the kibbutz way of sharing everything; in the 1950s kibbutzim were run on more strictly Communistic lines than today, which took some stomaching for a city child. "You have to understand," says Nurit, the elder sister of the Shomron family, who still lives on Hatzor, "for these children, it was like a punishment. *They* would feel guilty for, as they saw it, breaking up the family. Uri once said on TV that the kibbutz he stayed on was a terrible place. But then in the next sentence, he said, 'My family loved me very much.' And we did."

The kibbutz was a few kilometers back from the sea, overlooking the port of Ashdod and only a kilometer or so from a busy Israeli Air Force base. It is not set in particularly spectacular countryside, but in flat, hot fields, with industrial installations and pylons close by. But Nurit's mother, Tova, one of the founders of the community, had insisted from the start on planting beautiful gardens to counterbalance the functionality of the kibbutz, whose industries were cotton-growing and aluminum-smelting, and the noise from the airbase, as heavy freighters and fighter aircraft took off and landed. Thanks to Tova's determination to beautify the kibbutz, it was soon an overwhelmingly peaceful little paradise of pines, flowers and lawns. Yet a few years before Uri's arrival, it had not been so tranquil. In 1948, within days of Israel's independence, the advancing Egyptian Army, intent on destroying the new state, had come within a few kilometers of Hatzor, and ferocious land and air battles were fought around Tova's gardens before the invaders were beaten back.

Ironically, considering it was Tibor who had visited chaos upon the family, the location of Hatzor was more convenient to him than to anyone else. Not only was he stationed at an Army base just twenty kilometers away, but he had the use of military vehicles to visit Uri. For Margaret, Hatzor was two hours and two buses away—when the tricky rural bus connections worked—but she came regularly. Sadly, she sensed that Tibor's visits seemed to leave a greater impression on Uri than hers. He always came bearing some interesting military item for his son, and things were a little happier between the pair. Uri remembers one visit in particular: "Just after the Suez war, which we could hear faintly from the kibbutz, and I was very scared about, he had phoned to say he was coming, and I was waiting for him all day. I stood in the entrance to the kibbutz and eventually, from far away, I saw a puff of dust, and that was his Jeep. He was unshaven and dusty and he had his gun on him. He looked like he had come from war, and I was so proud. He was safe, and it was so unbelievable that he came straight from the fighting."

Margaret's visits were more awkward for Uri. She was always smartly dressed and wearing lipstick, which the other kibbutzniks laughed at. Beneath the surface friendliness and the socialist ethic, there existed quite a strong prejudice against the city children, the *ironim*, which made a homesick Uri still more miserable. Yet there were compensations in kibbutz life. The school-ing was much easier and less strict than in the city. The aluminum smelter had a yard filled with old airplanes, some of them military, there to be broken up. It provided an incomparable playground for any child with imagination. The little bit of farm work the children were required to do, such as orange pick-ing, was pleasant enough. The food in the large communal dining hall was ex-cellent and you could eat as much as you wanted, which Uri, who was fond of his food, appreciated. Hatzor also had a huge outdoor swimming pool, and a children's zoo with rabbits, chickens, goats, peacocks and a donkey, which Uri loved. He would still go out at night, however, to look at the moon and think of how it was shining over Tel Aviv, too, and that perhaps Tzuki was looking at it.

Like a lot of town dwellers transplanted to the country before him, Uri was horrified by the occasional violence of rural life. "I had a bad fright once. We were picking potatoes, and I was pulling out what I thought was the stem of the plant, but I was actually holding a poisonous snake, which was curled around the plant. It was a bad shock suddenly to be holding this sleek, slimy living viper in my hand. There was a tractor nearby and I dropped the snake and shouted, 'Snake,' and everyone was looking at it wiggle away. Then the guy on the tractor rolled over and cut its head off with a plough, and I really felt sorry and angry. I was sorry that I had made a live thing die because I alerted everyone that there was a snake."

Uri lived, in the kibbutz manner, in a one-storey children's house attached to his schoolroom. His contact with his "second family," as the host families on Hatzor were called, was therefore relatively limited, but he rapidly became fond of the Shomrons, and they of him. "My memory is mixed with what my mother told me about him, but I do remember him being a very beautiful child, with a lot of imagination," says Nurit. "Tibor I remember as tall and charming, always in uniform. He was about forty, which seemed old in my eyes. According to Uri's stories, he was a hero, but people used to gossip—as a reaction, I think, to the wonderful things Uri told about him—that he was just in the administrative part of the Army.

"His father used to buy him a lot of sweets, and Uri was naturally supposed to share everything with Eytan, my brother, who was Uri's age. But Uri would hide his secret little box of sweets and refuse to share. Yet, for me, that was un-derstandable. It was all the love he got. He could go to that box and feel the love of his parents, which he missed so much. His mother, particularly, was lost after the breakup of the family."

Tova Shomron was the one, as Nurit puts it, who was in charge of emotions in the family, and she gave a very good impression of loving Uri like a son, even though whatever she gave him inevitably wasn't enough. "I think it was Eytan, who was the middle child, who felt deprived, but instead of getting angry with his parents for allowing Uri to join the family, he would get mad with Uri," Nurit explains.

Even if he did resent Uri , Eytan Shomron became his close friend, which was a big thing for Uri because he was not enormously popular among the other children, who scoffed at Uri's stories and called him a liar. Eytan was different, a little more sophisticated. After rising to Lieutenant Colonel in the army, today he is a melon farmer in the Negev desert, and also a great expert on—and friend of—the Bedouin Arabs. Eytan runs desert tours for tourists with an academic interest in the ancient, vanished Nabatean civilization. Back on Kibbutz Hatzor, when he was ten, even if he secretly half hoped Uri's stories of the big world, the miracles of Tel Aviv, his father's acts of heroism were untrue, he also hung on every word. "We were good friends," Eytan says. "I don't remember there being any tension or problem with sharing my parents' attention with him. In a small community, on a kibbutz, it's not easy to be friends with someone who is not like everybody, who is exceptional, and Uri was exceptional. He came from the outside, and then became an outsider. He got this name for being a liar, but it's unfair. I can't put a finger on him ever lying."

In later life, too, Uri Geller's critics have derided him with non-specific allegations of lying, while friends maintain that he never lies. Geller's detractors also find endlessly amusing—not to mention highly instructive—his insistence that his psychic powers refuse to work unless those around him are friendly, if not actual "believers." Kibbutz Hatzor was the first place in which he found himself among rather unsympathetic people, somewhat averse to him personally, strongly averse to anything other than the black-and-white here and now—and positively against anything that smacked of religion, the unexplained, the paranormal or the supernatural. As a result, perhaps, of the bad vibes, or perhaps of Uri's instinctive sense that he was not going to find a receptive audience among these people—he puts it down simply to his depression and unhappiness—nothing "strange" happened to him during his entire year on the kibbutz.

Well, almost nothing. There were odd incidents, which ensured that the Geller boy's psychic powers were not unknown on the kibbutz, even if they were not given much credence, and tended to be elaborated upon by others only after he became world famous. A story went around, for example, that he accurately predicted an air crash at the neighboring base a few hours before it happened: "My brother Ilan remembers Uri telling him that an airplane was going to crash tomorrow, and it did," says Eytan. Curiously, Uri remembers saying in class one afternoon only that he thought "something" terrible was going to happen, not that it was a crash at the airbase just beyond the wheatfields. "I suddenly felt something very powerful in me, almost like a feeling of running out of the classroom. A very short time afterwards, we heard this huge bang. We all ran out of the studying bungalow and across the cornfields we saw smoke and we all started running toward this jet on the end of the runway embedded in the ground and the pilot inside with blood all over his face. It was quite something, the first time that I encountered someone dead or dying other than my dog. Actually, the pilot survived and months later, he came over to see us and tell us about it."

Uri did little in the way of spoon-bending and interfering with watches on the kibbutz, and nothing for his closest friend, Eytan, who saw him bend a spoon for the first time some forty years later. He was probably more astonished by it then than he would have been as a child. It is almost as if as a child Uri sensed that, if he left it for a few years, he would eventually have a far greater impact on someone he was keen to impress. The result was that, in his fifties, Eytan became a firm believer in Uri's powers. Many years after Uri left Hatzor, and was beginning his stage career, Nurit and Eytan had noticed that he was performing one night in a nearby village. A group of kibbutzniks trooped along to see the show, but Nurit and Eytan didn't bother. As fond as they were of Uri, they didn't then believe the stories of his powers, and were not interested in magicians' shows.

At least one former child on the kibbutz, though, has a vivid memory of Uri giving him a glimpse of his powers. Avi Seton, a year younger and now a management consultant in Portland, Oregon, was walking with Uri from the dining hall to the swimming pool one day when Uri suddenly said to him, "Hey, look what I can do."

"Uri took off his watch and held it, and the hands just moved without him doing anything. I'm not sure if he was sophisticated enough at ten years old for some kind of sleight-of-hand to be involved, and I clearly saw them move. For some reason, I got the feeling then and now that it wasn't something he could really *do*, but rather something that was *happening* to him. But the funny thing was that all I said when I saw this was, 'Hey, so what?' I think it was always going to be like that for him when he showed these things to kids. 'Hey, that's good, but you want to see how high I can jump?'" Why should Uri have chosen Avi to show him his secret ability? There are three possible reasons. The first was that Avi was another of the *ironim*, the transplanted city kids. The second was that Avi was reasonably friendly with Uri, and had once rescued him from drowning when they went swimming together in a rough sea. The third, although it is hard to know how Uri could have appreciated this other than through some overdeveloped childhood instinct, was that even at ten Avi was already more open-minded than the average kibbutz kid toward the new and the explained. Which was why, although he has never since seen Uri bend a spoon or do anything else out of the ordinary, he still feels at fifty-one quite sure that what Uri showed him was an example of a true psychic gift rather than a rehearsed trick.

Eytan Shomron meanwhile believes that all the time they were together, Uri was desperate to give his friend some indication that there was more to him than met the eye. "I remember once walking on a dirt road in a field of wheat when Uri asked me if I had the ability to know where the snakes were hidden in the grass, would it make me feel better? There were a lot of snakes, and they were extremely frightening, but I said, 'No, I wouldn't want to know.' It was such a strange question. Years later, I thought it was an attempt to hint at what he could do, to signal to me that he was sitting on a secret. I think Uri Geller lived in two worlds. He tried to share his imagination with people, but they couldn't accept it."

Chapter 3

Cyprus

"I wanted to share the secret of the powers with someone I didn't know too well."

Uri Geller on his thinking, aged fifteen

....

One morning Margaret Geller arrived on the kibbutz in her usual Saturday best for one of her slightly embarrassing visits. She was accompanied by a man Uri had never seen before. Heavily built and in his fifties, Ladislas Gero was another Hungarian Jew, a former concert pianist, who some years previously had formed a cabaret team with his wife and gone on tour to Cyprus. The couple had liked the lively, cosmopolitan island and opened a small hotel there, which, now widowed, he ran on his own. The notable thing about Ladislas Gero for the children of Kibbutz Hatzor was that he was wearing a tie, which many of them had never seen before. "What is that cloth hanging around his neck?" they demanded. It is not inconceivable that the older ones were being disingenuous—a cocky, kibbutznik way of demonstrating how different and inherently superior their radical lifestyle was to the fast and fancy ways of the city. What was notable about Ladislas Gero to Uri Geller, aged eleven, was not his necktie—as a big-city kid he was familiar with them—but that his mother had fallen in love with him, planned to marry him, move to Cyprus and take Uri to live there too.

The plan immediately appealed to Uri, because it solved two problems at once, as well as opening some important doors, which he did not yet know were ajar. For the moment, he was delighted to see his mother happy and to have an escape route from the kibbutz. Not only did Ladislas seem a decent enough fellow, if perhaps a little dull compared with Tibor, but he was also well off. The chance of an end to poverty seemed to have arrived with Ladislas Gero, which Uri appreciated.

What the boy could not know was that moving to Cyprus would mean that he would learn English in addition to the Hebrew and Hungarian he already spoke—and that many years later his fluency in the language would be his open sesame to an international audience. By the end of his teenage years, he was even thinking in English. Because Cyprus was a British colony, he also built up an affinity with Britain, which became increasingly important to him. His early memories of his father were pictures of Tibor in British Army uniform, and now he would get used to seeing the Queen on stamps and banknotes and the Union flag flying. They all left a stirring impression on him.

The move to Cyprus also benefited Uri with regard to his unusual abilities. At this stage, he was still uncertain whether his powers were an asset or an embarrassment: they were, he felt, too transient to rely on—they were not always at his command—and furthermore, he continued, as he still does, to insist that he had no idea where they came from or how he produced them. This troubled him at a deep level. Even when he could make strange things happen, as he hinted he could to his friend Eytan, there was always the possibility that other children would either fail to see what was special or shrug and say he was doing tricks. Uri needed an adult independent of his family to see what he could do, to believe in it and to reassure him that he was not a freak. At Terra Santa College, a strict Catholic boarding school on a hill high above Nicosia, Cyprus's capital, he found several such adults and children, who worked out, without his having shown them anything, that Uri Geller was a most unusual boy.

Establishing through third, preferably unrelated, parties that Uri Geller had special abilities as a child, whether of a conjuring or psychic nature, is crucially important in unravelling his life story. One day his major critics would assert widely and confidently in gossip, articles, interviews with journalists, books and eventually on the Internet that Geller's powers mysteriously manifested only in his early twenties, after he and a teenage friend came upon a magicians' manual and saw the makings of a wonderful scam. Since this assertion was so boldly made—indeed, it is one of the first precepts of Uri Geller's detractors—if it could be shown to be untrue, the process of *reassessing* Geller would have to begin.

It is indisputable that evidence of Uri's peculiar abilities in early childhood is a little hazy; witnesses were either too young to rely on, or related to Uri and bound (perhaps) to support him, or the accounts come from Uri himself. And while many of these latter pieces of testimony are often interesting, and give a compelling appearance of honesty on Geller's part, a single corroborative witness has to be worth ten George Washingtons. In Uri Geller's Cyprus period, from 1957 to 1963—which took him from the age of eleven to eighteen—we begin to encounter strong indications that he was a fully formed psychic, magician or *something*. Cyprus was also where two other major influences came into his life: sex and showbusiness. No wonder he looks upon those years as the time of his life.

Tibor drove Margaret and Uri to the docks at Haifa to board the ship to Larnaca. Uri discovered to his distress as an adult that Tibor had demanded Margaret hand over to him the key deposit on the Tel Aviv apartment as a condition of releasing the boy to leave Israel. Behind Uri already was his traumatic parting from Tzuki the dog, who was sent to live with a family friend on a farm. Uri kissed and hugged his dog and cried as he left him. Ahead of him were worries about how he would get on with his new stepfather and how he would survive in a country where Hebrew wasn't spoken. But Margaret told him that Ladislas had already bought a dog, and Tibor assured his son that he would be able to visit him in Israel, so by the time the Italian ship sailed, he was more excited than scared. At Immigration in Larnaca, a real surprise was awaiting Uri: a new name. "The officer looked at my name, Uri, and he said Uri in Russian is Yuri, and that is actually George. So, on the spot, they wrote down George and that was my name at school for the next seven years."

It was not difficult even for an eleven-year-old to grasp immediately that Cyprus was in a state of undeclared civil war. Margaret explained to Uri on the drive to Nicosia in a black Triumph Mayflower, that there were Greek and Turkish Cypriots, who lived separately in different villages and were routinely involved in atrocities against one another. And although the sight of a military presence was no shock to an Israeli boy, there were an awful lot of British troops around. The names and phrases that were part of the background noise during Uri's stay in Cyprus now sound like the scratchy soundtrack of an ancient black-and-white newsreel: Enosis, the movement to integrate Cyprus with Greece, Archbishop Makarios, Colonel Grivas, the EOKA terrorist leader, Prime Minister Karamanlis of Greece . . . Uri's teenage life was touched tangentially by them all.

Ladislas' small hotel was a pleasant fourteen-bedroom establishment at 12 Pantheon Street in Nicosia. It bore an ambitious name for a little place: Pension Ritz. Ladislas made sure that Uri's arrival there was happy: there was not one dog, but two waiting for him: a wirehaired fox terrier called Joker and a mixed breed terrier named Peter. Joker became Uri's special companion. A package was also on a table inside for him to open: it contained a blue model Cadillac, which he loved.

Uri was sent first to the American School in Larnaca, where he boarded and was not very happy. Most of his friends were English, though, and he quickly picked up the language. After a short time, the violence and fighting were bordering on civil war, there were frequent curfews, and for a few weeks Uri was brought back to the hotel. The Ritz catered almost exclusively for touring theatricals temporarily stationed in Nicosia to service its busy nightlife: singers, musicians, acrobats, jugglers and dancers stayed there, and Uri met and spent time with them during the curfews. He says he showed some his spoon-bending and watch-jumping, and they were duly impressed.

In the garage there was a bicycle, which Uri coveted. His stepfather promised he could have it for a bar mitzvah present, when he was thirteen, but Uri couldn't stop looking at it. The bike was immobilized with a heavy combination lock, and he wondered whether, since he could manage so many other mind-over-matter feats, he could crack the lock. After a bout of intense concentration, he says he finally got the combination, opened the lock, took out the machine and learned to ride it in a nearby cinema car-park. Ladislas was amazed that he had unlocked the bike and, taking the path of least resistance, meekly said that Uri might as well have it now. He sees it today as the first practical, selfish use to which he put his powers. (Incidentally Uri's bar mitzvah, in 1959, was a low-key affair, held at the Israeli consulate in Nicosia in lieu of a synagogue. A Jewish friend called Peter was bar mitzvah at the same time. With the bike already in his possession, Uri received as presents several books and a leather pencil case, which he treasured.)

The bicycle, combined with Margaret and Ladislas' laissez-faire attitude to bringing up Uri, opened up Cyprus to him. Between it and the rickety local buses to Limassol, the Troodos mountains, Famagusta and Kyrenia, the island became a paradise to him. With one of the world's major political crises going on around him, and the frequent grim scenes of violence he witnessed, he managed nevertheless to enjoy a glorious, free, independent teenage of scuba diving from lonely beaches, cycling in the mountains, messing around in junkyards and with motor scooters—and, as he got older, chasing girls. "I occupied myself with the things I loved, like my dog Joker, but while I was doing that the war was going on," Uri says now. "So I somehow carved myself a path and a system, maybe to build some kind of entertainment into my life that would shield me from the death and the destruction that was going on around us."

Terra Santa College was in a safe part of Cyprus, high in the hills a couple of miles from Nicosia. But it was not a place where Uri might have expected to be as happy as he was. It was strict, run by monks, had fairly primitive facilities and provided education of highly demanding, 1950s British standards, which came as a shock to many of its pupils, especially the few Americans. Yet almost from the start Uri was content there as a boarder. One of the first things he noticed at Terra Santa, and to which he unaccountably warmed, was that the pretty gardens at the modern school building's entrance were cut in the shape of crucifixes. The school had no other Jewish pupils, which might have made him lonely, were it not for one incident. "I was there because it was the best school in Nicosia," Uri says, "but one incident melted away any fear I had. One day Father Camillo, who was the headmaster, called me into his office and he locked the door. He said, 'Come close,' and I didn't know what he was about to do to me. Suddenly, he started unbuttoning his collar, and then he pulled out a bunch of little trinkets on a gold chain, a cross, a St. Christopher's medallion and so on. But among them was a little Star of David. He said, 'Look at what I am wearing. Don't be afraid of Jesus.' He wanted me to be absolutely clear that he loved and respected the Jewish people. And that was it for me. All the barriers that had built up between Judaism and Christianity disappeared, vaporized, and I realized there were no real religions, there was only one God and that was the God I believed in. I knew I was going to be fine at the school. And years later, when I went back to Cyprus, I heard from one of the fathers that before he died Camillo said his family back in Sardinia had Jewish origins."

Uri made up for lost time, almost instantly regaining the popularity he had enjoyed before the disastrous Torah-stealing incident back at Ahad Ha'am School in Israel. But he was still distinctly wary about what he did in the paranormal line—and for whom. A consistent characteristic begins to emerge in him even this early in his life: he seems to show different people different versions of his abilities. Leaving aside his enemies and those who are intellectually opposed to what he does, even his friends report widely differing personal experiences of him. Some friends, like Eytan Shomron, waited forty years after first meeting Uri to see him bend a spoon, then found themselves amazed and shocked by the experience; others were shown things to astonish them the first time they met Uri; yet others had been friends for decades without ever seeing him perform anything remarkable, even if they wanted to; another group makes a point of never wanting to see him do anything paranormal, explaining that they like him as a man with or without his powers, are worried that they might feel they have detected sleight-of-hand if they see him perform and that this would lessen their respect for him.

One of Geller's closest schoolfriends in Cyprus was a chubby Armenian boy, Ardash Melemendjian, who enjoyed dual renown at Terra Santa as a mechanical genius and a sexual prodigy. "I was one for anything on wheels and anything in a skirt," he jokes. He lives now near York, in northern England, where he works as a general repairman, is a prominent Freemason, is married to Janet, a local Guide leader, and speaks in a broad adopted Yorkshire accent with an Armenian twang. He is also an amateur rally driver, having worked for the Czech Skoda car company for many years as a technical representative—it was he who undertook the considerable technical challenge of preparing Skoda's first successful rally car. Although he has not seen Geller since they were young, they remain in contact by phone. He has only ever watched his old pal bend a spoon on television. And yet he is perfectly satisfied, even as a supremely practical and rational engineer by trade, that what he saw is genuine: "I have no doubts. I don't have to see it in real life, because of what I experienced with him at school," he says. "A lot of people will ask me if there is any trickery to it and I say, 'You believe what you want to believe. I think it's genuine. I know it's genuine, but I can't explain how he does it because I don't know.' It must be some sort of mental power that the rest of us are unable to exercise because we don't know these things.

"George Geller," Ardash continues, "would have been about twelve-ish when I met him. What was my first impression? That you knew him the instant you met him. It was some sort of magic that you couldn't explain with this feller. You couldn't help but like him and get on with him. He had this grace of making things nice, and people liked being with him. You'd never wrong him in any way, or do anything against him. Uri Geller was the ringleader, if you like. He got people gelling together, and when you made friends you made friends forever.

"And, yes, certain little things happened. The college was built in an area they called the Acropolis, all stone quarries and caves. We used to go down to these caves, Uri and several other kids. They were quite dangerous, and we were told at school that some boys had got lost and died down there once. But we'd pinch the school toilet rolls, put a stick through them and use them as a thread. Then we'd put old bicycle tires on sticks and light them as torches. But you could run out of toilet paper. One time on our return from the deepest caves we got badly lost. We were faced with three ways to go in the pitch black. Someone started to say something and suddenly Uri said, 'Shhh,' and everyone hushed. He thought for a minute and then said, 'This way!' and we went straight on or to the left, whichever the case was, and then we walked a long way before anything happened. But suddenly we saw a little circle of light, and it got bigger and bigger, and that was the exit. I'm sure the rest of us would have chosen another way. I don't know how he did it.

"There were other oddities which when you put them together, even back then, just made you wonder what *was* this guy," Ardash continues. "He never once got a puncture on his bike, and yet we used to ride through the same fields, the same thorn hedges. I'd get them all the time, and end up sat on the back of his bike, holding my bike while he was pedalling. We'd go to the cinema to see X-rated films. I'd go to buy my ticket and get told, 'No, you're too young—out.' He'd go to buy his ticket—and it would be perfectly all right for him, even though we are the same age and looked it.

"Another thing that we used to take for granted, never gave a second thought to—he never revised for anything. You'd find him sat down with a textbook that we were supposed to be studying and he'd have a comic inside it. But when it came to overall results at the end of the term you could bet your boots that he'd be top. I'm not very good at math, and we were doing an algebra exam. In one question, I kept getting this astronomical figure that I knew I shouldn't. Uri was sat next to me and said, 'Just copy me.' I said, 'What if Archie sees me?' Because Archie, one of the masters, used to throw whatever came to his hand, whether it was a piece of chalk or the rubber for the blackboard or a book and every time it was bull's-eye. I didn't like being hit by missiles in classroom. But Uri said, 'No, if he is going to see you, I'll give you a kick on your shin sideways with my foot.' So I was looking at his paperwork and copying down what he wrote in a slightly different way so that the teacher wouldn't cotton on that I was cheating. At the time I never thought anything about it, but years later, I started wondering how did he know to kick me if Archie is going to look? He would have had to have some sort of premonition. But he wouldn't tell me that's how he was operating, and I wouldn't know because we never thought of these powers that he has.

"Him and basketball was yet another thing. All right, he's tall, but basketball teams would always want him on their side. A group of fellers made two groups to play basketball, and whichever side Uri was on, the other side would say, 'No, that's unfair, you've got him. Every time he touches that ball, it goes through the net.' Yet he wasn't a keen basketball player. He played it as and when, whenever it was there. He didn't practice to be good at it or anything." (Uri maintains that he was able psychokinetically to edge the ball into the net. A Greek boy of Uri's time, Andreas Christodoulou, who is still in Nicosia and works as a maintenance contractor at Terra Santa, confirms this, and adds that "He would definitely move the hoop in a way, it looked as if it was vibrating without anybody at all touching it. You could see it move, I believe, a couple of inches when George was shooting at it.")

Uri also became famous, Ardash recalls, as a storyteller: "Mrs. Agrotis, our English teacher, would get him to stand up and speak for ages, and he would make stories up on the spot. A war story, a ghost story, anything. And I would be thinking, Wow, this is better than reading a book." But as for metal bending and interfering with clocks, he has no memory of Uri doing either: "If he had those qualities at school then he never showed them to me. I think he probably didn't because people would start getting dubious about him. Imagine two twelve-year-old kids and one rubs a spoon and breaks it in half. What does the other one think? That there's something wrong with him. As it was, everything he did we all took in our stride. It was only later on, when you think about it, that you think, How *did* he do that? Like his being ace in school, like finding his way out of the cave, like never getting a puncture, like the odd thing in the algebra exam . . . it's too much for one feller."

"The only one time I impressed him," concludes Ardash, "was when there was a particular type of speedometer I wanted on this armored car we used to pass in a scrapyard. I could see it from the fence, but inside the compound there were two Alsatians, one of them a real mean junkyard dog. So I started saving my sandwiches, and when I went past every afternoon, I would throw them over the fence. The dog would eat the brown paper bag, the sandwich, the tin foil—gone. This went on for three or four days and after that the dog would look at me going past at that time of the day and instead of snarling, its tail would waggle. I gained confidence. Then I'd pet the dog through the wire mesh, and finally I took enough sandwiches that the dog would take a few minutes to eat then. And while he was at it, I jumped over the fence, stole the instrument and jumped back again. Uri stood there watching me, leaned up against his bike. He just shook his head, astounded. 'I would have never done that,' he said."

Bob Brooks, now a criminal attorney in Los Angeles, gives a similar account of a charismatic, even if not necessarily psychic, young Geller. Brooks had come to Cyprus with his mother and stepfather, who was an entrepreneur. His stepfather had cut a deal with Brooks: if he stayed at the college a week, then he would have the option whether to stay on or to try somewhere else. "My first memory of Uri—or George—Geller was of him saving my life," Brooks says. "After crying for two solid days and being utterly miserable when I came as an immature twelve-year-old from Sherman Oaks, California, into this physically harsh regime with its Arabic toilets and intimidating six-days-a-week British public-school traditions, Uri befriended me. He was much older, at fourteen, and was nice and friendly and interested in me. And it worked. I liked him instantly. He invited me to his house and, all of a sudden, life was fun. Uri was the class monitor, who sat at the back and was held responsible for us. But he succeeded by strength of personality rather than bullying. He was taller and older than most of us, which helped."

Again, through Brooks, we hear nothing of unusual events. It is almost as if he was at school with a different Uri Geller from Ardash Melemendjian. "I do remember him complaining that watches would always stop on him," Brooks says. "One time he just nonchalantly took his watch off and said, 'That's another one that's quit on me.'" But of metal-bending, Brooks shakes his head: "I can't say I saw anything like that, no." And of Geller's basketball prowess? "Sure, I remember him shooting hoops, but not bending anything."

And here another consistent element in Geller's story forms out of the mist. Bob Brooks is delighted to confirm his great and continuing affection for Uri, but he is by no means an acolyte or a total believer. A lawyer with the skeptical view of the human condition that his profession encompasses, he cheerily refers to his late stepfather as "a con man, basically" and keeps a book on con men on the living room shelves of his California home. He couldn't help recalling, as he watched Uri's career develop in subsequent years, his friend's affinity with the showbusiness people who stayed at the Pension Ritz. Yet, he is anxious to emphasize that he does *not* think Geller is a con man although neither will he commit himself to accepting that he is an out-and-out paranormalist. It is probably fair to say that Brooks still does not know what his friend is.

"Uri visited me at the office in the early seventies and bent a spoon for me at that time, which was witnessed by four other co-workers," Brooks says. "Then he visited my home this past winter and bent a spoon for my daughter. This was done in our kitchen, near the washing-machine—Uri said being near metal helped him—in front of Samantha, Linda and myself. The way he did it appeared to be without any obvious use of force and without any attempt at sleight-of-hand. If it was a trick, it's the best one I have ever seen executed. Frankly I'm still amazed by how he did this. All of this stuff is contrary to my understanding of the physical universe and, while I do not wish to dismiss it all as merely a trick, I cannot find any other acceptable explanation."

Given these perspectives from two of Uri's closest schoolfriends, it is not hard to guess which of the two he has kept more closely in touch with: it has to be Ardash rather than Bob. Not so: it is Bob Brooks to whom he has remained closer, to whom he wrote frequently throughout his twenties and thirties, whose home he has visited, with whom he goes out to dinner when he is in Los Angeles. And Uri admits that he has a tendency to cleave to people who don't *quite* believe in him. "It's often those people I feel close to," he says, "the ones I feel I have yet to convince, and would dearly love to but can't. I don't really know why that is."

The thoroughly convinced Ardash, meanwhile, has had to resort to some fairly irregular means over the years to keep in contact with Uri. "About eight years ago I saw a newspaper spread about him, and he hadn't rung or written in a long time, so I thought, I am going to test your powers, mate. And I got the paper with his picture in front of me, his eyes looking at me, and I stared for about five minutes and said, 'If you've got anything about you, you get in touch with me.' The following evening, I get a phone call. 'What's the matter? What do you want me for?' It was Uri. I said, 'Nothing's the matter, I just want to say hello.'"

Joy Philippou, a teacher at Terra Santa, had no contact at all with Uri for forty years, until she wrote to him after seeing a newspaper article about him. Yet Mrs. Philippou, now in retirement in the southeast London suburbs, is as strong an independent witness of his early psychic prowess as could be found, someone whose account would provide a powerful dissenting note in any skeptical assessment of Geller—if anyone had troubled to talk to her.

"Uri was one of thirty children in my form," Mrs. Philippou recounts. "He stood out. You can't have gifts like that and remain anonymous. As he was a child he used this thing he had for pranks, for fun. For example, he did this clock-moving thing, not just on me but on other teachers as well. But for me, it took a long, long time before I put two and two together and realized that it was him who was doing it. I wasn't into the supernatural or anything like that, and I couldn't make out what it was. But whenever it was my turn to ring the twelve o'clock bell, I would have Uri fidgeting in the class, wanting to get out for lunch. The clock was behind me, an electric wall clock, about a foot in diameter. The class was in front of me, Uri sitting among them and he would be looking at the clock. I would check with my watch to make sure it was twelve o'clock, and it said the same. But as soon as I got into the staff room, they would say, 'Why have you rung twenty minutes early?' I would say, 'It can't be, look, my watch says twelve o'clock. But all theirs would be a quarter of an hour earlier than mine. It wasn't until I began to hear stories from other teachers that I began to find that Uri had something to do with this. One teacher had made him stay half an hour after every one else. She said, 'You won't go home until the clock says four thirty.' So he started to get up and leave, and she said, 'What are you doing? I told you four thirty.' And he said, 'But it is four thirty,' and she looked at the clock, and that's what it said.

"He also became famous because of his basketball playing. He *guided* the ball. He could shoot from almost anywhere. It never, ever missed the basket. Now that is a feat for an eleven-year-old. From one end of the court to another, over and over again. I thought it must be my imagination, but several people began to talk about it. Then I realized that this child really did have some peculiar power, particularly during matches, which it was important to win. Suppose he would shoot and his aim wasn't quite a hundred percent, and the ball was a few centimeters from the basket. He would definitely *do* something. We all saw the ball sway when there was no one near it, or sometimes the post would sway a little to the left or the right, whichever way he wanted it for the ball to go in. In truth, it was really scary. There'd be a great deal of talk and argument. People would say, 'Ah, no, it's just a fluke, someone must have pushed it.' But then you'd see it happen over and over again. We had very little contact with Father Camillo in the staff room. We mostly dealt with Father Kevin Mooney, who was head of the British section, and when we mentioned this extraordinary George, he brushed it aside somehow. It was difficult to convince him that something supernatural was going on. But most of us could see that what he was doing wasn't sleight-of-hand, and that this child had something extraordinary."

It is clear from Mrs. Philippou's recollection that it was the adults at Terra Santa who were more struck by the unconventional nature of Uri's apparent powers than the children. "I suppose when something like that happens, children don't necessarily understand it," she reflects. "They either make a joke of it, or they start bullying whoever it is. In Uri's case, it was the former. They would laugh at it. It was the children mostly who alerted me to the clock business. In the playground I seemed to see clusters of kids around him, and he would be doing something which they would be going ha-ha-ha at. But for them, it was a game. They didn't realize that there was anything beyond the ordinary. It was, like, he can jump five meters and I can't. What blew people's mind in the staff room was this ball business and the clocks moving. But also he could read other people's thoughts. If they played cards or guessing games, it was impossible to keep it from Uri, simply impossible. They just could not win. If people were planning something that wasn't to his liking, he would know. Of course, the children would say he guessed.

"As with all exceptional children," Joy Philippou summarizes, "some people loved him and others were jealous. But it wasn't like a persecution, as it is now, with everyone saying he is a charlatan, because he had nothing to prove then. He was just being himself. Every day he went to school and something new cropped up, and he just played about. I think he was discovering his own powers, and every time a new situation arose, he experimented with what would happen. Little by little you establish some sort of reputation. He didn't appear to use his powers to make people like him. The gut feeling that Uri brought out in many people was that they felt he did have something special. If nothing else, there was that intensity in his eyes. He has the same eyes now as he had then. I thought maybe he was going to be a fantastic poet, because along with this intensity there was an understanding that was far beyond his years. If you are sensitive to Uri's powers, this is a very powerful man."

The young Mrs. Philippou's fascination with Uri was probably exceeded by that of the more senior Julie Agrotis, an Englishwoman in her forties who was married to a Greek and taught English at Terra Santa. By Uri's account, Mrs. Agrotis took a more proactive interest in him, and he grew quite close to her. Mrs. Agrotis's curiosity was sparked when a story was going round the staff room that Uri's test papers in maths bore a striking resemblance—mistakes and all—to those of a German boy, Gunther König, whom Uri sat behind. Uri says he saw Gunther's answers "on this greyish TV screen in my mind" by looking at the back of the blond boy's head. He had first noticed this "TV screen" during his mother's card games back in Tel Aviv; it continues to be his description of how he senses the conventionally unseeable and unknowable. He says images tend to "draw themselves" on the screen rather than appear in a flash. Naturally, the teachers assumed he was copying by normal means, and made him sit in a far corner for exams, under individual guard. To the teachers' bafflement, the copying continued: Uri's answers in a weak subject mirrored those of whoever was top in it. (König, today a toolmaker at a Siemens electronics plant in Berlin, is one of the few ex-Terra Santa boys who remembers anything odd about Uri. "He used to sit next to me, but I wouldn't let him see my work," Gunther confirms. "But then I think he would look straight into my mind. I didn't actually think about it at the time, and I didn't talk about it with the other boys. I was just astonished." But König, like Brooks and Melemendjian, has no memory of Uri bending metal or deviating basketball hoops.)

Mrs. Agrotis was a popular teacher, renowned as a softie who never punished children. Nevertheless she had to take her turn in guarding the habitual exam "cheat." It was while she was doing so that Uri forgot himself and asked her about some incident in the market in Nicosia that was troubling her from the day before. She was alarmed, as she had been thinking about it at the moment he asked. On another occasion, he says, he saw the word "doctor" on his screen and, for a fleeting moment saw her in a surgery. He asked (a little cheekily, one would imagine) if everything had been OK at the doctor's.

Mrs. Agrotis and Uri started to have long talks together after class. It was some while before he felt confident enough to do it, but eventually, he showed her how he could bend a key and a spoon. She was astonished. She did a series of telepathy experiments with him, to what standard of rigorousness we will never know, but they left her baffled and wondering, more than any of her colleagues, just what made the boy tick. He would confide in her all his secrets, going right back to when he was a toddler and played with bullets. He told her about the episode in the Arabic garden, and insisted, with a conviction she may well have found eerie and disturbing, that he knew instinctively there was life on worlds far beyond our solar system. She would persuade Uri to retell his space-travel stories for the younger children. One day, Uri recalls, a teacher brought in four broken watches, which he was able to start ticking by passing his hands over them. Occasionally, when he was sent on some errand to the stationery supply room, he would hear the teachers discussing him in the staff room. One would say he was supernatural; another would insist that whatever had happened was coincidence. Someone else would say it was all trickery. He got a huge kick out of listening to them arguing and asking, "What is he?" since, he says, he hardly knew himself. "I was just a normal boy with friends, except I had a bizarre, weird energy coming from me, which seemed really to be mainly for entertainment purposes."

When he was alone plenty of strange things were happening to Uri and he did not tell anyone, even Mrs. Agrotis, about them. Life was taking him down an extraordinary path, and his experiences were so bizarre that he dared not speak about them for fear of being accused again of lying. Uri says now that what was happening then was only a taste of the weird things that soon invaded his life. He even speculates on whether he was being tested in some way (or even testing himself) to see if he could cope with more and more inexplicable events around him, and still maintain some credibility when he made some of them known. Once, he says, he got lost on his own in the caves and this time could not navigate his way out. He remembers praying to God for help, then hearing the distant barking of a dog. He followed the barking, to find that Joker had somehow made his way the two miles from the hotel to find him. Another time he was out driving in the mountains with a Hungarian friend of his parents, who was putting a new MG through its paces. While his companion stayed in the car, he wandered off on his own, only to find himself being held on the ground by men with guns. It seemed he had stumbled upon Colonel Grivas's secret EOKA guerrilla hideout. He was taken to see Grivas, who, he noted quite correctly, spoke Athenian Greek rather than the local variety. He told the terrorist, who had a large reward on his head, that he was Israeli, which struck a chord with Grivas. He approved of the Haganah, in which Uri's father had served, for its struggle against the British. He, too, had fought originally in British uniform, and was now obliged by nationalist politics to oppose his former comrades. Trusting the boy, Grivas sent him on his way.

The Hungarian was angry and worried when Uri appeared back at the car. Where had he been? Uri told him, but the man accused him of making the story up. Uri kept his cool: it did, after all, sound ridiculous. Why should anyone believe it? *Why* were all these things happening to him? And was he destined to spend his life either keeping secrets, or suffering the frustration of being disbelieved at every turn?

It was early in his time at Terra Santa College, when he was still twelve, that Uri's stepfather died. He remembers one of the monks Father Bernard, taking him out of a class to tell him that something had happened, and then receiving the news from a friend of his mother that Ladislas had suffered a heart-attack and was not expected to live. In the car back to Nicosia, he cried, not for his stepfather but for Margaret. His mother was on her own again, which meant he would no longer board, and would have to become a dayboy, like Ardash. He was happy about coming to live at home, but was immediately aware that he would become the man of the family. And he did. It was Uri who arranged to sell his stepfather's half of a music shop in the city, and plough the money into a smaller but better Pension Ritz in a modern villa he located on his bicycle. He organized the finances and the minutiae of the move, all in the middle of a civil war. It was little wonder that he matured so quickly—nor that he lived to such a large extent inside his own busy head.

Like Mrs. Philippou, Mrs. Agrotis lost touch with Uri after he left Cyprus and went back to Israel at eighteen—yet another of the "converts" to whom he did not feel the need to write. But when his fame was reported outside Israel in 1973, she wrote to a British newspaper from Nicosia. The letter is another compelling clue that Uri's powers were active much earlier than is generally credited:

Dear Sir,

Uri Geller was a pupil of mine for five years in Cyprus. Even while so young, he astonished his friends at the College with his amazing feats, i.e., bent forks, etc. The stories he told of the wonderful scientific things that could, and would, be done by him, seem to be coming true. I for one do believe in him. He was outstanding in every way, with a brilliant mind. Certainly, one does not meet a pupil like him very often. Yours sincerely, (Mrs.) Julie Agrotis.

Of course, few teenage boys or young men could countenance for long the idea of having psychic powers and not using them in the pursuit of the impulse that drives most such lads most of the time. Did Uri Geller use *it*—paranormal powers? oversize charisma? gift of the gab?—to launch him on his sexual career? Or did he need not to, nature having been especially kind to him in not spoiling his childhood good looks during adolescence? He does not normally downplay his psychic abilities, but he accords them a pretty low priority in his account of these adventures. Perhaps his assertion that, as far as women were concerned, he could do very nicely on his own without paranormal intervention was no more than macho teenage vanity, or perhaps it just happens to have been true. Or perhaps he felt he would be taking unfair advantage of girls if he used whatever it was he possessed to overcome them. Whatever, by his mid-teens, Uri was simultaneously in love with two girls, neither of whom was prepared to sleep with him. The first was Patty, the slim, blonde daughter of the coach of The Barons, a baseball team he joined on the American military base. He was too shy to speak to her, but she approached him, said she liked the way he played ball, and asked him out to a movie at the American club. Both in shorts, they got to the cinema late that evening and had to sit close together on a windowsill to watch a film whose title he can't remember. She put her hand on his leg, he put his arm round her. He was in love. They would swim together, dance and kiss, go bowling and eat hamburgers and hot dogs. He formed a lifelong attachment, concurrent with his love for Britain, to all things American, from the easygoing lifestyle to the material cornucopia of the PX store.

At home he was infatuated with a Greek-American girl over the road called Helena, who was dark and tanned rather than blonde, but as pretty and intelligent as Patty, and more intellectual, which appealed to Uri. He had been too

shy to speak to her, too, and had eventually faked a ball-over-the-fence incident while he was playing with Joker. The two got on well together. Whereas
with Patty, things barely got beyond kissing, with Helena, he pressed his case
a little further, although she, as he puts it, "was very successful at stopping me."
As happens with forces families, Patty's dad was called home a year or so into
their romance, and Uri did not hear from her again. He was happier with Helena, anyway. And then Eva, a German dancer with short, black hair, fashion-
ably cut, and expensive perfume, checked into the Pension Ritz.

Late one hot afternoon, with his mother away, Eva set about seducing the
tall, handsome Israeli boy, who was watching television listlessly. She told him
it was so hot that she was going to her room to change into a swimsuit. After
a few moments, he heard her calling to him through her closed door. She was
standing, he recalls, in a bikini and asking for some assistance with a bra catch
she simply couldn't close. As he was struggling, with uncharacteristic lack of
success, bearing in mind that the clasp was metal, she discarded the bra entirely and pulled him down with her on to the bed. From that point on, he relied on what he had seen in the movies and heard around and about. He
admits he was awkward. "Please don't tell my mother about this," he remembers blurting out. "I had become a man, but my emotions were those of an
adolescent," he says today.

Losing his virginity was a mixture of triumph and letdown, as it so often is.
He was just as enamored with Helena before as after. "Aye," recalls Ardash
Melemendjian, forty years later in his Yorkshire Armenian accent. "It's true.
He fell in love with his next-door neighbor. She was slightly older. Maria?
Anna? Anyway, he was madly in love with her. I used to say, 'Oh, come on for
goodness sake, *in love.* What does that mean?' He'd say, 'Don't you think she's
pretty?' And I'd say, 'Oh, all right, man, everybody's pretty.' I said to him, 'You
save your pocket money and I'll take you to a real pretty lady. So come the
time when we had a guinea each, we pedal up on our bikes towards the American embassy, where there were some blocks of flats. We park our bikes underneath there, into the lift, fourth floor, along the corridor and press on the
doorbell. An old lady comes and opens the door and says, 'Good afternoon,
boys, come in, sit down.' Next thing, an old boy comes out with a hat with two
feathers in the side, says, 'Have a good time, boys,' and takes his hat off and
bows to us, cheerio, and off he goes. He was Greek. Obviously he'd paid Lola,
had his fun and off he went. So the next thing I know, Uri is sat there, and his
knees are shaking with nerves. I could almost hear his kneecaps rattling. It's
August, scorching hot, so he can't be cold. 'What are you doing that for?' I ask.

'I can't help it. I know where we are I know what's going to happen.' Next thing Lola comes through, a big buxom blonde with lots of hair and blue eyes. 'Get inside there and undress yourself. I will be two minutes.' Uri says, 'You go first. I'll see you when you come out.' I'd already paid my guinea to the madam, and so off I went. I said to him before I went, 'If you're not here when I come back, I'll have your guts for garters, you'll be in big trouble.' He says, 'Right, OK.' Two minutes later I'm out and he's in. Two minutes later he's out with the biggest cheesy grin on his face. 'Yes,' he says, 'I can't wait to save my next guinea.' We can't have been more than fourteen, fifteen years old. She must have been old enough to be my mum. But you don't think about those nitty-gritty things when you're that age, do you? And anyway, he wasn't in love after that with the girl next door, the one called Maria or Anna. I think about it sometimes and the only conclusion I come to is that we had a very happy childhood."

The encounter with Lola—Uri's account is almost identical to Ardash's, although he thought it had happened a year or so later and that Lola's fee had been ten shillings, not a guinea—affected Uri quite deeply. "Helena and Patty, they were the girls I really loved but they were not really women that I would remember clearly. They really left no impression. Funnily it was Lola, the prostitute, who left an impression. Also, the German girl who seduced me. Having real sex was the first time I felt passion and the real sexual urge. Those are the moments you don't forget."

So did the young Uri use his talents to help him with women? "I don't think I could quite understand my powers then. If I knew then what I know today through life and experience, I would have probably sent my powers of telepathy to their mind and tried to seduce them and try and alter their thinking towards me. I would have tried at least to use it. I didn't need to, though, because I was basically a relatively good-looking guy. There was a stage when I was heavy, but I was always courteous and polite and nice to everyone, and they liked me for what I am. Now, I did telepathy, and I would bend things for their parents, who would instantaneously take a liking to me. So I would use my powers to impress not only girls but generally people around me, because I knew that the result was always positive. When you are surprised and astonished and bewildered about someone, you tend to want to talk to that person more, or be around that person more, find out about that person more. And that was very easy for me to achieve."

There was a whole other side to Uri's teenage activities on that all-liberating bicycle, to which Ardash was not privy. After Uri and his mother had moved to the new hotel, the business took a downturn. The warfare was becoming so intense and the curfews so frequent that foreign entertainers and theatrical companies were giving Nicosia a miss. The hotel, though, was close to the Israeli consulate, and attracted a few visitors from Israel. One was a tall, well-built man in the grain-buying business, Yoav Shacham. Uri became friendly with him. He enjoyed speaking Hebrew with an interesting man, who also knew judo and offered to teach him. But while they were practicing moves, Uri says he had the feeling that Shacham was more than a grain buyer. He used to get mail from all over the Arabic world and, moreover, Uri believed he could see on his mental screen his friend practicing with firearms and working with documents in some way. It occurred to him that Shacham was a spy, which appealed to his cinema-honed imagination.

One afternoon, Uri had to go into the loft, and found himself above Shacham's room. He overheard a conversation with overtones of espionage. Through a wiring hole in the ceiling he saw Shacham with a middle-aged Arab who, he gathered, lived in Egypt. The two were poring over and photographing documents, which Uri could see were in Arabic. The men were speaking quietly about such matters as the Egyptian Army, something happening in the Sudan and some business concerning agricultural machinery. Uri was thrilled and excited. The dramatic Israeli connection stirred him, and somehow, knowing that Shacham was a secret agent made Uri want to tell him more; confiding in nice Mrs. Agrotis was one thing, but telling a real Mossad agent was the stuff of his dreams come true. "I wanted to share the secret of the powers with someone I didn't know too well," he explains.

When Uri told Shacham what he suspected he was, the agent was horrified, and probably ashamed that he had failed so amateurishly to cover his tracks. He confirmed that Uri was correct, and appealed to his young countryman's patriotism to keep it to himself. Heaven knows what he thought when the boy to whom he had just been obliged to entrust his deadly important secret, said that he possessed inexplicable, magical powers. The Mossad man did not seem too pleased.

Uri asked him to think of numbers, which he guessed correctly each time. He made Shacham's watch hands move. Shacham invited him out for a walk. Uri told him as they walked that he would do anything to spy for Israel too. Shacham explained that he was far too young, but then truly put his life in Uri's hands. He said, "You can help me." A routine started whereby whenever Shacham was away from Cyprus Uri would cycle to the post office in Nicosia to pick up his mail from the *poste-restante* box and deliver it personally to the

Israeli consul. Loyally he told no one what he was doing, but made the mistake of wearing an Israeli insignia his father had won. The consul zoomed in on it and asked gently whose it was. Uri told him about his father being a sergeant major in the Tank Corps, and the consul smoothly extracted every detail from him.

Back in Israel, Tibor came home to find his apartment had been almost taken apart by intruders, although nothing had been stolen. He had no idea what had happened. The Mossad, it seemed, had been anxious to check that Tibor wasn't a double agent—as well as to warn Uri that he was playing with the big boys now. Meanwhile Yoav and Uri, his unpaid courier, became close friends. Uri met Yoav's fiancée, Talma, and Yoav promised Uri that when he had finished his military service at twenty-one, he would gladly help him get into the secret service.

If it was impossible for Uri to reveal any of this to his friends or family, one arena presented itself in which he could show off. It became known in Nicosia not that George Geller could bend spoons with the power of his mind but that he had uncommon motivational skills. "The hotel was also used sometimes by football managers and one of them was a Hungarian who trained a local Cypriot team. He used to take me every Saturday to psych the players up. When I learned I could influence a football team, it meant to me that I could also teach people. I also think I helped motivate a basketball team I played for. The first time I got into a newspaper was with that team, my name a millimeter high, with a picture of me running. It was a big deal to appear in the paper. I think they felt that part of my powers rubbed on to them and gave them extra energy. Who knows? Another Greek sports paper also carried a picture of the football team when it won the championship in 1963, and I'm in the photo."

As with all Israelis, as Uri approached eighteen and the end of school, there was no doubt what the next three years would bring for him: Army service. He was more than happy about this. Although he had been to Israel to see his father only twice during the seven years in Cyprus, father and son were still close, and Uri's male role models were his father and Yoav Shacham, both men of action.

After Margaret was widowed, Tibor had been over to stay in the new hotel, and husband and ex-wife were just about on speaking terms. Uri's immediate ambition therefore was to be a soldier, and then serve Israel as a spy, but his mother had more conventional hopes for her only child: "I would have very much liked him to become either a singer or a lawyer," she says today, "but as the main occupation, a lawyer. For he is certainly eloquent enough, thank God."

But would the Israeli secret service be too covert, too low-profile for a boy whose biggest thrills came from hearing himself talked about in the school staff room, and seeing his name in the local paper? His excitement since childhood at performing in front of an audience, his naturally extrovert personality and his contact with showbusiness types at the hotel combined to give him a strong impetus to perform in adulthood. Additionally, the violent circumstances of Cyprus in the fifties and early sixties had triggered in him a quirky—although hardly unusual—interest in the ghoulish. "Seeing death everywhere, seeing people being blown up and shot and body parts interfered a lot with my psyche," he admits. One of his first experiences in Cyprus was of seeing a young British soldier walking along a street with his young daughter on his shoulders, and an EOKA fighter coming out of a doorway and shooting the man in the back. He was deeply sorry for the man and the child, but was equally affected by the tragedy in a second way. "Witnessing someone getting killed when you are only twelve to thirteen, and daily waking up and opening the papers and seeing pictures taken in morgues becomes a powerful influence. There is one picture that haunts me even today. A whole Greek family was slaughtered in a village, and their bodies were thrown into a bath tub." Because of this slightly macabre tendency, he was fascinated by a picture in a book he had of a half-rotted Ancient Egyptian mummy. Much later, Tibor gave Uri a photograph he had taken in the Sinai desert of the top half of an Egyptian soldier, blown apart and burned black, his hands clawing at the air. Uri still has it among dozens of bags and boxes of family photos.

"My dream as a young man was to become a horror-film actor. There was a whole morbid side to my fantasies. I loved monster movies. My favorite one was *Tarantula* [a 1955 black-and-white film about scientists creating a giant spider that rampages through the desert]. When I was a boarder at Terra Santa, they took us to see it. For weeks afterwards, I was frightened to death in the dormitory by the monsters I thought were lurking in there. It was something that I built in my mind. It went to such an extent that I saw a comic at the American Club with an advertisement for these rubber horror masks and I ordered one from America. It took ages to come, but when it did, it was my most important possession. It had big bulgy eyes, big white teeth, blood dripping on its face and warts all over. I used to scare people with it. I loved scaring my mother's friends. I even went to one of those automatic photo machines with it on. It was a real fascination with horror. Boris Karloff and Peter Lorre were my heroes, in a way. That was what I thought would make me famous—being a horror actor. I knew there was something that could make me well known, and it was not necessarily my powers."

Chapter 4

Starting Point

"Look, look, it's bending . . ."

Uri Geller, as he held the author's spoon, July 1996. It wasn't bending.

. . . .

Do we believe what we see? Or do we see what we believe? When we watch a conjuror make a rabbit disappear, we know perfectly well that, in reality, bunny is safe even though he seems to have dematerialized. In other words, we see what we believe—that conjuring is a skill that enables people to create clever, convincing illusions. Uri Geller asks something different of us: he demands that we believe what we see, that we accept he is honest when he says he isn't cheating, and that he can genuinely do things that the most elementary physics states are impossible and, anyway, can be duplicated effectively by regular conjurors. It's a tall order, but over the decades tens of millions of people have been adamant that they witnessed something rare and special when watching Geller. Yet—and this is the fundamental question about Geller, the crux of the entire, almost fifty-year phenomenon—when he seems to do amazing things, do we merely see what we believe? Does Geller, by strength of personality, quickness of hand, or even some form of hypnosis, convince us initially that he has paranormal powers, then strike quickly while we are vulnerable and cause us to believe that an illusion he just performed was actually *not* an illusion?

The process by which I became interested in Uri Geller illustrates, I believe, most sides to these questions. When I started out, I do not believe I was receptive to him. I am not religious, had never had a psychic insight into any-thing, seen a ghost or experienced so much as a spooky feeling about some-one or somewhere. I had, I suppose, had the odd suspect ESP experience, but when pressed put each down to coincidence. I had never seen a UFO, and was deeply suspicious of those who claim they have, especially after once attend-ing, as a journalist, a meeting for UFO "abductees" in New York. All of the people there seemed to me to be in the throes of a complex rape fantasy, in which they convinced themselves they had been interfered with sexually by male aliens. Indeed, if there was one thing I found truly amazing about the paranormal, it was the astonishing number of people who *don't* have para-normal experiences, even though 70 percent of us apparently admit to believ-ing in them.

I was irritated, therefore, in 1996, when my son, David, then fourteen, be-came interested in the paranormal, and especially in Uri Geller, whom I had imagined was dead or in hiding somewhere, his trickery in bending spoons humiliatingly exposed decades ago by science. I was amazed to hear his name spoken at all by a fourteen-year-old. I was eighteen when Geller first became known in Britain, and considered myself rather above conjurors, pseudo-psychics, or whatever he was supposed to be: Uri Geller was someone irritat-ing fourteen-year-olds who were into magic harped on about. But that was in 1973. Geller must be about fifty now. Where had my irritating fourteen-year-old heard of the rogue? It turned out that Uri Geller had been bending spoons on an afternoon TV show and David was hooked, just as other boys had been in the heyday of flares.

Now, of course, the irritation factor was even greater, because of the World Wide Web, on which I was astounded to discover some three thousand sites concerning themselves with Uri Geller and almost a hundred thousand men-tions of him. David pointed me to Geller's Internet site, and told me that pub-lications from the *Sunday Times* to a computer magazine had that year voted Uri Geller's Psychic City site among the best in the world. I tried to explain postmodern irony to David, and how the more intellectual media were going through a phase of reassessing unfashionable seventies icons, like Max By-graves, Gary Glitter and, come to mention it, Uri Geller. He had to understand that it was all strictly tongue-in-cheek. Getting excited about Uri Geller's Web site was a just a sophisticated, grown-up joke like the revival of lava lamps. David didn't get it.

A few days later, on a warm May Monday evening, I had to drive out to a town near Cambridge on a story for the *Sunday Times*. I was going to see a millionaire electronics manufacturer called John Knopp, and David came along for the ride. Knopp was doing some interesting work, ended sadly by his death a year later, on a potential electrical cure for cancer. Although he was a country boy, who left school unqualified, conventional scientists I spoke to about him were anxious to explain that Knopp was a genius at observational physics. Michael Laughton, professor of electrical engineering and dean of engineering at Queen Mary and Westfield College, London, regarded him as "very likely the greatest inventive mind Britain has produced this century, a national hero, but an entirely unsung one." Another contact, a London University lecturer in physical chemistry, said of Knopp, "Any academic who looks down their nose at him because he doesn't have letters after his name and a string of publications is basically a prejudiced old git. He is very, very impressive."

But what impressed—or, to be accurate, depressed—me that evening was when John Knopp got talking to my son. "You know who you remind me of slightly, about the eyes?" he said, in his broad rural Essex accent. "You're a dead spit, you are, for my good friend Uri Geller." David was fascinated, as one might expect. Did he think Geller was real? he asked.

"Well," Knopp replied, "I used to think he was just an old magician, but I totally believe in telepathy and in people having a psychic affinity for certain other people, and I think he is genuine, yes. He made my key bend right here in my own hand while I was holding it, and there was *no* way on earth he could have done that by trickery. My argument with Uri is that I can't see the point of it. If he could straighten a bloody key, now that *would* be something." Before we left, John took our phone number and promised he would ask Geller to phone David.

On the way home, I restated my position: "Uri Geller is a proven fake. Don't waste your time thinking about him. He's a con man, he's history. I don't know what John Knopp was on when he told us that, and you'll never find out because Uri Geller is not going to telephone you. Ever." There was a moment's silence.

"OK," David said. "If Uri Geller is a proven fake, prove it."

A little annoyed, I started to search through various databases for recent articles from serious British newspapers and magazines. All had done their best to be scornful of Geller, but in each case, journalists had admitted to leaving meetings with him a little crestfallen because he appeared to be able to do just what he says—bend metal and read minds. It became more intriguing still. I was convinced that Geller's powers had never stood up to scientific scrutiny, but the evidence, forgotten or deliberately ignored by me and other rationalists, is almost precisely the opposite. As far as I have been able to discover, few scientists in thirty years have disputed after running tests on Geller that he has powers which, as they cautiously put it, are worthy of further examination.

The late Dr. Wernher von Braun, the renowned NASA rocket scientist and father of the US space program—not to mention the Nazi V1 and V2 bombs—was on record as saying, "Geller has bent my ring in the palm of my hand without touching it. Personally, I have no scientific explanation for the phenomena." Dr. Wilbur Franklin of the physics department at Kent State University in Ohio had announced after testing him: "The evidence based on metallurgical analysis of fractured surfaces produced by Geller indicates that a paranormal influence must have been operative in the formation of the fractures."

However, in the same articles, professional conjurors were also quoted: they opposed Geller doggedly and at every turn. They said he had managed to convince a gullible media and public that a variety of well-known, simple tricks are paranormal. The magicians insisted that they could do the same as Geller by using conventional sleight-of-hand methods. Now *that* was the kind of argument to which I was receptive. They explained, convincingly to me, that there was nothing to Geller's trick: all he did in essence was bend the spoon behind his back when you weren't looking. Nobody has ever *seen* Geller bend a spoon in front of their eyes, they stated confidently.

The scientific and journalistic accounts were a little troubling, though. I couldn't speak for the scientists, but I had worked with some of the journalists who reported being baffled by what they had seen Geller do, and knew them to be hard-boiled to the point of cynicism. One writer I didn't know had reported in 1990 in the magazine *Punch* that he had brought his own large tablespoon to Geller's house to try to catch him out. "He held it with one hand and stroked it with the finger of the other," he wrote. "It wilted like a flower. He gave it back to me, and it slowly continued to curl like a British Rail sandwich." A photographer from the *Independent* had come away from meeting Geller to find that the keys in his pocket were bent.

One of the most intriguing reports on Geller's mind-bending was in 1996 by Nigel Reynolds, the *Daily Telegraph*'s then arts correspondent, and someone I regard as sensible and grounded. Nigel gave over a lengthy piece to an investigation he had done into how an appalling play, which closed after a few nights at the Hampstead Theatre in London, attracted rave notices from all the critics who attended on press night. *Some Sunny Day*, by Martin Sherman, starred Rupert Everett and Corin Redgrave, and had a paranormal subject, which the producer asked Geller to advise on. The story Nigel Reynolds uncovered, with some difficulty—even Geller was cagey about it, he says—was that Geller was present on the press evening, and managed to "bend" the critics' minds.

The evidence seemed to be there in the newspapers. "It is fun and, in its demented way, original," wrote the *Observer*. "It's the superb playing which makes the evening worthwhile," gushed the *Evening Standard*. "Brilliantly witty new play," reported the *News of the World*. "The play left me in an accepting, upbeat mood, but I did wonder, I really did," said *The Times* man. Most enthusiastic of all was the *Telegraph*'s critic, Charles Spencer, who announced that *Some Sunny Day* was "Without doubt, one of the most entertaining and unexpected plays of the year."

Reynolds was fascinated by the notices, and how they contrasted with those of critics who came the next night when Geller was not present. "Absurd mishmash. If there is method in Sherman's madness, it escapes me," the *Sunday Express* reported. "I am not at all sure what this adds up to," concluded the *Sunday Times*. When Reynolds discovered Geller's involvement, he put it to Charles Spencer, his own newspaper's critic. Spencer was candid: he actually thought the play was "preposterous," and admitted that he "would not rule out at all" that his mind had been taken over by Geller's, even though he had not known the psychic had been in the theater. "There was definitely a good spirit, good vibes, in the air that night, and for a reason I can't explain, I was in an uncommonly good frame of mind," Spencer said. "I was writing for publication the next morning. I normally find that torture, and I am usually in a complete panic, but I was relaxed and calm that night." He even confessed that until he sat down to write his review, he had been unsure of whether to call the play a hit or a flop. And he was now "surprised" by the depth of passion he had felt for Sherman's play.

Even one magician, it seemed, as I ploughed on in my attempt to prove to my son that Uri Geller was a phony, had been convinced by Geller. Leo Leslie, a professional conjurer in Denmark and a leading light of the Danish Magic Circle, did tests with Geller in Copenhagen and concluded that he was genuinely beyond the abilities of a magician.

David was triumphant at my discovering all this, but meanwhile, another week passed, and Uri Geller still hadn't phoned. I might yet win the battle of wits with my fourteen-year-old. Perhaps he'd forget about all the pro-Geller stuff I'd found, and believe his father, when the promised phone call turned out to be more Geller moonshine.

But Geller did finally call. After talking with him for at least twenty minutes,

David handed me the phone, telling him, "I'm going to put you on to my dad. He's the journalist." I felt ridiculous talking to Geller. What was the point of it? I felt I was wasting his time. But Geller didn't seem awkward. He was pleasant and enthusiastic, with a light, Israeli voice. I apologized to him for David having taken up so much of his time, to which he protested that he had been delighted to speak to him. He promptly invited the whole family of five round for tea one weekday afternoon. I was even less comfortable at this, since David had obviously told Geller how implacably skeptical I was of his abilities. But I found myself accepting and making a date for a Tuesday a couple of weeks hence.

Perhaps Geller placed in my head the idea of writing a biography on him. All I know is that, in the space of a minute, I went from wanting to do nothing less to thinking it would be a good idea. The extraordinarily opposed position of Geller's supporters and detractors, along with the whole unresolved enigma of the paranormal, were deeply intriguing. And, although I had paid it no attention, there *had* been a remarkable revival of interest in Geller in the preceding months. There had been no mention of him for nearly a decade but now broadsheet newspapers and respectable magazines had been featuring him one after the other. The *Independent*, the *Daily Telegraph*, *The Times*, the *Sunday Times*, the *Sunday Telegraph* and the *Sunday Telegraph* magazine had all interviewed him in quick succession. In each case, the journalist assigned had concluded, often with some reluctance, that there just might be something in Uri Geller after all. Wouldn't it be interesting if I could prove conclusively that he was a con man? Or that he wasn't?

On the appointed day, the whole family drove to where Geller lives by the River Thames just outside Reading. We were late. There were plenty of jokes in the car about it not being necessary to phone to say we would be late as he would doubtless know already by his psychic powers. I still felt distinctly embarrassed about the whole thing. The chance that he would give this doubting Thomas the access I would need for a proper biography was, surely, minimal, and he would almost certainly be a control freak who would strike anything vaguely critical from the manuscript. I would mention the book idea, I decided out of politeness, but in such an unenthusiastic way that he would not take me up on it.

We didn't need to go through the charade. Mr Uri Geller was not at home. We learned this from a puzzled Israeli voice on the entryphone, which was on the wrong side of a fearsome-looking set of electric security gates. He was not expecting anyone, we were told. He had gone to London. He might be back tonight. We returned home in silence. My wife and I didn't say so, but we were clearly sharing a comforting thought: we had wasted an afternoon, but on the other hand, at least we wouldn't be hearing about Uri Geller again from David.

As we got home the phone was ringing. It was Uri Geller from his mobile, with one of the more impressive excuses I have heard for a missed appointment. It was the day before the Euro '96 football semi-final between England and Germany, and Uri had been to Wembley Stadium to plant energized crystals under the goalposts to help England because he was worried they were going to lose the following night. "You'll read about it all in the papers tomorrow," he said. He had completely forgotten we were coming, was terribly sorry, and reinvited us a week the following Sunday.

Minus my wife and younger daughter, who had both retired uninterested, we arrived at Geller's house mid-morning. Geller is a lean, intense man, who looked nearer thirty-five than fifty. He struck me, David and Ruth, who was then seventeen, as eager, quite disorganized, but very hospitable and thoughtful. We were introduced to his manager and brother-in-law, Shipi Shtrang, a smiling Passepartout, who straight away reminded me of a cautious Boo Boo Bear to Uri's impulsive Yogi. Then there was Uri's wife Hanna, a pretty, blonde, shy woman who, I felt, would be difficult to get to know, his mother Margaret, in her eighties and speaking only Hungarian, and the two polite, attractive and beautifully behaved children, Daniel and Natalie.

The house was huge and modern, in colonial style, with a sizeable gravel forecourt, several cars and dogs. Inside was immaculate, and full of strange New Age artworks and countless crystals—some enormous, near-man-sized specimens. It was plain that this was a household built by, inspired by and largely a monument to Uri Geller's gifts and talents, a place in tune, above all, to his needs and desires. Although there was an earnestness in all the New Age artifacts, there were also quirky things everywhere, which suggested a family with plenty of humor. Fixed high up on a wall in the entrance hall was what looked like a bicycle from the Starship Enterprise, an amazing space-age machine that Uri told us was the world's fastest bike; on display in another room was a huge, eight-foot-wingspan model of a Boeing 727 in an Arab airline's colors, which Uri had somehow acquired once. The furnishings throughout looked as if someone had run riot with an open checkbook in an extremely expensive store somewhere in the Mediterranean. The items were colorful, ornate and clearly costly—yet it was all comfortable in a way such millionaire homes often are not. There was a pleasant smell of some kind of incense in every room.

Uri asked if we minded him using his exercise bike while we had coffee. He is a fitness fanatic and a vegetarian. The exercise bike is in the conservatory, where we sat looking out over a pool, covered although it was the middle of summer, and across vast, trimmed lawns down to the river. We chatted over the whooshing of the bike, which was less off-putting than it sounds: he punishes himself on it for an hour a day, working up a sweat, but talking easily without puffing. He seemed to have guessed, or mindread, that I was thinking of writing a book on him—so much for leaking the idea gently into the conversation. But we left the idea hanging. He talked mostly to the children.

Uri doesn't need to be psychic to know that most social guests will be hoping that at some stage it will be showtime. As he was cycling, he tossed a pad and a felt-tipped pen to David, who was sitting a few meters away. "David, do a simple drawing on that while I turn away with my eyes closed," he instructed, "then place it facedown on the table, make sure I could never possibly see it, and try to transmit the picture to me mentally." David drew something, shielding it with his hands, although Uri had stopped cycling, turned his back to us and had his hands over his eyes. David placed the drawing facedown as instructed, and Uri turned round and started to concentrate.

I decided at this stage that it would be interesting to try to sabotage the supposed ESP demonstration by thinking of spurious images and beaming them in Uri's direction. Of course, if he picked them up, it would be the opposite of sabotage, and actually make a point to his credit, but it would be interesting all the same. I thought hard of hippopotamuses, dollar signs and Stars of David. I do not know why these images sprang to mind, but Uri asked quite sharply if I would stop "all that junk" because he couldn't read David's thoughts. Impressive, but a worthwhile gambit on Uri's part: maybe most journalists try to interfere in the way I had. If I had said, "What junk?" he could simply bluff that my mind was too active, and I should try to think of nothing.

David did another drawing as Uri looked away again. This time, after the paper was firmly face down, Uri turned round, smiling. "You've drawn a stick man," he said, immediately grabbing a pad and pen of his own from the untidy ledge above the speedometer of the exercise bike. "It's something like this." He scrawled briefly and the two held up their sketches simultaneously. Uri's was a perfect copy of David's—so exact that when we measured them, the height, 6 centimeters, and the width of the head, 1.8 centimeters, were identical. Uri cycled on for a few moments as we tried to work out if we had been fooled. Then he stopped, and asked the very thing we had, of course, been hoping for. "Would you like me to bend a spoon for you?" he asked. We would, we confirmed. "Just a minute, I'll go and get one," he said. At which point David, like half the visitors, I imagine, to the Geller place, produced one we had selected from the cutlery drawer at home. It was an oversized teaspoon, chosen because it was thicker and heavier than most. Geller's brow furrowed fractionally, in what I suspect is his customary reaction. "It's a little thick," he said, "but I'll try." He steered us all over to a radiator, saying it sometimes works better if he's touching metal. Then he put his right hand on the radiator—which at least kept it out of the way for illicit bending purposes—and held the spoon halfway down its handle between his thumb and forefinger.

I was amused to note that nothing happened. Fifteen or twenty seconds passed, the four of us in a close huddle. "Look, look, its bending," Uri said. If it was, none of the three of us could see it. "David, hold out your hand." He placed the spoon flat on David's hand. I dipped my head down to see if there was some slight bend which I could at least be polite about. Viewed side on, there was a barely perceptible warp of perhaps a few millimeters out of true. It was sufficiently bent, let us say, that we could have congratulated him, if halfheartedly. "Wait, wait," Uri said. None of us noticed if he was smiling or looking anxious, because we were staring at the spoon, wondering what precisely there was to wait for. What must have been two or three seconds passed, but seemed like much longer. And then, like a miniature Loch Ness Monster arching its back upwards, a point of couple of centimeters south of the spoon's bowl simply, spontaneously, and rather graciously rose, until it was bent at a ninety-degree angle and standing up from David's hand in an upside-down V. We gasped. To see a spoon bend in Uri's hand, as everyone has on TV, is one thing. It could be a special spoon, he could be in collusion with the TV people, anything. But to watch your own spoon actually in the process of bending and without Uri touching it at the time was truly disturbing. I picked it up to try to feel if it was at all warm, or had some caustic chemical on it. There was clearly no chemical. I touched the bend point to my upper lip, a specially heat-sensitive spot. It was cold.

Uri held the spoon to look at it horizontally as if to assess his handiwork and seemed particularly pleased. (Later I measured the bend: the tip of the spoon handle had travelled 12 centimeters under our gaze.) He signed inside the bowl with an indelible marker.

It was a remarkable moment, and I judged it time to leave, as we had now been at the house for over an hour. Ruth, either through teenage truculence or genuine puzzlement, had her arms folded, elementary body language that Uri noticed, because in the hall on the way out he touched her elbow, smiled, and said, "Ruth, there's something that will interest you in this room." He led us in, and gestured theatrically, as if introducing a turn on the stage, to a pair of chairs in pride of place, in the center of the sitting room. They were made of dozens of layers of crystal glass, laid horizontally one on top of the other. What was remarkable to Ruth and to me about the chairs, which had been made by an artist called Danny Lane, was that two months previously, on an A-level art trip to the Craft Council in London, she had bought a postcard showing one of them. She had liked it so much that she had put it up in her bedroom. A little shocked, we left and promised to keep in touch.

It had certainly been a persuasive finale. How could he have known that the chairs were special to her? Did he rummage around in her mind until he found some unusual item filed away within it that he happened to have in the house? Was it purely a lucky guess? What would have happened if she had shrugged and failed to react? A rigorous scientific approach, of course, would have to conclude that Geller must have surreptitiously applied an unde-tectable caustic chemical to our spoon when he held it, installed hidden miniature video cameras all over his conservatory, and burgled our apartment to see what we had on display in it before hurriedly buying two priceless arty chairs. My own version of rationality, however, could only deduce that we had either seen three genuine examples of paranormal powers, or some excep-tionally high-class magicianship. What militated against the latter was that the magicians whose comments I had read on the Internet mostly said that Uri was a very poor conjurer. The legendary Penn and Teller, for example, had de-scribed spoon-bending as "a lousy trick for lousy people." Could they really be talking about the same thing we had just seen?

I wanted to accept the rule of scientific law, yet what three of us simultane-ously saw Uri Geller do that morning calls two established facts into doubt—indeed, strictly speaking, disproves them. It is beyond question that rigid metal at room temperature cannot bend by its own volition, and silent mind-reading, without any known form of communication, does not and cannot exist.

The following week, early on Monday morning, Geller phoned me to ask if I had had any psychic experiences since meeting him. It often happened, he said. I replied that I had not, and had a strange feeling I was not going to. He either missed or ignored my little joke. Had I had any odd dreams? he contin-ued. I said that the previous night I had dreamed about an Alitalia A300 air-craft crashing after part of its tail was blown off. He said I should watch out because he feared something like it would happen in a few days. He added that he thought there would be a major earthquake on the west coast of the USA that week too. The following day, an earthquake measuring 5.7 on the Richter scale hit the west coast of Mexico. Well, all right. Then, on the Wednesday, TWA 800, a Boeing 747, crashed off Long Island after an explosion on board; it obviously wasn't Alitalia, but it was, as Uri pointed out excitedly, carrying a party of Italians on a cancelled Rome flight.

When he called I took the opportunity to say I had been thinking more about writing a serious, objective biography of him. Has the time not come, I argued, for Uri Geller, as a middle-aged man, to be thoroughly reassessed? He seemed receptive, but guarded. Over the forthcoming weeks, he warmed to the idea, finally accepting three weeks later. It was agreed, most crucially, that I would have his full cooperation, but would be at liberty to interview whichever of his fiercest opponents I chose. He would also have the right to read and correct the manuscript if it was inaccurate, but could not censor it.

Now I had to write a proposal and find a publisher. It was August, and we were going on holiday to a borrowed apartment in Torquay, on the Devon coast. Anxious to get my thoughts down, I slipped my new IBM Thinkpad computer into the car, and decided to get up early each morning, while the family were still asleep, to write the proposal. I had a lot to sort out in my mind even then, before I had started researching properly, about the experiences on 7 July at Uri's house, and the mass of material I had read on the Geller phenomenon.

The plan worked well. I got a couple of hours done before breakfast each day, and the children never even realized that their dad was doing what they hated—working when we were on holiday. On the fifth morning, I reckoned I would finish. Toward the end of the proposal on this last day of writing I mentioned that Uri was not the most intellectually brilliant of men; a fair observation, I thought at the time, but one, I supposed, that he might be hurt by. As I later discovered, he was extremely bright at school. At about 8 a.m., I finished, read the proposal, was happy with it and went to make some tea. While it was brewing, I went back to the Thinkpad to alter a couple of words. It was turned off. That was odd, I thought. I didn't remember doing that. I flicked the switch to reboot. Nothing happened. Assuming that the computer's battery had run down, I plugged it into the mains supply. The machine still refused to turn on. I checked the fuse in the power-supply plug. It was fine. I tried another socket, having first checked that it was live. Still no luck.

I began to sweat. For some stupid reason, I had failed to back up any of the proposal on to a disk. The IBM had been so reliable up to that moment that it had seemed unnecessary. I called the helpline in Scotland. They ran me through dozens of tests before declaring that the machine had suffered a major hardware failure and needed to go back to London for repair or replacement. "I hope you've backed up your documents," the IBM man said.

By now the family was up and wanted to go to our favorite beach, half an hour's drive away. David tried to get the Thinkpad working, to no avail. "Why don't you try the Uri Geller method?" he asked. "Just shout at it: 'Work! Work! Work!' Despite all I had learned in the past three months, this reference to Gellerana still irritated me, and I brushed it aside, but he persuaded me and, feeling rather foolish, I did it anyway. The computer came instantly to life, not even going through the reboot procedure, opening straight into the word-processing program, with the document before me. It was as if none of the trauma of the past two hours had happened. I put it down to coincidence.

The drama over, I saved the proposal to disk, then tried to fax it from the computer to my agent in London. This took another hour: after every page, the fax software went into spasm. Eventually it went across in eleven separate takes.

It was now 11 a.m. on a beautiful day, I was exhausted and far from popular with the children. My wife went into the kitchen to make some tea. Seconds later, we all heard a loud crash and Sue shouting, "Oh, my God." We rushed into the kitchen. A plastic wall clock had somehow detached itself from above the hob, where it had been hanging at a height of about two meters, traversed the room to a point just over two meters horizontally from where it had started, and smashed down on to the ceramic tiled floor—all without cracking or missing a tick. Although Sue was only aware of what had happened when the clock hit the floor, it seemed to have fallen impossibly: if the fixing had become loose, it would simply have slid down the wall and onto the work surface.

We assured each other that it was just coincidence that I had written an incorrect line about which Uri would have been angry, that the computer had malfunctioned in a bizarre manner, and that a clock, of all the clichéd Uri Geller things, had misbehaved seriously. But the spoon, the drawings, the glass chairs: did all these have a banal explanation too? Had three of us suffered a simultaneous hallucination when we believed we saw our spoon bend on its own? Had the identifying of so spectacularly rare an item special to my daughter been a confidence trick? Was I simply being open-minded and believing what I saw? Or had I started on the slippery slope downward toward unreason, toward seeing what I believed?

Chapter 5

The French Hill

"Kill the Jews wherever you find them!"

King Hussein of Jordan to his troops, on Radio Amman, 12:15 p.m.,
Wednesday, 7 June 1967, the third day of the Six Day War

....

Two almost concurrent rites of passage toward the end of 1963—Uri's
one-guinea afternoon tryst with Lola, the Nicosia prostitute, and the handing
over of his British GCE (General Certificate of Education) by Father
Camillo—marked almost the end of the Gellers' time in Cyprus. The island
had become too dangerous to remain there voluntarily: two hundred Turkish
Cypriots had been killed in intercommunity fighting, and hostile fighter jets
dispatched from mainland Turkey were making menacing passes over Nicosia;
three attempted Turkish naval invasions were only thwarted by the alert
American Sixth Fleet, and civil war seemed inevitable. The British colonial
secretary, Duncan Sandys, cancelled his Christmas holiday to fly to the island.
Shortly afterward, in the early spring, UN troops started to arrive, and Margaret and Uri began to settle their affairs in Cyprus. There was no longer any
point in being there: Uri was close to finishing school, there were virtually no
visitors, not even undercover Israelis, and certainly no travelling show people
to make the business worth running. Hotels were closing down all over the island. In addition, Uri would be eighteen soon and would have to return to Israel for his military service.

The Pension Ritz's shabby furniture was sold off, and the building returned to the landlord. Margaret's friends in Tel Aviv located a modest city-center flat for her to rent. Mother and son shipped their heavy goods, including a white Vespa scooter Uri had bought, ahead to Limassol. On the day of sailing, they got cars to take them, their suitcases and Joker to the port, where a mini-disaster ensued. The Customs officers decided to examine the suitcases slowly and carefully, and somehow, the ship, with dog and most, but not all, of the Geller household aboard sailed for Haifa. Uri suggested cheerfully that as they had some money they could fly, but no aircraft was leaving for Israel for another two days. They spent that night back at the Ritz, camping in the empty hotel with the owner's permission.

Soon afterward the Gellers, plus Joker, were reunited in Israel, and installed in the flat. This was a little cramped and dingy, but in a reasonable location on Trumpeldor Street, five hundred meters equidistant from the beach and the central business, restaurant and entertainment hotspot of Dizengoff Circle. It was an exceptionally noisy street, narrow and with buses roaring past every couple of minutes. But immediately opposite it, behind a three-meter-high stone wall, was a relatively quiet, and very grand, ancient graveyard, where many of the famous pioneers of the Israeli state rest in a semblance of peace.

Practically the first thing Uri did was to ditch his adopted Cyprus name. George Geller was no more, and he doesn't welcome even old Cyprus friends using the name today. ("I called him George on the telephone once, about five years ago," says Ardash Melemendjian, "and he said, 'Don't call me that. My name is Uri.' I replied, 'OK, I didn't know you minded.' I was surprised by how he obviously felt about it.") However, coming back to Israel was not really a matter of reestablishing an old identity. Uri had left Israel as a bewildered, confused and unhappy little boy and was now a rather more confident young man. He had no particular old friends to look up and, indeed, at this point, had the choice of reinventing himself as pretty much anything he wanted. He was an Israeli, but also an outsider because he had spent his formative years abroad. He was a loner, too, for at least three reasons: he was an only child, he had no friends in Tel Aviv, and he felt haunted by his perplexing supernatural powers. The idea of being in the Israeli secret service seemed more suitable than ever. But Uri knew from Yoav Shacham that he had to build a shining Army career before the Mossad would consider him; and if he didn't manage to become a James Bond he was perfectly willing to set his sights on the Army and follow his father. But the problem was that Uri was no great soldier. He could do the physical stuff easily but his innate individualism, which had rejected the communalism of the kibbutz, made the Army and the ethic of teamwork highly unappealing. The Israeli Defense Forces and Uri Geller were not, at the end of the day, made for one another.

For the moment, however, in the spring of 1964, Uri couldn't wait to get into uniform. He kicked around happily all summer and autumn, awaiting his eighteenth birthday, doing odd jobs to make money to help out his mother, building a social life and going through his Army medicals. In the evenings and at weekends, he played basketball again, and became known for what was called his "golden left hand." But, psychic prodigy or not, for the time being Uri Geller, international superstar-to-be, was just another Mediterranean teenager whizzing noisily and irritatingly around the streets on a scooter. "My first job was as a construction-site worker," he recalls. "I used to carry cement in buckets from the truck to the building site then pour them into the site. Every bucket weighed about a hundred kilos, but it was fun. I looked at it positively, and I started bringing some money home. My second job, my father arranged for me. I was to be a desk clerk at a hotel in Eilat. So I went down and had the time of my life, because there were hippies there and all kinds of beautiful girls from all around the world. I was seventeen and had my own room in the hotel. It was warm in Eilat, there was the beach, and every night I had another girl."

Back in Tel Aviv after the summer, the Vespa came into its own. "I worked as a delivery boy delivering architectural plans in long tubes around the city. I had a really bad boss. He was just ruthless. I was so angry at him—everyone was—that one day when he asked me to make him tea I peed in it. I am a good-natured person, but I needed revenge on that occasion. I could have done a lot of mind stuff to him. Today, knowing what my power can do is awesome, but I don't think I realized then that I could activate these powers. And, anyway, I don't seem to be able to do anything negative. And making my boss's watches and clocks move, I think, would only have entertained him rather than angered him." (It was interesting that the thought of using or attempting to use his mental powers for malicious purposes had not occurred to Uri more often in his youth. He is able to rationalize things now, as an adult, and conclude that, for some reason, he seems unable to do harm; however, there must have been a certain frustration on his part as a boy that he could "bend" basketball rings in his favor and snap spoons in half for entertainment, but not, say, snap his boss's brake cable.)

As the time of Uri's military induction approached, he toyed with alternative specialties to apply for within the forces. He had enjoyed scuba-diving in Cyprus, so he liked the idea of becoming a frogman, or flying, or above all, being a paratrooper—a suggestion Yoav Shacham had made to him back in Cyprus. Tibor pressured Uri to achieve what he had been unable to. Tibor Geller was one of life's master sergeants, able, brave, long-serving, but never quite officer material. He thought it was his strong Hungarian accent that had held him back. He told his son that he would love him to be an officer. The Paras appealed to Uri for the best of reasons: he loved the image—the green beret, which was exchanged for red when you got your wings, the different shirt from what the regular grunts wore, the special maroon boots with crêpe soles. The Paras' mystique was part of the image. They were a volunteer force within the professional Army, trained in the art of killing swiftly and silently, with unconventional weapons, often as the enemy slept. Tibor warned Uri that the Paras would be tougher than he could imagine, but the boy's mind was almost set.

December, the month of Uri's birthday, came, and he went off by bus to the processing center in Jaffa, was allocated service number 971171, and by the end of the day was settling into a tent with seven strangers at a boot camp. A flurry of mustachioed, yelling sergeant majors and frantically running recruits, it contained blocks where rookies could volunteer for the different branches of the services. A poster of a para about to leap out of an aircraft nearly dissuaded Uri at the last, but a couple of days later, Uri was on the back of a truck heading for Netanya, where the Paratroop training camp was. Weeks of running around the base with a 20-kilo kitbag (for the first three months you weren't allowed to walk anywhere), of obstacle courses and lengthy marches (which Uri hated) led to the purpose of it all: the first parachute jump. Paratroopers had to make seven jumps before they could wear the red beret. Recruit Geller's first jump, on a hot day at some nearby sand dunes, went perfectly. From then on they got progressively worse.

On his second he panicked and fell clumsily, jarring himself. A subsequent jump, at 4 a.m in the Negev desert, almost killed him. He had been edgy beforehand: he had dreamed the night before that he was going to die that morning. For once Uri did not accept this as a supernatural warning. He says he appreciated that dreaming of dying on a jump was fairly normal for a paratrooper. But as he and his colleagues were on the way to the airfield, a white dog ran out in front of their truck and was killed, which added to his unease by reminding him of the death of his first dog, Tzuki. Thoroughly rattled, he messed up the jump, banged into the side of the airplane and went into a spin. His main chute failed to fill properly with air, leaving him in the graphically named and deadly "candle fall." He failed to deploy his reserve chute properly, and was convinced as the desert floor approached that he was milliseconds from death. But at the last instant, the big chute opened and he landed, praying that he would never go through such an experience again. It did not stop him from completing the course and he got his wings—and his coveted red beret.

Immediately after this came a fascinating incident to which there was not a single witness—but which both skeptics and believers may feel proves their point. Practically nothing psychic, by Uri's definition, had happened to him or around him since he came back to Israel. He puts down the disappearance of his powers to pressure of time: "You are constantly occupied and busy in the Army. You wake up at four thirty in the morning, you have to clean your gun, you have to shine your shoes, you have to quickly have breakfast and get off to maneuvers. This is a non-stop three years. There is no time for anything except maybe to write a letter. My big moment of freedom was when I was able to slip to the canteen and buy myself the equivalent of a Mars Bar and take off the thin silver foil wrapper and just indulge in the taste of that chocolate melting in my mouth. That was my pleasure. There was no time for thinking."

Uri's first assignment as a Para, he says, was a 110-kilometer march into the Negev as a heavy-machine gunner, carrying with two other men a Browning machine gun weighing some 40 kilos. The gun broke down for transport into three parts, body, legs and ammunition, of which the heaviest was the body, which was his responsibility to carry. Worse still, it was his job to parachute-jump with it which, Army tradition maintained, was the hardest task in existence. The plan for the exercise, which would, if successful, gain him his corporal's stripes, was this: once down in the Negev, the team would be taken by truck further out into the desert with kitbags, then make a jump with the Browning equipment and march back ten kilometers to their base camp with it.

Let us say at this point that all young men, in virtually all societies, are adept at thinking up dodges from their responsibilities; it is almost part of the young male condition to circumvent imposed roles. Yet Uri Geller in his paratroop unit was—or, perhaps, should have been—an unusual young male. Here he was, a volunteer in a crack unit, with his own military reputation at stake, by which he set great store. Here he was, too, with his much-loved and admired father's standing in the Army at stake, and his relationship with his father, *and* his standing in the eyes of his other significant role model, the secret agent Yoav Shacham, whom he planned to emulate and to whom he would be going for a job. Here he was, additionally, with a small part of Israel's precarious security in his hands; for an Israeli, in an imperilled, besieged nation, to duck and dive on military service is a much more serious matter than say, for, a US serviceman to do a Sergeant Bilko and have a free ride at the expense of Uncle Sam. But, bearing all this in mind, Uri decided to cheat—big time. He hatched a plan to get off a duty lightly—yet in being rescued from the consequences of his dishonesty, he experienced what he regards as the second most profound paranormal occurrence of his life. It was topped only by a staggering, and in this case semi-witnessed, event many years later in New York.

His cunning plan of deception in the Paratroopers was not only fool-hardy—he could have been flung in a military prison for months and suffered a lifelong stain on his record—it will also reflect rather poorly, for some crit-ics, on how he should subsequently be regarded in his psychic career. If, after all, we are to believe what we see in Uri Geller rather than see what we believe, we need to know that he is fundamentally honest; if we are accept him as a sep-arate species from the run-of-the-mill conjurer, we are required to believe him when he protests his innocence of conjurers' tricks. Yet what he did on a tough Negev Army exercise, albeit as a young, inexperienced former Tel Aviv street urchin, was not just fleetingly dishonest but was carefully prepared and aimed to pull the wool over several people's eyes. All a little disturbing—except for one major point: this account of what happened does not emerge as the result of surreptitious investigation. Geller tells it himself. Whether we believe the para-normal part of it or not—and he admits candidly that it takes some believing—it is his own account. And if a miscreant is honest about his own dishonesty, for many people a certain superstructure of trust is immediately constructed. Thus it may even be (if we rule out some complex double bluff) that by ad-mitting the shady circumstances that preceded the following, Geller will gain some credibility.

This, then, was Uri Geller's plan, and how it fell bafflingly apart. The Browning gun body, he realized, when he looked carefully at its construction, could be broken down still further. If the heavy barrel *inside* the outer casing, and the mechanism that fed the ammunition through were removed, the cas-ing, full of holes to cool the barrel, could be placed in its canvas bag so that it looked from the outside like the full body, but weighed considerably less. Since the exercise of dropping with the full body of the gun was purely a fitness test, and they were not going to need to use the Browning after they landed, and since he was still edgy about parachuting after his near-lethal tangle of a few days previous, why not remove the innards of the gun and leave them in his kitbag at base camp? He could then carry the canvas bag easily on the ten-kilometer hike after the jump. He ran through the physical reality of this tempting plan as carefully as any magician plotting a complex stage illusion. He would have to make certain that none of his comrades got to carry the bag, as they would be likely to feel it was underweight, and he daren't risk anyone discovering his secret. But—significantly again, for his critics—he calculated that he could get away with it.

The moment of the jump came, and passed safely. The case, which was heavy enough, he winced, without its essential contents, was strapped to him for the jump, and let loose on a five-meter cable for the landing, to avoid him being injured by it on impact. He packed up his chute and slung the useless Browning over his shoulder for the march. Soon came the first problem—and with it, the first indication to Uri, perhaps, that people could be convinced to see (or in this case, feel) what they believe. Seeing Uri striding ahead robustly even though he was supposedly carrying the lion's share of the Browning, one of his pals insisted on helping him: "Look at poor Geller, they were all saying, he's carrying that bloody thing on his own." So, wary of protesting too much, he let his friend carry the bag up a hill. But far from working out that Uri had cheated the young man marvelled that he had never before been able to carry this part of the gun further than a few hundred meters without a rest. Now he could. He must, he puffed, as he handed the canvassed gun back to Uri at the top of the hill, be getting stronger. Uri was trying, he now recalls, to suppress laughter, when he saw something that almost made him pass out with fear.

A Jeep scrunched up alongside the group of men as they rested on a cliff edge. In it was a general. Uri knew at once that his game was spectacularly up. Very occasionally, on such a dummy run, the commanders would spring a surprise on a random bunch of soldiers, and put them through a full-blooded maneuver, in which they would have to shoot with live ammunition at an imaginary enemy ambush. It was an excellent way of keeping them on their mettle even during a relatively benign training routine, as well as giving them a chance to try their skills against the kind of danger that might well face them one day; in 1966, Israel had not been at war for ten years, since the Suez campaign, but a well-armed and angry enemy was never more than a few kilometers away, even in the heart of the country, down in its southern desert.

The staff officers ordered Uri's platoon to spread out and set up the guns, ready to fire. He was scared, and began to shake. He did not even want to take the empty gun case out of the canvas. As he did so, his mind racing to think of some way out of such appalling trouble, he could see daylight through it. His companion handed him the ammo belt; he fed it into the useless shell of the gun and cocked the non-existent mechanism. He looked again through the lid of the gun, in despair now, at the first bullet waiting to be fired by nothing, hoping ridiculously that something might have changed, or that it was a bad dream he was about to wake from. The first group were ordered to fire their gun; the end of Uri Geller was seconds away. The way ahead was clear; he would be taken away, court-martialled and jailed, then, at the end of what would have been his military service, he would be dishonorably discharged. His father would never speak to him again. He would have no friends beyond the riff-raff he met in the prison camp—if he was not kept in solitary confinement. His mother would doubtless take pity on him, but would never be able to hide her tragic disappointment, let down first by her husband, then her son. If he were lucky, a job as a street cleaner or a lavatory attendant might be his into old age. If he could not find anyone to trust him that far, he might end up joining the few tramps and bums who existed even in such a young, vital country. The general and the staff officers were hovering just behind him, their decorations gleaming in the sun. As his mind was in freefall, the sergeant major continued barking orders: "Company B . . . FIRE! . . . Company C . . . FIRE!"

He had a brainwave: it was not likely to work, but it was evidence, for all the good it would do him, of the quick thinking he was capable of when his back was against the wall. He decided to take his small side arm, a standard-issue Israeli-made Uzi, and surreptitiously place it next to his dead Browning. When the order came to fire, he would pull both triggers. The report of the Uzi would be feeble and too sharp to be mistaken for that of the Browning, but in the noise, confusion and cordite of so many heavy machine guns firing simultaneously, he might just get away with it. A bit of chaos, instinct told him, might work wonders at concealing what he was doing, perhaps even from the eagle-eyed top brass behind him. After all, they weren't expecting the *wrong* sound to issue from Soldier Geller's Browning. They were expecting the *right* sound. And it was just possible that they might hear what they believed.

He heard the command to fire and pulled both triggers. What unfolded in the next few seconds was a sequence he claims he still relives more than thirty years later. He insists vigorously that it was neither a fantasy nor a daydream. Yes, he knows he was always famed for his imagination as a child; he admits willingly that he had a wondrous ability as a young teenager to spin compelling stories out of nothing and to keep an audience rapt; he needs no reminding that what he maintains happened out in the Negev sounds suspiciously like one of his science-fiction flights of fancy.

But *both* guns fired. The spent cartridges spat out of the Browning until there was no ammunition left. His first thought was that God had intervened and, as he has never had any other explanation for it, that tends to remain his belief. An officer behind Uri, impressed no doubt by the young man's gusto at loosing two firearms simultaneously, even leaned down to tap his helmet and say, "Good shooting, soldier." Trembling, Uri put his hand on the hot gun, which was now dripping black oil, and kissed it. There had been an incident not unlike it once in the past when, as a boy, he had visited his father, who was in charge of the gun storage at his base. Having checked carefully that a machine gun was empty, Tibor let Uri handle it as a treat. Uri pulled the trigger, and a single bullet shot out. Badly shaken, Tibor put it down to a mistake, and Uri to just one of the strange things that happened to him around metal. The incident with the Browning, however, was immense in comparison, yet there was no one he could tell, not even in the rush of satisfaction and good humor that swept through the men as the officers drove off, leaving them with the march back to camp. He had told his closest Army friend, Avram Stedler, something of his powers, and his dream of being a spy, but knew that if he tried to tell even Avram such a story as this, he would probably lose his friendship.

What happened, or what Uri perceived had happened, would already be enough to unhinge most people. When Uri got back to the camp, he was naturally anxious to examine whatever it was he imagined he had so deceitfully left in his kitbag. And now came, if such a thing can be imagined, a still greater shock. He peeped into his kit and saw the barrel and firing parts of the gun, exactly where he had left them. He went back to the canvas bag to look at the Browning again. The casing was empty, just as it had been on the cliff edge when the general and the officers pounced on his unit. He returned to the kitbag and drew out the internal gun parts. The apparatus had been clean when he left for the exercise a few hours earlier; it was now oily and blackened—just as it would have been had it been fired. Yet, by any rational standards, it had not left the kitbag.

This sequence of events gave Uri a few things to think about as he cleaned the gun. His mind was full of Cyprus, of the light in the Arabic garden when he was five, of the bent spoons and the telepathy with Mrs. Agrotis. What had occurred presaged the kind of bizarre madness that happened around him—much of it with witnesses—over the coming decades. But in his tent in the Negev, anxious as he was to unburden himself, there was nobody with whom he could share it. Was there *anyone* to whom he could talk about it? Perhaps Yoav, if he saw him again. But that would mean admitting the dreadful deception to his hero. "I knew no one would believe me. What would I say to someone? That I left the barrel in my kitbag and then it reappeared shooting? I just decided not to think about it because it might make me insane. I thought, Maybe I am crazy and I never really hid the barrel, I only think I did. But I know I didn't. I *am* a logical person. I know my deeds. I don't take drugs, I don't drink, nothing can alter my consciousness or subconscious or clarity and thinking. When something like that happens you are amazed and shocked, and because of the shock you erase it and try not to think about it anymore. Lots of soldiers find all kinds of tricks to ease their struggle through the military. If *I* thought that I was going crazy, what would others think?"

His military service continued untouched by paranormal phenomena. He got his corporal's stripes, and was recommended for officer training. Sometimes, he says, something like a knife would bend on the table in front of him without him trying to do anything. But as long as it went unnoticed by his colleagues, such an event served as a micro-reminder of what he now strongly believed: that he was under the protection of some outside force, which was unfathomable but at least was not malevolent.

He went off to officer training school. Out on a field exercise in teeming rain one day, he was overjoyed to come across Yoav Shacham, doing a stint as a Paratroop officer. Uri told his old friend he had joined the Paras on his advice. He asked if Uri was still doing telepathy, and said again that his abilities could be put to good use in due course. Uri confirmed that he still dreamed of being a spy, but Yoav encouraged him to put all his effort into officer school, then to go back to the Paratroopers and establish a fine record. They parted. A short while later, two tragedies struck. First, while Uri was at home on leave, Joker had to be put down by the vet: he was in pain, dying of old age, Uri had to stop himself crying in the street outside the vet's—always a Para, even on home leave. Then, as soon as he got back to camp, he picked up a newspaper to read of the death of an Israeli officer during a cross-border raid into Jordan. He was the only casualty and had been killed by a bullet in the head. He was named as Yoav Shacham.

By Uri's account, the bereavement caused his performance at officer school to tail off sharply. He fell asleep on a night exercise, had to be kicked awake by an officer, and was thrown off his course the next day. "Yoav was the key to the door for my future," Uri says. "His death in this really small raid sank me into despair, firstly because I loved him, I cared for him, and then because I knew my career was down the drain. Only he really knew of my powers. So I couldn't care less anymore about officer school, and, apart from telling my father, who was devastated but advised me to try again, leaving and going back to my unit was a great relief. A big responsibility was lifted, and I felt fine about it."

A certain interesting dissonance surrounds two areas of Uri's time at the officer training school, and, as with his admission of cheating over the Browning incident, there is scope again to look at both in several ways. What follows can be seen as both pro- and anti-Geller—depending, as so much depends in assessing the Geller phenomenon, on one's own viewpoint.

The first question concerns precisely why he left officer school. Uri says that his departure was under a cloud, but a rumor persists in Israel that there was more to it than his simply falling asleep on an exercise. "When Uri left," says Eytan Shomron, his childhood pal from the kibbutz who briefly bumped into Uri at the training school, "his friends in his platoon said that when he did the sociometric tests, when you had to make a list of your best friends, he was the lowest, and that was why he was thrown out. I'm not at all sure it was the truth, but that's the rumor."

Another ex-student at the academy, Miron Givon, who was actually on Uri's course, although not in his classes, fleshes out the story a little: "Uri Geller's reputation as a potential officer wasn't really very good," he says. "He was one of the first cadets whom the cadets themselves recommended—under this new system of appraisal they brought in—as not suitable to be an officer in the Israeli Army.

"I don't think he enjoyed the reputation of a serious person. At that time it was very important that you had to be an example to everybody, and what I heard was that he wasn't always very loyal to his friends and he tried to do everything for his benefit and not for the good of the group or the team or the class he worked with. You have to understand that, at that time, most of the cadets came from either the kibbutzim or the *moshavim* [collective villages], as I did. So Uri was from a completely different part of the society, which meant that he wasn't regarded from the start as classic material for an officer. We always tried to volunteer for all kinds of missions without thinking about ourselves. We thought it was a good cause. We were very naïve at the time, but he wasn't the type to jump if he wasn't going to get some benefit out of it."

A note might be appropriate at this point about the question of rumor in Israel: there is a saying that goes, "Two Israelis, three opinions." National generalizations are always dangerous, but Israelis themselves complain about the extraordinary disputatiousness of their people, along with their predilection for gossip, often malicious and based in jealousy, at every level, from the coffee bar to the Knesset, the Israeli parliament. This is partly because Israel is a far smaller country than people realize. However, there is a deeper, more pervasive culture of embroidering truth for the benefit of the listener, which comes as a surprise to those who expect this technological, modern nation to display every characteristic of the West. In the West it is assumed, often wrongly that people mostly tell the truth about each other. In Israel, at the most important level, people are honest—there is, for example, almost no street theft, and among friends there is a profound code of truthfulness—yet to strangers, or when the truth matters less than telling a colorful story, tongues wag unfettered.

This problem has led to deep difficulties for many unwary and gullible folk, especially foreigners, who have tried to research Uri Geller's background. Some ten years after the events at which we are now looking, a respected Tel Aviv magazine published what appeared to be a devastating exposé of Geller. The piece is still bandied about by some as the definitive proof of his fakery. However, eleven years later, the then editor had admitted publicly that the entire story, quotes, sources and all, may well have been made up. Later still, there was great excitement when one of Uri's former managers admitted to having connived at helping him cheat. He eventually apologized, said he had been upset with Uri over a financial matter and had invented his story for a payment. Needless to say, the story of Uri being thrown out of officer school has been seized upon widely, in various exaggerated forms, by those anxious to construct a case against him. They often say that he was "cashiered" from the Paratroopers, which is, of course, a lie—even though, by his own admission in the Browning gun case, he should have been.

However, one item of gossip in Israel about Uri's military service that is of considerable interest, yet has been missed in the past, turns out to contain an element of truth. The story has it that, in bored moments, at the officers' training school, Uri would sometimes perform card tricks. Now many young men take an interest in cards—but Uri is particularly anxious to distance himself from routine conjuring skills. To be sharp with cards is the last thing he needs to be known for. He says it is possible that he did mess around with cards—in childhood, helping his mother win money at games, after all, had been a part of his life; but he has no memory of being adept with them. Yet Miron Givon, who left the Army a lieutenant, read economics and business management at the Hebrew University, and now imports kibbutz-manufactured plumbing supplies to Britain, has a clear recollection. "I remember Uri well from among the 120 other cadets because even at that time he had started to do his tricks, or whatever they can be called. I don't remember any spoon-bending, but he did card tricks, at which he was quite good.

"He also used to perform seances. People would sit round a table and he took a cup and put it on the other side and everybody put his finger on this cup and it started to move around the table and tell all sorts of stories about everyone round the table, and what may happen in the near future and all those kinds of things. I don't think we took it too seriously. It's hard for me to say whether he did. The interesting thing was that he said, 'I am not a magician,' and what I think about Uri—and I never changed my opinion—was that he tried to be very honest. That was my feeling. He said he believed he had some kind of extra powers that everyone has, but not everyone can utilize yet. He didn't try to play God at all, and to me, some of what he did looked like magicians' tricks, but I'm not sure. Maybe he's right. Actually, it's not something which bothers me too much. But I don't have any answer for it." Uri explains today that what appeared to colleagues to be tricks really were telepathic demonstrations.

Relieved that the strain of officer school was over, Uri accepted that he would not become a great soldier. During a week's leave, he helped his mother move into a smaller, quieter apartment on a street called Merkaz Ba'alei Mlacha, just a few blocks from his childhood home, and a few meters from the lively Sheinkin Street, now one of the most fashionable in Tel Aviv. Margaret was now in her mid-fifties, supplementing her seamstressing by waitressing in a coffee shop, which Uri found distressing. He wished he could make some money so that she could stop working, but knew there was nothing he could do about it until he got out of the Army. He made up his mind that then he would.

People's life stories in times of global trouble always have a micro and a macro level. Uri's return to his unit, his head full of career plans for the following year, when he finished his service, came a few months before the 1967 Six Day War with the Arab countries. Israel was on the point of having to fight for its life in what promised to be a David and Goliath struggle far more unbalanced than even Britain's lonely fight against Nazi Germany.

Israel's forces were, in many ways, a motley crew, made up of dozens of different nationalities. Many of the more senior soldiers were concentration-camp survivors, and they had been trained unconventionally compared to most armies. Their equipment came from mixed sources, and much of it was obsolete; their supplies of fuel and munitions were limited. Ranged against Israel were the armies of fourteen encircling countries, thirty times greater in number, and equipped with the latest Soviet weaponry, much of it tried and tested to the highest contemporary standards in North Vietnam against the Americans. The Egyptians, Israel's most populous enemy, had the benefit not only of the Soviets behind them but of a large number of high-ranking former Nazis, who came to Cairo to give quiet military and propaganda advice. It was public knowledge that Israeli intelligence calculated that if war came the Jews would have to begin to push back the Arab armies on every front within ten days to stand a chance of survival. It was a ridiculously unrealiztic target and, consequently, there was a widespread fear that Israel faced extermination—which today, when Israel is perceived internationally as the aggressive Goliath of the region rather than its David, is often forgotten.

With the war brewing, Uri was sent to a unit training to use a fleet of new French light armored attack vehicles. But while there, he came down with pneumonia. He was in hospital for a month, where they were already taping up windows and preparing emergency operating rooms, and then went to an Army convalescent station for ten days. There he met an already engaged girl called Yaffa, an Army officer who helped run the convalescent unit. Yaffa had black hair, green eyes and a beautiful body; within hours of meeting, Uri and she went to her room, made love together and he fell deeply in love with her. In the intense few prewar days they spent together, she said she loved him too, but felt she could not break off her engagement to a man she had known since she was thirteen. Nevertheless, when Uri had to go home for two days prior to returning to his new base, they made elaborate plans to keep in touch and see each other whenever they could. She gave him a list of everywhere she expected to be in the following months, and he left. It was two days before the Six Day War broke out.

The sirens ordering all Israeli services personnel to report to their units went off throughout the country early in the morning of Monday, 5 June 1967. Uri leaped onto his Vespa and ran every red light in the city, his hand permanently on the scooter horn. Because he had not finished the course, it was decided to put him in charge of eight men in a command car rather than to let him drive one of the new armored vehicles. By late afternoon, all ready and dressed in camouflage gear, he and his platoon sat and waited for orders. Even the officers did not know which front they would be sent to—the Golan Heights to fight the Syrians, Sinai to engage with the Egyptians, or the border with Jordan, whose armies were the best trained and technically competent of all the Arabs, and comprised by far the most dangerous of Israel's enemies in close ground combat. Like every citizen in Israel, Uri Geller and his platoon listened to the news on transistor radios. It was eighteen hours before they got their orders, during which much happened, as the waiting soldiers heard on the news. Squadrons of Israeli jets had burst out of bases that most citizens did not even know existed, and in three hours of the early morning had destroyed on the ground almost every gleaming new Soviet MIG the combined Arab air forces owned. Flying their sleek French aircraft in eight missions back to back, in radio silence and as low as 150 meters, the air force pilots, who ranged from tanned teenage kibbutzniks just off their tractors, to sequestered E1 A1 707 captains in their forties, to grizzled middle-aged RAF veterans, destroyed three hundred Egyptian planes (of which just twenty were in the air), fifty-two in Syria, twenty in Jordan and seven in Iraq. The first part of the Israelis' master plan, total air supremacy, was therefore theirs before suppertime on the first day. Israel was saved; now the country's military commanders wanted to make further wars unnecessary by pushing their enemies back from their borders. That meant ground fighting, which would take another five days.

The land battles, however, were a much harder matter than pulverizing the Arabs had been from the air, and none of the ground attacks the Israelis undertook was more difficult than defense minister General Moshe Dayan's bold attempt to take east Jerusalem and the entire west bank of the river Jordan, which had been a source of constant bombardment from the Jordanians for years. King Hussein already felt badly let down by Colonel Nasser over Egypt's military collapse within hours of the war starting, and the Sandhurst-trained monarch badly wanted his troops to give a better account of themselves.

At three in the morning of Tuesday, 6 June, Uri's unit was ordered to head for a point between Jerusalem and the town of Ramallah to the north of the city, to try to prevent the tough Jordanians getting supplies through to their renowned legionnaires in Jerusalem. Although he did not know the entire picture, he formed part of the northern jaw of a pincer movement designed to encircle Jerusalem. Ramallah was a cool summer retreat favored by rich Arabs, where King Hussein had been building a summer palace until the war intervened. On the slow journey across country to Ramallah, which took all of Tuesday, Uri thought continually about Yaffa, about his mother and father and about the strong possibility he sensed that he would be injured. He had a feeling at the same time, he says, that he would not be killed. Somewhere on the road, where they were refuelling the vehicles from a tanker, Uri saw Avram Stedler and became convinced that his friend was going to die. "Avram," he called out, "can I shake your hand?" Stedler was puzzled and asked why. "Just shake hands with me, please," Uri demanded. He felt sickened, he says, by the burden of knowing something he should not.

At lunchtime on Wednesday, 7 June, King Hussein made a stirring broadcast to the men of the Royal Jordanian Army over Radio Amman. "Kill the Jews wherever you find them," he said, in his deep, restrained baritone. "Kill them with your arms, with your hands, with your nails and teeth." By that night, Hussein had given up the struggle but in the afternoon at a spot called Tel el Ful, near an elevated position known to the Israelis as the French Hill, several of his loyal units attempted to do their king's bidding when they ran into the outfit in which Uri Geller served. They ambushed it and nearly wiped it out. Sheltering in a graveyard, as hastily called-in Israeli tanks engaged with Jordanians and Israeli aircraft bombed the enemy with napalm, Uri took a bullet or shrapnel through his right arm. Another soldier tore off his shirt to see if the profuse blood was coming from anywhere else but saw it was only a flesh wound and tied up his arm. Minutes later, Uri watched as one of his group's semi-light armored cars came head to head with a Jordanian Patton tank. It might have been his vehicle, had he not caught pneumonia and been deemed too out of practice after his long sick leave to be on board. As it happened, the car contained Avram Stedler. Avram, who was the gunner, could only fire his shell to within a few meters of the tank, where it exploded harmlessly. Then Uri saw the tank fire at the armored vehicle from close range and watched, helpless, as Avram's vehicle tilted and shuddered. What he describes as a strange rattle could be heard from inside the car, then a rumble, followed by smoke and flames. Uri and another soldier ran to the wreck to see if anyone was alive. The bodywork was red hot. The driver and the captain were dead, but Avram was still alive. As they pulled him out, what must have been an Israeli tank shell, fired from a distance away, hit the Patton and destroyed it. The shock wave knocked Uri's rescue party off its feet.

"I saw Avram's left leg was blown off," Uri recounts. "He was very pale, but conscious. As I dragged him, all he cared about was his penis. He kept saying, 'Is my thing all right, is it still there?' I opened his trousers and looked. It was all blown away with the leg. I lied to him, and said everything was fine. We got him to a house. He asked if there were helicopters coming." Uri grabbed a walkie-talkie with two bullet holes through it and called into the dead radio to pretend to ask for a helicopter with a *chovesh*, a medic. "I said a helicopter was on its way to pick him up and he'd be fine. Later on, of course, I found out that he'd died right there."

There were urgent things to attend to. The fire that was still pinning down the group was coming from a Jordanian pillbox above them, and Uri decided to lead a party up to knock it out. As they sneaked up the hillside, a soldier jumped from behind a rock and shot twice at them from thirty meters, but missed. Uri pulled his gun up to waist height with his uninjured left arm and looked the soldier in the face. He noticed he had a mustache before he fired accurately, killing him instantly. Some moments later, in the confusion, with explosions and flying bullets all around, he was hit again, this time badly, by lumps of metal flying off another stricken enemy tank, or possibly a ricochet. It was never established which. He felt a blast, sensed something enter his left elbow and the left side of his forehead, and, as he blacked out, assumed with resignation that he was dead. He remembers being surprised at how easy death was.

He was next aware of being in bed. The first thing he noticed was that everything around him was clean. His arms were both bandaged, as was his head. He heard from the radio that the war was not quite over, but was moving rapidly toward victory. He thought immediately of Yaffa. He saw other wounded soldiers in beds around him, most hurt far more seriously than him, and requested a phone. He called his mother to say he wouldn't be home for a while but he was fine. He didn't say where he was, as he knew Margaret also had her ex-husband Tibor to worry about—his father was fighting somewhere, probably in Sinai. Then he phoned Yaffa and, to his delight, reached her. He immediately went back on his resolve not to tell her where he was. She wanted to see him as soon as she could.

Uri had been lucky, the wounds stopped short of being serious, although his left arm needed an operation to remove the shattered bone and much more attention before it worked again. More than thirty years on, he still cannot fully extend it. During his weeks in hospital, he thought a lot about the Jordanian he had shot. "It was a split second. You don't have it in your mind that you are killing a person. You don't think. You just know that if you don't pull the trigger, you will be killed, and you are saving your life. I still have a recurring dream of that Jordanian soldier coming to me. He grabs my lapel and shakes me, and he is crying. He actually talks to me in Arabic, but I understand him. He says, 'Why? Why did you do it to me? Why did you take my life away from me?' I don't say anything and he is shaking me and I am horrified and I wake up. I don't wake up in any great sweat, but I am disturbed, and that day I feel depressed."

In hospital other things from his past swam into his mind. He wanted to contact his old friends from Cyprus, especially Ardash, who had left the island for England and had not exchanged addresses with Uri. One day, at his digs at number 13 Landsdowne Road, in Chingford, east London, Ardash received a letter from Uri, writing from his hospital bed. In his reply, Ardash asked how he got the address. "He said he thought of it while he was in bed in hospital. How could he have known my address?" Ardash still wonders. "I was living with my brother's parents-in-law."

Uri's military service wound down gracefully. He left hospital with his left arm in a cast, but the right healed. He was finally awarded his sergeant's rank, and as part of his recuperation, he spent the rest of the summer as an organizer at a holiday camp for children. He saw Yaffa when he could, but the relationship was clearly doomed. He was discharged, wounded, by the Paratroopers, as his fitness rating had gone down and went to the induction camp where he had started his service. Here, he resumed light duties, while still receiving physiotherapy. He was quite happy. He was assigned a job tracking down Army deserters. Normally he would have been expected to do this travelling around on the bus, but instead found an old BSA motorcycle, got his father to fix it up in his tank workshop, and set himself up as a sort of DIY military policeman. "I had this helmet and I felt superior on my motorbike. The camp was attached to a hospital, and there were beautiful nurses there. Every morning whenever I wanted to pick up a girl or find some new girlfriend, I would ride the bike between the nurses' bungalows. I would look very impressive, just like my father."

As for being exactly like his father in terms of staying on in the forces, if only in some minor NCO capacity, the injured left arm put paid to that—and in a socially acceptable way. Flunking the Army was one thing, but being a wounded veteran was another. Uri had cause to be rather pleased with the way things had worked out. "You know who really saved my life?" he reflects. "It was the officer who kicked me awake and said, 'Uri, get up,' when I fell asleep. If I had not been booted out of officer school, either I would have died in one of the wars or I would now be some general in the Israeli Army with an Army house, a little Renault and a driver. I met the guy who woke me up in New York once, in the lobby of the Lexington Hotel. I was already on my way to stardom and he was working as an El Al security man. I walked up and said, 'Weren't you the guy that kicked me and woke me up?' He said, 'Yes, Uri, of course.' So I shook his hand and said, 'Thanks for starting my career off.'"

Hanging around for official discharge on his last day as a full-time soldier of the Israel Defense Forces, Uri met a younger man, Ygal Goren, whom he had never come across before. In the odd way that these things sometimes work out, the two young men got on, and Goren is one of the few Army pals whom Uri still looks up when he is in Israel. There was a strong link between the two: it turned out that Goren had also been fighting near the French Hill the day the Israelis took that terrible pounding from the Jordanians, and had been wounded close to the same spot. Yet, oddly enough, they did not discover this until several years later, when they were talking, as they always do, about their Army days, a period Goren has noticed that Uri seems to find especially important to him. Goren went on from the Army to the Hebrew University to study political science, became a journalist, rose to be the diplomatic correspondent of Israel Television, and now has a private TV documentary production company in Tel Aviv.

Not knowing that they had nearly died in the same Arab village, or of the strange powers Uri believed he possessed, what stuck in Goren's mind after meeting him in 1968 was an odd thing his new friend had told him within minutes of meeting. "To tell you the truth," Ygal Goren says, "I didn't know what this twenty-one-year-old was talking about. I was laughing at him, just to myself. I had asked him, as you would anyone on their last day in the Army, what he was going to do now. And he just said to me, straight out, 'Ygal, I am going to be rich and famous.'"

Chapter 6

Word Spreads

"The jeans, the T-shirt, the simple, amazed nature . . . it was a brilliant idea."

Guy Bavli, Israeli magician—and skeptic

. . . .

By his late teens events and circumstances had conspired to make Uri Geller something of a loner. But in the summer of 1967, as he was recovering from being shot up in Jordan in the Six Day War, he met the man who became his devoted and loyal *de facto* kid brother, lifelong business manager, friend and confidant. Or, to put it another way, if by any chance Uri Geller *has* been pulling the wool over the world's eyes these past forty-nine years, Shimshon Shtrang is the one person on the planet who, as they say, knows where the bodies are buried.

It was a curious meeting, which these days might even raise a cynical eyebrow or two. Shipi, as Shimshon has always been known, was thirteen; Uri was twenty-one. Shipi had been sent by his parents for ten days to a children's camp an hour out of Tel Aviv called Alumim. Uri, with his arm still in plaster, and hence not ready to return to the Army, was a camp counsellor.

Uri was not taken on that summer to instruct in any particular subject, but just to supervise in the dining room and to keep the children occupied and happy. One of the best ways he had found to while away a few hours was to take a group out on to a patch of grass in the middle of the camp and tell them some of the stories he had made up back in Cyprus for Mrs. Agrotis's younger pupils. Among the children at Alumin, Shipi Shtrang was most responsive to

Uri's imaginative, scary science-fiction tales, and was constantly nagging him to tell another story.

Uri didn't only tell gripping stories. As a paratrooper, albeit an injured one, he organized some unusually exciting and ambitious outdoor games. "I remember very vividly that we used to go at night into the orange groves and Uri would divide us into two groups," says Shipi, an easygoing, smiling, patient man, who speaks slowly, says little, and has a certain aura of wisdom about him. "One group was supposed to be looking for us, capturing us. I'll never forget Uri had this idea. He got us to lie down under the orange trees. It was cold and at night, and it was really scary. We were thirteen and this was Israel, where there are always terrorists, and it was all up near the border, and the next thing I knew I was captured. Two guys pulled me out and they hit me with an egg over my head, and I can still feel the yolk running down my face."

What really fascinated Shipi about Uri Geller, however, and what had him chattering excitedly to his parents on the phone in the evenings about the wounded soldier who was looking after his group, was not that he told good stories or invented great activities. It was that the soldier had been performing some extraordinary mental experiments with his group. "In between the stories, he would ask someone to think of something or draw something," Shipi explains. "The whole subject of telepathy and mind-reading was really new to us, and I suppose we looked on it as magic tricks, as part of entertainment. But it was amazing."

More amazed still was Uri, who was staggered by the results he could achieve with telepathy when he conducted tests with children, and most especially with Shipi. Shipi would get numbers that Uri had written down and sealed in envelopes; he would go upstairs in a nearby building, draw his own pictures and apparently be able to transmit them to Uri outside on the lawn. Uri started showing the children his bending ability, and again, when Shipi was close by, or holding the spoon or the key, the distortion in the metal would far exceed that which occurred with any of the other children. The two experimented with nails, watch hands and any metal they could lay their hands on. "It seemed to me that Shipi was some sort of a generator to me, like a battery. The telepathy between us blew the other kids' minds because I didn't know him well. It wasn't as if we were friends or relatives." This symbiosis between Uri and Shipi would later become a matter of fascination to skeptical investigators, who wrote (100 percent incorrectly) that Uri could *only* function when Shipi was with him. The story, still quoted as gospel truth by some eminent researchers, circulated that Uri's "psychic" abilities first came to light during this summer camp, that Shipi showed Uri a book on magic, and that the two jointly cooked up the charade which became the Uri Geller stage act. Some researchers even claim to know which book it was: a magicians' textbook called *Thirteen Steps to Mentalism*, by Tony Corinda, which was published in England in 1958.

Today, even friends of Uri have an in-joke that, actually, Uri *is* an impostor—and that it has been Shipi all along who is the psychic. But the myth that the Uri Geller phenomenon only started at Camp Alumin when he and Shipi met has enduring appeal to its believers. Yet it is not, even for the devout skeptic, a very likely story. For one thing, there are too many pre-Shipi witnesses to discount, who attest to Uri demonstrating either paranormal effects or unusually precocious acts of magicianship in childhood. For another, struck as Uri was by young Shipi's complementary abilities in the psychic field, he was only a thirteen-year-old child, and hardly the type of person to whom a serving Paratrooper would look for career advice. For yet another, Uri being Uri, he was rather more interested in Shipi's nineteen-year-old sister, a pretty green-eyed honey blonde with a touch of the Faye Dunaway about her.

Uri Geller first met Hanna Shtrang at a parents' day, when the Shtrang family came over from Tel Aviv to see Shipi. "We were all sitting on the lawn and I introduced my sister to Uri, they talked a little bit, and that was it. My sister used to be like a hippie, she had little round John Lennon-style glasses, and long hair and was into the Beatles," says Shipi. Uri and Shipi demonstrated some of the psychic stuff they had been doing together in the camp, and Hanna was hooked, even though with her the experiments did not work particularly well. For the next twenty-four years, Hanna, then a supervisor at a Motorola electronics office in Tel Aviv, was Uri's on-off girlfriend, then full-time lover and mother of his children; the couple married in Budapest in 1991. "Hanna invited me over to her house that first time we met," Uri says. "I liked her very much, but I had a girlfriend at the time, so I didn't take it too seriously. But neither did I forget her."

When Shipi went home, he and Uri swapped addresses, and Uri promised to look him up. Although Uri had been aware of his powers long before Shipi came on the scene, and was clearly shopping around on the paranormal fringe in early adulthood, Camp Alumin was the scene of a revelation in the summer of 1967: there, he grasped the entertainment value of what he could do. "I suddenly felt like an entertainer for the first time in my life," he says. He also understood that, even if things had worked out in the Army, he was far too extrovert for the anonymity of the secret service. In his last weeks at the camp, Uri was thoughtful; he shone at entertaining, and had ever since he had told stories to Mrs. Agrotis' pupils. Was there the basis of a bizarre new stage act in his special abilities? In his last few months in the Army, he gave it a great deal of thought.

Although at home Shipi talked endlessly about Uri Geller, and Hanna was more than keen to hear from him, Uri was tardy about getting in touch. He had grown to superman proportions in Shipi's mind; he was his hero. Yet Shipi found, to his distress, that people laughed at his stories about Uri, and said it was all trickery. He insisted it was real, and promised that one day he would bring this amazing man to meet them. By a lucky chance, he was able to do just that a short time later. Uri's father was based in an apartment in the suburb of Givatayim, which he seldom used, so Uri took his girlfriends there. He was once giving a lift on his scooter to a girlfriend, when a few yards from the apartment, he nearly ran someone down in the street. It was Shipi. "I almost fell off the scooter," Uri says. "He jumped on me, and I said, 'What are you doing here?' and he said, 'I live here.' He lived about a hundred and fifty meters away from my father."

A few days later, Shipi invited Uri to the Shtrang house, where he talked some more with Hanna. From then, Uri gradually became almost an adopted son of the Shtrangs, with undertones of a romance between him and Hanna. He had other relationships on the go with glamorous girls in the city, but Hanna was increasingly his central point of reference. As he puts it tellingly, "I loved Hanna in a different way. She was fragile and a good girl, and we were very close." Shipi slipped into the role of slightly put-upon little brother. Once in a while, Uri would let him come out on the Vespa with him, but, as Shipi says, "Basically, he met my sisters. They used to go over to his father's flat dancing and would never let me come. I used to get hurt by that."

It was not long before Uri was doing his psychic stuff for the whole Shtrang family and their friends. "We started getting more amazed at it," says Shipi, "And when he explained to us that it wasn't a trick, even my parents began to believe in it. My father was a welder with this huge conglomerate, building bridges. He used to work a lot in Eilat and came home at weekends. My parents were regular people. They were not philosophers. I think to begin with they didn't take much notice of the things Uri could do. But when we got to do it under better conditions, and he would tell someone to go out of the room and he would still read their thoughts, they started to see there was more to it."

Uri was now working out the rudiments of a stage act, and Shipi, although he was still only a schoolboy now of fourteen, was quietly engaged on the same project. "When he got back to school Shipi obviously told all the kids and the teachers that there was this guy who was his instructor who can do telepathy. One of his teachers told him to ask me to come over to the school." In fact, none of the teachers had believed Shipi, but he had prevailed upon them to ask Uri Geller to come as a speaker. Uri would even be paid twenty-six lira (about four pounds) from a speakers' petty-cash fund—the first money he ever received for a professional engagement, and the first time he had ever been on a real stage. "I had nothing prepared or rehearsed. I just walked up, and there was a blackboard and I said, 'Right, somebody come up and write a color or a city or a number and I'll turn away and you'll all project it into my mind. So right there, I formed myself an act, starting with telepathy, which really impressed everyone. Then I did the rings—spoons weren't in my thing then. Everyone was wearing rings, so I started bringing people on the stage and bending the rings. I was obviously a natural-born ham, because I really found myself enjoying it."

Shipi, too, was enjoying it from the audience; he could see a showbusiness phenomenon in front of him, who was here because of him. Particularly delicious was watching his teachers and friends, who had sneered, change tack during the two-hour show. "I kind of accepted the phenomena now. It just became very natural. What amazed me was the different ways everybody reacted," Shipi says. Some people, he noted, would refuse outright to believe what they saw, while others would demand to see more and more, as if just one more demonstration if they watched it *very* carefully could help them work out in their own minds if they were being entertainingly duped, or if this was a real scientific phenomenon.

The teachers asked intelligent questions, the same as everyone had for years. Did he guarantee it wasn't a conjuring trick? How did these phenomena start? What else could he do? Interestingly, although Uri mentioned the spoon breaking in his hand when he was four or five, he had not yet made the final mental breakthrough of seeing that spoons, banal and everyday objects as they were, would make a wonderful central image for him to project his act.

What Uri says amused him about all this earnest enquiry, of course, was that he knew there *was* no explanation to give the school audience. This was just the stuff that had been happening to him since he was a child. There had been long periods when he experienced no phenomena, but something now—perhaps his contented state of mind, or that he was surrounded by enthusiastic, receptive children, or Shipi's presence, whatever—was making it possible for him to produce them more or less at will. Cynics would say the only important factor was that he needed to earn a living when he left the Army. But he realized that if people were dubious or suspicious of him it didn't matter: they would still pay their entrance fee to see him, even if it was only to go away thinking he was a novel type of trickster. Controversy, Uri and Shipi learned in the space of that afternoon, was not a drawback. It was their act's biggest asset.

And yet while Shipi was making big plans for the act, Uri still thought of his paranormal party trick as nothing more than a money-spinning sideline. Israel, with its famously high cost of living and high inflation, was a hotbed of what we would now call multi-tasking. Uri had his military service to finish, and the offer of a job—in the export department of a friend's father's textile business. (He took it at the beginning of 1969, as it gave him a chance to capitalize on his good English.) He also had a mightily complicated love life to attend to, and two second-string sidelines developing nicely—as a male model and, almost, as an actor.

Modelling was one of the funnier interludes in Uri's life. "It came about through another girlfriend who was a model," he recalls. "She had a shoot one afternoon, and I drove her there on my scooter and I went into the studio with her. The male model never showed up, so the photographer looked at me and said, 'OK, you do it.' I said 'Me?' I didn't really know that I had good looks. I only realized it when I saw how wanted I suddenly was for all these adverts." The advertisements look unbelievably naïve today: it was only the late 1960s, and Israel, for all its technological and intellectual sophistication was still in many ways a typically Mediterranean country, with an eye for the gaudy and unsubtle. "The first picture I was in was for a company called Ata that made towels, and it was shot on Tel Aviv beach," Uri says. "The photo was of me standing with a girl and a child at sunset, and wrapped around us is a big towel. It was unreal how the assignments started coming, from one photographer to another." The Ata ad was run in all the newspapers; today it looks like a rather bad holiday snap. Subsequent advertisements Uri starred in were aesthetically no better. There was one dreadful studio shot for King's Men deodorant, in which Uri is seen beaming as he applies it, watched adoringly by some forgotten sixties beauty with long false eyelashes, and her head at the level of his crotch. In another, for a clothing company, he is seen in the latest, swinging Terylene jacket apparently caught in the act of either doing the Twist or hailing a taxi—it is hard to tell which. He also modelled for postcards: one, of Uri and a girl in Army uniform, posing with Jerusalem in the background in about 1970, could still be found until recently in the more flyblown souvenir shops in the Holy City.

Although it may seem in retrospect like a carefree hobby, Uri took his modelling seriously. He still has a notebook from 1969 with every job he did carefully recorded with the name of the photographer, the address, the telephone number and how much he was paid. He had no way of knowing if this might prove to be his destiny: "To me, you have to understand, the modelling was like a whole new world opening to me. Remember, my real dream, my real yearning, was to become a horror-film actor, and I always looked for some sort of a window, a hatch that would lead me into the world of movies. One time an Italian movie production company came and they wanted me to act in a film. I don't know why that never materialized. I still wanted it so badly that I went through what was supposed to be a screen test, but was actually a rip-off. In the street that I lived on there was a producer who used to do screen tests. He would put up a camera and film you, and say they would check your acting out later, when they had found a movie for you. I felt so high about this that I did it a few times. But I never saw the film. Later on, I found out that there was no film in the camera. The guy was charging young kids who had a dream and cheating." (Alert skeptical readers will wonder why Uri was cheated in such a simple scam; others will be encouraged by his honesty in admitting that even psychics can sometimes miss a trick.)

The appearance of the advertisements had a couple of immediate benefits for Uri: he was recognized in the streets, which he enjoyed; and his pulling power with women increased, sufficient to complicate his emotional life to a ridiculous extent. Although he had shied away from pursuing Hanna because he "already had a girlfriend," it would seem that he was really trying to give her special consideration, protecting her from becoming involved with him for the present. He had already decided that Hanna was his best long-term bet as a life partner, but he still had fields full of wild oats to sow, and had no wish to put her through the serial infidelity to which his father had subjected his mother. He was still seeing the now married Yaffa, as well as a succession of Tel Aviv beauties and models. In addition, he had met a new girlfriend in a pavement café. She was an exceptionally pretty part-time model and beauty queen, with huge, grey-green eyes and a fascination with the supernatural, UFOs and psychic abilities. Her name was Iris Davidesco, and she and Uri fell in love. They spent hours walking on the beach, sitting in cafés and talking about the paranormal, as well as having innocent fun watching the world go by. They once starred together in an advertising photo for a brand of beer. An early problem in the relationship came as a shock to Uri; he had thought Iris was eighteen or so but, in another uncharacteristic failure of psychic powers, he only later discovered from her parents that she was just fifteen. Understandably they disapproved of him. "It wasn't easy to maneuver between the people I loved, and believe me, I truly loved them all. But each love is different. I still somewhere in my heart love Iris, and whenever I remember Yaffa, there is a little thing in my heart too. You can't erase these things from your inside. I told Hanna that someday I'd marry her, because I knew that Hanna was the only girl who was really stable for me."

Amid all this glamour and emotional drama in 1968 and 1969, Uri's professional psychic career was inexorably forming out of the mist, in great part thanks, incredibly, to the steady, focused approach of Shipi. Shipi had been so delighted with the initial performance at his school in Givatayim that he arranged for more shows in other schools, as well as demonstrations at private parties. The increasing frequency of his appearances made Uri more and more confident that he could summon up the phenomena on demand within a reasonable margin of error. To those who reject the paranormal hypothesis, this could equally be seen as a training period, but what was certain was that if Uri was to make his living at this someone, either he or the mysterious external powers that he was convinced were the source of his abilities, needed practice.

By the middle of 1969, the bending of spoons and keys was increasingly forming the central plank of Uri's performances; there was something about the spoon in particular—its familiarity, its novelty as a stage prop—which resonated with people across all sectors of society. And the strange, unprecedented show the boys had put together was playing amazingly well with both upmarket and downmarket audiences. Was it a science project? Was it a magic show? Who cared? It was a unique happening for your party. While Shipi got Uri bookings in the Tel Aviv suburbs, Uri, partly through Iris's connections, partly through his own, cracked the smarter set in the city, the photographers, models and showbusiness parties.

There was very little money in it—Uri still rode to performances on the Vespa from Cyprus—but there was a joint conviction between Uri and Shipi that a profitable little sideline was practically within their grasp. Uri began seriously to think that capitalizing on his strange abilities could make him rich—rich enough, he dreamed, to keep his mother and perhaps even to open a little coffee shop. And he had already developed a taste for material ostentation: he bought his mother a TV, himself a fancy hi-fi, and, always a big eater, indulged his appetite for copious quantities of food. The son of his employer had a big Plymouth, which he allowed Uri to drive. "I used to come and take Hanna for a spin in the Plymouth all over Tel Aviv," Uri recounts. "It was automatic, and a really big deal, with power steering and those big wings with the red lights." By late 1969, with his face appearing regularly—albeit anonymously—in artistically dreadful but highly visible advertisements, and his performances becoming quite a cult thing in and around Tel Aviv, Uri was perilously close to being famous. It was the best thing he had ever known in his twenty-two years—he had fame, money, as much sex as he could handle with the pick of the Tel Aviv *belle monde*, and even a pretty, sensible girl waiting in the background to settle down with him and have his babies. What more could a young man want?

"Israel is so small that it spread like wildfire," Uri says, and even his critics in Israel agree he became a minor sensation. "People were saying, have you heard about this guy, he does these amazing things? Suddenly from these little parties, the publicity added to the word-of-mouth buzz. A newspaper wrote about me, because there was a journalist in the party, then suddenly every newspaper was writing about me."

He started doing semi-professional shows in local public halls—the first was in Eilat in December 1969, when he was approaching his twenty-third birthday. The element of controversy, which Uri and Shipi had realized was such an asset, was a gift for publicity. Theories abounded in the press as to what this man Geller's trick could be. Lasers, chemicals, accomplices in the audience and mirrors were all put forward. Uri continued to insist that it was all "real," but a large proportion of people disbelieved him, assuming that this was just part of his patter. Importantly, though, even the skeptics were fascinated by his act. He was managing, he estimates, a success rate with the bending, telepathy and watch stopping and starting of seventy to eighty percent. Who had ever heard of a magician whose success was based on his tricks only working some of the time? Even the cynics had to admit it was a devastatingly clever idea. Shipi and Uri joked that half the people buying tickets to the shows were merely nosey about how much money the new phenomenon was making, and wanted to count customers to assuage their curiosity.

Uri Geller still wasn't a big name, but as word about him spread the question of professional management inevitably arose. Shipi would have been ideal for the job, but at fifteen, had to concentrate on his schoolwork. Small-time managers offered their services, and suddenly, thanks to their efforts, he was being booked into big theaters, and getting big audiences. "Although I was basically ripped off, I didn't care. From earning next to zero, I was making three or four hundred lira a night. The money was motivating me. I was throwing bundles of cash around my room." He bought a second-hand Triumph Spitfire and told Margaret she could stop working if she wished. If Uri's mother and father still thought he was basically a naughty boy who broke all their cutlery and had never grown out of this bad habit, now they had to be impressed. In fact, both had come to believe in his special powers.

The performances were pulling in some money, but it was private parties that upgraded Uri's social standing at a dizzying rate. Perhaps the most unlikely new friend he met at an exclusive social gathering was the dean of the law school at Tel Aviv University, Dr. Amnon Rubinstein, an academic with a flair for the media. He wrote for a number of newspapers and hosted a popular TV talk show called *Boomerang*, which covered the arts, science and intellectual matters. Rubinstein was not only convinced by what he saw, but went on to become one of Uri's great champions.

Now a prominent left-wing member of the Israeli parliament, the Knesset (he served as a greatly admired minister of education in Yitzhak Rabin's Labor government), Rubinstein was introduced to Uri at the party by a friend, a respected novelist, Ephraim Kishon, who had been deeply impressed by what he had seen of Uri's abilities. "Everyone was skeptical in the beginning, but these were amazing things we were seeing," Rubinstein recalls in his office in the Knesset building, overlooking Jerusalem. He speaks about Geller with great passion.

"I had no specific interest in psychic things. I am a totally rational, skeptical person. So I am not a fall guy, but I am open-minded, and I saw things that I couldn't explain. I first saw him at Kishon's place and I immediately saw that there was something in it, that this was not mere conjuring. He was not a trickster. I imagine the spoon-bending is some sort of strange energy which we haven't even begun to measure, but I suspect it's subject to rational terms. I have since seen Uri do it hundreds of times. It had become almost routine. A magician told me that Uri supplies his own spoon, which is not true, but anyway, that wasn't what interested me so much.

"The thing that amazed me more than anything else is that he could write something ahead of time on a piece of paper and hide it, and would then tell me, my wife or my children or my friends to write whatever you want. It started with a very limited scope—any number, any name or any capital city, and without exception he was right. He could somehow plant a thought right in our minds. Then he moved on to drawings, and again, was right in detail, every time. To me this is much more significant than spoon-bending. This was one single phenomenon that cast doubt on many of the foundations of our rational world. There are things that cannot be repeated by any trick. It's one thing to be a David Copperfield, but here was something that was done in my own home, not in another environment, on a stage that was organized and controlled as someone like that would require. There was nothing there that could deceive me, and it happened so often. We invited him time and time again. All sorts of people got involved, and overnight he became a celebrity. Then he developed it. When I met him he was very limited, but then his powers increased. He came into my office once, and one of the professors came in and said, 'You're Uri Geller, but I know your tricks.' So Uri said, 'OK, think of a number,' and he said, 'Ten thousand three hundred and something,' and Uri opened up his palm and it was written there. My colleague was staggered." (The question of Uri's powers increasing as he became more famous has not been seized on by skeptics. On reflection, it could have been due to either increasing confidence or increasing trickery—but talented athletes also build their skills repertoire *and* their basic aptitude as a result of playing in higher leagues.)

The power and vehemence of the reaction of an *ad hoc* coalition of magicians and scientists against Uri Geller as early as 1969 was remarkable: his professional career had barely begun. By 1970 the man who became his first serious manager had never heard of him. Yet the word was getting round rapidly among Israeli magicians that a dangerous trickster was at large, claiming that he had paranormal powers. Spoon-bending was a novel trick, which had never been seen before in magic, but for many skilled sleight-of-hand conjurers it was no great shakes. They were soon tripping over themselves in the race to duplicate Geller's trademark effect, and none found it difficult to come up with something that looked similar. Compared to the elaborate trickery they were used to, seeming to bend a spoon was nothing at all, and it frustrated them immensely to see this upstart youngster rising to fame solely because of it. The older magicians were also baffled by how Geller could be so successful when he looked so scruffy and amateurish, "like a kibbutznik," as one schoolgirl, who met him at a party, puts it. Where was the hocus-pocus, the top hat and the showbiz pizzazz? They felt that he was letting the side down by not according the craft its due pomp and ceremony. But the younger aspirants saw the new phenomenon differently. One successful young Israeli conjurer, Guy Bavli, who as a toddler rated Uri Geller as his hero, thought his informal style was his greatest trick. Bavli, who at the age of twenty-eight often plays Caesar's Palace in Las Vegas, expressly does not believe Geller is a para-normalist yet, a little alarmingly, compares him to Moses. "Here was a simple person with a stammer, who suddenly started doing amazing things—parting the Red Sea, apparently conversing with God. He wasn't a performer, and neither was Uri. The jeans, the T-shirt, the simple, amazed nature . . . it was a brilliant idea, and I admire him enormously for it."

Scientists began to join the onslaught at the behest, largely, of journalists assigned to reassess the Geller phenomenon after the first flush of media excitement had passed. Established scientists were not inclined to believe what they saw, or to express doubts on the fundamental laws of physics over the phone to a reporter; they suggested conjuring as an explanation. Conjurers were only too delighted to concur that the Geller effect could be created, or duplicated, as an illusion. At this early stage, for science there was no further case to answer—a cause had been found for the effect. The subtle point that replication by itself meant next to nothing—that just because there are wigs doesn't mean there's no hair—had not yet taken root.

Uri's appearance on Rubinstein's *Boomerang* program, in accord with the show's name, came back on him. In the interests of balance, Rubinstein had invited a number of voluble skeptics into the audience. Assuming that a civilized discussion would ensue, he started the show to find anti-Geller people howling Uri down. "It was the first TV show I had ever done, and it would have been OK if they just didn't believe me," Uri says, "but they were attacking me, really violently, with personal abuse. It was the first time I'd had direct, physical contact with these people, and I was really scared. Then I realized it was in my power just to walk off, so I did. Amnon followed me out of the building and he actually started crying, because he believed in me so much and it totally devastated him." The taped show was abandoned and never aired.

"He was very infantile," Dr. Rubinstein recollects of Uri's personality, "but highly intelligent and knew how to sell himself. He had a commercial knack. His intelligence was basic, animal intelligence, what you might call emotional intelligence. He was not a great thinker, but he was not a fool. He was very limited in his education, but it was easy to see how he caught on. He also spoke English very well from the start, which was important, and he knew how to handle audiences and journalists. The remarkable thing about his personality is that he makes friends very easily. When he first started I hadn't seen him do a public appearance, but people told me he would win the audience over in no time."

Ephraim Kishon, who was probably the most distinguished journalist as well as novelist of his day in Israel, seemed to have taken it upon himself to conduct the young Geller on a Cook's tour of the country's elite. There may have been a touch of the Hungarian old-boy network operating here: Kishon was of Hungarian extraction, as was Yosef Lapid, a bright young broadcaster working then at the Army radio station. Lapid, who is known as Tommy Lapid, and is now the Ephraim Kishon of *his* day, was introduced as a young man to Geller at Kishon's house. "I was one of the first to interview him," Lapid says. "We did a number of experiments with Kishon, but it was something he did in my car which I found remarkable."

Lapid had a brand-new Ford, of which he was especially proud. With Uri blindfolded, at his own request, with a sweater, and Lapid "frozen with fear," Uri drove the car nearly five hundred meters across the center of Tel Aviv in busy nighttime traffic, from Sderot Hen to the town hall on Ibn Gvirol. At one point, he ran over a newspaper in the street, and panicked. "I think he thought it was a person." Lapid laughs. "I'm telling you this despite my not believing in these things. But if it was a trick, it's one I've never been able to fathom."

Just as magicians had no difficulty in duplicating Uri's spoon-bending, blindfold driving was an unwise skill for him to demonstrate. It was already a favorite standby of regular magicians, who exploit the sightlines a poorly tied blindfold permits. It may be that Uri saw and heard the newspaper he drove over in Tommy Lapid's car. Yet on other occasions Uri did it with tighter and tighter blindfolds, with the windscreen blacked out—and on pitch dark, unlit desert roads at night. But although he could do it better and more convincingly than the average magician, demonstrating blindfold driving as a paranormal event still led him directly into the magicians' trap. It was almost as if he was unaware of the standard repertoire of illusionists—or that he wanted to give the impression that he was unaware of it.

As he was cutting his unlikely swath through Israel's intelligentsia, Uri's relationship with Amnon Rubinstein was scraping the rocks. One of the agents he was working for at the time observed that if there wasn't more substance to his routine, people were going to get bored with it. He suggested that Uri "fatten up the act" by the inclusion of a trick he had devised. Uri claims that he balked at the suggestion on the ground that the point of his act was that it was genuine. But the agent, Baruch Cutani, who has since died, appealed to Uri's desire to make more money, as well as warning him again that his livelihood was at risk if he did not innovate. Cutani's plan was to watch audience members as they got out of their cars outside the theater, write down their licence-plate numbers, and pass these to Uri, having shepherded the stooges to specially reserved seats. It wasn't a sophisticated con and, as ever, Uri's agreement to go along with it can be subject to several interpretations. It could be the key proof that, by nature and training, he was a trickster. Yet many of his magician critics were arguing that he was already a *sophisticated* magician; if that were the case, surely he would not have needed to fall in with an overcomplicated yet unconvincing plan such as Cutani's? The decision to go with Cutani's idea could equally be viewed as evidence that he really knew nothing about magic and, as a rash, naïve young man, was prepared to seize any opportunity to rake in money. Or perhaps he tells this story about himself because deviously he *wants* us to believe he was hopelessly unaware of the wiles of conjuring. Whatever, it came perilously close to losing him the support of Dr. Rubinstein, probably his most important champion.

He began to use the licence-plate trick in his act, which seemed to go down well. Now, while we may be dubious over quite why Uri tells this story apparently against himself, two things we know for sure: first, the fraud was not discovered, even by his pursuers, since none of the debunking accounts have mentioned it; second, after a few successful evenings, we know that Uri went to confess his guilt to Dr. Rubinstein. He says he went disconsolately to the law professor's office and told him "to forget Uri Geller, that Uri Geller is no damned good." He explained what the agent had pressurized him into doing. Rubinstein took him by the shoulders and said, part menace, part disappointment, "Uri, you've done things neither you nor I can explain. You don't need to add tricks to it. All right, that's a trick. But how did you do all the other things? The spoons, the keys, the numbers and drawings you beamed into my head?" Uri replied, with what many people regard as his strongest, least challengeable explanation, "I don't know."

Rubinstein confirms this account: "Uri said, 'I am a fool, I can't explain it, I got bad advice.' I was very mad at him for this. I gave him a piece of my mind. I said he had deceived me. Even before that I began to suspect that he was using trickery, maybe mixing it in with the other things. There were a few things that I thought were foolproof, which couldn't be done by trickery, and now he was admitting to one. But then he was a young boy. To me the precognition is much, much more important. I asked him, 'How do you do it, and why is it so accurate, why can you predict what I will be doing in two minutes?' He said, 'Because I see. It is very disturbing.' He said, 'This is not a trick.' He was adamant about that." Rubinstein suggested to Uri that, in the light of this mistake he had made and the uproar his paranormal claims were making, he must sooner or later legitimize himself by having his powers tested by scientists. Uri took the message on board, although it would be a while before he did anything about it because, by luck, nobody had caught his hand in the till—and there was still plenty of money to be made, largely as a result of the timely intervention of Mr. Miki Peled, who was establishing himself as a rising star among young Tel Aviv theatrical agents.

It was bound to happen sooner or later that Israel's emerging Mr. Showbiz would cotton on to the Uri Geller phenomenon. Peled, who was thirty, had just staged a big charity evening at the prestigious Mann Auditorium in Tel Aviv, and was talking after the show in the Scala coffee shop with Shlomo Hillel, the police minister and various actors and other artistes. For an hour, Peled recalls, most of the talk was about Uri Geller, of whom he had, curiously, never heard. "People were so excited talking about this boy, and I asked them who he was, and where I could meet him. They didn't know, but a friend of a friend had seen him at a party, where he'd amazed everyone. It was said that his mother worked in an espresso bar in Allenby Street. The next day, I told someone from my office to try to locate her. There were only five or six coffee bars on Allenby, and they found her."

Peled got Geller to come round to his busy ground-floor office close to the town hall within two hours. "Uri was wearing a short-sleeved shirt—it was summer—and the first thing he asked was whether I knew what I had in my briefcase. I did, of course, and he wrote on a piece of paper a complete list of everything, in detail. It included some medicines, some pictures of my family, bills, the exact number of keys. He knew everything, I couldn't believe it, and also he knew all sorts of things about me. Two hours before he had never heard of me, and neither of us had any idea we would be meeting. There was no possibility for him to have looked in my briefcase."

Obviously, the idea of a show was paramount in Miki Peled's mind, even though he was primarily in the music business. But one thing was obvious to his experienced eye, which was not entirely so to the other agents and managers who had dealt with Geller. He was not yet a performer. Peled explained this to him and how, as a producer, he could transform Uri Geller into a professional stage act, without dictating that he include conjuring tricks, or putting him into a tuxedo and top hat. Nuances of presentation made the difference for Peled between a one-season novelty act and a showbusiness phenomenon. Uri was impressed by someone he saw as much as a mentor as a meal ticket.

Peled offered him a formal management contract, but instead the two agreed that he would buy a hundred shows. "If I manage him, I can make ten percent, but if I produce I can make ten thousand percent. I asked him how much he wanted for a show, and he said two hundred dollars. I agreed, of course, and started work." Did Peled believe in his new protégé's psychic powers? "I didn't in the beginning," he admits today. He never once saw a Geller spoon in the act of bending on its own, the rare but far from unique phenomenon so many people have been certain over the years that they witnessed. He did not even bring a spoon of his own from home for Uri to bend. It was as if Peled was unwilling to tempt fate by examining too closely the goose that he was convinced was about to go into full-time golden-egg production. "When we were kids, we used to go and see magicians, but everybody could tell how the trick was done. And none of them could do anything like Uri Geller.

"No, no," Miki Peled corrects himself. "Many, many people were *like* Uri Geller and did the same kind of tricks, but I never saw the same. For twenty years since Uri left Israel, people have come to me saying they know Uri's trick, and show me, and every time, it was never the same. It was always *like* Uri Geller. How many people have there been who are *like* Elvis? Even in Israel we have about ten. And another ten *like* Tom Jones. These *like* Uri Gellers always had to touch the things they bent, but Uri could do it from twenty meters away. I always check how they do it and it's easy to see, every time.

"I sometimes thought it was a freak and would stop. I preferred not to investigate," Peled reflects. "I preferred to believe he did it with his power, and if you ask me now, I think he did. It's hard to say, 'I believe,' because I'm ashamed to believe. People are afraid to say they believe in Uri Geller, when you have the newspapers saying he's a liar. Sometimes you feel like you're against the world. Let's say I am against the possibility, but I believe he has something which nobody else has. It has taken me many years to decide, but I am now sure he is real."

Some time after it was reported in the Israeli press in 1970 that Miki Peled was now working with Uri Geller, Peled received a remarkable phone call. It was from a Professor Yitzhak Kelson, a physicist at Tel Aviv University. "He told me he could prove to me that Uri was a liar," says Peled. "Maybe at this time I was kind of looking for somebody to show me that it was a trick, because I couldn't swear it was the truth, yet I had no evidence it was a trick. He invited me to come and see him in his house, and he was really angry with me. He said because of me people might believe in Uri Geller, this liar, this trickster. He was a very strong personality and I was convinced that Professor Kelson was right and Uri was a liar.

"I came home and was devastated. I said to my wife, 'Listen, Uri Geller is a liar. He's cheated us. I think I should finish my relationship with him.' That evening, Uri Geller was performing in Gedera. I phoned the theater and said, 'Uri, after the show, please come to my house.' When he came, he realized I was upset, and I told him the professor had said exactly what he was doing. I said, 'I'm your friend, I'm your agent. I expect you to tell me, at least, the truth. I don't want to get the information from other people. I don't care if it's a supernatural power or a trick. For me it's good business. But I feel insulted that you don't behave to me as a friend, as a brother, as a father. And he said, 'Miki, this Professor Kelson is talking nonsense. I'll meet him and convince him he's mistaken.' So now I was confused. 'Ten minutes before, I felt you were a liar. Now I don't know. *Please* tell me how do you do it.' He said, 'I don't know how I do it. Sometimes I don't do it. I can never explain to anybody how I do it. My mother doesn't know how I do it.'

"Two weeks later," Peled says, "we had a show in Jerusalem, and this professor came with all his colleagues from the university. They told Uri that they would be in the first row and would take pictures and tape the show, and make a big story in the newspapers about how he cheated. Uri said, 'Please do.' And some of them went on the balcony with a telescope. After the show I said to Kelson, 'Do you still think the same as two weeks ago?' He said, 'No, I think maybe it's a different trick. But our theories of physics don't accept his apparent abilities.' We never heard another word from him."

Like many of the scientists who pitted themselves against Uri Geller, Professor Kelson was a lover of magic shows, and had even learned to perform some tricks himself. But keen as he was to spread the word against Uri in 1970, three decades later he is anxious to distance himself. "At one time, I believed it was important to persuade people that this was nonsense," he said warily, at his office at the university. "Now, I try to disengage myself in a totally neutral manner. I'd rather not even be mentioned in connection with your book. My energies are not channelled in that direction anymore. It's obviously fraudulent, and that's it." An unambiguous, yet oddly enigmatic epitaph.

Just as Elvis Presley had to do his Army service despite his world fame, Uri, as a minor celebrity, was required every year to serve in the Israeli Army reserves. As he was still unable to extend his damaged arm, he would have been put on fairly dull duties, had not the Army heard of his unusual entertainment value and swiftly placed him in a unit that entertained troops all over the country. This was a godsend for two reasons: it helped Uri become better known to people in captive audiences, who ordinarily might not have been interested in seeing him; it also gave him a chance to bypass the conventionalities of rank and hobnob with high-flying officers and generals, thereby extending his assiduous networking still further.

Among the kind of fans he might not have expected were two Israeli Air Force pilots, Gideon Peleg and Dov Yarom, both of whom now fly 747s for El Al, and remain his strong supporters. When he first met Uri in 1969 Peleg was a lieutenant colonel. "I met him at a party and later flew him to a show at an Air Force base at Sharm el Sheikh in the Sinai," he says. "There were two hundred or so of us at the show, a mix of soldiers and pilots. I don't know what they thought they were going to see, but I remember they were very impressed by him. At first I was very skeptical, but then I admired him after I saw what he was doing, and I went with him to many shows and we became friends. As a pilot, you are very used to watching. I have to watch maybe two hundred instruments for the slightest deviation or change, so I think I see pretty well. And in all the hundreds of things I have very carefully watched Uri do, I have never seen anything underhand. Nothing.

"Privately, he did many things like driving a car blindfolded. He told me that he could see the road through my eyes and asked me to concentrate on the road. Things would move on the shelves in our apartment when he was there. Sometimes we'd visit him and on the way home say something about him, and he'd call us later and ask why did you say so and so like that after you left? When we were staying at a friend's apartment, there was a big old clock that hadn't worked for a few years and he made it move—he didn't touch it, just put his hands close to it. One day, I remember, somebody showed him a picture of a group of people, and he pointed to some of them and said that this one has an injury on his left foot, that this one was very ill a few years ago, that this one broke his left hand. They were all correct. This guy that showed him the picture was amazed. Uri didn't know anybody there. Of course, I have seen the spoon-bending on its own many times—these are the simple things that he does. But once, when we were talking about Uri in the kitchen when he was hundreds of miles away, a fork started bending, right there in front of us. I still have it, it was amazing. It was on the counter and suddenly we saw one of the tines just bend forward, several centimeters, completely on its own. But it wasn't scary, because we were used to these things after a while.

"Of course, I read all the newspapers at the time, and sometimes people told the press that Uri Geller takes some of his own people to every show, that he had a code routine with someone in the audience. Because I was skeptical I started looking out for these people. I would drive him or fly him to shows, and there would be no one. Shipi wasn't there—I didn't know Shipi then. It was just him and me. He was doing a show in a different place every evening, and if he was cheating he would have needed a big group of people working for him. The idea of him having confederates in the audience is wrong. It's a fantasy. If I had seen anyone assisting him, I would have left him and never gone to a show again. I wouldn't have associated with him anymore.

"He told me that when he was young he started to feel that he had some sort of powers. He once said that he could make people stumble and fall when they are walking, but he wouldn't do it because he is not that kind of person. I think," Gideon Peleg concludes, "that he can read your mind from your sub-conscious. Sometimes when you talk to him, he suddenly asks you something very strange that happened to you a few months or years ago, something that you almost don't remember. Sometimes he knows in detail about things that you have never talked to him or anyone about. It's God's gift, I think."

Peleg's first wife, Leah, a medical secretary, was around for many of these strange occurrences. (The fork-bending incident Peleg related was with his second wife, Ofrah.) Leah Peleg's first experience of Geller was being with him on a kibbutz in the Negev, and seeing a needle break in half without Uri touching it. She was a witness to him blindfold-driving on unlit Negev roads, when even a peek from under the blindfold would have been of little use to him, and saw Uri start the antique clock to which her ex-husband referred.

Leah Peleg also became friendly with Tibor Geller. "He was very dignified, clever, very tall, very, very handsome. You don't often see people like this, so straight and honest. Once a month I went to visit him in Hayarkon Street. Every time I came, he would escort me to my car, a Ford Capri. One time, I held my keys in my hand, and we were talking about Uri. Tibor said that he loved him very much but regretted a few things. He had never talked with me so seriously about things which happened in the past. And my car key broke in two, a big, heavy key. Uri's father was very calm. He just said, 'Oh, it's Uri. I hope you have a spare key.' I did. He wasn't surprised. He just said, 'Yes, it happens.' He believed in him. He had no theory about Uri's powers. All he said a few times was that there was some gypsy blood in the family, from back in Hungary."

Dov Yarom, now also an El Al captain, was a major in the Air Force when he heard about Geller in 1969, and got to know him in parallel with Peleg. "We used to do Friday-night parties at the base, and I was in charge of organizing one particular evening. Uri Geller was just starting out, so I went to visit him at his mother's home to see if he would be a good entertainment to hire. I found a very nice, polite chap, who held the doors open for you. I told him I was a pilot in the Air Force, and we wanted to invite him to our base, but there might be a security problem. But he explained that he was already security cleared. So I said, 'OK, can you show me something?' We were sitting head to head, and I didn't know about the guy. He told me a lot about himself, and was very confident, very persuasive, but I had to see. So he took a piece of paper and he tore it with his hands into a few pieces, put them on the table in front of us, and started concentrating. He put his hands twenty or twenty-five centimeters above the pieces and they started to float above the table, not very high, but moving. That was good enough for me. There was no fake involved, they really moved. I am very skeptical, I am very fond of magicians, but I always keep in mind that they create illusions. It didn't matter to me at the time if it was an illusion or a fake or the real thing. But, as far as I was concerned, it was a real power. The same things have happened to me with a magician, but it's definitely not the same experience that I had personally with Uri.

"He took me over to the window of this four-storey building and he told me that he is fascinated by the powers he has," Yarom continues. "He told me wonderful things, astonishing things. He looked out of the window and said he can decide whether someone will fall in the street, although he didn't do it for me. Anyway, we invited him to the base and did all the usual stuff he does in front of the audience, but more amazing things happened later. We went to the house of one of our navigators. There were five or six couples there—that evening was the first time Gideon and Leah met Uri. So he started with bending a little spoon in his hand. It was very intimate, just us sitting having coffee and cake. He bent it in front of us. Really, it was unbelievable. He was holding it between his thumb and little finger and he had no power to bend it physically. And we actually saw the spoon bending. Another thing which amazed me was how astonished and happy he was when he succeeded. He didn't react as if he took it for granted that it would work. But more striking still was what happened to the wife of the navigator who had invited us. She had very nice glasses on her head and he told her to take them off, to put them between her hands and cover them. Then he floated his hands over her hands, and said, 'I have to concentrate, help me with this,' and then he said, 'Open your hands,' and she opened them and her glasses were bent. We were all astonished. She was not annoyed—there was no problem rebending them. I know he wouldn't do anything harmful. Many years later, when I was flying for E1 A1 and Uri was a passenger one time, he came on to the flight deck and showed everybody there the things he could do. I knew there was no way he would be a danger in the cockpit; I don't know, perhaps that shows that I was still a little skeptical, after all."

One intriguing assertion Captain Yarom made about Uri at this stage is that the Israeli military became nervous about him as he darted from base to base, apparently overturning the laws of nature at every stop. "He definitely had connections with some very high-ranking officers in the Israeli Army, but as far as I know the Air Force regarded this phenomenon called Uri Geller as a security problem. What they found a little frightening was that people believed in him so much. They were afraid of a Pied Piper effect, that people would follow him blindly. Because this guy was very persuasive, very trustworthy, and very dominant and strong in character, if you are in charge of an Air Force that is dealing with a very technical, very real world, you don't want people to believe too much in a paranormal phenomenon. It's very nice if you go and see a magician, but it's totally another thing if someone convinces you he has real paranormal powers. In fact, it was the Air Force that first took the initiative of trying to debunk him. They brought a few guys together who did something like Uri Geller did, bending spoons and driving blindfold—these three guys, I remember, were called the Ayalon Trio—and they were taken round the Air Force bases of Israel to say what Uri Geller does is a trick." (Eytan Ayalon was indeed a magician, who launched a high-profile campaign of duplicating Geller's effects. He trained two young men to act as fake psychics, grew a beard and announced in the press that "Uri Geller will disappear." If Uri did not announce himself as a fake within a fortnight, they said, they would "reveal all." Ayalon spoke of his regret at this, but said it was a matter of "saving the Israeli people." A left-wing magazine renowned for exposés, *Haolam Hazeh*, also spoke of Geller, the "telepathic impostor," as "a national menace.")

In barely two years from being an obscure wounded war veteran and promising a fellow soldier that he was going to become rich and famous Uri had nearly achieved both. To have upset stage magicians along the way was hardly surprising but to have been seen by the military and academic establishment as a living threat to national morale must have been beyond even Uri's fruitful imagination. He had made powerful friends in high places, but powerful forces were also working against him.

They did not always, however, have quite the desired effect when they did so. Captain Yarom's suggestion that the Israeli Air Force used magicians to forestall any possibility of its elite flyers starting to believe in the paranormal is echoed, with an interesting and amusing twist, by Roni Schachnaey, the Grand President of the Israeli Society for Promoting the Art of Magic. Schachnaey recalls that he was contacted by the Air Force in 1983, and asked to go down quickly to do a show at an F16 fighter base in the south of Israel. He is a mentalist, a magician specializing in the simulation of psychic effects such as ESP, or extrasensory perception and psychokinesis, the moving of material objects by mind power. Mentalists often leave it to the public to judge whether they are using trickery or genuine psychic powers, or sometimes, as Schachnaey did on this occasion, will claim that their performance is psychic, then explain later, to make a point, that it was really done by non-supernatural means. Uri Geller, of course, is regarded as a mentalist—at least by mentalists.

The Air Force base, Schachnaey recounts, had recently received an entertainment visit from a South African Israeli, who did an updated Uri Geller-style act. The F16 pilots were knocked out by it, to the extent that senior officers telephoned Schachnaey and asked him to do an Ayalon-style magician counterstrike. He tried out on the assembled pilots and their wives a new and impressive trick he had devised. He got one of the men to sign his name on two blank cards and place them at either end of a stack of similar blanks. He then asked the airman to bundle up the stack of cards and place them at some distance from the audience but in full view of it. This done, he asked the same man to pick any woman from the audience. Schachnaey then took her through a lengthy rigmarole, asking her first to name her favorite childhood book, and finally, to remember her favorite phrase from it. The woman chose the phrase "daisy chain." Schachnaey asked her to go over to the stack of cards and flick through them. She found a card in the middle of the pack with the phrase "daisy chain" written on it.

"From that point onwards," Roni Schachnaey says, "I had these fighter pilots open-mouthed. But the funny thing was that instead of taking the point that some of these psychic effects can be done by trickery, they started saying the South African guy was a fake and it was me that was the real thing."

Chapter 7

Fame and Friction

"I don't predict. Why don't you ask Uri Geller?"

Prime Minister Golda Meir, asked at a 1970 press conference about Israel's future

....

Renown and notoriety for Uri Geller were running almost neck and neck in the middle period of his celebrity in Israel, from the end of 1970 to 1972. He managed a spectacular feat of headline grabbing at the end of September 1970, when Gamal Abdel Nasser, the Egyptian leader, died unexpectedly in Cairo of a heart attack. It was one of the biggest news stories imaginable for Israel: his brand of Soviet-backed nationalistic socialism had been a thorn in Israel's side since 1954, when he had become president.

The big news from Cairo occurred shortly after Miki Peled became Uri's manager, and upgraded the polish and theatricality of his act. The new partnership was going well, and some theaters across the country, which had previously enjoyed thirty percent occupancy rates, were reporting full houses for Geller. But however much more dramatic Uri had become in his presentation, nothing quite prepared Peled for the display of sheer hamming he displayed on the night of 28 September in a small but prestigious Tel Aviv auditorium, *Tsavta*. From his seat in the stalls, Peled truly believed the boat that had so recently come in for him was on its way back out—under full steam.

Some way into the show, Uri stopped suddenly in mid-act, looked ill, sat down and asked if there was a doctor in the house. As a doctor came up from the audience, Uri announced that he was unable to carry on because some enormous historic event was about to happen. He said he believed Nasser had just died or was about to die, promptly stopped the show, and asked the three-hundred-strong audience if they wouldn't mind leaving. As they were filing out, looking puzzled and murmuring, Miki Peled was not a happy impresario. "I just thought, That's it. That's his last show. Saying Nasser is about to die is not like saying it's going to rain tomorrow. There happened to be a journalist in the audience called Ruth Hefer, and I believe she went to the phone in the lobby and phoned the newsdesk at her paper and Israel Radio to ask what was going on. I think she came back and said there was nothing at all on the news wires about anything happening to Nasser.

"I was really concentrating more on Uri. He was really not well. The doctor had taken his pulse and it was 160 or 170. If it was all an act, it was crazy. This wasn't something where he could say, 'Oh, sorry, I made a mistake.' He was putting all his money on one number. If nothing had happened, people would have laughed for years. It would have been a grand finale."

Nearly thirty years on, it is practically impossible to establish the exact timings involved, but the Israeli papers over the next few days were full of the story of Uri Geller predicting the death of Nasser twenty minutes before it was announced in Cairo. Some stories said that someone backstage had been listening to the radio and whispered to Geller on stage that Nasser had died. The theater director gave a well-reported statement in response to say that nobody had been backstage to tell Geller anything, and the story passed, as these things do, into a sort of uneasy mythology, with some people believing it, others deeply doubtful, and nothing really settled. A strike against the story's veracity is that Ruth Hefer, who would have been most likely to recall the precise details, admits to being hazy about them. Since 1970, she has dropped out of journalism, split up with her husband, Chaim, a well-known Tel Aviv columnist, become a fashion designer, and now runs a stall in the flea-market in Old Jaffa. "I was certainly in the audience, and I certainly remember Uri Geller saying Nasser was dead and hearing the news later that he had died," she says. "But what I remember most was the shock. So I can't be absolutely sure that I went all the way and made the phone calls. It's very possible, as I was writing for papers then, and the feeling I have at this distance is that, yes, he was well ahead of the news breaking."

Uri, as might be expected, maintains that it was just an inexplicable feeling he had, and the whisperer-behind-the-curtain theory is very doubtful. He did not pretend to be a clairvoyant, so why would some backstage person, in the unlikely event that he was listening to the radio, tell a man in the middle of a spoon-bending, watch-starting, telepathic demonstration about the news from Egypt? It might have brought the whisperer a bawling-out from the star for putting him off his stride. Occam's razor aside, the whisperer theory becomes less plausible still if we accept the dubious idea that Geller always had someone on standby listening to the news in case some world-shattering event occurred during the act, on which he could then capitalize. The risk of making such a drastic intervention as pretending to become unwell and throwing the audience out because he had heard a faint message about Nasser would seem too great even for a rash performer to take. What if someone in the front row had heard the whisperer? What if the news, or indication of its imminence, had already been on the radio before the show, and somehow Geller had missed it? Short of being able to quiz his informant through the curtain, as a journalist would—Was the news confirmed? How could he be sure this was the very first inkling and hadn't been mentioned on any radio or TV station earlier?—it is hard to imagine how he could possibly have been confident enough to gamble his entire reputation and career on this one long shot. For it to be a trick and succeed, he needed more than just the audience to leave the theater and hear on their car radios that Nasser was dead. There had to be a reasonable interval before anyone heard the news; there had to be no possibility of a credible witness coming forward to say they had heard someone tell him of it. Apart from anything else, he had no need to take such a chance. His star was in the ascendant.

But whether it was a genuine psychic premonition, a mad guess, or an outrageously reckless piece of opportunism—and perhaps you would need to be psychic anyway to know if such a risk would pay off—the Nasser incident turned Uri Geller into a nationwide celebrity. For anyone who had somehow not heard the showbusiness buzz and also missed the Nasser story, the prime minister, Golda Meir, ensured Uri's elevation to stardom. Asked three days later by a radio journalist at a Jewish New Year press conference to speculate on how the next year would work out for Israel, Meir, who was probably delighted at the chance to avoid giving an answer and to sound clued-up, said, "I don't predict. Why don't you ask Uri Geller?" He responded later by saying that he wasn't in the habit of predicting either. Perhaps Meir had even crafted her comment as an ironic put-down to Geller for public consumption, and she had meant that only a charlatan pretends to be able to predict the future. But it didn't matter: it was taken as a *de facto* acknowledgment that Israel had its own psychic superstar and Uri basked in the glow for years afterward. "There was absolutely no question about it," says Miki Peled. "From the moment of the Nasser incident, he was the most famous guy in this country, and even now, in a way, he still is. It was from this point that he became a phenomenon."

Increasingly busy and famous, Uri's social and love life were rather neglected. Iris, still almost a child, was virtually his shadow, showing a neediness and dependence that were getting him down. She wanted to know everything he was doing and where he was at all times and, partly because his true love was still Yaffa, and partly just because he was a man of twenty-four, he found this constant pressure increasingly wearing. Whenever he saw Yaffa, which was rarely, he reaffirmed that he loved her, and told her all about Iris, without ever telling Iris about Yaffa. The imbalance between the story each woman was receiving—leaving aside Hanna Shtrang's background role—was the kind of moral conflict many young men can cope with for a while, but the relationship with Iris was petering out. Eventually Uri finished with her, a blow from which she never quite recovered, ending her days lonely and drug-addicted. She died on his birthday three years ago, in her forties.

Uri had been unhappy about leaving Iris, and deeply saddened when he discovered she had fallen on hard times and died; he still felt tenderly for her. Yet, her clinginess aside, it is easy to understand how for someone in Uri's extraordinary position, a love affair with a teenager he had met in a café, and which seemed a good idea at the time, must have come to feel increasingly unsuitable. It would, perhaps, have been asking too much of him not to feel that he had moved on. The élite of Israeli society, right up to the prime minister, was flocking to him for private audiences after meeting him socially. "I was now getting invited to really important parties, with lawyers and judges and generals. That's where I met Golda Meir. She did a hidden drawing, and I read her mind. But the only problem was that she did a Star of David so I didn't really have to be very psychic to know what she'd drawn. I always laugh at that."

There was a story in the newspapers that the pen of Shimon Peres, later to be prime minister, had broken in two in Uri's presence without him having touched it, and that Moshe Dayan, coming to the end of his time as defense minister, had been meeting Geller secretly. "I did meet Golda Meir after she mentioned me, but on a very confidential basis," Uri says. "She and Moshe Dayan wanted me very much to work for the Israeli secret service, and to see how they could utilize my powers. Then, putting aside the secret stuff, Moshe Dayan utilized my powers to find him archaeological remains—illegally. I was really young and naïve and I didn't know—here you are talking to *the* Moshe Dayan, the national hero, and he asked me to locate things for him. I used to spend hours over maps, and I know his garden and his house were just riddled with antiquities." Dayan, according to a remarkable account by Guy Lyon Playfair in *The Geller Effect*, a fine 1986 book written with Uri, had initiated the contact by inviting Geller for lunch at a steakhouse called the White Elephant at Zahala, where he lived. Geller did telepathy with him, both the routine way and the "reverse" method, which had so bowled over Amnon Rubinstein. Uri remembers Dayan's single eye "flickering and gleaming"—and that the defense minister let him pay the bill.

A couple of weeks later, Dayan asked Geller to come to his house. This time, Dayan said he had hidden a photograph in the room, and asked Uri to indicate where it was, and to describe the photo before he had looked at it. Uri relates that he "dowsed" for the photo, using his hands, and pointed to one book on a shelf. Dayan confirmed he had the right spot and asked him what the photo showed. He asked Dayan to "project" the image to him, then described an Israeli flag. Dayan laughed, which caused Uri to wonder if he had blundered, then turned to page 201 of the book, in which was placed a small snapshot of a flag flying over the control tower at Lod airport. As Uri tells it, Dayan said, "You've proved yourself, Uri. I don't want to see any more. There's no need for you to bend anything. Now, what can you do for Israel?" Soon after the meeting Uri was invited for a chat with the head of the Mossad, Aharon Yariv, at a coffee shop on Ibn Gvirol in Tel Aviv.

"Golda believed in these things," Uri continues, "and she wanted to know the overall picture of Israel's future, and how many more wars were in store. She was very much for peace, and I told her I could see Israel signing peace treaties with all our Arab neighbors. I actually predicted—but I don't know if it was a logical conclusion—that we were going to sign a peace treaty with Egypt first. I met Golda three times. Once in the Beit Sokolov, which is the press center, once at the house of a friend, a general, and once on an Army base, in a conference room in the barracks. I never visited her home. And the only time I bent a spoon for her was after the telepathy, at that little party." (Conspiracy theorists may well conclude from the anxiety of politicians to talk to Uri that they know more than they let on about his powers; non-conspiracy theorists may conclude simply that politicians are deeply superstitious people.) Interestingly, his political connections in Israel seem to have been maintained—and to transcend left–right differences. While all the above were of the Israeli left, Uri has friendly contact today with Yitzhak Mordechai, who served as defense minister in "Bibi" Netanyahu's right-wing government. Mordechai has been to visit the Gellers in Berkshire.

In October 1970, following closely on the Nasser "prediction" and Meir's comment about Uri on national radio, *Haolam Hazeh,* the popular magazine that had called Uri a national menace, carried an unsigned attack on him, quoting mostly from the magician Eytan Ayalon. Ayalon was openly promising a witch-hunt against Geller—his phrase. Geller's transgressions were (a) claiming to be a psychic, (b) poking his nose into Israeli politics and, (c) "He started to hurt our earnings. That is why we decided to hit back."

Another unconventional circuit besides the military with which Uri started working early in his career, and in which he was still playing after Miki Peled came on the scene, was the universities. Here, he often found himself causing rifts between students who believed in him and others who did not. Ygal Goren, who had last seen him on that final day in the Army and been baffled by his confident announcement that he was going to become rich and famous, caught up with him at the Hebrew University, en route to his own career as a political journalist. "We were shocked," Goren says. "It was very impressive. I remember people saying he was a sophisticated magician, but it didn't matter to me, because he was going to become the biggest magician in the world, and I was very happy for him. I saw him a lot after that. He's a nice guy, a good guy. I like his energy and happiness, and he helps people. Jealousy is a big thing in Israel, and people were always going to try to damage him."

A student event that went less well, in retrospect, for Uri, and gives a further impression of the depth of feeling developing against him, occurred at an engineering outpost of Haifa's Technion, Israel's answer to the Massachusetts Institute of Technology (MIT), in Beersheba, in the south of the country. A student called Sam Volner booked Uri as a pre-disco entertainer. He did his usual act in front of 300 engineering students and, as Volner recalls, it went well. "The paranormal was a new phenomenon in those days," says Volner, now a diamond dealer in Los Angeles. "This was something out of the blue. It wasn't a regular magician with pigeons and rabbits. It was somebody from another world, right down to the casual clothes he wore for a performance. It was weird, and amazing to watch. There were big arguments for weeks afterwards among us, but I'd say the majority of the students thought he was real. However, one guy, a mechanical engineering student called Uri Goldstein, wasn't happy. He didn't believe, so he found a lawyer who was interested in some publicity and sued the promoters for his money back."

The following year, in July 1971, the case came before the civil court in Beersheba. Goldstein alleged breach of contract, the *Jerusalem Post* reported in a single paragraph item, "in that he promised to perform feats of telepathy, parapsychology, hypnotism and telekinesis, while in fact he merely employed sleight-of-hand and stage tricks." With Uri absent from the court to defend himself, the summons having been sent to Miki Peled's office and either lost or ignored as trivial, Goldstein was awarded by default 27.5 lira for breach of contract. The money—around three pounds—was apparently paid into the court anonymously and the case settled. "I think Uri Goldstein's case began seriously, but it was really a student joke," Volner says. "I remember Uri Geller, when he heard about the judgment, wrote a very funny letter to a newspaper. He used a phrase I still remember. He said, 'Why should I argue with a horse?' Trivial as the case seems—the ruling can hardly be said to have been the product of a sustained argument by one side or the other—it is seized on even now as the definitive debunking of Geller, and the reason he left Israel a few years later for Europe and America. Various publications over the years have stated that Geller was "convicted in a court of law for pretending to have paranormal powers," and have accorded great significance to the Beersheba ruling. This seems a substantial exaggeration, even if based on indisputable fact.

A curious insight into the case now, particularly in the light of the airline captain Dov Yarom's belief that the Israeli Air Force had decided at a high level to use magicians to debunk Geller, comes from Uri Goldstein, who today works as an air-conditioning engineer in Petah Tikva, a town to the east of Tel Aviv. Goldstein rejects the idea that his legal case was a student joke. He says that he had decided to bring it as soon as he saw the posters announcing Geller's forthcoming appearance, and admits having bought his ticket with every intention of saying afterward that he had been swindled. "I didn't believe in all this nonsense about telekinesis, so I talked with my lawyer and said we would go and see the show and ask for the price of the tickets back. It wasn't a question of the few lira. It was the principle." A week or two after the Geller show, Goldstein recalls, another show was announced in a hall in Beersheba by Eytan Ayalon, the magician Yarom believes was used by the military as the spearhead of its surreptitious campaign to discredit Geller in case he started turning airmen into paranormal believers. Goldstein took a group of fellow science students to the hall, and went up to see Ayalon at the end of the show. "Ayalon said, 'OK, why don't I come to your house? Bring some of your friends, and I'll show you all Uri Geller's tricks.' And he did. He came back with about twenty students and showed them everything. It was very interesting. It proved that Geller was just a magician."

All this could be tossed off lightly as good, publicity-attracting hurly-burly, but subsequent events were much more damaging for Uri. Rather quietly, before he teamed up with Peled, he had been doing some performances in Italy. They had not been a success, and were to lead to a near catastrophe. All the indications from the start were that Italy was going to be bad news. The interpreter had not been able to translate him understandably into Italian, and the audience gave every impression of being unmoved by the effects.

He had been depressed by this first foreign venture, and decided that, confrontational and argumentative though Israelis were, he should never try to work outside Israel. One man in the Rome audience however, was impressed, and asked to meet Uri for lunch the next day. He picked him up in a Rolls-Royce, gave him a tour of the city, and explained that he was keen to get Uri to Monte Carlo and to America—especially to Las Vegas. Not unnaturally, and again not really needing psychic powers, Uri had enough imagination to smell Mafia. He was scared, and politely explained that he had a lot of engagements coming up in Israel, and that if he ever got back to Italy, he would, of course, look the man up. Uri was already having problems in disengaging himself from his current manager to start working exclusively for Peled. He was sure that the manager, who had arranged the Italian trip, was cheating him, and he was terrified of getting sucked into some Mafia operation based around using his powers to fleece Las Vegas casinos.

The following morning, when Geller was checking out of his hotel, the desk clerk handed him an envelope someone had left for him. It contained the keys to a car, and papers registering it in his name. Outside the hotel was a brand-new Alfa Romeo Spider. Even more paranoid now about the Mafia, he gave the envelope back to the receptionist, and asked him if later that morning—preferably well after the flight to Tel Aviv had left—he wouldn't mind phoning the number on the papers and asking for them to take the car back with his most gracious thanks, but no thanks. He heard nothing more from the Rolls-Royce man. (On a subsequent visit with Miki Peled to Venice, Uri couldn't nevertheless resist a session in the casino, which led to yet more Mafia fears. Gambling was an anomalous area for Geller. He had always, or so he says, had an instinctive belief, perhaps merely superstitious in nature, that he was not "supposed" to use his abilities to make money, yet he was now making a good living using little else, with no deleterious effect on the powers, so in spite of himself he kept being drawn to casinos. "A casino is a most dangerous place to try tricks," says Peled, who was with Geller. "He made a lot of money on roulette. I remember it was thirty-six thousand dollars. Whatever number he said would come up came up. But I advised him not to go back. It could have been very dangerous to win any more. The Mafia would find out about him again, and come to ask if Uri could help them. I was with my wife, and she said she would leave Italy if he went back. But it was difficult to tell Uri, because he liked money *very* much.")

Uri's undoing in Italy came not from Mafia threats, genuine or imagined, but from a very real piece of amateurish stupidity on behalf of a young Israeli, Rany Hirsch, who was with Uri as representative of his pre-Peled manager. It was well into Uri's Peled heyday back home, but Uri was in the country again fulfilling some previously agreed dates. "Rany had all kinds of bizarre publicity-stunt ideas," Uri explains. "He said it would be great if Uri Geller could meet Sophia Loren, which he actually pulled off. I went to her villa and met her, and it was all fine. But stupid Rany, because she wouldn't allow us to take a photograph with her, stayed in Rome when I went back to Israel, went to some photographer and had a photomontage forged of me and her. It was so obvious, a fool could tell it was a montage. I woke up one morning in Tel Aviv and, as usual, went down to buy the morning papers and there was I with Sophia Loren on the front page and a headline shouting, 'FORGED!'"

The newspapers fed off the scandal for days. Years later, Hirsch wrote a cringing acknowledgment and apology that the whole mess had been his doing, but it was a gift to the skeptics in Israel, and a bad blow to Uri's credibility. "He was not psychologically prepared for such a blow," says Amnon Rubinstein. "I said again that the only way he could repair all the damage that had been done was by going overseas, to an American or English university, and have scientists examine him."

Characteristically, Uri put on a brave face over the Loren fiasco. "I was shocked because it wasn't my doing but, funnily, it just shows you again that all publicity is good publicity, as long as you are not some kind of murderer or have done something really bad. Because being on the cover of the paper actually led to more interest, more bookings, there wasn't really any damage—but what Amnon was saying again about trying to get some kind of scientific study was making me start to think very hard about the nature of these powers, about what I really was."

Uri's experience to date with scientists had not encouraged him to see them as his salvation—Professor Kelson, the physicist who had been quoted rubbishing him in the Israeli newspapers, even Uri Goldstein, the mechanical engineering student and his lawsuit. So on the one hand he wondered if maybe Amnon was right, and on the other whether he should phase out his show-business career and go back to regular employment and a normal life.

Uri was not totally sucked into the spiritual world of ghosts, seances and unexplained powers, and consequently removed from the world of practicality. Oddly, perhaps—although not to those who suspect him of being a regular magician, with the considerable mechanical aptitude that that requires—Uri Geller was a bit of a backyard mechanic. As a boy he had removed an electric motor from a ventilating unit to power up his mother's old pedalled Singer sewing machine, and had fitted an ungainly outboard motor to his bike in an (unsuccessful) attempt to make cycling up the hill to Terra Santa College in Nicosia a bit less arduous. Even when his performing career was developing, he retained an affection for mechanical tinkering, and therefore had a natural affinity with a slightly older man called Meir Gitlis, whom he had met at a party in his teenage years. Gitlis was an electronics wizard, who had his own little workshop at his parents' house, close to Margaret and Uri's flat, and a neighborhoodwide reputation for repairing almost anything electrical. He saw something of Uri's paranormal abilities, and was immediately fascinated by them.

It was Gitlis, indeed, who became the first scientist ever to examine Uri's strange aptitudes. Their informal experiments had two lasting results: the first was that Uri was not a complete laboratory virgin when he was first tested seriously by professional scientists; the second was that he and Gitlis continue to be partners in an electronics business, Nachshol, which Gitlis and his sons run from his combined home, laboratory and factory in a pretty rural village a few miles east of Tel Aviv. Gitlis, who is now fifty-four, is a gadget fanatic, his shelves groaning under his thirty inventions, most of which are in production. There's a thermal diamond tester, an electronic handheld dollar-bill tester, a gold tester and a cellular phone radiation shield, some manufactured under the Uri Geller Enterprises label. The company is currently selling a Gitlis-designed earthquake early-warning gadget in California, a sensitive metronome-like device that detects micro-tremors and could give up to thirty seconds warning of a coming quake.

"At the beginning, I refused to believe in what he was doing," Gitlis says. "When he was young, Uri was always very naïve and excited when something he tried to do worked out, but I was still very suspicious. So, just after he went into the Army, I asked him if I could do some tests on him. The result of this was that I measured a voltage from Uri's body of about ten times more than average. What was more surprising was that he could make the needle of a compass move, even if it was your compass, and you put it where you wanted it. The compass could be on the table and Uri half a meter away from it and he could still make the needle move. It was unbelievable. I checked him carefully for metal and for magnetic fields, in case he had some magnet hidden, but there was nothing. And anyway, he was too far from the compass for a magnet to affect it. I often photographed the spoon-bending. I was looking for the trick, but there wasn't one. I saw the spoon bend on its own many, many times.

"I told Uri always, 'Look, I am a technical man. I believe only in what can be tested and seen.' I often asked him when we were young, 'OK, how do you do it?' It took me a long time until I believed that he was really doing it. I've seen magicians on TV saying they can do the same as Uri, but I can always see the trick. It's easy. But not when Uri does it. If you tested Uri and the magicians side by side, there would be no competition. My older son was very suspicious of Uri just like I was, and recently, he did a telepathy test with him where he controlled all the conditions. He went into another room and, although the door was closed, surrounded himself with books so Uri wouldn't even be able to see if he was in the same room. Then he drew a car with a certain number of windows and lights and antennae. Then he went back to where Uri was and gave him paper and a pen. And Uri drew the identical car, with all the same antennae, the exact same length, only higher. Uri was on his own, without Shipi. These people who say he can't do it without Shipi are liars. They're just jealous.

"A lot of other things have happened to me with Uri," Gitlis continues. "We went to see our accountant only a little while ago to talk about something Uri wanted to do, which was to give all the royalties from our cellular-phone shield, a lead protection from mobile-phone radiation, to a children's charity. We were sitting in the accountant's office and Uri was under a light-fitting high up on the ceiling, which was held up by a chain. And as he was sitting there one of the links of the chain snapped. The accountant said the light had been there for twenty years without a problem. Uri also always phones when we're talking about him, we're very used to that now.

"I once asked a neurologist I know what he thought the mechanism might be, how Uri works. He told me that he believed the two halves of our brain transmit to one another on a certain frequency of some kind, and that Uri may have the ability to tune in to frequencies that are not his own, that his brain is like a scanner for these brain transmissions. He believes a very small number of people have this ability."

It was, then, with Gitlis' small-scale, informal scientific experiments in mind as reassurance that such work might not be too terrible, that in 1970 Uri considered whether and how he might give a part of himself to science. He mulled in particular over how this might affect his performing career and his bank balance. Even with Miki doing well financially out of him, Uri had been able to buy a small penthouse apartment for himself and his mother on Yesha'yahu Street, in the swanky north of Tel Aviv, and was driving his dream car. (This transport of delight was a Peugeot 404, more a Third World idea of a luxury limo than an ostentatiously smart vehicle of the sort one might expect a young star to opt for. "I don't know what made me buy a 404." He laughs. "I think it was the nice ads in the newspaper. When you opened the door you were supposed to get hit with a burst of the fragrance of leather, but it was the worst car in the world. It hardly had the power to climb up the long, slow road to Jerusalem. I used to stop for hitchhikers, and the car would struggle up the hills.")

The Peugeot was not the most psychically inspired choice Uri could have made, but these were dog-days for him in many more important ways. There is something quite melodramatic in the decline of Uri Geller at this time. "I started ebbing away in Israel," he acknowledges. "My performances had a limit—I could do telepathy, I could bend a spoon, I could warp rings, I could hypnotize, and that's where it ended. A magician could write new acts, get new magic, do new tricks. I couldn't because I wasn't a magician. I was amazed when I started seeing the auditoriums emptying on me. 1971 was as incredible for me as 1970 had been, but already I was being attacked and questioned. 1972 was when I was over and out. People had seen me over and over, they were shouting, 'Hey, Uri, we've seen that.' Managers could no longer put me up in big theaters, so I started being booked into discotheques and nightclubs, underground, smoky places, with dancing and striptease and clowns, jugglers and acrobats. I was suddenly just another act. No one would pay attention to me, and I really felt the pits."

Chapter 8

Getting Weirder

"It was us who found Uri in the garden when he was four."

Message, supposedly from the planet Hoova, received by Dr. Andrija Puharich in the early hours of 1 December 1971

....

It was perhaps because he was in a steep decline by the summer of 1971—playing too many tacky clubs, wondering whether he should become a laboratory guinea-pig, in love with a married woman, worried whether he could support his mother long-term—that on Tuesday, 17 August, Uri Geller fell into the Svengali-like clutches of Dr. Andrija Puharich of Ossining, New York.

Puharich proved both a blessing and a curse for him—and no less for me. Damaging or embarrassing revelations are supposed to be the flesh on the bone of biography, but in researching Uri Geller's life story, his close connection with this strange Croatian Serb medical doctor, wonderfully idiosyncratic material though it provided, was curiously depressing. This was not simply because I had developed a respect and fondness for Uri, and was sad to see him smeared by association, nor because Puharich had even done him any great harm. It is because I am sure that Andrija Puharich became a deluded paranoiac. Uri is not so certain, and goes along with—or at least acquiesces to—much of Puharich's peculiar input into his life. More important, the Puharich connection is a gift to the more dogmatic of Uri's opponents; not a bad thing, perhaps, except that I believe it also detracts from the process of assessing him fairly.

There are subtleties beyond the simplistic "Geller teams up with eccentric, therefore he is a charlatan" line of argument. I would suggest, for example, that while he may have been ill advised to associate so closely with Puharich, his loyalty to such an unlikely mentor is anything but evidence for the prosecution. After all, Uri stands accused by his detractors of being a cunning deceiver, not of being gullible or impressionable. But there is no avoiding it: Puharich remains an embarrassment to those who have tried to give Uri Geller a fair hearing. Charles Panati, a long-time science editor of *Newsweek*, knew Uri in the mid-seventies and edited—at some cost, he says, to his credibility as a science journalist—*The Geller Papers*, a book collating all the then existing scientific research on him. Panati met Puharich and recalls him as, "Very, very strange indeed. I don't think I'd ever met anyone quite like that."

Yet Andrija Puharich was not a rogue or a charlatan, even if he did indulge himself from early on with one classic charlatan characteristic: the use of several different first names. Born Karel Puharich in Chicago in 1918, he liked to be called Andrija at home, but changed his name to Henry at high school to sound more American. As a doctor and presenter of medical papers, he was always Henry K. Puharich, reverting only occasionally to Andrija for his less conventional work, such as that on Uri Geller. A polymath, Puharich was a school academic and sporting star, and went on to do a first degree in philosophy at Northwestern University in Evanston, Illinois. He worked his way through college as a tree-surgeon and entered the University's medical school in 1943.

While he was a medical student, he was a prominent wrestler, and continued with graduate studies in philosophy. His first medical assignment was as a second lieutenant in the US Army Medical Corps, from which he was released—on medical grounds, with a chronic inner-ear infection—in December 1947. From the start of his medical career he was deeply interested in parapsychology and ESP although he continued to lecture and publish papers in conventional medicine. He was also a formidable electronics genius, who hero-worshipped and seems to have modelled himself on another Serbian American, the brilliant inventor Nikola Tesla.

Just like Tesla, Puharich was megalomaniacal, neurotic, obsessive, self-destructive. Like Tesla, Puharich patented dozens of inventions, many based on the newly discovered transistor technology; among his patents were micro in-ear hearing aids (which worked by electrically stimulating nerve endings in the bones of the skull), a device for splitting water molecules, and a shield for protecting people from the effects of ELF magnetic radiation. Similarly, like Tesla, Puharich was adept at living royally on other people's money, although

left Margaret Geller on the promenade, Tel Aviv, late 1940s.

below Tibor Geller, in British Army uniform, North Africa campaign, 1942.

Baby Uri Geller in a tin bath.

Tibor and Uri, aged 2.

above Achad Ha'am School, Tel Aviv, 1954. Uri, aged 8, is second row from top, far right.

right Uri in 1956 on Kibbutz Hatzor with the Shomron family. Eytan (top, centre) was his special friend. (It was while copying this photo that the author's defunct camera exposure meter temporarily began working again).

below Downtown Tel Aviv, 1998. The Geller family apartment was on the third floor of the block in the centre. The modern bank building to the left of the photo is on the site of the Arabic garden where Uri believes he had his strange UFO experience, aged 3 or 4.

The suave Tibor, in Israeli army uniform and cravat, with Uri, aged 12, 1958.

Cyprus, 1959, with Joker, Uri's fox terrier.

Joy Philipou, one of the teachers at Terra Santa College, Nicosia, who took a special interest in Uri's powers.

Two of Uri's Cyprus schoolfriends, Ardash Melemendjian, handyman, at his home near York, and Bob Brooks, criminal attorney, in Los Angeles.

left Yoav Shacham, the Mossad agent who recruited 16-year-old Uri as an unpaid, bicycle-riding courier in Cyprus. Yoav is with his fiancée, Talma, and Uri's mother.

below Special agent Geller in Cyprus with another unidentified Mossad man.

below Uri, aged 17 in 1964, on the steps of the Pension Ritz, Nicosia. He would soon be returning to Israel and starting his military service.

right and below Back in Israel, Uri enjoyed playing basketball and riding his Vespa scooter with his friends.

Uri, with an interesting army haircut, 1966.

above Paratrooper Geller, on exercises.

right After the Six Day War, Uri had a brief career as a male model. He is seen here in a stylish, tailored Terylene mod jacket.

below Uri with his early girlfriend, Iris Davidesco.

right 1969. Uri with Hanna Shtrang, now his wife, and her little brother, Shipi, who, while still a schoolboy, devised Uri's stage career. Shipi is now his manager.

1970. Part of Uri's early stage performance was as a hypnotist.

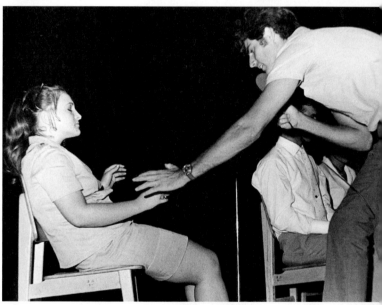

While officially denouncing Uri as a mere magician, the Israeli air force was secretly using his powers for military purposes. Here, he is seen engaged in operations some-where over Israel.

Miki Peled, Tel Aviv's Mr Showbiz, in 1998. Until Uri left Israel, Miki was his agent.

below Uri's shows in Israel brought him a cult-like following. Here, he is psycho-kinetically mending broken watches brought to him by audience members.

Uri with Dr Andrija Puharich, the strange American medical doctor who discovered him in Israel, and brought him first to Europe, then to the USA.

Uri with
Muhammad Ali.

Uri in Munich, 1972,
undergoing informal
testing by Dr Fried-
bert Karger of the
Max Planck Institute
for Plasma Physics.

Uri being laboratory
tested in France, at the
INSERM Telemetry
Laboratories of the Foch
Hospital, Suresnes.

both men died in abject poverty. And while Tesla hobnobbed with the likes of Mark Twain and Rudyard Kipling, fifty years later Puharich became friendly with the enigmatic novelist, Aldous Huxley.

In 1954, while the Godalming, Surrey-born Huxley was living in California, he published his second best-known work after *Brave New World: The Doors of Perception*, an account of his tripping on mescalin. The book became a Bible of the sixties counterculture. He had borrowed the title from yet another strange man, the nineteenth-century poet William Blake, who wrote: "If the doors of perception were cleansed, everything would appear to man as it is, infinite." (Yet another peculiar man, Jim Morrison, borrowed from Huxley for the name of his cult rock band, The Doors.) It was Andrija Puharich who introduced Aldous Huxley to drugs, or so believes his fourth wife Rebecca. Whether or not Puharich procured Huxley the four-tenths of a gram of mescalin he took on a bright May morning in 1953 which inspired him to write *The Doors of Perception* is not recorded. However, the drug blew the writer's mind, and nearly two decades later, Uri Geller, or so it seems, blew Puharich's mind—more or less permanently and without using drugs.

Between Huxley and Geller, Puharich had done enough to merit a full biography of his own. By the seventies, when he sought out Uri, he had adopted a rumpled, Einstein look, frizzy-haired with a crooked bow-tie, but in the sixties, when he first became peripherally well known in America, he was a dark, intense, dapper little doctor, renowned as an author of books on the paranormal and as an occasional face on TV. In the early 1950s he served in the Army again and in 1952 presented a paper entitled "An Evaluation of the Possible Uses of Extrasensory Perception in Psychological Warfare" at a secret Pentagon meeting. In 1953, he lectured senior US Air Force officers on telepathy, and the staff of the Army Chemical Center on "The Biological Foundations of Extrasensory Perception." Back in civilian life, he starred in an episode of *Perry Mason* as a scientist on the track of a paranormal phenomenon. A TV documentary, which appeared in an ABC-TV series called *One Step Beyond* in 1961, followed his expedition to a remote village in Mexico to investigate a local mushroom, which was rumored by the Chatino Indians to induce extrasensory perception in those who consumed it. It had been the subject of Puharich's first book, *The Sacred Mushroom*.

It was as a distant result of a lecture Uri gave to science students in the spring of 1970 at the Technion in Haifa that Puharich and he became a team. Many months after the lecture, according to Uri, a retired Israeli Army colonel and Mossad agent called Yacov came to see him, saying that his student son had been at the Technion event, and had been especially impressed. The colonel had told an Israeli researcher friend in Boston, Yitzhak Bentov, about Geller and Bentov wanted to know more. Uri liked the colonel's laid-back approach, he recalls, and broke a pin the colonel had in his fist. The colonel left, and posted the broken pieces to Bentov in the States. What Bentov, who worked for the Mossad and had good CIA contacts, made of the snapped pin is not clear, but he seems to have found something of interest in the structure of the break. In 1985, ten years before his death, Puharich recounted in a videotaped interview-for-posterity that Bentov stood up and talked about Uri at a November 1970 conference in New York for "alternative" scientists, called "Exploring the Energy Fields of Man." Delegates at the conference had been bemoaning the lack of a scientifically validated exponent of psychokinesis. As a result of what Bentov had to say, Puharich says he was mandated by the conference to go to Israel to seek out and assess Uri Geller. Bentov would ultimately be instrumental in Uri coming to be studied in the USA. In 1979, he died in a Chicago airline crash.

The mission was just what Puharich needed. He was in search of a new protégé. He was just getting over the death in a car crash that January of a Brazilian "psychic surgeon," Arigo, whom he had been studying and writing about for several years. Arigo had the facility, or so Puharich was convinced, to perform major surgery in seconds while in a trance and with the use of no instruments other than a rusty knife. A later Mexican psychic surgeon Pachita, whom Puharich also studied, could perform even more complex operations without anaesthetic or sterile procedure. Puharich claimed to have witnessed him do kidney transplants, and Pachita operated successfully on Puharich's continuing inner-ear problems.

By way of getting Uri interested in doing some scientific research, Puharich had enlisted the help of someone he believed might impress him: Dr. Edgar Mitchell, the lunar module pilot for the Apollo 14 Moon landing. He had been the sixth man to walk on the Moon just a few months earlier. Mitchell was a highly unusual recruit to the ranks of paranormalists. A science graduate twice over with an additional Ph.D. from MIT, where he taught inertial guidance and interplanetary navigation, he had been a Navy pilot and an aerospace test pilot, and was technical director for Navy collaboration in the US Air Force–manned Orbiting Laboratory Program when he joined the astronaut corps in 1966. Despite being as practical an empirical scientist as any of his training would be, Edgar Mitchell was also fascinated by what he believed, both before and after his astronaut career, to be the bigger picture: the view of the universe that accepted the existence of ESP and psychic phenomena. While on the Moon, he quietly carried out an extracurricular and informal ESP card-guessing experiment with four friends on Earth, which he felt was mildly successful, but nowhere near as spiritually uplifting as seeing the world from a quarter of a million miles away.

After serving as a back-up crew member for Apollo 16, Mitchell retired and went full-time into psychic and parapsychological research, writing a lengthy scientific book, *Psychic Exploration: A Challenge For Science,* which earned him the soubriquet "half-assed-tronaut" from his non-admirers among convinced scientist and magician skeptics. Puharich had met Mitchell twice in 1971 while he was raising funds for his Uri Geller expedition, as a result of which Mitchell wrote to Uri recommending Puharich and enclosing a signed photograph of himself on the Moon.

It was, therefore, with some hope that Andrija Puharich found himself at 11 p.m. on a hot Tuesday night in a seedy Old Jaffa nightclub called Zorba, watching Uri Geller perform as the climax to a succession of second-rate singers, jugglers and other cabaret turns—and being distinctly underwhelmed by what he saw. Uri knew from Mitchell's letter that Puharich was coming, but had not expected him to turn up at Zorba, and was embarrassed when he did. Months later Puharich admitted to Uri that he had been pretty sure at the end of his evening at Zorba that Uri was no more than a routine magician, and that he had wasted his trip. Keen though he appears to have been to believe anything going, Puharich was not entirely undiscriminating. The year before he discovered Uri, he had been up to the north of Canada to meet an eighty-year-old man called Arthur Matthews, who had just published a book called *Nikola Tesla and the Venusian Space Ship.* It was Matthews's contention that Tesla, Puharich's exemplar, had not died, as history recorded, in 1943, but was living aboard a UFO, which occasionally landed in Matthews' backyard. And it was Puharich's conclusion, after meeting him, that Matthews was quite mad.

Initially dubious though he was of Uri too, Puharich installed himself in a friend's apartment, and over the next few days did some preliminary tests with him. It seems he was determined to "get a result" if there was one to get. Nevertheless, he did so with the reputation and methods of the good, pedantic, plodding scientific researcher that he was. He kept meticulous notes in tiny handwriting on his experiments. No tape-recorder or film camera could be mentioned without its make and model number; all times were accurately recorded to the second. The culture of precision note-taking was second nature to Puharich; he also kept detailed written records of every sexual encounter he had enjoyed with his succession of four wives and countless beautiful, young, impressionable (and usually rich) girlfriends, who were attracted by his renown as a sort of hippie scientific icon.

Puharich mailed his notes on Uri's science-busting feats back to Ed Mitchell in the States; Uri jokes now that Mitchell must have thought Puharich was running clinical trials on some new form of marijuana over in Israel. It is undeniable that what Puharich reported looked rather like the result of some Aldous Huxley–style drug research—and this was before his work in Israel with Uri turned seriously unorthodox, as it did later that year.

It started routinely enough. Puharich explained to Uri that the tests would be lengthy and occasionally boring, but that this was necessary, thanks to the scientific convention that extraordinary claims require extraordinary proof. With Yacov, the retired army colonel, and an Israeli friend as assistants, Puharich asked Uri what he would like to do first. Uri suggested some simple telepathy. He wrote something on a pad, placed it face down on the table and asked Puharich to think of a number, then another, then another. Next Uri asked him to pick up the pad. On it were already written the numbers, 4, 3, 2, which Puharich had had in his mind. Uri laughed, apparently delighted that it had worked. Like Amnon Rubinstein before him, Puharich was immediately more impressed by this than he had been by the spoon-bending, which he had seen at the night-club and regarded as inconclusive. "That's pretty clever," Puharich reports that he said. "You told me this would be telepathy, and I, of course, thought you were going to be the receiver. But you pulled a switch on me."

Uri explained why he had done it this way round: if he had told Puharich to try to receive the numbers, he might have fought him. "In this way, you participated in the experiment without prejudice," he said. Puharich asked if he could turn on the tape and camera. Uri assented, but added, "You probably think that since I sent those numbers to you so easily, I might also hypnotize you to see and do things that are not really there." Puharich noted that from then he felt that the two of them would get along fine. After an hour of swapping numbers, colors and single words telepathically, Puharich and his assistants agreed that, even if this was not a proper controlled experiment, they were satisfied that it was genuine telepathy. They asked if Uri could receive or transmit more complex data; he replied that he stuck to simple information because then he could be judged either wholly right or wholly wrong, with no gray area, as would be bound to occur if he tried to transfer whole concepts or stories.

Then Uri asked if anyone had brought a broken watch. Yacov's female friend said she had one that was not broken but that she had allowed to stop. Puharich asked to inspect it. With the camera running, he shook it. It ticked for a few seconds, then stopped. Uri refused to touch it. He told Puharich to give it straight to the woman. He placed it in her palm, which she closed. Uri put his left palm over her hand, without, Puharich said, touching it. After thirty seconds, the watch was running, and continued to work for another thirty minutes before it stopped again. Meanwhile, Uri asked Puharich to take off his watch, a chronometer, and hold it in his hand. Puharich noted the time on it as 2:32 p.m., Uri held his hand over Puharich's for ten seconds and told Puharich to check it. The time on the watch was now 3:04, but what surprised Puharich more was that the stopwatch dial on the watch face had similarly advanced thirty-two minutes. For both dials to have advanced by the same time, the whole apparatus would have to have run for thirty-two minutes. "This complex feat of psychokinesis was unparalleled in my experience, or in the literature, for that matter," Puharich concluded.

The next day, Puharich repeated the telepathy tests with the same success, then asked Uri to concentrate on a pair of bi-metal strip thermometers. Even from across the room, he was capable of raising the reading on whichever of the instruments he selected by six to eight degrees. Thoroughly convinced that Uri Geller possessed startling telepathic and psychokinetic powers, Puharich started to interview him about his past, and about his views on his powers. He was impressed and surprised by the depth of introspection that Geller had achieved. The burden of Uri's idea was that telepathic waves travel faster than light, which meant that, once the light barrier was overcome, he could see into the past and the future, and teleport materials instantaneously. He also believed that the particles that existed beyond the speed of light were too small yet to have been discovered. On the question of teleportation, he did not discuss his extraordinary incident in the Army with the heavy machine gun parts, which had apparently teleported to him, but did tell Puharich that when he broke a ring it often lost weight, and when he snapped a jewellery chain, a link was frequently found to have vanished.

He also speculated, Puharich reported, on the source of his powers: perhaps he had inherited them by some genetic fluke from a previous human civilization, for whom they were commonplace; or perhaps his ancestors had interbred with extraterrestrials; or maybe there was a warp in the makeup of his brain. He said mysteriously that he didn't want to talk about his fourth idea, except insofar as it was related to the second, and that, "They are somewhere out there. They have their reasons," with which he returned to the experiments.

He promised to crack but not break the ring of Yacov's wife, Sara, and did so. Puharich relates that he sent the ring to Dr. Anton West, a metallurgist at the materials science department of Stanford University in California. Several months later, he was informed that electron microscopy had shown the fracture in the ring to be of an unknown kind.

For a few more days, Puharich repeated the same tests determined not to be fooled. He needed to go back to the States with sufficient evidence of Geller's abilities to guarantee that, with Edgar Mitchell's help, he could drum up financial support to do further research in Israel and America. Thus it was that he doggedly prepared the ground, at least through Bentov's secret negotiations, for Uri to be tested by Stanford Research International, a vast laboratory and think tank in Menlo Park outside San Francisco, with considerable and globally reported success.

But before that breakthrough, Puharich returned to Israel in November 1971, to try to find some answers to the fascinating scientific phenomenon he seemed to have uncovered in the Zorba night-club the previous August.

Perhaps I am being disingenuous in saying "try to find some answers." I hope this does not do a disservice to Puharich, who died in 1995, but there seems a distinct possibility that already he had a clear idea of what he believed he was on to. The mysterious reference Uri had made in August—"They are somewhere out there. They have their reasons"—had revived in Puharich's mind something he had encountered in 1952, when he was just an Army medic with an interest in the new field of parapsychology.

At a party in New York in 1952, he had met Dr. D. G. Vinod, a professor of philosophy and psychology at the University of Poona, in India. Dr. Vinod was on a lecture tour organized by the Rotary Club. He, like Puharich, was interested in matters such as ESP. Two months after meeting Dr. Vinod, Puharich bumped into him on a train. During the journey, the Hindu scholar did a past and future life reading for Puharich by holding his right ring finger at the middle joint with his right thumb and index finger. Puharich found Vinod's past reading uncannily accurate. On New Year's Eve 1952, Puharich invited the Indian to his home in Maine, where at 9 p.m., the Indian went almost immediately into a deep, hypnotic-like trance. Although Puharich, with his big, sleepy eyes and slow speech, was a superb hypnotist, on this occasion, Vinod went under spontaneously.

While he was in the trance—we must assume with Puharich recording him on some early form of tape or wire-recorder—Vinod apparently took on a deep, sonorous voice. He spoke in perfect, unaccented English, quite different, Puharich reported, from his normal, high-pitched, soft, Indian-accented speech—even if, from what Puharich wrote down of it, a distinct tone of Indian English will be discernible to some. "M calling," Dr. Vinod apparently said. "We are Nine principles and forces, personalities, if you will, working in complete mutual implication. We are forces, and the nature of our work is to accentuate the positive, the evolutional, and the teleological aspects of existence." He went on in this vein for ninety minutes, interspersing his monologue with references to Einstein, Jesus, Puharich himself, and a mathematical equation which, amusingly, when examined later by mathematicians, was found to be slightly wrong.

After listening to Vinod in such trances for a month, Puharich and a group of helpers were satisfied that they were being spoken to through Dr. Vinod by an extraterrestrial intelligence, which Puharich named the Nine, supreme alien beings, who had decided to save Earthlings from the disastrous consequences of their wars, pollution and so on. Puharich was convinced that the beings were using automated, computerized spacecraft to effect changes on Earth, including the contact and training of selected humans—starting, of course, with himself.

At the end of January 1953, Vinod went home, and Puharich heard nothing more from him. Remarkable though the experience of being contacted by extraterrestrials must have been, Puharich seems to have shelved it for nineteen years, until, in November 1971, the Nine spoke to him again in Tel Aviv, through the medium of a hypnotized Uri Geller.

For his second trip, Puharich had rented a sixth-floor apartment in the upmarket area of Herzliya, north of Tel Aviv, about a mile from the Mediterranean. He set up camp from crates loaded with the latest in magnetometers, cameras, tape-recorders and countless electronic gadgets Uri could not identify, and started work again. It was agreed between the two men that Uri would give Puharich three to four hours a day, but that this might have to happen at odd times as Uri was continuing his shows and public demonstrations.

Again, the experiments started with what now passed for routine stuff, Uri accurately picking up three-digit numbers from Puharich's mind while in another room, and moving a compass needle through ninety degrees; the latter, Puharich was intrigued to note, worked better when Uri put rubber bands tightly round his left hand as a tourniquet to block the return of blood. The compass-moving seemed to exhaust him: he complained to Puharich that he found it much less strenuous if he had a crowd of people around him, on whose energy he felt he could draw. Puharich was especially fascinated by Uri's ability to bend a thin stream of water from a tap with his hand held a few centimeters away. This, he commented in his notes, was easily done by anyone with an electrically charged piece of plastic, such as a comb, but with a finger such an effect was unheard-of. The electrical charge on Uri's skin, Puharich further noted, seemed to disappear when it was wet. Another simple test Puharich devised was to see whether Uri could direct a beam of energy narrowly, or whether he produced a random, scatter-gun effect. He laid out five matchsticks in a long row, on a glass plate monitored by a film camera. Uri was able to move whichever matchstick he chose up to thirty-two millimeters.

At one stage, Yitzhak Bentov came to join in the tests with two old friends who in the 1940s had been students together at the Technion and like him, worked for the Mossad. With four researchers poring over him, Puharich noticed that Uri was getting bored. He and Uri had a "where do we go now?" discussion. Uri laid out his problem with scientific work. Despite the advice of Amnon Rubinstein, he still could not see the point of it. He elaborated eloquently on how nothing mattered to him as long as he was making money, and had the freedom that went with it. As he saw it, his life had been a constant struggle to assert his freedom. When the chance came to show off his powers and make money at the same time, he grabbed it. "I want to be known. I want to be successful. If you want to work with me, you will have to deal with my need for fame and fortune. That's it," he concluded to Puharich.

Puharich and Bentov were saddened by what they saw as the small-mindedness of this "unabashed egomaniac," as Puharich described him. They all went out for dinner. On the way home, late at night, Uri insisted on giving a display of blindfold driving. This did not impress Puharich—he knew it was an old magician's trick and how it was done—but he was surprised by how accurately Uri drove, at up to fifty m.p.h. for three kilometers. At one point Uri said he could see a red Peugeot coming: such a car then appeared from round a bend.

Back at the apartment, Bentov started a late-night conversation about the soul, and how he believed Uri's was more evolved than other people's but had become coarsened by poverty and struggle. He did not have to be so selfish and financially obsessed, Bentov said.

Uri seemed mildly interested, and asked how he could find out about his soul; Puharich leaped at this and offered to hypnotize him. Uri was reluctant at first, but Puharich was already compiling ever more detailed notes with a view to writing a book on his Uri Geller experiences. He convinced Uri that hypnotism would be the best way to go back to his childhood and recall vital material he had forgotten; Uri said he knew about hypnotism—he sometimes performed it on stage—but that he was not susceptible to it, although he would happily give it a try.

As the guests left the apartment, one of Bentov's friends took Puharich to one side and said, "You know, we have a word in Hebrew for a kid like Uri—*puscht*, a punk. He really is insufferable. I don't know how you can be so patient with him." Puharich noted that he replied, "I feel he is so extraordinary that he is worth almost any effort."

On 30 November, Uri was doing a performance at a discothèque in Herzliya. Puharich and Bentov were planning the first hypnosis session with him that night, and went to see him. Later Puharich reported having been so depressed by the tawdriness of the show, just as he had been by Uri's cabaret performance at Zorba, that he had almost wondered if he wanted to continue any longer with the experiments. Nevertheless, Uri turned up at his apartment with Iris and lay down on the living room sofa at just after midnight. Puharich asked him to count backward from twenty-five, and was pleased to note that by the time he got to eighteen, he was in a deep trance. He remained in it for an hour and a half. From this point, I have to warn, we are entirely dependent on the late Dr. Puharich for detail. Many, Uri included, find the account bizarre and unbelievable. It troubles Uri to this day.

Once he was fully under, Puharich asked Uri where he was. He talked initially about being in the caves in Cyprus, with Joker. "I come here for learning," Uri said. "I just sit here in the dark with Joker. I learn and learn, but I don't know who is doing the teaching." Puharich asked what he was learning. He replied that it was a secret, about people who come from space, and that he would tell Puharich all about them, but not yet. He lapsed into Hebrew, with Bentov doing a running translation, and talked about trivial childhood incidents. Finally, he spoke of the light in the garden opposite his parents' flat in Tel Aviv. He named the day it happened as 25 December 1949, a date that obviously has enormous resonance, although not throughout Israel, of course, where Christmas Day is just another working day. Uri described the light he saw in the garden as a large, shining bowl, from which emerged a figure with no face but a general radiance. The figure raised its arms and held them above its head, so that it appeared to be holding the sun, at which point he passed out from the brightness.

According to Puharich, at this point, a mechanical, robotic voice could be heard in the apartment, which came either from Uri or from directly above him. It spoke for a couple of minutes, after which Puharich ended the session and woke Uri. He told him about the strange voice, which Uri clearly did not believe. Puharich played him the section of the tape leading up to the voice's intervention, where his own voice could be heard describing the garden incident. Uri became agitated; he did not remember any of the long hypnosis. As soon as the mechanical voice spoke, Puharich reported, Uri ejected the tape swiftly, took it in his left hand, and closed his fist over it. It vanished. He rushed out of the apartment and ran away. Puharich, Bentov and Iris searched everywhere, worried that he might still be partially in a trance and could hurt himself. After half an hour, they found him, as Puharich put it, "like a standing mummy." They took him back to the apartment, and decided that he should go home and sleep. Iris agreed to drive him, albeit that she did not have a license, while Puharich and Bentov decided to reconstruct all they could recall of the strange voice's words while the memory was still fresh.

Their reconstruction ran: "It was us who found Uri in the garden when he was three. We programmed him in the garden for many years to come, but he was also programmed not to remember. On this day, our work begins. Andrija, you are to take care of him. We reveal ourselves because we believe that man may be on the threshold of a world war. Plans for war have been made by Egypt, and if Israel loses, the entire world will explode into war. There will be one last round of negotiations that may not avert war. America is the problem. The negotiations will not succeed. The Egyptians have, as of now, no fixed date to start the war. The critical dates as seen by us are: 12, 15, 20, 25, 26 December 1971—or nothing at all."

Puharich and Bentov stayed up all night discussing what they might be dealing with. The following day, Puharich was alone in the apartment, catching up on his sleep, when Uri arrived, seeming, Puharich reported, unusually relaxed, as if things had taken a distinct turn for the better. Earlier Puharich had placed a specially machined steel ring, made by Bentov in his workshop, into a wooden microscope box. Puharich was not sure why he had put it in the box: he had planned to get Uri to bend it. But Uri asked suddenly, "Why did you put the ring in the box?" Puharich said he didn't know. Uri demanded that Puharich get out the movie camera and take a film of him putting the ring in the box. Puharich did so. Uri placed his hands over the box for around two minutes and told him to check the box. The ring had vanished. "This was the first time I had experienced an object vanishing where I was certain there was no deception involved," Puharich wrote later.

Puharich's work may indeed have only just started, according to the Nine, but for most people, the first hypnosis session is where the usefulness of Puharich's account of his Geller experiments seems abruptly to end. While his reporting on events up to this moment has a truthful feel to it, it then spirals downwards into a bad-movie imbroglio of UFOs appearing all over Israel, of objects moving of their own volition about buildings and the world, of Mossad spies, of top-level meetings with anonymous Israeli security chiefs and an averted world war. For instance, he recorded that one day, he took a brass ink refill cartridge with the number 347299 on it, put it inside a ball-point pen, then put the pen in a wooden box, all in an attempt to produce a variation on the disappearing-ring phenomenon.

When Uri held his hands over the box, the pen stayed put, but the cartridge vanished. A few days later, on the night of 9 December, Uri felt an inexplicable urge to go to a certain point in a suburb east of Tel Aviv at night. He drove out with Puharich and Iris, and there, above a building site, the three saw a bluish pulsating light. He felt drawn to the light and told the others to stay by the car. As he approached, he saw a massive object and, in a near-trance, sensed he was being drawn into its interior. He believed he could make out control panels inside the object. Then a dark shape approached him and put something in his hand. Seconds later he was outside again, and running up to Puharich and Iris. Puharich checked what Uri was holding. It was a brass ball-point ink refill cartridge with the number 347299 engraved on it. The tape-recorder continued to issue its communiqués, summoning Uri to a UFO fly-past here, a teleportation there. Yet every tape made of the voice conveniently disappeared, just as the first one had. By both Puharich's and his own description, Uri seems to have tagged along as a bewildered passenger on a magical mystery tour produced and directed by the good doctor. Yet questions of whether he was Puharich's acolyte or Puharich his, of precisely where the power lay in the relationship, of whether Uri Geller was out-conjured by Puharich or the two were co-conspirators—or perhaps, even, whether the whole thing was genuine—are still up for debate today.

Puharich claimed in his notes that Uri started relaying messages regularly from the Nine. Sometimes, the voice would come out of his Sony tape-recorder in the same monotonous, automated tone. The mysterious aliens, from a world called Hoova, and sometimes calling themselves Rhombus 4D, had designated him and Uri to carry out a variety of tasks, which would test their faith and abilities. The Nine had assigned the pair a central role in preventing war, as well as making them foot soldiers in a grand design for Earth, which they admitted was principally for their own needs and benefit, but would also be the greatest thing ever for mankind. They reassured Puharich through Uri that they had been directing his life and career for decades, as well as Uri's; their city-sized spacecraft, called Spectra, they explained, was responsible for Uri's odd powers, and the way mankind received Uri Geller would determine whether and how their Earth development program would continue, and the ultimate fate of humanity. For some subtle, cosmic reason, Uri was being sent into the world under cover of a clownish, comic act.

Maybe it was just a weird symbiosis between Uri's and Puharich's fertile imagination, each sparking the other off in an atmosphere of increasing hysteria. Puharich became utterly entranced by his watch, whose wild, erratic hand movements in Uri's presence were for him the everyday calling card of the Nine. The two men also experienced extraordinary teleportations almost daily. On one such occasion, they have both reported, an electrical massage machine Puharich had left in New York appeared in its box in working order in the Herzliya apartment. Puharich logged every minuscule detail in his extraordinary 1974 book, *Uri*, a work that, page by unreadable page, became less credible and more damaging and embarrassing to its subject.

To take Andrija Puharich apart intellectually is almost too easy, yet to dismiss him as a madman is far too simplistic. He *was* a real scientist; he delivered Geller with great success to a worldwide scientific audience. The majority of his note-taking has that ring of pedantic accuracy about it, whether it reflects objective truth or not. Indigestible though his book *Uri* is, he was not a relentlessly earnest or humorless man. Nor did he lack worldly wiles: he orchestrated Uri's appearance on every US TV talk show.

"Was it a mistake for Geller to link up with Puharich?" ponders John Hasted, an atomic physicist, and retired professor of experimental physics, at Birkbeck College, the University of London. "No, it wasn't. No one else could have got other people interested. Puharich was a medical electronics man, a reputable electroengineer, and that was the whole criticism of him. They thought he was so good at putting transmitters inside gold teeth that Geller did his telepathy that way, which is rather absurd although it is perfectly possible. He was also very personable but not absurdly so, and a very *nice* man."

What the Puharich/Geller story most likely illustrated was the progressive diminution of Puharich's rationality as he led the all-too-willing young Israeli entertainer into an ever-deepening, hypnotically induced *folie-à-deux*. Michael Rossman, a science writer and teacher, educated at Berkeley, California, wrote an eloquent 1979 article on Puharich and Geller which, while not uncritical, may have got to the nub of the matter.

Puharich records for us the precise times of his watch stopping and starting, an obsessive litany, clinging to this incongruous reed of objective data like a man drowning, the scientist stripped back to his most primitive reflex: measure something, something outside the self. The chaos he faces is real before his eyes; but it is also within him . . . The story I read in his book is not, perhaps, the one Puharich meant to write. True, he warns us at the start that *Uri* is less about Geller than about the Nine, a group of approximately omnipotent entities from another dimension or plane, whose guidance he and Geller have come to accept and serve. But I read the book instead as a drama, candid and historical, about the states of mind of men confronting the unknown. . . .

If one does not simply dismiss Puharich as a crackpot for this account of the Nine, but instead reads *Uri* seriously, as the drama of the muddling of its writer's mind and will, one must ask why his pot cracked in this particular way. The question is not minor, for in nosing around circles of psychic research I have met a number of others whose minds have been muddled (if muddle this be) in a strikingly similar fashion. Perhaps their patterns of reaction give better clues to what they are reacting to, than do their researches themselves. And surely Puharich is a prime case to study, given the precise way in which he blew his scientific cover on the eve of a long-pursued triumph.

When he had been in his early thirties, Puharich had been able to cope with and set aside the spooky Dr. Vinod experience. In his fifties, when he encountered Uri Geller, he fell apart. If even a quarter of what he relates about UFOs, the Nine and the increasing interest in him of the Israeli secret service is true, I will owe him a posthumous apology, but it is hard not to see him as just another deluded soul, riven with obsessions and conspiracy theories. Conditioned in the fifties to be politically wary—he was branded a Communist for his association with Yugoslav friends in America of Marshal Tito—Puharich reported in *Uri* that the Mossad persecuted him in Israel. When he brought Geller to the US in 1973, his suspicions focused, in classic paranoid fashion, on the CIA and FBI. (He, or the Nine, may have had the FBI in mind when they said that their planet was called Hoova—as in J. Edgar Hoover.)

To get a final firm fix on Puharich at this stage in the Uri Geller story, we must spin forward a couple of years in the narrative. Puharich had bought—with whose funds is not known—a magnificent fifteen-room house with six acres, a brook and a pond at 87 Hawkes Avenue, Ossining, New York. This became his base for what was, at his Geller apogee, a virtual Puharich cult. It was known in Ossining as a hangout for oddballs, otherwise "the

Turkey Farm" or "Lab Nine." In early 1979, in his role as a UFO contactee, Puharich discovered that Moscow was beaming powerful signals at the Satanic-sounding frequency of 6.66 Hertz into the brains of Americans. The signals were designed to make those who received them feel constantly depressed. Puharich sent this vital information to President Carter, to Prime Minister Trudeau of Canada and—for some unclear reason—to the British opposition leader, Margaret Thatcher. He received no reply from any of the three, but a few weeks later his house burned to the ground. He claimed to have evidence that the CIA had arranged for the fire, but had subcontracted the job to the Palestine Liberation Organization, which in turn had assigned it to a notorious IRA terrorist.

In fear, Puharich, his wife Rebecca, and their daughter (who is now a stand-up comedian in London) fled to Mexico, where they lived in rustic poverty, fearing assassination—until Rebecca began to suspect that the whole thing was a fantasy on her husband's part, phoned her father in Baltimore and asked him to drive down as soon as he could to pick up her and the child. "Andrija was always starring in his own drama, but it was a drama of his own making," Rebecca reflects today. In the divorce hearing, he claimed she was a CIA agent; she replied tartly that it was a funny sort of CIA agent who bore the subject of her investigation a baby. He said later that she was also the best wife he had ever had, and he wanted her back.

The clinching evidence for me against Puharich is linguistic. I think the full extent of his self-delusion has to be read between, as well as in, the lines he attributed to the Nine. How curious it is that when Dr. Vinod is the mouthpiece of the superior beings, they speak in unaccented English, yet when they speak through Uri Geller in the seventies, it is in the style of the Daleks in *Dr. Who*. The vocabulary, too, at this time, is distinctly 1971. At one point, speaking through Puharich's tape recorder, the mechanical, synthesized voice of the Nine slowed down to automaton speed to say: "We are com-put-er-ized completely com-put-er-ized. We are com-put-er-ized, we are com-put-er-ized." That may have been the way we imagined computers behaving in 1971, but it is hard to believe that the computers of a supercivilization from the planet Hoova would still be droning on in this distinctly seventies science fiction way.

The most devastating linguistic clue, however, that Puharich was himself simulating the voices of the Nine—although how he made Sony tape recorders seemingly speak with their voices, and how he made the cassettes disappear is unknown—comes from Rebecca, who is now back in Baltimore, married to a wealthy attorney, LeRoy E. Hoffberger, and has founded a superb museum of modern, visionary art there. Rebecca Hoffberger recalls that when she got home from Mexico she found a message on her father's answering machine from Puharich, speaking in a strange robot voice: "It was saying, 'This—is—Doctor—Andrija—Puharich. You—have—stolen—the—following—items—of—video—equipment. If—you—do—not—return—these . . .' and so on. Of course, I hadn't taken anything. We just wanted to get out of Mexico before he found out we'd gone. But it was very, very odd. He was very paranoid. If you were against him, you were from the CIA. But he loved Uri. He knew he was the real thing, and in that respect I still agree with Andrija."

Uri Geller's attitude to Puharich over this bizarre period in Israel is best characterized as that of a favored nephew defending an eccentric, erratic but brilliant uncle, to whom he owed a great deal, and with whom he had a special intellectual connection. He declines to dissociate himself entirely from Puharich's wilder theories. He appreciated the American's approach from the outset. "Here he was, this good-looking Einstein, full of joy and fascination and interest. There was something about him that said to me, 'This is an important man that I have to listen to.' He was almost like a guide to me." Liking Puharich was one thing, but most important for Uri was that he was prepared to accept as reality his childhood Joan of Arc vision—and to run with it.

The centrality to Uri Geller's life of the light he saw nearly fifty years ago in the Arabic garden on Betzalel Yaffe can never be underestimated. One evening when he phoned me to reply to a couple of earlier questions, he said out of the blue: "I've been meaning to ask. What do *you* think I saw in that garden when I was four?" Taken aback, I replied that it could have been a dream, or some kind of childhood fit, or a UFO, or possibly God. It was really very hard for me to tell. He said he understood my uncertainty.

With Andrija Puharich there had been no such hesitancy. While the rest of the world was still struggling to believe or not to believe in Uri's powers, Puharich was managing to persuade him to believe in a Uri Geller of Puharich's most idealized imaginings: exit Svengali, enter Dr. Frankenstein. The vision in the garden and the ensuing feeling of difference that this had engendered in Uri as a boy served as the starting point for Puharich to gain his compliance in the construction of a new version of himself as a higher being. The extent of Uri's affirmation of this idea of himself has varied over the years.

If we accept that Uri was telling the truth, and all the phenomena were merely something that happened to him rather than that he contrived, it is hardly surprising that he would trust the belief of a highly qualified foreigner that he was under the control of aliens. Neither would it be amazing if, from time to time, he had his doubts about the theory. Frankly, even if his powers were a trick, the degree to which it had already worked over the twenty years he had been preparing it, and the volume of affirmation he had received from the public that he had paranormal powers, might be enough to make anyone wonder if they really were "special," even if their "miracles" were faked. It is likely that many witch doctors, shamans and miracle-working gurus, who learn their trade systematically, come eventually to believe they have special powers.

"Such bizarre things started happening when Andrija came into my life," Uri attested one day, as we were walking his dogs along the river Thames in a rainstorm. "Like the incident with the massage machine. I wanted one so badly, and he was wishing he had brought his over with him, so one morning his materialized from New York to Israel. I wake up and there is a massage machine in front of my bed. When this kind of thing happens, you either think you are totally out of it, or you have to accept it, because it is a fact. I questioned his credibility, I don't question my own sanity. I had gone through a war and gone through Cyprus, crazy things had happened since childhood, I read minds.

"Look, sometimes I think there are no in-betweens here. It's either I really saw what I saw and it was there in physical form or not. But, then, many a time the idea sneaked up on me that maybe he managed to hypnotize me to such an extent that he actually implanted these ideas and images into my mind, so when, for instance, we saw this huge disc in the Sinai desert, it was really my imagination and it wasn't there. Then there were other times when I thought he had sprinkled my food and drink with magic mushrooms. Then again, my relationship with Puharich was a very long one, and you can't poison food every time you plan for Uri Geller to see something. And yes, there is supposed to be a phenomenon where your mind or your subconscious can put itself on magnetic tape. Maybe Andrija found a way either by hypnotism or by triggering some ability in me to create those tapes. But then the voices I heard *were* very real. So it was seeing, hearing, touching and smelling, and as far as I feel, it was a fact I saw these things.

"You must understand," he continued, "because we were in this situation it looked quite normal to me in a way. Yes it was bizarre, but it was normal. But to the outside person, who was not involved, it looked total madness and hysteria. From the day I met Andrija he was very accurate. He kept diaries. He was a hundred percent sure that an extraterrestrial intelligence was working through me, using me as a vehicle for them to achieve certain things here. There was some sort of code system through his watch. OK, in a very strange way, I disconnected myself from that scene while it was going on. I let things happen. The UFO in the Sinai, another one that I have seen with Iris in the suburbs of Tel Aviv, they were all happening to me, and I took it very naturally, just said to myself, let it happen.

"When he hypnotized me, some of the voices came through me, but I was awake when I heard the words come out of the tape recorder. Did I hallucinate? No way. But because of the way the tapes *in* the machine dematerialized every time they should have been recording the voice from Spectra, I suspected Andrija, because he had come with his own tape-recorder, a Sony. Once, when he wasn't in the room, I opened it with a screwdriver just to satisfy myself that this wasn't a trick tape recorder that could gulp down a tape and make it disappear. Yes, then I thought Andrija was tricking me. He was totally immersed in me, Uri Geller, for no monetary reason. I had to tell him that if he wanted me out of Israel, I wanted to buy my mother an apartment before I left. He actually loaned me money with which I bought my mother an apartment. It was new for me to see such a non-financial motivation.

"Now when Andrija's book came out and I was being interviewed, I was very supportive to him. I had to go along with his idea, because I was a believer, because he painted the canvas and I interpreted from the canvas. But when I parted ways with Andrija years later, I had to stay in the balance, meaning if I would have disputed what he had written, it would mean that I was just some kind of conspirator along with him, and I lied and all that. But because I still very deeply believe that what was occurring between me and Andrija was real, I couldn't brush it aside. If you look at an interview in its entirety, I would go on about ninety percent about my powers and abilities and that would give a little opening of about ten percent to the possibility that these voices were some kind of an extraterrestrial intelligence. I never said that this was a hoax from Andrija or that it wasn't real, or that this was his imagination. I said it exactly as it happened. What can I do when Andrija opens a Sony tape, a new one, in front of my very own eyes, tears off the cellophane, puts it into the tape recorder, presses the button to record and a mechanical voice comes on?

"This is the big difference between me and many other paranormalists. They think that paranormal powers come from within you, whereas I say that's possible, but I believe that in my case, it is coming from outside, from a thinking entity, and that it is it which decides what to do. The fact is that here I am, after nearly thirty years, and I am still in contact with something. If that's controversial to some closed-minded skeptics, fuck them. The fact is that these things are still continuing to happen to me—and not only to me."

Chapter 9

An Agreement to Fantasize?

"The rational, orderly, common-sense world of experience is a sham: behind it lies a murky and paradoxical world of shadowy experience and shifting perspectives."

Professor Paul Davies, physicist

....

You may have noticed that the word hypnotism has begun to creep into the Uri Geller story like an uninvited guest at a party. Early in my research I had wondered idly whether the explanation for what I saw Uri apparently do—make a spoon bend of its own accord in the flat of my son's hand—might lie in the field of hypnosis. The idea seemed too ludicrous, however: in corny fiction and bad films hypnosis is credited with far more than it can achieve. But I have also seen and admired the British stage hypnotist, Paul McKenna, apparently induce a ridiculous private fantasy—be it riding a horse or swimming underwater—in a stage full of people. Perhaps Uri Geller is more of a mind-bender than a spoon-bender.

Strongest among the competing theories I had thus far considered as an explanation for the Geller phenomenon was the idea that Uri's ability to bend metal with the power of his mind exists in the majority of us, and that he somehow triggers our subconscious to cause us to produce such effects. This *could* be the answer for the huge number of anomalous events I was told about that had happened at some distance from Uri.

If we accept that mind-power could bend metal, a subconscious triggering mechanism in third parties has, surely, to be the only way to explain for example, how the El Al captain Gideon Peleg had seen a fork tine bend spontaneously when he was talking about Uri, who was several hundred miles away from him. Then there are the thousands of reports from dozens of countries of people's broken watches and clocks coming to life, and their cutlery bending and leaping about when Uri appears on television. The same happens every time he appears on radio or TV. Recently a couple from Leeds, in Yorkshire, both highly educated crossword compilers for several quality newspapers, heard Uri on a local radio station asking people to get their broken watches working via his powers. The wife had an old battery-operated Sekonda, which had stopped, she estimated, over two years earlier. For amusement, she tried to give the watch the Geller treatment by clenching her hand over it and shouting, "Work!" Not only did it come to life, she says, but it started to tell the same time as the kitchen, microwave and oven clocks, all of which were two minutes fast. A month later, the watch was still working perfectly.

"I am completely astounded by it because I am a total skeptic. I still can't believe that it happened," the woman told me.

Her husband added, "We always thought he was a charlatan and, in a way, we still do. We are both quite rational and deeply skeptical, but then we are also both religious people, who believe in the possibility of miracles. I have to dismiss as unbelievable the 'obvious' explanation, that my wife got the watch going and set it by the kitchen clock then played a trick on me. It is logical and plausible, but incorrect."

Surely not all such people can be imagining things? James Randi, a charismatic Canadian magician-turned-crusader against all forms of what he believes is charlatanism, laughs and said they most certainly can. He claims that he was once on a New York radio program pretending to be a Geller-esque spoon-bending psychic, and received scores of calls from people reporting healed watches and destroyed cutlery. Randi, who has spent twenty-five years doggedly campaigning against Uri Geller, is a colorful, engaging character, a former escapologist, who has been adopted as the unlikely figurehead of a confederation of anti-Geller magicians and scientists.

The possibilities of Randi's radio experiment are intriguing, so long as he is telling the truth. Unfortunately, Randi is a self-proclaimed con man; although he now describes himself as such ironically, to demonstrate that all magic is a confidence trick, he also has a self-defeating tendency to stretch the truth, albeit in the pursuit of what he believes to be a greater truth. Randi subscribes to the view that the callers to the New York radio station imagined the phenomena, or were simply lying. But what if, believing that he was a "real" psychic, they accepted a hypnotic suggestion that their spoons would bend and their watches restart, and thereupon triggered in themselves the Geller effect on metal? Or if, under the power of Randi's suggestion, they all believed they had seen such phenomena, even though they had not occurred?

Of course, being *told*, even by the steadiest and most reliable of witnesses such as Captain Peleg, about such wonders as objects bending and changing at a distance, is fascinating, but not nearly so much so as seeing the phenomena for yourself.

An hour before I left my office on the morning of my first interview with Uri in 1996, he phoned to ask if I minded conducting it as he went on one of his daily Thames-side walks—the pattern into which we settled for two years. This meant that Uri would have to wear a remote microphone for my tape recorder clipped to his lapel as we walked. In 1981, I had bought an expensive Sony electronic mike with a tiny windsock that would have been ideal for an outdoor interview, but it had not worked for at least ten years. For some reason, I had never thrown it away. I had occasionally bought it a new battery to try to goad it back into life, but to no avail. It was dead. When Uri said we would be doing the interview on the hoof, I went to my local electronics shop to buy a new microphone, only to find that such things were unknown in suburban high streets. Back in the office, I found a cheap old mike in a drawer. Next to it was the fifteen-year-old Sony; out of curiosity, I tried it and was alarmed to find it working perfectly. It has continued to do so ever since, right through all the Geller interviews, indoors and out, all over the world, in all weathers.

An old camera also underwent a mysterious rebirth. I use a second-hand Pentax Spotmatic with a close-up lens when the need arises to copy pictures for my books. The meter has not worked for several years, but this hardly matters, as I have become adept at judging exposure. One morning, I was on Kibbutz Hatzor, where Uri lived for a year as a child, when Nurit Melamed, the elder sister of his then best friend, Eytan Shomron, produced a tiny but excellent black and white snapshot of Uri and the Shomron family in about 1957. She did not want to part with it, but was happy for me to copy it. The light level in her house was low, however, so we took it outside, where the midday sun was dazzlingly bright. I realized I had never copied a photo in such light, and was unsure what exposure to use. For once, I could have done with a working meter. Peering through the viewfinder at the old photo of Uri's intense eyes, I suppose I should have expected something odd to happen, but I didn't, and proceeded to guess a variety of exposures. It was while doing so that I noticed the dead meter needle was suddenly working; I had no memory of ever seeing it move from its resting point. It gave me a perfect reading and continued to work for the rest of the day.

The following morning, I awoke in my hotel to find that a sandstorm had blown up. I jumped up to take a photo through the window of the extraordinary swirling yellow dust outside. As I picked up the camera, the strap caught round something, and it hit the hard floor with a horrible crack. The Pentax was undamaged—apart from the meter, which stopped again, and has not worked since.

A key factor of these phenomena, if such they are and not just coincidence upon coincidence, always seems to be an element of the unconscious. It is no use hoping or assuming that your faulty camera or microphone will suddenly work because you are using it in some connection with Uri Geller. But if you aren't expecting anything, something odd seems to happen, even though curiously you don't associate it with Uri. When I was copying the photo on the kibbutz, and told Nurit that my camera meter had just come to life when I needed it, it was she who pointed out the Geller connection.

Another day, Uri came to see me in my office—he was passing by in the late afternoon. The next morning, a previously reliable wall clock he had been sitting under was twenty minutes slow. Assuming that the battery had run down, I checked it on a tester, but it was fresh. I threw out the clock. It was only several hours later that the connection between it and the world's most renowned psychic interferer with watches even struck me.

While professional magicians would dismiss the idea that Uri can hypnotize others to make Geller-type effects take place through their own subconscious efforts, one or two of those I interviewed hinted that when we see a spoon bend so dramatically, it is an illusion as the result of a suggestion by Geller. Mass hypnotism occasionally crops up as an explanation for such anomalies: in 1863, D. D. Home, a Scottish psychic, who was never discovered to be a fraud, performed a series of table and cloth levitations in France, as well as extending his own body by several centimeters, and placing his head in a pile of live coals and emerging unmarked. These experiments, and others by Home, were observed and written up by Sir William Crookes, a distinguished physicist, and Lord Adare, a *Daily Telegraph* foreign correspondent. A commentator in the scientific journal *Nature* at the time posited the theory that Home was a hypnotist—or a werewolf. In London, over a hundred years later, the science-fiction novelist Arthur C. Clarke, years after seeing his door key apparently bend under Uri Geller's gaze, changed his mind and said that he had been mistaken: he believed he might have been in a hypnotic state when he made the observation.

But even having suspected that hypnotism might provide an answer to the Geller enigma, I was still shocked when I learned later from Uri that Andrija Puharich was a master hypnotist, and when I came by chance upon the first evidence that Uri himself had been honing his hypnotic skills in the early seventies, I experienced what felt then like scales falling from my eyes. Subsequently Uri mentioned hypnotism in an interview, but did not dwell on the subject. This might have been because it was not very important to him, but I wondered if this was something he preferred not to be too well known about him.

I discovered more about Uri's dalliance with hypnotism through an Israeli investment management MSc, Yael Azulay, whom I met at an afternoon workshop Uri held at Battersea Town Hall in London in 1997. Yael got up to tell Uri that she had met him in 1972, when she was a schoolgirl. He was friendly towards her, but I do not think it was in his plans for me to take her number and visit her. Yael is a great admirer of Uri Geller, but her story was quite different from what I had expected.

Although by the time Yael met him Uri was already famous, and well into his bizarre Puharich period, he was still attending the more upmarket student parties in his continuing effort to convince the next generation of influential Israelis of his powers. Yael was at an elite private high school, where she was worried about some math exams. She was at a friend of a friend's party late one night at a villa in a smart Tel Aviv area, when, she recalls, "Uri just arrived. I remember someone saying he is likely to come and you must see this guy. People were hyping him up and talking about how he does all these magic kinds of things. He just arrived and the music stopped and he was trying to grab attention because obviously he had an audience. He wanted to talk to us, to get something going. It's not unusual at Israeli parties if somebody wants to say something or they have had enough of the music just to come in and do as they want. Uri had short hair, and was wearing a loose, baggy, checked shirt with buttons down the front and denims. He looked like a kibbutznik. He didn't come across as a very powerful man. He had presence, yes, but he was just like someone who was playing around. He said, 'Does anyone want to do some hypnotism?' in a very inquisitive, almost childlike, way. Obviously I volunteered. I wasn't working at all at school, and I was worried about it. He had a pendulum, and said, 'I bet you that with this pendulum I can have you asleep within seconds.' It seemed to me, throughout the whole time he was hypnotizing me, I was not asleep. I am quite aware of what was going on. Everybody was watching. He asked me if I wanted anything in particular and I said, yes, I wanted him to make me pass my exams the next month, to make it so I could get really good marks in maths. I was very skeptical of the whole thing. I didn't believe that he had managed to hypnotize me, but I did immediately start working damned hard. And I don't know how, but the exact questions I had revised came up in the exam, and I got a really good mark of ninety-five percent. Of course I made the connection when I got the mark. What I liked was that he didn't make me do anything under hypnosis. He inserted messages in my mind. He said, 'Just believe that you are going to do well,' but he wasn't looking for a product there and then. He didn't even ask me to let him know what results I got."

If his hypnotic exploits are really a skeleton in Uri Geller's cupboard, and not merely just another of his abilities, it may seem curious that his critics have not made more of it in all their ceaseless attacks on him. Insisting, as they do, that Geller bends spoons behind his back while you are not looking is less than satisfactory for those who fail to see anything of the sort. Hypnotism would seem an acceptable, rational explanation for what so many people see, or believe they see, in his presence or with him consciously or subconsciously in mind.

The problem for skeptics here is that, by and large, they believe hypnotism, too, is a fraud, and therefore cannot cite it as a rational explanation for Uri Geller's repertoire. They argue that research with thousands of subjects has shown reliably that only fifteen to twenty percent of the entire population is capable of going into a deep hypnotic trance, and that only another thirty percent can be hypnotized at a lighter level. Additionally, they say, it is not even known what a trance is. No instrument has been invented to measure whether someone is under hypnosis or not, and there is a good reason for this: there is no indication that there would be anything for such a machine to measure. Some modern brain-scanning experiments have indicated that the brain activity of a hypnotized person is significantly different from that of a person told to pretend to be hypnotized. But the evidence is tentative. Psychologists can show that the "altered state" supposed to be characteristic of hypnosis can be faked. So much for the kind of controlled, laboratory tests that skeptical, empirical science demands before any new effect can be accepted as proven. Hypnosis happens when all parties to it consent willingly, and this does not make it a scientific phenomenon.

"I am convinced," James Randi told me in his Fort Lauderdale office, "that hypnotism is an agreement between the hypnotist and the subject to fantasize. I have never seen anything done during a so-called hypnotic trance that could not be done out of a hypnotic trance."

At his office desk in Loughton, Essex, Mike Hutchinson, a close friend of Randi, a major figure in the British skeptic movement and an implacable opponent of Uri Geller, was still more forthright: "Hypnosis is nonsense," says Hutchinson, who left his job as a wood-veneer merchant a decade ago to become the UK distributor for rationalist books from America. "Let's get one thing straight as far as hypnosis is concerned, there is no such thing. There is no hypnotic trance. Perhaps if you use the word suggestion, I can go along with it. I know somebody who is a stage hypnotist, who used to use this so-called trance, but now he does his act without using the hypnotic trance—and gets the same sort of results."

In 1995 Randi went as far as to include hypnosis in a book called *The Supernatural A–Z*. Under his scrutiny it did not emerge well. Such apparent successes of hypnotism as weight-loss and cessation of smoking, he wrote, might just as easily be attained by religious inspiration, "or the intervention of another mystic-sounding but ineffective therapy . . . This is an idea professional hypnotists do not care to hear."

Morris Goran's 1978 book, *Fact, Fraud, and Fantasy, The Occult and Pseudosciences*, is a recommended text for convinced skeptics. In it, Goran includes hypnotism with pyramidology, palmistry, numerology, I Ching, the tarot, Scientology, witchcraft and astrology. A 1990 book James Randi especially recommends, *They Call It Hypnosis*, by Robert Allen Baker, a psychologist, propounds the theory that there is no such thing as a state of altered consciousness produced by hypnosis, and that what we term hypnosis is in fact a mixture of social compliance, relaxation, and suggestibility. This, it is argued, can account for many occult phenomena, such as past-life regression, UFO "abduction," channelling and speaking in tongues. *Bizarre Beliefs*, by Simon Hoggart, a political journalist, and Mike Hutchinson, examines hypnotism alongside crop circles, Nostradamus, "evidence" of a living Elvis Presley and the curse of Tutankhamun. (An oddity to note here, perhaps, is that Mike Hutchinson's ex-wife was a white witch. When he brought this up in our interview I suggested lightheartedly that, as he is a highly knowledgeable rationalist and his wife was a witch, the reason for their split was clearer than in many divorce cases. He shot me a meaningful glance. "It was better than if she'd got into Catholicism," he said. It turned out that he supported her, had been delighted when she got into a good coven in nearby Leyton, and has written in qualified support of white witchcraft in a skeptics' magazine.)

To appreciate hypnotism's status for skeptics, it is important to realize that when this strange new mental process was discovered two hundred years ago, it was the spoon-bending of its day, and its proponent, a Swiss-German mystic and physician, Franz Anton Mesmer, the contemporary Uri Geller.

There are striking parallels between Mesmer and Geller. Both are flashy, commercial, controversial, and were publicly accused of fraud. Both became celebrities and were sought out by other celebrities. Both arguably hit upon a new scientific effect—but seem to have missed out on understanding what made it work. Mesmer was the talented son of a game warden, and was flamboyant, rather opinionated, forceful and given to the dramatic. At twenty-three, as a medical student, he came up with his early ideas on hypnotism. He first called his practice "animal gravitation," then changed its name to "animal magnetism," magnetism then being a fashionable explanation for "life, the universe and everything." For centuries, magnetism had been regarded as an "occult virtue" and accredited with all manner of crazy qualities; once it was better understood, from the early seventeenth century, people liked to use magnetic attraction as a metaphor for all kinds of effects that had nothing to do with magnets. For Mesmer to tack "magnetism" on to his theory was much like attaching the prefix "cyber" to some new concept today.

When Mesmer hypnotized patients to produce "crises"—what we would call trances—to cure various ailments, he used a combination of magnets and his own charisma. It hardly mattered that the magnets were an extraneous gimmick. Not even Mesmer seemed aware that it was he—"the magnetizer"—who was the significant ingredient in animal magnetism. Nor was it realized that the practice of curing ailments, both physical and mental, by unleashing the power of the subconscious had been used by shamans, medicine men and witch doctors for thousands of years.

Shortly after he set up in medical practice in Vienna Mesmer became the man of the moment. There, and in Munich, he demonstrated the art of "magnetism," and was a sensation, with hundreds of happy clients to swear by his cures. Not surprisingly, Mesmer, a cantankerous maestro much given to tantrums, eventually attracted professional skepticism and outright opposition, just as Geller did centuries later. At the age of forty-three, in the wake of a slightly over-ambitious, and unsuccessful, attempt to cure a Viennese dignitary of blindness, he decamped for Paris, and became a controversial sensation all over again, only this time in an even bigger way.

He opened a clinic on the Place Vendôme, which he equipped with a *baquet*—a tub of water filled with iron filings and pieces of glass, with iron rods protruding. Patients were required to grasp the rods while sitting in a circle connected to each other by a cord. The room was darkened and full of mirrors; Mesmer would appear dressed as a wizard, touching or simply staring at his clients as soft music played. Some would fall asleep, others go into convulsions. And hundreds claimed to be cured. Such a furor ensued that Mesmer soon had to move into bigger premises, with four *baquets*. He even introduced an economy class for those unable to afford the personal attention of the master. He "magnetized" a tree, to which thousands of the poor and sick attached themselves with cords—shades of Uri Geller's power crystals. A large proportion of those who used it claimed to be cured, probably by self-hypnosis.

Le magnetisme animal was the talk of France, ridiculed by doctors, respectable scientists and satirists, discussed in hundreds of books and pamphlets, but patronized by the wealthy and powerful—Marie Antoinette for one—as well as the poor. Mesmer, as a man of science as well as a doctor, craved scientific validation, but the professors refused even to discuss him, let alone investigate his claims. They held that he and his preposterous theory were a gigantic hoax. The Royal Society of Medicine in London discussed examining Mesmer's methods, but he soon blew up over the suggested experimental protocols, and the Society had nothing more to do with him.

The accusations of charlatanism did nothing to dim Mesmer's star. The richer and more famous he became, the more miraculous cures were reported. Eventually, in 1784 the King, Louis XVI, intervened. He appointed a royal commission to establish whether Mesmer was a charlatan or a healer. On the panel were Antoine-Laurent Lavoisier, the celebrated chemist, Benjamin Franklin, physicist and statesman, Jean-Sylvain Bailly, the astronomer, Joseph-Ignace Guillotin, inventor of the guillotine (seen at the time as a great advance in humane execution) and Antoine Laurent de Jussieu, a botanist.

The commission utterly debunked Mesmer. It ripped apart the concept of animal magnetism, found that the fluid in the *baquets* was not magnetic, and showed that a susceptible subject, when offered four trees, only one of which was "magnetized" was sent into a trance by all of them. It refused to consider the evidence that a huge number of people believed themselves cured by Mesmer, and effectively sent him packing into obscurity and exile. Of the nine commission members, only the botanist, de Jussieu, published a dissenting opinion. He was convinced from what he had seen that Mesmer might be on to something genuine.

A combination of Mesmer's rampant commercialism, his showbiz pizzazz, his fanaticism and the poor standard of his scientific explanation for his own work ensured that he was designated a fraud. Yet a large body of his more open-minded supporters believed—rightly, as it turned out—that he was on the track of something, and they continued to use and develop animal magnetism, still without knowing what it was.

Skeptics aside, today hypnosis is pretty much an established treatment, "officially endorsed," as the *Encyclopaedia Britannica* confirms, "as a therapeutic method by medical, psychiatric, dental, and psychological associations throughout the world." Some hypnotists in Europe still describe the "community of sensation" between hypnotist and subject, likening it to a magnetic force. Experiments by Soviet researchers have suggested that hypnotism can work over long distances, of a thousand miles, in one case, and that hypnotic suggestion may even be transmitted by some electromagnetic means. In more conventional arenas, hypnotism is used in preparing people for anesthesia and childbirth, in enhancing drug response and reducing dosages. It is routinely used in the management of extreme pain, especially in cases of terminal cancer. It is excellent for nervous dental patients, and works well on high blood pressure and headaches.

Although Freud used hypnosis for a while, he turned against it. Partly as a consequence of this, modern psychotherapists do not fully approve of it because it relieves only symptoms and not the causes of neurosis. Although controversy continues to burn over the question of stage hypnotists, and whether their performances are dangerous, few medical doctors, and still fewer practitioners in the psychological sciences, have any doubt at all that hypnotism is "real."

Real, yes, but could it have caused a skeptical journalist and his two teenaged children to believe simultaneously that they had seen the same spoon bend when it hadn't? I found that the answer to that depended on who you asked. For Mike Hutchinson, the idea was inconceivable—not that he was in any way suggesting that the spoon-bending we saw was real. "A mass hypnosis, of three people?" Hutchinson reflected. "Suggestion, perhaps, but if you are thinking about being put into trance, then no."

On the phone from New York, where he is establishing himself as the star of stage hypnosis he has been in the UK for many years, Paul McKenna took an on-the-fence position, but not an uninteresting one. "Three people to see the same thing? Definitely, I think it's possible, if the operator is skillful and slick enough," he said. "There are all kinds of examples of mass hallucinations. It's less common than one person seeing something." Could Geller have learned to hypnotize the unsuspecting in an instant, as McKenna seems to? "It seems in my stage show to some people that I have more power than I really do," McKenna admitted. "It looks as if I can just walk up and snap my fingers, but that's not actually what takes place at all. Because of the environment, the context in which the show is taking place, the cards are so stacked in my favor that I appear to be able to do these things. Some research in Australia has shown that if you give people a big title, like professor, doctor or his lordship, they appear taller to others. We distort reality in our mind with our preconceptions. But at the same time, on anecdotal evidence of spoon-bending, I'd say I'd have to keep an open mind. I've seen magicians bend spoons and fool me, but not the way Uri does it, where people see it bend apparently by itself. So what you saw could have been real."

Dr. Graham Wagstaff, reader in psychology at Liverpool University and a leading authority on hypnosis, had a third view. He gave evidence in Paul McKenna's favor at the July 1998 court case in London in which a man who believed McKenna had turned him into a schizophrenic unsuccessfully tried to sue him.

"It wouldn't be unusual for three people to think that's what they've all seen if that's what they expected to see," Wagstaff postulates. "Or maybe you *did* see it, but it was an illusion, or maybe it's a problem of memory, that you all remembered it wrongly. But as for hypnosis by Uri Geller, you'd have to have a pretty way out, eccentric view of hypnosis to believe people can be hypnotized without being aware of it. It won't wash with the vast majority of the scientific hypnosis community, even those who really believe there is a hypnotic state. To them, a hypnotic state is something like focusing your attention, not some weird thing, some strange suggestible state that you fall into and then you're at it. You have to *believe* you're being hypnotized."

In talking to Graham Wagstaff, I became aware of a fascinating difference between him, a professional skeptic, and myself, an amateur. He believes that things happen to all of us that the likes of Geller and Puharich—and, latterly, I—would regard as "strange" and spooky, but that a *proper* skeptic retains his skepticism at all costs. "We all have these experiences," Wagstaff says. "One of my favorites was when the wing mirror on my car got mended by itself. It was in about 1975, when I lived in Newcastle, and, no, I wasn't on drugs. I had a Ford Anglia, and the mirror was dangling off. Then one morning, I came along and it wasn't dangling off. It was mended. That's how I remember it. I do a bit on cars, and I'd looked at it, and I couldn't see how anyone could fix it. I'm not suggesting that anything weird and wonderful happened, but that I suppose I must have seen it wrong, or I'd made some sort of mistake, or my memory was playing tricks on me or something like that. I went through everything. None of the neighbors knew what had happened. I was quite worried about it. It's quite possible that some good Samaritan mended it, but I would have thought it was beyond repair. It was hanging down. But I'm a real skeptic so there must be some explanation."

Uri Geller, meanwhile, does not believe hypnotism plays a part in spoon bending. "It's all very well saying people imagine they see the spoon bend," he says. "But how do you then explain that the spoon actually *is* bent, and you can take it home with you?" It is a cogent enough point.

Chapter 10

Germany

"The powers of this man are a phenomenon that in theoretical physics cannot be explained."

Dr. Friedbert Karger, physicist, the Max Planck Institute for Plasma Physics, Munich

....

The end of Uri's harrowing, futile relationship with Yaffa came in the middle of his extraordinary adventures with Andrija Puharich but not as a result of the bizarre turn his life had taken. The illicit extramarital affair had finally become intolerable for Yaffa, who decided they should not see one another again. Uri had no doubt that he loved her, and was heartbroken by her decision. Even though he had one night stands with other women, and Hanna Shtrang was still quietly in the background as his on-hold marriage partner, the split with Yaffa played a considerable part in his decision to leave Israel in the summer of 1972, when he was twenty-five.

Amnon Rubinstein had long ago counselled him to be tested scientifically overseas, and now Puharich was increasing the pressure on him to ease up on the showbusiness razzmatazz and become a serious fish in some bigger pools. It seems almost that Puharich tacitly acknowledged that his own eccentric reputation precluded Uri from being taken seriously until he had been tested by independent researchers. However, Uri's experience abroad was minimal. He had not been successful as a performer in Italy, and he was distinctly nervous about submitting himself to the scrutiny of US scientists who might be less friendly than Puharich. He worried that his powers might desert him outside Israel. He decided he would like to go to Europe first, in a kind of step-by-step approach to America. He wanted to meet some scientists there, who had expressed interest in him, and perhaps try some performances.

Germany might seem an odd place for an Israeli to go to further himself, but several factors had led Uri to this decision. An Israeli friend, a singer called Zmira Henn, had a boyfriend already working in West Germany as an impresario. She suspected that Uri would get on well with Yasha Katz, and could come to a good business arrangement with him. Also, in common with many native-born Israelis, Uri did not have quite the post-Holocaust horror of Germany by which so many European Jews understandably are haunted. Germans tend to respond to the friendliness of Israelis by being especially welcoming in return. And, as his mother had been born in Berlin, Uri felt some affinity with the country.

He was seen off by an odd party of well-wishers, consisting of his divorced parents, Shipi's parents and Hanna. With Uri on the flight was Shipi, who had finished school but still had some time to go before he was required for his Army service. It looked very much as if Shipi was going to be Uri's personal and road manager. Now a smart seventeen-year-old, he was, to all intents, Uri's kid brother.

It was a poignant parting from Israel for Uri. He had a lot to think about. "I like to have these in-built safety devices in my mind so I made two vows as I walked up the steps of the plane. I swore that every day, whatever happens to me, I will look at my life as one big holiday. The second thing, I would thank God for what he had given me, and when the moment comes when it ends, I will always be grateful. You see in the back of my mind I always kept a little room of fear that it might end and I might have to go back and work. To me it was such a splendor and a privilege to wake up in the morning whenever I wanted to, I didn't have to go to work. The days of me running around in Tel Aviv being a messenger boy on my Vespa really were over. I could do whatever I wanted, because everything around me was paid for."

Uri and Shipi did not fly initially to Germany, but to Rome, which Uri knew, and where a friend had lent them an apartment. There, Uri rented a car and he and Shipi took a leisurely drive north, stopping off in St. Moritz, where they met two Australian girls with whom they spent some time. Enjoying the mountain scenery, the luxury and wealth all around them, they continued to Munich, where Yasha Katz was waiting for them, a friendly-looking man of nearly forty, Uri observed, with a crinkly face. Uri liked him immediately. Katz had an entire show tour already planned but, more important, he introduced

Uri to friendly tabloid newspaper coverage—to which he took an immediate liking.

In Israel, the popular newspapers were always a little prickly about him, although not necessarily in the good sense of being cautiously skeptical. As so many Israelis point out, there is a jealous streak in their national culture that manifests as a desire to be spiteful about anyone successful. Geller had fallen foul of this—and of the perils of the "instant expert" black-and-white school of journalism. This dictates that if an academic with halfway decent-looking qualifications is prepared off-the-cuff to be derogatory about someone, what he says counts instantly as the totality of expert opinion.

In Germany, almost from his first day, thanks to Katz's introduction, newspapers saw Uri as good news, and did not naïvely assume that because one scientist had dismissed him as a magician, all would do the same. In Uri Geller, the Munich newspaper *Bild Zeitung*, the first in Germany to go big on him, found a fascinating story of the paranormal personified in a character of a tabloid editor's dreams: young, handsome, heterosexual, earnest, articulate and even from a favored country—Israel was all the more favored after the terrorist massacre of Israeli athletes at the Munich Olympics, which coincidentally occurred while Geller was living in the city.

Bild Zeitung went ahead with a six-part Uri Geller series, and even found some informal scientific backup for him from a serious physicist. At one point one of the paper's journalists asked if Uri could do some really big stunt, such as stopping a cable car in midair. "My powers were in tip-top shape," Uri said. "And I wanted to prove myself. I wanted to show the Germans the power of the mind and I did things for them that I doubt I can do today, but they just happened, one after the other." After several tries, Uri succeeded in doing just what the journalist had suggested. The car controller told the reporters on board that the main power switch had simply flicked off. It was a most unusual incident, he said. The story made headlines all over Germany; Uri repeated the feat with the escalator in a department store. More headlines. He bent the mayor's wedding ring in the middle of Munich, and a set of handcuffs at a police station—after he had been strip-searched for any illicit conjuring aids. Then *Bild Zeitung* took him along for an informal meeting in a hotel with a thirty-two-year-old physicist who worked at the Max Planck Institute for Plasma Physics at Garching, just outside Munich.

Although he was infinitely more mainstream than Andrija Puharich, Dr. Friedbert Karger was still not quite an everyday physicist. A specialist in thermonuclear fusion research—the study of high temperatures—he has also studied psychology and philosophy, and has spent most of his professional life examining paraphysics, and especially poltergeist and other psychokinetic phenomena, alongside his conventional work at the Institute. Five years before Uri arrived in Munich, Karger was one of two physicists from the Max Planck Institute allowed to use the Institute's apparatus to assist in the investigation of what remains the most validated poltergeist case in parapsychological history. (Anxious not to lose government research grants, the then director of the Institute, a believer in some aspects of the paranormal, permitted the equipment to be used as long as it was clear that the two young scientists were doing the poltergeist research on their own behalf rather than that of the prestigious laboratory.) A nineteen-year-old secretary in a law firm in Rosenheim, a small town in southern Germany, was causing unparalleled havoc without seeming to do anything deliberately: disrupting electrical supply and telephone lines, sending hanging lights swinging as she walked down a corridor and so on. Fakery was never proven, despite intensive sleuthing by scientists, journalists and police, and the effects moved with the young woman when she changed jobs until they finally faded out.

Friedbert Karger's whole perspective on physics changed. "These experiments were really a challenge to physics," he says today. "What we saw in the Rosenheim case could be a hundred percent shown not to be explainable by known physics." Because he had been brave enough to say so, it was natural that *Bild Zeitung* looked to Karger to do a preliminary assessment of Uri Geller. He came prepared with a ring, which he handled cautiously, never taking his eyes off it or letting it leave his hand. Uri touched it gently in Karger's palm and concentrated on it. The ring rapidly bent out of shape and cracked in two places. Manfred Lipa, Karger's colleague from the Institute, examined the ring for tool marks and found none. Karger also brought a diving watch, which Uri altered without any detectable trickery. The journalists asked Karger if the damage to the ring could have been caused by strong pressure. He said it could not. By a laser? No, Karger replied. The only possibility was that Geller had tried some form of hypnosis, but he considered that unlikely. Karger summed up: "The powers of this man are a phenomenon that in theoretical physics cannot be explained. It is like atomic science. At the turn of the century, it was already known as a reality. It was just that, at that time, one could not yet explain it in terms of physics."

A quarter of a century on, had Friedbert Karger altered his view? He had, after all, become skeptical about some of the indiscriminate enthusiasm surrounding supposedly paranormal phenomena. "I came over to England to go on a David Frost show on firewalking." He laughed. "I demonstrated that it has nothing to do with paranormal abilities, and that anybody can do it. One can explain it with physics. But, of course, after I had done firewalking myself on the show, people said, 'Oh, you must also have paranormal abilities.' It was very funny. But Uri Geller? No, the pre-experiments I did showed me that there were really some abilities in his case. Now, I didn't do anything in laboratory. And I think what he does on TV may be something else—it's a pity he uses his abilities in shows and that kind of thing—but what I saw him do, especially with the diving watch, which is extremely difficult to change the time on, was very impressive. He moved the hands by one hour, and we could observe both him and the watch at all times, so it was not possible for him to do any tricks. Naturally, many of my colleagues said the usual thing, that he was doing good tricks and nothing else, but they had not done experiments with him, and I had.

"I think he has both psychokinetic and telepathic abilities," Dr. Karger maintains. Asked what the physical mechanism might be that explains how Uri's effects work, he prefers not to speculate but hints at the way in which his thinking has been going, which is that the Uri Geller effect, poltergeist effects, and even stranger paranormal anomalies might all be one and the same. "It seems that we have really to change our way of looking at these phenomena," Karger says, "because I have found that they are connected with such strange things as life after death. It's unavoidable that you come into contact with these things when you investigate such cases. Things like psychokinesis don't exist in isolation—and you are totally helpless when you use only known physics. Many very well-known physicists have done this work, you know. Einstein investigated spiritualistic mediums, and Pauli and other Nobel Prize winners did similar experiments. If you are ignorant of these phenomena, it's easy to dismiss them, but if you have seen the phenomena you have to ask the questions I have."

Uri Geller as a poltergeist phenomenon? It is certainly a new and interesting idea, which could explain many of the bizarre things that seem to have happened when Uri and Puharich were together in Israel. Poltergeists (German for "noisy spirit") have been known and spoken of in dozens of cultures, and are regarded as a major area for parapsychological research, the problem being that the majority of cases examined are easily discovered to be dubious. Most poltergeists are centered, as was the one in the Rosenheim case, on adolescents or young adults, the very people who, spurred on by horror films and TV documentaries, are the most likely to fake poltergeist phenomena as an attention-seeking strategy. The kind of children and adolescents in the better-documented poltergeist cases, however, tend to be genuinely unhappy as well as attention-seeking. As a child Uri, of course, was unhappy and lonely at times. He was also an admitted attention-seeker. What is most curious when pursuing this line of thought is the number of his friends who characterize his boundless enthusiasm and energy, his impatience, his incaution and often crazy, ill-advised ideas—along with his affectionate nature, generosity and many other good qualities—as distinctly adolescent. Now if Uri, as an unhappy child, attracted the attentions of a particularly strong poltergeist (rather than those of the crew of the spaceship Spectra), is it possible, then, that he is still haunted by such a presence? He often speculates, when pursuing, as he still does, his controlled-by-extraterrestrials theory, that he might be under the power of some maverick UFO crew, who are, basically, having a laugh at his, and humankind's, expense. This, he feels, explains the trivial—or "clownish," as he calls it—nature of so many of the effects that "happen around him." But how much better, perhaps, would be a poltergeist explanation: that it is a poltergeist, not an alien, which has the sense of humor, and continues to exercise it through Uri Geller, the world's oldest teenager?

Oddly enough, as a showbusiness tour in the summer of 1972, rather than as a publicity bonanza, his German interlude was not very successful. In Munich, he appeared at the Hilton Hotel and was the hottest ticket in town, but elsewhere the tour met with a mixed reception. In Hamburg, he found himself booked for ten days into a magicians' spectacular, which he was most unhappy about, although he was gratified, he said, to find his fellow performers fascinated by how he did his "tricks" without any special equipment or sleight of hand. That was the first sign he had had that some magicians might come to accept him as *not* being one of their own.

The real difficulty in Germany for Uri was that Yasha Katz had overextended himself with promises. "He was a good man, but he did want to earn a *lot* of money through my talents. He and another guy both had these tremendous dreams and visions of becoming multimillionaires from Uri Geller, and they planned the big shows and auditoriums and record deals. Yasha promised me a lovely little sports car, an Opel GT, when I arrived, but it never happened, so from the financial point of view, it was all a little disappointing."

Yet those few months in Germany were successful from the social point of view. The parties back home at which the elite of Israel had gathered and clamored around him had represented an extraordinary social boost for a young man, but Israel is a small, villagy place with only a fuzzy, indistinct class system. In Germany, Uri began his assault on the Matterhorn of social climb-ing: the world of jet-setting European socialites. In Munich, he found himself invited to every reception and cocktail party worth being seen at. Which was how he came to enjoy a passionate affair with Brigitte Bardot's sister-in-law, Eleanor "Lo" Sachs. Lo Sachs was married to Ernst, whose brother Gunter was married to Bardot. Gunter and Ernst were the only shareholders in a huge motor-accessories business, and were among the richest men in Europe. While Gunter amused himself as an international playboy, Ernst was a quieter, duller workaholic of thirty-nine who was usually away on business. It is not hard, then, to see how a flamboyant young Israeli psychic superstar of twenty-five would have provided an interesting summer distraction for the older Frau Sachs. They lived in a huge, antique-laden mansion in Grunwald, close to Franz Beckenbauer, the German football star. Uri and Shipi were invited there frequently before his affair with his gracious hostess began.

"I guess in Yaffa I had seen the mature woman. She was older and wiser, she really wanted me as me and not for anything else," Uri said. "Maybe this is why I was attracted to Lo too, except she was German and very beautiful and very, very rich. I was looking for security and a mature love affair. Lo must have been close to forty. It was an astounding thing for me, because in Israel, although I was making good money and I managed to buy my mother a penthouse, but a tiny one, suddenly I was brought into this palatial house in the outskirts of Mu-nich with its indoor swimming pool, outdoor swimming pool, suites, silver and gold everywhere. She introduced me to all the Guccis and Schmuccis and Fendis. I had no idea about such things. I was totally drunk in these surround-ings and I liked it. It was almost power. She was mingling with royalty and politi-cians and singers and actors, and there were football players going through the house, and parties with caviar and champagne.

"You must understand that Iris and Hanna and Yaffa were all beautiful young girls, but we were all very simple. We didn't know more than what was around us in Israel. At those times, the late sixties and the early seventies, it was even a big deal to have a black-and-white television, never mind dish-washers and washing machines. Those were unheard of. And then suddenly you are catapulted into surroundings where those things are totally normal and standard. It was ridiculous. I also loved the openness and the cleanness and the meticulous Germanic ways, everything working, the streets clean, the post office working. I liked the clinical cleanness. All that appealed to me.

"Lo was still married to Ernst, but he had an Italian girlfriend and didn't seem to be living in the house. He even gave me his cufflinks as a gift, twenty-two carat gold, studded with diamonds. And, yes, the gigolo in me woke up. When I was still struggling, I sometimes had this notion that I would marry someone rich, and if that didn't work out, I would just become a gigolo. Lo and I used to go to restaurants, and she would order caviar and she would buy me shoes and clothes. One day, we walked into a shoe store and she bought me these beautiful long boots. Then as we were sitting in the restaurant she tucked five or six hundred marks into my boots under the table so that I could pay the bill, so it didn't look like she was paying it. I was living a fantasy. There was a total detachment from my past. I disconnected myself from Iris, who loved me madly, and from Hanna and from everyone in Israel. For a while, I didn't want to hear about Israel any more."

The summer idyll could not last long. Andrija Puharich was urging Uri to get on a flight to the States and start seeing a line-up of interested scientists he had contacted. And then, while he was hanging out at the Sachs home one afternoon, something reminded him sharply of his roots, and made him realize that he needed to be getting on with the more serious side of his life. "Lo had a Ping-Pong table," he related, "and I was in the attic either looking for the balls or the rackets to play Ping-Pong and there I stumbled on these pictures of Gunter and Ernst's father—and Hitler. It was unbelievable. There were all kinds of Nazi swastika signs and documents and books that blew me away. You can imagine a twenty-five-year-old Israeli standing in an attic in Munich with all this Nazi paraphernalia around me, and I am sleeping with this woman and I am taking her money. I think it shook me back into reality and out of the fantasy I was living. I didn't raise it with Lo, though. She was good to me and I couldn't blame her or Gunther or Ernst for their father being a friend of Hitler. But it was enough for me."

Chapter 11

I Wanna Be in America

"We have observed certain phenomena for which we have no scientific explanation."

Preliminary statement from the Stanford Research Institute regarding its work with Uri Geller

....

The composition of the strange Team Geller that headed for the USA from Germany in October 1972 to begin the eleven-year middle phase of Uri's career explains why the Geller phenomenon was seen and sneered at by many as a circus. It consisted of Uri, the eighteen-year-old Shipi, who had been exempted from Army service on medical grounds, Andrija Puharich, who had flown over from the States to accompany the party, Yasha Katz, whom Uri still wanted around—even though he had not quite delivered what he promised in the way of bookings or sports cars in Germany—and Werner Schmidt, an impresario, who had produced the German versions of *Fiddler on the Roof* and *Hair*. After meeting Uri in Hamburg, he wanted to make him the singing star of a psychic musical, which included a demonstration of Uri's powers. Schmidt came to try to make his musical happen, while Katz was to organize a lecture tour to make enough money to keep the team together as Uri submitted to the exhaustive round of scientific investigations Puharich had arranged.

The team grew bigger in the States, with such glitzy additions as the beautiful Japanese-American Melanie Toyofuku, who was working in film production in Rome but had previously been an assistant to Puharich. Uri and she soon became lovers. Another female team member was Solveig Clark, a Nor-wegian-American executive with Revlon who had a consuming interest in the paranormal and was in love with Puharich. Also attached to the group, if not on the road with it, were Dr. Edgar Mitchell, and a New York society couple, Byron and Maria Janis. He was an international piano virtuoso who had been trained by the great Vladimir Horowitz, she, the daughter of the film star Gary Cooper.

While Dr. Mitchell had had some of his formative thoughts on the para-normal while walking on the moon, Byron and Maria's interest stemmed partly from an extraordinary coincidence, one they are convinced is more than pure chance. In his twenties, Byron had become one of the world's lead-ing exponents of Chopin. When his career was well established, he discovered in France two unknown Chopin waltzes, written in the composer's own hand. Six years later, he found different handwritten versions of the same waltzes in a library at Yale University. What makes the Janis/Chopin connection truly strange, however, is that Byron Janis happens to be the precise double of Frédéric Chopin.

In the USA, then, Uri was collecting around him, just as he had in Israel, an entourage of high-profile, interesting friends, some with a tendency—al-though he has never encouraged this—to regard him perhaps, as a guru. All became fascinated by him after seeing him carry out the procedures he had been doing since childhood. They believed what they saw, and felt that Uri's powers were evidence for there being "greater things in Heaven and Earth than are dreamt of in our philosophy."

In America, Uri received scientific approbation at an awesome level—both before and during his crucial tests at the Stanford Research Institute (SRI) the scientists, albeit handpicked to an extent by Puharich, rolled over for him.

In December 1972 Edgar Mitchell announced: "Uri is not a magician. He is using capabilities that we all have and can develop with exercise and practice." After a brief spell of testing, during which Uri moved a watch ahead, broke a ring and concentrated on a needle until it broke with an audible crack, Dr. Wilbur Franklin, of the physics department at Kent State University, said: "As a result of Geller's success in this experimental period, we consider that he has demonstrated his paranormal, perceptual ability in a convincing and unam-biguous manner. The evidence based on metallurgical analysis of fractured surfaces [produced by Geller] indicates that a paranormal influence must have been operative in the formation of the fractures."

At Mitchell's suggestion, the Geller entourage went to see Dr. Wernher von

Braun, the renowned NASA rocket scientist, at his office at Fairchild Industries, where he was vice-president. Uri asked von Braun to take off his gold wedding band and hold it flat in his own hand while Uri held his hand over it and concentrated. To his delight—as he was keen to impress von Braun—the ring obediently warped into an oval shape. He also restarted von Braun's faulty electronic calculator. Von Braun said: "Geller has bent my ring in the palm of my hand without ever touching it. Personally, I have no scientific explanation for the phenomenon."

Other scientists, too, were enthusiastic after their first meetings with Uri. William E. Cox, of the Institute of Parapsychology at Durham, North Carolina, reported: "I have failed to conceive of any means of deception in the static PK tests with Geller, nor have magicians I have consulted." Dr. A.R.G. Owen, of the New Horizons Research Foundation in Toronto, concluded: "Metal objects were bent or divided [by Geller] in circumstances such as to prove conclusively . . . that the phenomena were genuine and paranormal." Dr. Thomas Coohill, a physicist at Western Kentucky University, said: "There is no logical explanation for what Geller did here. But I don't think logic is what necessarily makes new inroads in science." William A. Tiller, Professor Emeritus in the Department of Materials Science and Engineering at Stanford University, concluded in a letter to Uri: "I have always felt that you are able to perform the phenomena ascribed to you, at least under favorable conditions." Dr. Elizabeth Rauscher, a theoretical physicist at the Lawrence Berkeley Laboratory, at the University of California, Berkeley, pronounced Geller, "one of the most powerful men alive today." (A note of caution here, maybe: Rauscher lived for many years with Andrija Puharich; she is, however, a highly respected scientist.) Jule Eisenbud, MD, associate clinical professor of psychiatry at the University of Colorado Health Sciences Center, described a Geller key-bending episode. "The Yale key at no time left our sight from the moment it was removed from the key ring and placed on the typewriter frame to the time when the splined end had bent upwards. Our attention was not distracted and the key was not altered in position, accidentally or otherwise. We were all looking carefully for magician's tricks and there were none. Everything occurred exactly as I have described. As a result of this personally witnessed experiment in clear, unequivocal conditions, I am able to state with confidence my view that Mr. Geller has genuine psychic capability."

Uri's progress through the US was not restricted to academic departments of science: he was also making himself known to the "alternative" community. At what would today be called a New Age center in Silver Spring, Maryland, however, he was presented with an unusual request. A scientist called Eldon Byrd lived nearby, had read in the local newspaper that Uri Geller was coming to town, and wondered if he could spare him fifteen minutes.

Byrd was a lieutenant commander in the US Naval Reserve, who had left the full-time military to work as a civilian strategic-weapons-systems expert at the nearby Naval Surface Weapons Center. He had top-secret security clearance, and contacts high in the CIA and its Defense Department equivalent, the DIA, the Defense Intelligence Agency. Byrd was becoming increasingly interested in non-lethal weaponry, especially biological warfare; he saw it as more humane to infect an enemy with *reversible* illness than "to punch holes in their body and have their blood leak out." In 1970, to further his knowledge, he took a graduate degree in medical engineering at George Washington University, in Washington, DC. Later, he became involved in still more rarefied areas of defense: the use of electromagnetics as a weapon to confuse people, again as a reversible process, and experiments on thought transference.

In the early 1970s, various sections of the American military were studying different areas of "alternative warfare." According to Byrd: "The Army even started spending money to see if you could instrument plants on the jungle trail as intrusion detection devices, and they determined that, eighty percent of the time, plants could detect the presence of a human being who was bent on harm versus one that was friendly. That started me on the realm of the weird. Uri Geller was an anomalous phenomenon, and I particularly wanted to see if he could interact with a new metal, which had been discovered here at the laboratory."

The new metal, called nitinol, an alloy of nickel and titanium, had a unique property: it possessed a mechanical memory so that whatever twisting and distortion it was subjected to it sprang back to the shape at which it had been forged. It is now used, for example, in orthodontic braces and unbreakable spectacle frames, but was then known only to metallurgists. "I thought this was neat," Byrd recalled, "because, here was something which was not generally available, so the probability of Geller ever having even heard of it was very slim. If he could do something to it, it would be an indication that he had the ability to do something very strange."

With Shipi, Puharich and several other members of the entourage in attendance, Byrd handed Uri a length of nitinol wire he had taken from the lab. Uri asked if, first, he could play some games. Byrd said, "He wrote something on a piece of paper, handed it to me and said, 'Put this in your hand and don't look at it now. I'm going to think of a letter, and I want to see if you can pick it up.' He closed his eyes, but nothing was happening in my head. So I thought, maybe I have to close my eyes for this to work. I closed them, and bam, there's a big green R lit up in my head. So I said, 'I guess it's an R,' and he said, 'Yes, open the paper,' and it was an R."

Byrd asked Uri if he could do it the other way round. "I had been an amateur magician, so I knew a few tricks. He said, 'Make it something in this room,' but I knew that trick, so I thought, No, I'm not going to make it anything at all. I kept my paper and my pencil down below the lip of the desk, so he couldn't see the tip of the pencil running around, because if you're really good you can tell by the way the pencil moves what the picture is going to be. I just randomly started drawing something, an ellipse with a circle in it and then a dot in the circle. He quickly sketched something on the back of an envelope and said, 'What is this? A button?' He had drawn exactly what I had, but put four dots in the center, because he was thinking of a button. Then we compared them, and they were exactly the same size."

Then Uri stroked the nitinol wire, Byrd says, until an odd little lump formed in it, which failed to disappear. Byrd left, promising to let Uri know what his colleagues at the lab made of the wire. That night, he and his then wife, Kathleen, were up until late, transmitting increasingly complex pictures to one another flawlessly. "I thought, man, somehow Uri tuned me up and I can even transfer the ability to my wife. But the next day, we tried again, and it wouldn't work."

At the laboratory Byrd's colleagues examined with an electron microscope the nitinol wire Uri had handled: they said it seemed to have been stretched at that one point, but that this could easily have been due to a flaw in the metal. Byrd went to see Uri again, this time with wires he had scored with a razorblade in binary-coded decimal numbers. "One of the criticisms that magicians had was the switch. They'd say, 'How do you know he doesn't already have a supply of nitinol wire, and he has already bent these things?' I now had a mechanism for knowing that these were my wires."

Uri bent them successfully so that they did not spring back into shape. "I took them back and asked the lab to do a total analysis. They came back and said that the only way these wires could have changed their configuration is to have heated them to 400 degrees, left them at the same temperature and then reannealed them in some kind of oil. Uri had had some very profound effect at the molecular level in the memory of this shape-memory alloy." Further crystallographic examination of the wires showed that the crystals which contained the metal's memory had increased in size—which would have required

Uri to have raised the temperature of the metal to 900 degrees C. "He also altered the lattice structure of a metal alloy in a way that cannot be duplicated. There is no present scientific explanation as to how he did this," Byrd concluded.

Byrd wrote a paper on the trials, which was reviewed by his bosses and cleared for publication—the first time parapsychological research at a government facility had ever been so accepted. "Boy, did that story get the skeptics going." Byrd laughs. "They tried everything they could think of because that was the most threatening piece of evidence to them." (So frustrated, it seems, were skeptics by what they believed was flawed research that several years later, the magician James Randi, when he had become a respected leader of skeptical opinion, said in an unguarded comment that Byrd was now in jail for child molesting. He was repeating gossip he had heard on the highly unreliable skeptics' grapevine. Byrd, who was neither a child molester nor in jail, sued Randi for libel, which almost destroyed Randi financially and considerably damaged the skeptics' movement.)

As Byrd got to know Uri better, his conviction grew that the powers were genuine. "The magicians say that if they can replicate what Uri does with the spoons, then that proves that it's a trick. But a couple of years later, I saw another thing that blew my mind and proved beyond all doubt to me that he could bend spoons with some unknown kind of energy. It was in a restaurant in London, in front of a group of us. One of the waiters recognized him and asked if he would bend something. Uri said, 'Go to the kitchens and bring back a knife.' The waiter held it with one hand and Uri put one finger on top of the blade. Everybody was crowding round waiting, and he stroked it a few times. And over a three-second period, we watched the knife blade curl up all by itself. No magician can do that. I have also seen Uri touch a seed and in a second or two, it sprouted an inch. The first time he did this, and it sprouted just a little bit, was on Japanese television. They had the camera on his hand, and it started to sprout right in front of your very eyeballs. More recently, he touched a seed and it sprouted over an inch with leaves on it in a second or two. It was incredible."

Uri's apparent ability to make a seed sprout came to light when Edgar Mitchell suggested on a hunch that he try. I have seen him do it: he takes a scattering of radish seeds from what I assume—wrongly, perhaps—to be a standard, sealed pack. He holds them in the palm of one hand, stroking them gently with one finger. After thirty seconds or so, I saw one of the seeds pop with a visible shudder, as its epidermis appeared to burst, shoot emerged and grew within about half a second to approximately three millimeters complete with two tiny folded leaves.

Although the phenomenon was superficially as remarkable as spoon-bending, I was suspicious that perhaps radish seeds have a natural tendency to sprout suddenly in a warm spot. I called Simon Vyle, assistant head of the Chelsea Physic Garden in London, who confirmed that radishes indeed germinate quickly—sometimes in as little as twenty-four hours. However, he said, "No seed will sprout as quickly as a few seconds, whatever it is." After meeting James Randi in Florida, I e-mailed him to ask how he believed it was done: "An already sprouted seed will hide easily between the fingers, and Geller always uses radish seeds, which sprout within a few hours," Randi replied. "Easy to prepare by simply dampening a tissue in a plastic bag, adding seeds, and carrying the packet about with you until needed." It would be interesting to know how Randi would explain a hibiscus bush Uri's gardener showed me. After being touched by Uri, one sprig has always produced purple flowers, while the rest of the bush is covered in white blooms. Simon Vyle confirms that, short of complex grafting, no natural phenomenon he knows could produce such a freak. "I'm a skeptic, me," the gardener, Joe Thompson, whispered to me. "But the things I've seen here beggar belief."

At the end of 1972 Uri Geller finally got to the SRI. The rumor that he was to be tested in the electronics and bioengineering laboratory of such a prestigious establishment had spread throughout a bemused scientific world, as well as the conjuring fraternity, parts of which were becoming more furious by the day at the seriousness with which he was being taken. The view among magicians, as reflected in letters to their magazines, was that there was still time for the Israeli to confess his fraudulence and that, if he did, he could come to be regarded as a good old boy who had taken America for a brief ride; the status of conjuring could only increase if he came clean. If he persisted with his paranormal claims, though, magicians would be obliged to campaign ceaselessly against him, if only because he represented a grievous threat to their trade. Uri knew that how he performed at the SRI would be crucial to his future in the States, and that failure here would almost certainly wipe him out worldwide, as well as bury forever the fledgling academic study of *psi*—the blanket term for parapsychology and the paranormal. The pressure on him was immense: if he was a charlatan, he would have to contrive yet cleverer ways to cover his tracks in a fully fledged laboratory setting.

There was little encouragement for Uri from the mysterious voices on Puharich's tape-recorder. The machine warned Uri, he says, to meet scientists only socially. Already as scared of the laboratory as a patient might be of an operating theater, Uri decided at Puharich's house at Ossining, where the team was living, not to go ahead with the tests. A row ensued, in which he hurled a sugar bowl at his mentor. As he did so, a grandfather clock shifted across the hall and smashed, with Melanie and Shipi as witnesses. In the middle of the following night, Uri and Shipi, asleep in their rooms, woke to hear the tape recorder voice boom, "Andrija must write a book." The Ossining commune interpreted this to mean what it stated, and that the *Spectra* crew had finally approved the SRI program.

It was with this in mind that Uri, Shipi and Puharich flew two days later to San Francisco. They were met at the airport by Edgar Mitchell, Wilbur Franklin and the men who would be examining Uri over the next couple of weeks—and ultimately putting their reputations on the line to support him—Dr. Hal Puthoff and Russell Targ.

Hal Puthoff was a senior research engineer at SRI and a specialist in laser physics. He held patents in the field of lasers and optical instruments, and had co-written *Fundamentals of Quantum Electronics*, a textbook on the interrelation between quantum mechanics, engineering and applied physics. He had been a lieutenant in naval intelligence, handling the highest category of classified material, a civilian operative of the National Security Agency, and, in the early 1960s, he had been involved in the development of ultrafast computers for military use.

Russell Targ was a senior research physicist and an expert in plasma physics, like Friedbert Karger in Munich. Like Puthoff, Targ was an inventor, who had been a pioneer in the development of lasers. When he heard that Puthoff was doing high-level research into psychics he had sought him out for two reasons: first, he already had an interest in psychic research; second, which would serve him well, he was a keen amateur magician. He had grown up in New York, where he was a regular in the magic shops on 42nd Street, and prided himself on knowing the field of professional magic well.

Since 1946, SRI had been part of nearby Stanford University but in 1970 it had become an independent think-tank, laboratory and problem-solving organization. Its 2,800 staff members worked in a hundred different disciplines on the seventy-acre site in Menlo Park and at other locations around the US and overseas. The Institute worked on contract for both private industry and government, including secret defense work, although the identity of the client who had instigated the investigation into Uri Geller (as well as other psychics who were examined as part of the same program) has until recently remained a closely held secret. Back in the early 1970s, the official line was that the work was sponsored by an Edgar Mitchell foundation and a New York paranormal-investigation group.

Uri's testing at SRI fell into two parts: the first took place in late 1972, the remainder in March 1974. Clearly, Puthoff and Targ had taken advice on the conditions that helped psychics to perform. "They tried to make the environment very at home," Uri said. "They had a living room setting with paintings on the wall and all those homely kind of features so that I would feel good. They had all the equipment in another room. Everything was wired. It was really very professionally set up, to have it under totally controlled conditions."

The main thrust of the work took place over five weeks up to Christmas 1972. The investigation's findings were released in a multilayered fashion. Before the work was even finished, a statement was issued early in 1973 that, "We have observed certain phenomena for which we have no scientific explanation," which alerted the press. This publicity taster from SRI was a two-edged sword as far as Uri was concerned, for it started *Time* magazine on what would be a devastating story, debunking both him and the SRI work.

Late in 1974, the cream of the SRI work was published in the British science journal *Nature*. A more wide-ranging analysis was contained in a film made by the Institute, *Experiments with Uri Geller*, which, Puthoff and Targ explained on its release, had been made to "share with the viewer observations of phenomena that in our estimation clearly deserve further study." Further observations, meanwhile, which Puthoff and Targ deemed too anecdotal for the film—or were noted informally without the cameras running—are still emerging twenty-five years on, as the two physicists reveal them.

The findings sent to *Nature* were relatively modest, and concerned telepathy only. All the same, the journal's editors warned in their preamble to the article that it was "bound to create a stir in the scientific community," and added, candidly, that the paper would be "greeted with a preconditioned reaction amongst many scientists. To some, it simply confirms what they have always known or believed. To others, it is beyond the laws of science, and therefore necessarily unacceptable."

The first conclusion of Puthoff and Targ was that Uri had succeeded partially in reproducing randomly chosen drawings made by people unknown to him, while he was in a double-walled steel room, which was acoustically, visually and electrically shielded. The chance of him doing as well as he did by coincidence was calculated at one million to one, but he had done only as well as chance in trying to establish the contents of sealed envelopes. In another test, though, in which he was asked to "guess" the face of a die shaken in a double-sealed steel box—so that the investigator could not possibly know the position of the die either—he answered correctly eight times out of ten. What was especially interesting was that on the two occasions when he did not give the answer, he had not attempted one, saying that his perception was not clear. The die test, again, represented a million-to-one chance. In an informal run of the same experiment, Uri correctly predicted ten out of ten die positions—a one in a billion chance.

The rest of the *Nature* report concerned another psychic called Pat Price, a former California police commissioner. Price was a "remote-viewer," and in perceiving and describing in detail randomly chosen outdoor scenes from many miles away, he beat odds of a billion to one. A third test was performed on six unnamed psychics to see if their brainwaves could be measured in responding to a flashing light in a distant room: only one showed a measurable reaction in his brain.

Targ and Puthoff's conclusions were buttressed by several caveats: they explained the security precautions they had taken, and made it clear that their aim was no more ambitious than to establish whether paranormal phenomena could be scientifically tested; they had no mission to "prove" the paranormal. They also speculated that "remote perceptual ability" might be available to many of us, but that the perception is so far below what most of us are aware of that it is either not noticed or it is repressed. They made the point that, although they had seen Uri bend metal in the laboratory, they had been unable to do a full controlled experiment to support a paranormal hypothesis of metal-bending.

The SRI film went much further than the report. Uri was first shown sending numbers to Puthoff, Targ and Franklin, along with Don Scheuch, vice-president of research at SRI. Then he is shown playing what the experimenters call "ten-can Russian roulette," in which he successfully finds a steel ball in one of ten cans without touching them. He graduates from doing this by holding his hands over the cans, to detecting which contains the ball as he walks into a room and sees the cans lined up on a blackboard sill. He also succeeds at the same test when one of the cans contains room-temperature water. When faced with a line-up of cans, one of which contains a sugar cube, or a paper-wrapped ball-bearing, he says he cannot be sure. We are told in the film that whereas "officially" SRI could only report him as having achieved a one in a million chance, in reality, and taking all the tests into account, he had defeated odds of a trillion (ten to the twelfth power) to one against correctly guessing the cans' contents.

In psychokinesis (PK), which the experimenters did not explore in the *Na-*

ture article, the film showed Uri decreasing and increasing the weight of a one-gram piece of metal on an electronic scale covered by a bell jar; all Puthoff and Targ's precautions to preclude fraud by such methods as tapping the bell jar or even jumping on the floor are shown. In another PK test, Uri successfully deflects a magnetometer to full scale, having first been checked for concealed magnets with the same instrument. In another test, he is seen deflecting a compass needle, although the experimenters make the point that they are not satisfied by this test—not because they have evidence of Uri cheating, but because they discover that a small, concealed piece of metal in some circumstances, can produce the same effect.

On the question of spoon-bending, the film steers on the side of caution; although, as Puthoff and Targ show, Uri succeeded in bending several spoons in the laboratory, he never did so on film or without touching the spoon, and the question of whether it bent because he has exceptionally strong fingers and good control of micro-manipulatory movements, or whether the spoon "turns to plastic" as he claims, was not resolved. The same problem applied to the filming of him bending rings. For the experiments, SRI had manufactured rings that required 150-pounds force to distort them; they certainly ended up bent, but the laboratory had no film or experimental findings to confirm how they became so, and they were in Uri's hand when the distortion occurred. Of course, the mystery of why the spontaneous version of Uri's metal-bending, in which he does not handle the spoon, is never captured on film is *the* consummate weakness in the Geller phenomenon.

It was not, however, because the SRI team failed to capture spoons in the act of bending that the reaction to their work was so violent. As *Nature* had hinted, the skeptical counterattack was fierce. Indeed, even the coolest reading of events in late 1974 would have to be that the response to the article was beyond what might have been prompted by an ordinary piece of disputed scientific research. To be fair, the magazine, in the preamble, accepted that the Puthoff/Targ paper had its shortcomings. A skeptical professor of psychology, Ray Hyman of the University of Oregon, had, unlike other critics, visited SRI and pronounced that, from his observations, Geller was doing what any magician could, and was clever enough to fool the scientists. (Hyman was a watchful amateur magician like Targ, but he observed that Uri's eyes were blue, when they are in fact brown.) At its extremes, the criticism of SRI had a shrillness reminiscent of religious fundamentalists with their core beliefs under attack. Skeptics found fault with the experimental protocols, the conclusions, anything on which they had data, plus plenty on which they did not.

A massive wrangle—still being fought on the Internet—concerned a tiny hole in the wall of the sealed "cage" that had been built to shield Uri from electronic or any other outside signals, which might help his psychic senses. The hole, a few centimeters from the floor, was there for wiring to pass through, but Uri was said by his critics to have received all his information through it in code, or by whispering (nobody actually explained how this could have been done), courtesy of Shipi who, at eighteen and in a foreign country whose language he barely spoke, was credited with almost superhuman power in his ability to out-fox a lab full of Ph.D.s, conjuring buffs and experienced assistants.

Another theory put forward, and still held by many to an extent which would rival any *X-Files*–obsessed paranormal-conspiracy enthusiast suggested that, as Puharich was a miniature electronics expert, he must have fitted one of Uri's hollowed-out teeth with a radio. In the 1960s Puharich had filed three patents for tooth radios, which stemmed from his interest in hearing aids. The tooth radio theory, however, presupposed much more chicanery by the Geller team. Hidden radio or not, they still *somehow* had to find out what the secretly made drawing was, or which die-face was upward in a sealed box, then *somehow* transmit this information to Uri, even if he was in a radio-dead Faraday cage. Even James Randi conclusively squashed the tooth radio idea in an open letter to the British Magic Circle magazine, *Abracadabra* although he vowed in the same letter to "stop Geller *at all costs*." But neither Randi's letter, nor an examination of Uri's teeth for radio equipment by a New York dentist has destroyed the myth and *New Scientist* once even published alleged drawings of Geller's tooth radio!

If one thing became clear as a result of the SRI experience, it was that some anti-Geller skeptics spoil their case for others, and even make Uri look better than he necessarily deserves, by being outstandingly gullible: they seem to believe anything another skeptic tells them. The similarity in this respect between dogmatic paranormalists and dogmatic skeptics is a mirror of the personality similarities in politics between those of the far left and the far right and just as former left-wingers make the most fervent Fascists, devout skeptics have been known to become equally committed believers on the strength of a single experience of Uri Geller or someone like him. While I was writing this book, Uri was invited to dinner at the home of a mutual friend. Another guest was a famous British engineering industrialist who, when he heard that Uri would be there, scoffed and said he was a "a total fraud." Yet having seen him bend a spoon at the dinner table, he asked him if he could repeat the exercise in private, in the kitchen. A couple of minutes later, according to my friend, the industrialist emerged and said, "I've seen all I need. It's real." He has been a fervent (albeit anonymous, at his request) believer ever since. An interesting case of the reverse process is provided by Dr. Susan Blackmore, senior lecturer in psychology at the University of the West of England, Bristol. When she started out as a parapsychologist in 1973, she was a hippie, convinced of psychic powers, tarot-card reading, witchcraft, crystal balls and out-of-body experiences. Today, however, she is convinced that there is less to the power of the human mind than she thought. She is now a dogged—some might say dogmatic—skeptic, who has less belief in such areas as spiritual healing than thousands of doctors, and she opposes many forms of alternative medicine available on the National Health Service.

The skeptics also argued that the SRI film cameraman, an ex–*Life* magazine war photographer, Zev Pressman, had not really taken any of the forty hours of footage edited down into the film, and that he had been forced to say he had shot it; in fact, a group of conspirators in league with Uri had contrived it. If the story is true, then someone must have had a great deal of leverage over Mr. Pressman for, even in his mid-eighties and frail, he insisted to me, at his home at Palo Alto, a few miles from SRI, that it was his film and his alone, and he has a clear recall of several other feats Uri achieved. Pressman was so keen to talk about his Uri Geller experiences that he even rounded up his neighbor, the then head of information at SRI, Ron Deutsch, now also retired, for our morning-coffee meeting.

Pressman and Geller spent a lot of time together during the trials, talking for hours in Pressman's workshop. Pressman had wanted to bring something obscure to work to test Uri's telepathic powers, of which he was deeply skeptical. Hunting around in his garage, he came upon a strangely shaped roller-skate key, of a type, he reckoned, had disappeared around the 1930s. He had it in his pocket for their first meeting, and asked Uri to describe it. Uri immediately executed a near-perfect drawing of it. After that, Pressman says, he saw spoons bend "dozens of times," and both witnessed and videotaped an SRI stopwatch apparently materializing in midair from Hal Puthoff's briefcase, before dematerializing, then materializing again, and dropping down gently onto a table. Unlike the forty hours of raw footage, which to this day Pressman has no idea of the whereabouts of (it is thought by Targ and Puthoff to be under lock and key somewhere in a US government vault), copies of the videotape still exist. But they are, of course, said to be fakes, which Pressman was made to say were genuine, and even SRI was clearly too unsure about the segment being a Geller-inspired hoax to include it in their completed film.

Reflecting in old age on his time with Uri Geller, Zev Pressman veers inter-estingly toward the "mixed mediumship" hypothesis—the theory that a lot of genuine psychics muddy the waters for themselves by also being skilled in magic. Pressman believes, he said, that Geller's repertoire is a mixture of con-juring tricks and the paranormal: "He's very slick, he's fast, and he knows when and how to move. But it wasn't a question of belief in him. It was talent. The guy was good. No, he wasn't good, he was perfect, and I don't mean as a magician. I couldn't explain what he did. He couldn't explain it. He just said, 'I don't know how this happens.'" Another peripheral player in the Geller story at this time, Bob Williamson, the manager of the hotel where Uri was staying, took a similar view. As skeptical as anyone when he met him, and aware of the accusations of fraud, which were mushrooming in the media, he saw Uri bend a spoon and a key, and slowly became convinced: "I felt I hadn't been hearing the truth. To me it was simple. If one man could bend one key one time without using physical force, then that was a major event on Earth."

Press reaction to the SRI tests and the *Nature* article was largely favorable. The *New York Times*, not known for jumping to rash judgments, opened an editorial in November 1974: "The scientific community has been put on no-tice 'that there is something worthy of their attention and scrutiny' in the pos-sibilities of extra-sensory perception." The leader writer pointed out that Geller's reputation "is deeply clouded by suspicion of fakery," but picked up Puthoff and Targ's point that most people perhaps had ESP but were not aware of it. "Scientific orthodoxy has grown increasingly remote from the in-terests and beliefs of a generation of Americans," the editorial went on to warn. Leaving aside "junky pop-occult literature," college bookstores were full of texts by serious mystical thinkers, such as Gurdjieff and Ouspensky, so, the *Times* believed, "The epithet 'non-scientific' is no longer a sure ticket to obliv-ion." The newspaper's conclusions were that "The essence of science should be receptivity to new ideas," and that the editors of *Nature* had taken an im-portant step to stimulate scientific discourse.

Over a year before the *Nature* article appeared, *Newsweek* magazine cau-tiously welcomed the SRI work, but that other rock of quality American jour-nalism, *Time*, was less impressed. Ron Deutsch at SRI had been warned by the magazine's science editor, Leon Jaroff, that, although *Time* was reporting the SRI/Geller work closely, it was not likely to be doing so favorably. "The people at *Time* were adamant that Uri was a shyster," Deutsch recalled. "Leon, in par-ticular, felt he was a phoney." Nevertheless, as *Time* had established contact over a long period with Deutsch and SRI, Uri accepted an invitation to the magazine's Sixth Avenue, New York, offices to give Jaroff and the other editors a demonstration.

He arrived with Puharich—not, perhaps, a good idea, since Uri already suspected that the meeting would be something of a lynch party. Jaroff had lined up James Randi to pose as a *Time* reporter, for his first close-up inspection of Geller, the man who would become his bête noire—not to mention his livelihood—until the present day. Uri did not seem to recognize Randi and, as might be expected, Randi saw precisely what he believed he would: that Uri's bending of a fork and a key were due to sleight-of-hand. His confirmation of this spurred Jaroff to write a damning story based, maybe, on what he, too, had expected to see. The story, which labelled Uri "a questionable night-club magician" had its debatable factual points, although in the context of an attempt to unmask an alleged trickster, its central ethic, the ambush by James Randi, was well within the Queensberry rules of journalism. Some of the article's other assertions might not have survived the rigorous fact-checking *Time* now insists on. It was said, for example, that Geller had "left Israel in disgrace," for which evidence is lacking; it was also stated that scientists in Israel had duplicated his feats, which is difficult to support.

As ever, there was a complicated and intriguing backdrop to the *Time* affair. According to one of the reporters who worked with him, Jaroff had a deep-seated private distaste for parapyschology, because he and others on the magazine associated it with the occult, and the occult with Fascism. Another *Time* writer said privately, it has been reported, that SRI's parapsychological research should "be destroyed." And Uri's case was not helped in the eyes of Jaroff and Co. by Hal Puthoff having been a member of the controversial Church of Scientology, albeit at a time when thousands of other West Coast professionals were. He had long since resigned from it and he had joined an anti-Scientology pressure group.

More amusingly, the publication of the edition containing the March 1973 story rubbishing Uri—"The Magician and the Think Tank"—had been fraught with Gelleresque incident as the *Time* publisher wrote in his letter to readers. Leon Jaroff's clock radio failed to go off on three mornings running, causing him to be late for work each time. "Even more bizarre," the publisher continued, "was the mysterious force which glitched *Time*'s complex, computerized copy-processing system on copy night—at almost the precise moment that our psychic phenomena story was fed into it. Against astronomical odds, both of the machines that print out *Time*'s copy stopped working simultaneously. No sooner were the spirits exorcised and the machines back in operation than the IBM computer in effect swallowed the entire cover story." It took thirteen hours and two overhauls to get the story back. Uri claims that, some days before the magazine was due to appear, he stood on his Manhattan balcony looking toward the Time-Life building and willed the machinery to go wrong, visualizing the magazine rolling off the presses with column after column simply repeating his name. A fanciful theory, yes, but is it *just* possible that he liberated some force in Leon Jaroff's mind, and that of others in the *Time* office, which became a mischievous ghost in the machine?

I e-mailed Leon Jaroff to ask if he still felt the same about Geller as he had in the early 1970s and how he viewed the Time-Life (now Time-Warner) group's subsequent reporting of matters paranormal. In 1996, another—highly positive, on this occasion—*Time* cover story examined research by scientists into the effect of prayer and spirituality on illness. The article, by Claudia Wallis, centered on research into the beneficial effect of prayer on Aids patients by, ironically, Russell Targ's psychiatrist daughter Elisabeth, who is clinical director of psychosocial oncology research at the California Pacific Medical Center in San Francisco. "Twenty years ago," Wallis wrote, "no self-respecting American doctor would have dared to propose a double-blind, controlled study of something as intangible as prayer." Among several medical academics, she quoted Jeffrey Levin, a gerontologist and epidemiologist at Eastern Virginia Medical School: "People, a growing number of them, want to examine the connection between healing and spirituality," Levin said. "To do such research is no longer professional death."

In April 1998, *Time* carried a nine-page story on the Shroud of Turin, the overall impetus of which, beneath the balanced reporting, was largely in favor of its authenticity. CNN, Time-Warner's TV news network, regularly brings Uri Geller into the studio as a paranormal commentator. And in June 1998 *Life* magazine carried a mammoth 5,000-word assessment of paranormal research, which included a respectful passing mention of Uri Geller and this assertive quote from a leading parapsychology researcher in the US: "I don't *believe* in *psi*," said Richard Broughton, of the Rhine Centre at Duke University. "It's not a matter of belief. It's a matter of data."

Jaroff's reply to my e-mail was this: "In brief, I am still pro-rational and, until someone comes up with solid evidence of any paranormal phenomena, I still consider *psi* to be a combination of nonsense and wishful-thinking—sort of a religion substitute. As for Geller, he had demonstrated time and again that he is an excellent magician and a total fraud. Actually, however, he is a phenomenon, of sorts." (Jaroff has admitted ruefully at a skeptics' convention in the late

1970s that it was his assiduous debunking efforts which, by putting Geller in *Time*, effectively made him a superstar.)

Yet what Leon Jaroff would have made of some of the events "backstage" at SRI during Uri Geller's time there, as will be described in the next chapter, hardly bears thinking about.

Chapter 12

I Spy

"These are the names of the men which Moses sent to spy out the land."

Numbers 13:16

....

One day, Uri was having lunch in the SRI canteen with Russell Targ and Edgar Mitchell. They had been talking about Mitchell's epic walk across the Fra Mauro region of the Moon the previous year when Mitchell mentioned the expensive Hasselblad camera he had left up there. Uri, as ever with an eye on the main publicity chance, hatched the idea of trying to bring the Hasselblad back to Earth by some method of teleportation. (Whereas the camera has not yet returned, the idea has: to haunt Uri for having dreamed it up.) Within minutes, right there in the canteen, something apparently manifested itself in the presence of Targ and Mitchell.

Uri had ordered two desserts, the second of which was vanilla ice cream. In the first spoonful, he bit hard on something metallic. He spat it out to find a tiny arrowhead, which Mitchell looked at and said, "My God, that looks familiar." Uri, meanwhile, had called over the waitress and suggested that the canteen warn its supplier about foreign bodies in their product. She asked him if she could take away the offending item; he refused, thinking he would need it for claiming compensation if his tooth was broken. Back in the laboratory, the three were talking when they saw another small piece of metal fall to the carpet. They picked it up. Together, the two pieces made up a tie-pin. According to Geller and Targ, Mitchell looked shocked. It was a tie-pin he had lost several years before.

Russell Targ still lives close to the SRI, and has recently retired as a senior staff scientist at Lockheed Martin, the aerospace corporation, where he worked for twelve years developing a new laser-based air-safety system, only announced in 1998 and called Lidar. Lidar is a form of radar that detects clear-air turbulence up to ten kilometers ahead of an aircraft, and may be fitted to commercial aircraft in the near future. Targ, a rather magisterial, imposingly intellectual man, is so proud of his anti-turbulence device that he has the license plate LIDAR 1 on his motorcycle.

Although the more mystically inclined of the SRI Two, Targ is also the more reluctant to attribute too much to Uri Geller. We met in Beverly Hills, where he was on a tour promoting a fine new book he has co-authored called *Miracles of Mind*, which explores "non-local consciousness and spiritual healing." Available chiefly in alternative, spiritual-type bookshops, *Miracles of Mind* contains just two brief references to Uri Geller—and none to Puharich. "I don't regret having given him a platform, I think he is a fine fellow, an admirable character and a nice man, and I have no problem with the work I did with Uri," Targ said. "In the laboratory, he demonstrated various kinds of perceptual ESP comparable to what we saw from a number of other people. I would say that Uri was certainly better than average, but by no means the best we have seen. The fact that some of our remote-viewers were able to provide precise descriptions of what was going on in the Soviet Union and China and other places, which were later verified by satellite photography, makes it quite ordinary that Uri Geller can look in a closet in another room and describe what's on the wall. Geller's miracles are of very small note compared with the architectural accuracy provided by a number of other people from thousands of miles away.

"Spoon-bending, however," Targ continued, "is something which did not occur at SRI. We worked for five weeks intensively in an effort to elicit spoon-bending from him, but that did not happen for us, for whatever reason. It happened numerous times during informal sessions, but for a scientist, what doesn't happen in the laboratory doesn't happen.

"I don't rule out the possibility of Uri being able to bend a spoon paranormally. I have seen evidence, under somewhat better-controlled conditions, of spoons being bent in the hands of other people who were caught by surprise by the bowl of the spoon suddenly getting soft and rolling up. So it is not that I am categorically saying there is no paranormal spoon-bending—I think there probably is—but I couldn't say that I have seen Uri do it. Most people have paranormal psychic abilities, so it would be silly to say that the world is filled with psychics except for Uri Geller."

Hal Puthoff runs a private science research institute in Austin, Texas, working in a field so audacious and advanced—it is known as Zero Point Energy and concerns, ultimately, harnessing hidden energy in the vacuum of space to power spaceships—that he is expected by many to win a Nobel prize before he retires. I was told that, while Targ had already retired but was still involved in parapsychological research and would be happy to discuss Uri Geller with me, Hal Puthoff was a different matter. He works in a rarefied, but conventional, area, writes for respectable scientific journals and magazines such as *New Scientist*, and would most likely want to avoid talking about Geller.

He was, indeed, hesitant, but I sensed he had plenty of new insights to shed on the events of the early 1970s. First we talked about his work in the exciting area of extracting energy from "nothing." Ironically, perhaps, a major part of Hal Puthoff's job today is debunking crazy inventors who think they have discovered free energy—although he made it clear that he sees no difference between that function and what he was doing at SRI with Uri Geller and other psychics. "This is the hardest thing to get across to people," Puthoff explained. "My position is that I am a total skeptic, and that's a sword that cuts both ways. I am skeptical about *psi* phenomena existing, and similarly, I am totally skeptical of the skeptics who, without evidence and without investigation, dismiss it out of hand as being an impossibility. I have had some fairly acrimonious interaction with skeptics on the basis that they should have *supported* the SRI effort. In the laboratory we found these phenomena sketchy, unreliable, but nonetheless there was something there. I imagine there are some honest skeptics but for a lot of them it's an emotional issue."

Puthoff began to investigate psychic claims "on a lark," yet there was a deadly serious side to what SRI was doing. It is only recently, since part of his work at SRI became declassified—for which he had campaigned—that Puthoff has been able to reveal that the whole Geller program was requested and paid for by the CIA, and later passed on to the DIA. It turns out that the intelligence community was being seriously rattled by the Soviets' use of psychics for military purposes. It was believed that the information leaking out of the Communist bloc was largely disinformation, and that the psychic spying they were rumored to be engaged in was probably mere propaganda. However, it was seen as a good idea to launch a low-profile academic study of psychics, but in an out-of-the-way center where it would be under the control of CIA operatives and secrets-oriented scientists, like Puthoff, rather than glory-seeking university professors. The operation to discover whether there was potential in "remote-viewing" of distant targets continued in fits and starts until 1990, under a variety of names—Operation Stargate and Grillflame among them.

Where Uri Geller, who was by this time one of the best known—and ego-maniacal—celebrities in America, fitted into this hush-hush approach takes some explaining. For one thing, the Mossad, with whom US intelligence had friendly although mutually wary links, had informed the Americans that Geller was very interesting indeed. There is even evidence that some unfortunate Israeli spook was assigned the job of sifting Uri's toilet waste for shreds of anything it might reveal about his nefarious purposes. The Mossad once confronted him and Puharich about a photocopier brochure which Puharich had had mailed from the States; Uri had feared the security people would discover it and assume Puharich was an American spy. He tore it up and flushed it, only to find it painstakingly reconstructed back at Mossad HQ when he was summoned there to explain it. The Mossad's conclusion, however, seems to have been that although Puharich might be nutty he was bright and of no danger, but Geller was a potentially powerful military weapon who had proved himself useful in secret military tests. At the same time, though, he was a flamboyant showbusiness personality who, in terms of keeping a secret, was likely to be as much use as a giant megaphone. Their recommendation to the Americans, therefore, was to test him and use him, but to be careful.

As Hal Puthoff tells it, a veritable circus ensued. Geller was not to be told that he was just one of many psychics to be tested; for publicity purposes, however, it was to look as if he was the only one. That way if, as suspected, he was found to be a conjurer, the Russians might believe that the Americans had given up as soon as they had started. It would also provide an easy answer to be given when the rumor got around, as it would, that "something" was going on at SRI: they would say that they were just checking out Geller. Additionally, the Israelis had to be watched in case they were planting him as a known fake; there is said to have been an understanding that Israel, preparing for the Yom Kippur War, was letting the US look at him in exchange for use of American spy satellites as they passed over Arab countries. Another complication of which Puthoff and Targ needed to be aware was that rival parts of American intelligence might want to sabotage the CIA/DIA's work at SRI. Another still was that Uri Geller might, after all, be a magician who had fooled the Mossad and was now out to fool *them*.

"Before Geller came, someone showed up from Israeli intelligence," recounted Puthoff, a pixie-like Californian with a dry sense of humor. "They were interested in what we were going to do. They had used Geller in field operations and were impressed by what he had done, but they had never done anything scientific with him, so if we were going to generate scientific results, they were very interested in them."

Once it was clear that the Israelis were monitoring the SRI tests, the security around Uri increased. "We were doing our own security at SRI, but we were reporting to the CIA, and they wanted to be sure that we were taking every possible precaution. We were stationing people on the top of SRI buildings looking for people on the top of other SRI buildings. We did all kinds of things," Puthoff continued. "Another concern was that he was working for Israeli intelligence, and that they were just out to prove that he was a superman in order to scare the Arabs, and that therefore he might be something like the six-million-dollar-man. He might have implanted receivers, he might have a whole shadow team with eavesdropping equipment. So we tore apart the ceiling tiles every evening looking for bugs. Our concern that this was an intelligence plot resulted in our paranoia being much deeper than the typical skeptic would say. We were sure there was a scam."

Inside the lab, the "enemy" in a sense, was Uri. "What was not appreciated at the time, when everybody thought we had been fooled by a magician," continued Puthoff, "was that we were looking for magicians' tricks beyond anything Randi ever thought of. Of course, we looked at everything Randi had said, like Shipi probably had a signalling system to signal into the sealed room. Well, the thing wrong with that was that Shipi was in the sealed room with him on our insistence, because we were more worried about it than Randi was. We covered everything Randi later said was wrong with the experiments, but in ways he doesn't know. We were salting magicians in as physicists and lab people while he was doing the experiments. We had an expert in psychic magicianship come in and carefully view videotapes of experiments, and he couldn't work out how they were done."

Of course, trying to fool Uri Geller is not easy, as Puthoff noticed. "He is one of the brightest people I have met. He is very quick on the uptake, he doesn't miss a thing, and for those who would say that he is a magician pure and simple, he certainly sees things that the ordinary person doesn't. We might walk by a laboratory where I had a couple of agents hidden in the back with thirty other people, and Uri would walk by and point to them and say, 'Who are those two guys?' As far as I could tell, they looked just like everybody else."

There were, too, the suspected destabilization attempts by other parts of the US government machine to deal with. Puthoff tells of a visit from George Lawrence, the director of the Pentagon's Advance Research Projects Agency.

Lawrence brought with him Professor Robert Van de Castle of the University of Virginia School of Medicine. Van de Castle was a psychologist with a particular interest in sleep and dream research, parapsychology and psychic research. The three-man ARPA team, which also included Ray Hyman, the skeptical psychologist from Oregon, wanted to see the Geller experiments, but Puthoff and Targ objected. "We were still paranoid that there was a big operation against us, and maybe ARPA and Geller were in cahoots, so we wouldn't let them be in our experiments," Puthoff said. "What we offered instead was they did their own. So they did some experiments with Uri, but not under control. Uri did very well reproducing pictures from sealed envelopes, but someone from *New Scientist* ended up interviewing George Lawrence, and he said, 'Oh, yes, we went there and all we saw was tricks.' The implication was that they had seen our experiments, but they only saw their own."

According to Van de Castle, even those experiments had satisfied him that Geller "was an interesting subject for further research." He says that Geller had sensed that Lawrence and Hyman were hostile to him from the start, and that he had asked if he could do something alone with Van de Castle, "because he liked me and I was different from the others." Lawrence, Van de Castle says, was convinced before he even went to SRI that the trip was a waste of time. In addition, late the night before, Lawrence had eaten a large Chinese meal, and in the morning was complaining of diarrhea and fatigue, and was highly irritable. He later wrote a scathing report on the visit for ARPA, which formed a large part of Leon Jaroff's *Time* article. Van de Castle complains that he told *Time* of his conclusions from the visit, but that they were given a scant few lines compared to Lawrence's heavily critical comments.

Hal Puthoff explains that several experiments he and Targ did at SRI were never published. "Once we said, 'Uri, we have a physics colleague on the East Coast who we'd like you to show what you can do.' Now in fact, this was the CIA contract monitor. We phoned him at the agency and said, 'Just put something on your desk and we'll see if Uri can get it.' Uri is sitting there in our lab struggling to try and get whatever it is, and he keeps drawing something, crumpling it up and throwing it away. We were there for an hour, and then finally he said, 'I give up. This is all I am getting, but it doesn't make any sense,' and he had written the word 'architecture' across the back of this paper and made a drawing that looked like a plateful of scrambled eggs. So we asked the guy what he had on his desk. He said it was a medical textbook which he'd opened at random to a section on 'Architecture of the Brain,' next to a picture of a brain. There was no possibility that there was collusion between them."

As for psychokinesis effects, Puthoff confirms that the formal SRI tests were a disappointment. "Under camera conditions, the spoons just didn't bend. Informally, my father's keepsake ring distorted into a heart shape but Uri stopped it because he didn't want to break it. One of the things I found the most striking in an informal setting was early on, before we had started the experimentation. Russ is used to seeing how magicians handle cards, and decided to bring along a fresh pack he had bought on the airplane, a pack he knew hadn't been tampered with. Russ said by handing them to Uri and watching, he would be able to tell if he was a practiced magician. So we were sitting round the table chatting, and Russ takes the cards and rips open the cellophane and says, 'Uri, do you ever do anything with cards?' and hands him the deck. Uri says, 'No, I'm not into cards,' and he reaches out to take the deck and clumsily drops part of it. Now our observation was that the cards appeared to fall and land and go partially *into* the table and fall over, so what we ended up with was several cards whose corners were cut off where they appeared to go into the table. A whole piece of the card was missing. In the deck, of course, the cards were in order, and we had a certain place where they began to be slightly chopped, and the next one was a little more chopped and so on, from ten percent of a card up to thirty or forty percent. There were about six or seven cards with parts missing, and they were the ones that gave the impression of having dug 'into' the table. We all saw it—it was very startling.

"Russ scooped up the cards immediately. The question was, how did that happen? Without a doubt, there was no chance for Geller to substitute cards or to distract us while he cut pieces off. This was a one-second event. The only thing we could figure, since we weren't yet ready to believe that something so magical had happened, was that when the cards went through the machine in the factory, a certain set went through at an angle and got cut. So Russ checked with the card company, and asked if they ever had runs in which some of the cards get chopped. They said never, they had all sorts of procedures to prevent it, and it would be detected if it had occurred. Even on that basis, you have to say that the synchronicity that one of the few decks that ever got chopped should end up in Uri Geller's hand is unbelievable. But that's the kind of thing that happened around him.

"Another thing that happened was when everybody was over at our house for dinner, and my wife had made some mayonnaise, and set the spoon in the sink. We ate, and later when she went back, that spoon was all curled up but the mayonnaise on it had not been touched. It's hard to believe, not that it couldn't have been done. Uri would have had to go in there, bend the spoon, then go to the refrigerator, find more mayonnaise, swill it around, make sure it had untouched mayonnaise on it, and put it back in the sink. And we always watched him like a hawk. We always traded off that if one of us went to the bathroom, the other would watch him. Even in informal situations, myself, Russell, my wife, other friends we had over, I gave them all tasks; you concentrate on spoons, don't let them out of your sight, you concentrate on when he does drawings.

"Back at SRI, we were going to have Uri attempt to deflect a laser beam. This was a complex experiment, and he said, 'How will I know if I am successful?' We said, 'You see this chart recorder over here. That line is a recording of the position of the laser beam that is picked up and if you deflect the laser beam it will show as a signal on the chart.' He said, 'So what you want to see is a signal on this chart recorder. OK, one, two, three, go!' And the chart recorder went off scale, came back and was burned out. We took it to the repair shop and some of the electronics had been blown out. OK, so it could have been a coincidence, or our paranoid theory could have been correct, that he had some EMP pulse generator buried in his body somewhere and he stepped on a heel switch and made it blow. Or maybe he had just demonstrated a genuine PK [psychokinesis] event. But it is not a real event from our standpoint as scientists. It is one of those unrecorded events, so I don't know what to say about the PK claims. But I have no doubt that he has genuine powers in the *psi* area."

To place into perspective Hal Puthoff's position on Uri Geller, it is important to note, as Puthoff pointed out at our lunch, that Geller was only a part, arguably a publicity front, of a larger, more secret, remote-viewing program, and that both he and Targ are generally happier discussing remote-viewing as a whole than Geller alone. Both men tend to take an "oh, yes, and then there was Uri Geller" attitude to their work in the early 1970s. "Remote-viewing involved millions of dollars and training dozens of intelligence agents even as late as 1985," Puthoff explained. "And it worked. One of the Russian hypotheses was that it was transmission from brainwaves, so we even did some remote-viewing from a shielded area on a submerged submarine several hundred meters down, suspended midway between the surface and the bottom of the ocean off Catalina Island, southern California, five hundred miles from where we were." The results, which Puthoff presented at a symposium of the American Association for the Advancement of Science in 1981, were almost as good as remote-viewing results on land.

Did Puthoff, then, ever regret becoming involved with Geller? "I don't have any regret," he shot back, "because it was fascinating, and I know there is enough genuine stuff relevant to physics. It opened my mind. We are going to look back and see that twentieth-century science was pretty primitive, just as we look back and think that eighteen- and nineteenth-century science was primitive. I feel it has been a privilege to have been exposed to twenty-first-century physics ahead of time."

Targ came away with a rather different perspective. He was fascinated, above all, not by details, not even by any explanatory mathematical equations that the Geller experiments might have yielded up, but by the bigger picture still: "Modern physics talks about non-locality, which pertains to the idea that there is an element of conductivity in the world beyond what is obvious," he explained. "There are experiments that show, for example, that photons which set off in opposite directions at the speed of light still appear to have an interaction or an effect upon one another. It is said that there is a non-local connection between them. Photons at the speed of light should not still be interacting according to classical theory. Quantum theory, however, predicts that there will continue to be an interaction, and indeed that interaction is seen.

"This is in perfect agreement with what the Buddhists said 2,500 years ago. The central idea of the Buddhist tenet was that if you only knew one thing it is that separation is an illusion, that we misapprehend the world we live in, and there is significantly more connection between the consciousness and the physical universe than it seems. The Indian guru Patanjali, who was Hindu, wrote a book which he called *The Secrets of Patanjali*, and is available today as *How To Know God*, translated by Christopher Isherwood, in which Patanjali writes that a person seeking transcendence will encounter the abilities to see into the distance, see into the future and see into bodies—and this is available to the quiet mind. This was all five hundred years before the time of Christ that Patanjali provided the tool-kit for psychic functioning. So you could say we spent twenty million dollars of the CIA's money and twenty years of our time demonstrating that Patanjali got it right. That's our accomplishment—that we replicated his teachings. He totally understood psychic abilities."

Although Puthoff and Targ are still happy to support Uri Geller, there is a sense in which they continue, just a little, to damn him with faint praise. Specifically, both are agreed that, looking at the remote-viewing program as a whole, the star of that program was the former Burbank, California police commissioner, Pat Price. Price was one of the elite psychics put on an unofficial CIA payroll and employed through a distant outpost of the agency at Fort Meade, Maryland, as a remote-viewer. He had a string of successes, but died under what are claimed to be suspicious circumstances in Las Vegas. (It is rumored that he was so good that his heart-attack death was faked to fool the Russians, and he continued to work for many more years. He is said to have been buried in a closed casket; Hal Puthoff, however, was at the funeral and says it was open, and with Pat Price inside.)

Although Puthoff and Targ are unanimous that Price was the best remote-viewer in the US psychic program, that conclusion is disputed by Dr. David Morehouse, a forty-three-year-old career Army man, who believes he developed psychic powers as a result of being hit on the helmet by a bullet during a training exercise in Jordan. That Morehouse was recruited into the remote-viewing program at Fort Meade is beyond question, but he is controversial: he has written a book, *Psychic Warrior*, on the program, and had dealings with Hollywood over it, which has rendered him to some extent a pariah for breaking ranks so publicly. Nevertheless, what he has to say about Uri Geller is interesting. He works partly as a writer, and partly teaching American police departments on the use of psychics, and is highly regarded in his field.

"I came to know of Uri when I was in the remote-viewing unit because one of the first things you were required to do was go through the historical files, and in these files were constant references to Uri and Uri's early involvement at Stanford Research Institute," Morehouse says. "It was very clear in all of the historical documentation, the briefs that were passed on to the intelligence community, that Uri Geller was without equal. None of the others came even close to Uri's abilities in all of the tests. What interested me was that this was not a phenomenon that was born in some back room behind a beaded curtain by a starry-eyed guy. This was something that was born in a bed of science at Stanford Research Institute, being paid for heavily by the CIA. And, also, there were two laser physicists, not psychologists but hard scientists, brought in to establish the validity and credibility, to see if it works as an intelligence-collection asset, and if it works, to develop training templates that allow us to select certain individuals that meet a certain psychological profile, and establish units that can gather and collect data using certain phenomena. And their answer to all those things was yes. If Targ and Puthoff had said, 'Well, yes, there is a little something to it, but we can't explain it, it's not consistent and isn't of any value,' well, fine, but obviously it met all the criteria and twenty-odd years later they were still using it."

Like Morehouse, Uri too, feels—a little peevishly, perhaps—that there has been a retrospective attempt to play down his achievements at SRI, and suggests that, grateful as he is to Puthoff and Targ for their continuing support,

right Col John Alexander, a specialist in the study of death and other spooky subjects. He taught spoon bending to US Army officers. Photographed in his Nevada research institute, 1998.

far right Uri with Senator Claiborne Pell (with black glasses), chairman of the US Senate Foreign Relations Committee and others in Geneva, 1987. Uri was brought in by Pell to try to influence the Soviets to sign a nuclear non-proliferation treaty. They did so the following day.

Gary Sinclair, south California therapist extraordinaire, who teaches spoon bending.

above Uri's last laboratory test, with Prof Zvi Bentwich, at the Weizmann Institute, Rehovot, Israel, in 1987. The results amazed Bentwich, professor of medicine at the Hebrew University, Jerusalem.

El Al 747 Captain Gideon Peleg, who has experienced fork bending under Uri's influence at several hundred miles' distance.

Mangled cutlery from the collection of Jack Houck, a California engineer who also believes he can teach almost anybody to bend metal.

Uri on the celebrity trail in the 1970s: with Elton John …

Henry Kissinger and Rosalynn Carter (with bent spoon)…

Salvador Dali … and John Lennon

left More lab testing in London, 1974, with Prof David Bohm (left) and Prof John Hasted (right).

below Uri with an incredulous Johnny Carson on the NBC *Tonight* Show in 1975.

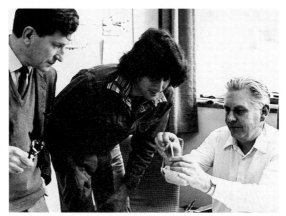

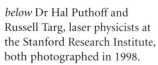
below Dr Hal Puthoff and Russell Targ, laser physicists at the Stanford Research Institute, both photographed in 1998.

below Uri with Carmen Romano de Lopez Portillo, the first lady of Mexico, 1976. Uri was suspected of having an affair with her. He denies it, but had to leave the country in a hurry after a London gossip column exposed their holiday together.

Shipi's Minox spy camera captures Dr Wernher von Braun and Apollo astronaut Edgar Mitchell in a NASA installation with Uri and a bent key.

right Meir Gitlis, Uri's electronics business partner in Israel. Meir did the first ever scientific tests on Uri in the mid-1960s.

below Magician Roni Schachnaey, Uri's old nemesis in Israel, now living in Scarborough, North Yorkshire.

below Uri with David Blaine, the cult American magician, in the summer of 1998. Blaine, who is a close friend of Leonardo di Caprio, flew over to Britain to meet Uri, his hero since childhood.

above James 'The Amazing' Randi, at his Fort Lauderdale, Florida, office.

right Michigan sociology professor Marcello Truzzi, another vigorous Geller enemy turned friend.

Uri and David Berglas, master illusionist and president of the Magic Circle. Berglas was once a Geller detractor, now a close friend.

Left to right Uri, Yuli M. Vorontsov, First Deputy Foreign Minister of the former Soviet Union, Anthony Lake, Clinton's former National Security Advisor, Sen. Claiborne Pell, former head of the U.S. Foreign Relations Committee, Al Gore

Uri with Ehud Barak,
Israel's new Prime Minister

Uri with the the Spice Girls, 1998.

'It's a good thing we called in Uri Geller!' Cartoon from the London *Evening Standard*, at the time of Euro '96. (*Cartoon by Patrick Blower © Evening Standard*)

left The spoon that led to the writing of this book. Geller appeared to make it bend in front of Jonathan, Ruth and David Margolis – without touching it as it did so.

above Here's one I prepared earlier … the heavy duty spoon Jonathan Margolis bent after coaching by Cyberphysiology therapist Gary Sinclair in California.

above David Margolis drew the left hand figure out of Geller's sight; Geller drew the one on the right seconds later; the head and body length dimensions are the same to the millimetre.

right Ruth Margolis bought ten of these postcards, of a chair by Danny Lane on a sixth form trip on May 8th 1996. Two months later, Uri Geller, sensing she was not quite convinced by him, led her into his sitting room saying there was something that would interest her there. In the centre of the room were two of the Danny Lane chairs.

below right The first time Geller dropped into Jonathan Margolis's office, in June 1998, Sue Margolis happened to take this new light bulb out of its pack at their home a few streets away. It *could* be a coincidence. There again …

The Geller family, summer 1998. Left to right: Shipi, Margaret, Hanna, Uri, Daniel, Natalie.

they might still be under obligation to the CIA to keep some material on him secret: "There was a lot of stuff at SRI that was very strange, like the stopwatch materializing out from Hal's briefcase and appearing over the experiment table and then falling on the table. I have seen the videotape of that because they played it back over and over. Then I bent metal under running water for them. I have never seen that film either, and you can actually see coins and spoons bending. Then there was the bending of the rings. Those were heavy, thick rings. There was no way that anyone with physical force could bend those, you'd have to really hammer it, but if you hammer a copper ring, you will see indentations. I know for certain they never found impact on those rings. They will probably deny this, and some of these things happened off camera and not under controlled conditions, but I always wonder, where is the stuff that was filmed under laboratory-controlled conditions? Why did they take it away? It probably exists somewhere in the dungeons of the Pentagon. Maybe they were afraid of the public knowing for a fact that Uri Geller is genuine. Maybe there was a plan to debunk me purposely, so I would come to depend on them."

One of Uri's most disturbing stories from this time was of being spirited away to a government installation where an unusual request was made: "I can't tell you where it happened. All I can say is that I was asked to stop the heart of a pig, and I knew that the final target was really Yuri Andropov, the head of the KGB. They were ultimately asking me to see if the power of the human mind could stop the human heart. I went into the room and talked to one of the scientists and said I wasn't interested in this at all, because it isn't in my nature to do such a thing. That was the time when I was becoming a vegetarian, and I was very quiet and very shocked. I asked to leave and they drove us—because this was a base outside a certain city—back to the hotel, and then I just flew back to New York. That was when I decided not to do any more scientific work, because I felt that the whole thing at SRI was really leading to that. Perhaps it was only one man's obsession. I don't know. They wanted to see what the power of the mind could do which was impossible physically or electronically. If they could find someone who could concentrate on a picture like some voodoo thing and stop someone's heart, bingo. They'd have a tool in their hands."

Further backing for Geller's having been known to the CIA, and a matter of interest and concern to it—if not for working on its behalf, as Uri claims he did—came from Edgar Mitchell and Eldon Byrd. "After the Geller work," Mitchell said, "I was asked to brief the director of the CIA, Ambassador

George Bush, who later became President, on our activities and the results. In later years, during the Brezhnev period, I met with several Russian scientists who not only had documented results similar to ours, but were actively using psychic techniques against the US and its allies."

Byrd said, "I eventually ended up briefing a director of the CIA, I briefed people on the National Security Council and I briefed Congressional committees because of some of the results we got." He also recounted two examples of Uri apparently working with Israeli intelligence—both of which Uri predictably denies. "At the beginning of July 1976, Uri called me when he was in New York and said he had had a very strange encounter that evening with someone who said they were from Israel and would he like to do something beneficial for his country. They wanted him at a certain time the next day to concentrate on some latitudes and longitudes, and to think, break, break, break. He asked what was there, and this person said if whatever was there broke, it would be good for Israel. He asked me if I thought he should do it, and I said I don't know why not, it would be interesting to try and see what happens. He called me, all excited, later on and asked if I'd heard what happened. The successful Israeli rescue raid on Entebbe had taken place, and he was sure the coordinates he had been given connected with it in some way. [An Air France airbus, hijacked by Palestinian terrorists, was given shelter in Idi Amin's Uganda and a hundred Israeli passengers were held hostage. A daring Israeli rescue mission swooped in by air to save them.]

"Uri kept saying, 'The radar in Entebbe, there must have been radars there. Can you find out if there were radars at these points?' I said I'd try. I had contacts with people at the CIA. I called them and asked them could they find out if there were radars at these latitudes and longitudes, as they were roughly on the way from Israel to Uganda, and if they could find out if the radar was really knocked out or not. They called me back and said they didn't have any information about that, they said the raid as far as we know was conducted underneath the radars anyway and we have no indication that there were radars at those points and whether they were working. But Uri had called me beforehand to tell me about this, and then the raid happened, so I thought that was pretty good." Byrd was not suggesting that this proved Uri's psychic ability, but that the incident implied that the Mossad were indeed in contact with him.

"In June 1981," Byrd said, "Uri was secreted out of the country by the Mossad, dressed as an airplane mechanic for an El Al flight. In the 747, there is a way from the cargo hold up into the cabin. That way, they got him in and out without going through Customs or immigration. He told me they took him back to Israel and flew him over some place in Iraq two days in a row and said they wanted to know where a certain installation at a nuclear-power plant was from his psychic impressions, and he told them. By gosh, just a day or so after he told me that, they bombed it."

As far as Uri working for the CIA is concerned, Byrd was less sure, yet his account continued to be highly illuminating. "I got a call a couple of years after I met Uri, from someone in the CIA. They wanted me to come over. I went down to Virginia, and they said, 'We understand you had an interaction with Uri a couple of years ago, and what did you do with him?' So I told them about the telepathy. And they said, 'So you say it was a green R that came in your head?' I said yes, and they looked at each other. I asked if there was some-thing significant about the color and they said yes.

"Another time," Byrd continued, "Uri asked me to check with my CIA guy, because he was living in the States and had the benefit of being here, and wanted to do something like work for the CIA on a project or something. So I passed that along to them and they said, 'No, we won't do that.' I said, 'He's offering for free, why not?' They said, 'We have had bad experiences working with double agents, so we don't do it.' They said they knew he was working with the Mossad. They verified what Uri had been telling me. I said he'd never told me he was working with the Mossad. There were a couple of instances of requests, but that doesn't mean working with or working for. They said, 'No, we know he works with the Mossad.'

"Later on, my contact person, who was head at the time of a division called Life Sciences, was regularly asking me if I knew where Uri was and what he was doing. Finally, I said, 'Why are you so curious?' They said they were as-signed to keep track of him. I said, 'This implies that you know he's for real.' They said, 'Of course we know he's for real.' I asked how they could determine that. They said they'd tested him without his knowing who they were. He had been told to call a certain telephone number when he was on the West Coast doing experiments, and there was a scientist in Washington, DC, who wanted to do a very quick experiment with him. My guy said he was the scientist. Now, this guy had a medical doctorate, and he also had a Ph.D. in neurophys-iology, and his expertise was forensic medicine. He was the Scully of the *X-Files*. He said he had seen a tape of Uri cheating, but it didn't make much difference because they'd seen him make spoons and forks bend on their own, so they were convinced that he was for real, but this time they were taping it under a certain set of protocols, and they said the proof to them that Uri was not a magician was that when they caught him cheating the way he did it was so naïve that a magician wouldn't have thought he could get away with it."

When he described the surreptitious test on Uri by his contacts at the CIA, Byrd was referring, of course, to the same incident as Hal Puthoff: the book the agent had on his desk was *Gray's Anatomy*, and the telephone test was the one that convinced the CIA that Geller was for real. "Rick," as Geller always knew the CIA contract manager, tried another test across the States with him on another day. He was at home with some sealed numbers in envelopes. From California, Geller told him that something had happened in his house in the Virginia suburbs of Washington involving shards of glass over some smooth green surface and a dog with a square face. Rick went into his den to find that his white bulldog had knocked over a lamp with a glass dome, and the glass splinters were lying across a bright green carpet.

Rick, whose similarity in function, if not form, to the fictional Agent Dana Scully of the *X-Files* has already been noted by Eldon Byrd, was soon to be dragged into something infinitely stranger involving Uri Geller, as documented by the science writer Jim Schnabel in his excellent 1997 book *Remote Viewers: The Secret History of America's Psychic Spies* (Dell Publishing). One of the most secret nuclear-weapons facilities in the USA, the Lawrence Livermore Laboratory, was an hour or so from SRI. By 1974, according to Schnabel, who writes for such journals as *Science*, *New Scientist*, the *Washington Post*, and *The Economist*, a few staff at Livermore had become concerned that if Uri Geller was genuine he was a danger to national security. It wouldn't take more than the movement of a few grams of nuclear material by a few centimeters, after all, to set off, or sabotage, a nuclear weapon.

Although the whole world now knew that Uri was being tested at SRI, and a select few knew that the work was government funded, it would still have been considered unseemly for the Livermore Laboratory to do any official work on him. In between scientific engagements, he was still a showbiz animal, hopping from talk show to celebrity party and back to talk show. Consequently, a small volunteer group of physicists and engineers at Livermore, with Rick's knowledge, embarked on a series of experiments with Uri, during evenings and at weekends, in an old wooden barracks on a low-security part of the former naval air base.

The tests were designed to succeed in the psychokinesis area where SRI had failed, Schnabel said. As experiments, they largely failed. Uri could do everything he was asked to do in the way of metal-bending and computer disk wiping—so long as he was allowed to touch the items he was working on. But a psychological phenomenon developed among the researchers. Hysteria mounted among the group when a security officer was speaking on the phone to Uri, who proceeded in mid-conversation to give him a detailed description of three minor family dramas yet to occur. The following Saturday all three happened to the officer. Then, in the makeshift lab, an infrared camera started recording, for a few seconds at a time, unexplained patches of radiation high up on a wall. Shortly afterward, an audiotape picked up a peculiar, unintelligible metallic voice, which no one had heard when the tape-recorder was on.

In the following days, some members of the team and their families began to experience a fuzzy gray 3-D hallucination, or vision, of a miniature flying saucer hovering in the center of various rooms. Other visions, the scientists reported, in mounting terror, took the form of giant birds, which would walk across their gardens, or, in the case of one physicist, Mike Russo, and his wife, at the foot of their bed. After a few weeks, according to Schnabel, another physicist, Peter Crane, called Rick at the CIA, almost in desperation. Rick came down and met him in a coffee-shop in the town closest to the lab. Later he met the other team members, and was astonished to find them sweating and weeping openly as they described what had been happening. Knowing from his medical training that group hallucinations were rare, and additionally, from their high-security clearance, that all the affected Livermore personnel were known to be unusually psychologically stable, Rick reportedly doubted the hallucination theory. When he examined the metallic-voice tape, he became even more puzzled. One of the few recognizable words on it was the codename for an unconnected top-secret project, of which he knew, but of which no one at Livermore could have an inkling.

Shortly afterward, Russo received a phone call from the metallic voice, which was insisting that the Livermore group cease its work on Geller; the scientists, who were only volunteers, agreed with alacrity, whereupon the phenomena gradually stopped. One of the last visions, according to Schnabel, appeared to a physicist, Don Curtis, and his wife in the center of their living room, and consisted of a holographic false arm, in grey suiting material, with a hook for a hand. This prompted Rick to ask Puthoff and Targ for a meeting when they were next in Washington. He seemed to think privately that the SRI men, both laser physicists, were playing some kind of holography prank on their scientific colleagues at a rival lab, and he wanted them to know that the joke had gone too far. Late at night, as Hal Puthoff confirms today, Rick told him and Targ the whole bizarre story of what had been happening at Livermore, hoping, presumably, for a confession. As he talked about the arm, apparently, a sharp, aggressive knocking was heard on the hotel-room door. By now, Puthoff and Targ suspected Rick might be playing a practical joke on *them*. Rick answered the door to a middle-aged man in a grey suit, who wandered stiffly into the room, stood between the beds and said, in an odd, slow voice, "I guess I must be in the wrong room," before walking out again. All three men noticed as he left that one sleeve of his suit was empty.

The Livermore events are unique in the Geller story in that they are the only instance of anything that might be described as evil happening around Uri. Could it be just possible that something—from Uri's subconscious, from the Livermore people's subconscious, from Andrija Puharich's bag of electronics tricks—objected to Uri working with men whose job was producing nuclear warheads? There is no answer to the question, but it seems odd that something so frightening to others would happen, just this once, when Uri was working within a few hundred meters of such weapons. "I have no explanation for what happened at Livermore," Uri says today. "I wasn't even aware of it at the time. I can only think it happened because I was in this place where weapons of mass destruction were made. For me what was so weird was the birds. The senior physicist was called Ron Hawke. I'd been dealing with Eldon Byrd over at the Naval Surface Weapons Center in Maryland—and I'd been living with Andrija on Hawkes Avenue in Ossining. I don't know what was going on."

In a couple of years, Uri had gone from being a nightclub turn in Israel to the periphery of the American nuclear machine. He had become a matter of fascination to the CIA and senior military figures were briefing senior politicians about him. He was still living in Puharich's cultish compound up in Ossining, and believed, rightly or wrongly, that he was under the control of extraterrestrials. On top of all this, he was a major showbusiness personality, who rarely passed a week—especially after he had been featured in *Time*—without appearing on TV. It is not an unreasonable speculation that if everything he did was a fake, the strain of keeping up appearances would surely have killed him or driven him into a mental institution; but what about the opposite, if he knew in his deepest self that what he did *was* real, that all those people trying to prove he was a fake were doomed to failure? Could being genuine have been as great a personal cross for Uri to bear as being a fraud? Could it be that he found some comfort in people believing he was just a conjurer?

Eldon Byrd has an interesting reminiscence on this question: "I always remember that Uri had this box. He may have got rid of it now. When he showed it to me, he said, 'You know, if the world really *knew* I was for real my life wouldn't be worth a nickel. There would be people trying to kill me if they thought I could really do what I say I can do.' He opened the box, and in it he had a fork, and in the handle of the fork there was this fingerprint I took to be his. I said, 'How did you do that?' and he said, 'I was thinking, melt, melt, melt, and it got soft.' I said, 'Just give me that, no magician can put their fingerprints in stainless steel. There's no way of doing this. It's mind-boggling. Give it to me, and we can analyze it. But Uri said, 'No. That's going to prove for good that I am for real, and I don't want people knowing that.' He was very, very paranoid about that."

Paranoia that the Russians, or even the Arabs, would kill him was one reason why he may have shied away after 1974 from any further laboratory testing. Another was boredom. The amount of time he spent wired up in laboratories in the early 1970s is astonishing, as Charles Panati of *Newsweek* discovered in researching his 1976 book, *The Geller Papers*. On top of SRI's and Eldon Byrd's work, Panati published papers from academics including Wilbur Franklin at Kent State ("Fracture surface physics indicating teleneural interaction") from Dr. Thelma Moss of the Neuropsychiatric Institute at UCLA's Center for the Health Sciences, from Dr. Coohill at Western Kentucky University, and from William E. Cox at the Institute of Parapsychology at Durham, North Carolina. In Europe, Uri underwent testing at Birkbeck College and King's College, both part of London University, and at the INSERM Telemetry Laboratories of the Foch Hospital, Suresnes, France. In South Africa, he was examined by Dr. E. Alan Price, a medical doctor and research-project director for the South African Institute for Parapsychology, who painstakingly documented over a hundred cases—which took up sixty pages of Panati's book—of Uri's effect on members of the public and university staff as he travelled across the country on a lecture tour.

Uri Geller was a handsome, wealthy young man in his twenties on the loose in America, with little real interest, according to his best friend Byron Janis, in being anything other than an unusual kind of rock star. While he was on the Holiday Inn trail around the States, he was able to attract as many women as he wanted, although he denies being on the rampage. "I had very stable relationships with girls. And then once in a while, yes, I would sleep with groupies because it was comfortable and offered passion and sex. I could have had anyone if I wanted to. The girls just appeared automatically, it was easy. There were even stories about girls having orgasms when they were watching me in shows.

"The government saw that they couldn't really control me because I was really on an ego trip and into making money and showbusiness. I didn't want to sit in a bloody laboratory without getting paid and doing this constant work, and I also noticed that wherever I went to do scientific work, they always wanted me to do the same thing over and over again. If one laboratory validated me, another one wanted to validate the validation. It was never ending. They didn't know how to handle Andrija, and they didn't know how to handle me."

The US government, to be fair to it, was not the only body of men and women which was finding Uri Geller a little tricky to deal with in the early Seventies. There is evidence that the restaurant servers of America, too, had difficulty in knowing how to handle the world's foremost contorter of cutlery. A story told by David Doubilet, today one of *National Geographic*'s top photographers, but then a young freelancer on assignment to photograph Geller for a Boston magazine, has amusing echoes of the Uri of 20 years previous, when Tel Aviv cafe owners would get angry at his childish coffee spoon-mangling efforts. Doubilet and Geller had become friendly, even though the photographer was annoyed when Uri twisted his apartment door key so badly that the top broke off. When Uri wanted to buy a new camera one day, Doubilet took him to a store he knew where he could get a special professional's deal, after which they went for a late lunch together at a hamburger restaurant on 53rd Street. "We were in a booth at the back of the restaurant," Doubilet recalls, "we ordered a couple of tuna salads, and Uri started playing with the cutlery from the other tables. The forks soon look like something by Salvador Dali. Anyway, the waitress came by and said, 'What are you doing with the forks?,' except this being in New York, she said 'fawks.' She got more and more annoyed. 'You boys, stop fooling around with the fawks,' she said when she came by again, only this time, Uri had a big lump of tuna on the fork he was eating with, and it suddenly seemed to bend and catapulted the tuna onto one of her shoes. Now she'd had enough, and threw us right out of the restaurant. We paid on the way out, and she was still muttering about us fooling with the fawks. Uri was fine about it; he just thought it was pretty funny."

Chapter 13

Gathering Clouds

"They are ill discoverers that think there is no land, when they can see nothing but sea."

Francis Bacon (1561–1626)

....

When the *New York Times* welcomed the SRI's excursion into psychic research in its editorial of 6 November 1974, but referred to the "high-risk element" of Puthoff and Targ's *Nature* paper, it put down this hazardousness to one of the test subjects being "a performing magician named Uri Geller, whose reputation is deeply clouded by suspicion of fakery." That such suspicion existed in the States was the triumph of a short, bearded magician, born in Toronto as Randall James Hamilton Zwinge, the son of a telephone company executive. In his forties when Uri Geller became well known, Zwinge was known in a small way in the US as James "The Amazing" Randi.

Randi, a complex live-wire, was a bright high school dropout who had run away at seventeen to join a circus. He claims to have been taken in his youth to a spiritualist church in Toronto and, with his sharp eyes and high intelligence, to have caught the preacher cheating at an attempt psychically to read the contents of sealed envelopes. He further claims that he disrupted the service in protest, and was locked up by the police for four hours until his father came to pick him up. He says that this incident was the source of his trenchant antipathy to those claiming psychic powers, although it did not stop him from doing that himself. He built a career in Canada touring rural towns in Quebec and Ontario as "Prince Ibis," a bearded, turbaned mind reader, posing as a psychic. In the States, he became an escapologist of fair to middling success, say other magicians. Many amusing and embarrassing stories circulate of James Randi failing to escape from his bonds. His magic, too, was said to be adequate, but no more. He spent some time in the road crew for the rock star Alice Cooper, choreographing the stage effect in which Cooper was guillotined.

It is no exaggeration to say that the biggest break Randi ever had was when *Time* drafted him in to pose as a staff member to help Leon Jaroff on his 1973 Uri Geller story. Randi, with his antithesis to the paranormal, was predictably unimpressed by what he saw of Geller at the *Time* office, announcing, "He'll never go anywhere with that act," which he later called the worst prediction he ever made. Geller went on, in Randi's words, to become the "psychic superstar of the century." Of course, now that he had shed his Canadian past as a psychic, Randi was under no pressure to be an accurate predictor of the future and was forgiven this miscalculation. As befitted a man with an IQ of 168, he turned it to his own advantage. He even instituted an annual "Uri Award"—a bent metal spoon on a homemade plastic base—which he has the *chutzpah* to say he presents "for incompetence."

As we know, Randi became Uri's internationally famous nemesis, and built a totally unpredicted showbusiness career—and later, something near academic eminence—as a debunker not only of Uri Geller but of all paranormal and religious activity. The basis of Randi's new career was the principle that "it takes a thief to catch a thief." His intellectual starting point was that all psychics and all paranormal phenomena *must* be fraudulent. In 1950 he himself had successfully fooled the public and the media in Canada that his mentalist act was genuinely psychic, and as a result he was convinced that scientists, journalists and the public were hopelessly under-equipped to detect such fraudulence. Such observers, he argued, were fatally inclined toward seeing what they believed. The people most likely to have the eyes, the experience and the knowledge to see the truth behind Uri Geller, healers, practitioners of alternative medicine, hypnotists, astrologers, spiritualists, clairvoyants and religion were stage magicians.

Coattailing on Geller's career—how lucky for Randi that Geller had not flopped after all—Randi, too, became a star. With a little practice, he learned to bend a spoon and do other tricks that looked remarkably like elements of Uri's repertoire. The premier TV talk-show host Johnny Carson, who had had training as a magician, had taken to Randi some while before Geller came on the scene, and went on to have him more than thirty times on to his NBC *Tonight* show. He gathered acolytes and admirers from academia. Of course, when such people praised Geller, skeptics accused them of being naïve; if they praised Randi, however, an illusionist who was proud to call himself "a char-latan, a liar, a thief and a fake all together," they were applauded for showing proper discrimination.

Randi's supporters were every bit as prestigious as Geller's: the Canadian could match Nobel prize-winner for Nobel prize-winner, professor for pro-fessor. Dr. Maurice Wilkins, the Nobel laureate and codiscoverer of DNA, went on record as saying: "Mr Randi, you've told us what you did was accom-plished by trickery. But I don't know whether to believe you or to believe *in* you." Ray Hyman, the skeptical psychologist from the University of Oregon, affirmed that, "Randi can straighten out the bent minds, but only for those of us who have the courage to face the facts as they are, rather than as they would like them to be." Martin Gardner, a columnist for the *Scientific American*, was cheered that Randi, "has done more to damage parapsychology than any one person in the last fifty years." Dr. Christopher Evans, a psychologist at the Na-tional Physical Laboratory in England said: "Randi knows, in some ways, more about human nature than a psychologist." Leon Jaroff saluted him for his "devastating blows to the pseudo-science of parapsychology." Isaac Asimov at-tested to his combination of "sanity and a sharp sense of magicianship."

An odd case was that of Carl Sagan, professor of astronomy and space sci-ences at Cornell University, who thanked Randi for performing "an important social service." If scientists and the public could be fooled by Uri Geller's con-juring tricks, Sagan—who never met or saw Uri perform—asked, "what more dangerous political deceptions must we already have swallowed?" Curiously, Sagan seems to have later changed his mind about the relative value of faith and empirical truth, with which skeptical scientists are meant to be exclusively concerned. Sagan's 1986 novel, *Contact*, and the superb film of the same title, which he coproduced, amount to a plea for faith in a discovery made by the protagonist even though the evidence for it was unsatisfactory. *Contact* is con-cerned closely and reverently with a cluster of matters skeptics are supposed to consider taboo—God, intuitive feelings—and the specter of unconven-tional scientists being marginalized and persecuted by their peers for stepping out of line with conservative, established ideas. The film ends with a definition of what skepticism should be: the desire to continue looking for answers.

In 1976 Randi was instrumental in the setting up of a pressure group called CSICOP (the Committee for Scientific Investigation of Claims of the Para-normal), with its magazine, the *Skeptical Inquirer* and a loosely connected publishing company, Prometheus Books, which is preeminent in the publica-tion of rationalist literature. In 1986, after his debunking business had fallen on hard times and he had been forced to sell his home in New Jersey, Randi was awarded $272,000 by the MacArthur Foundation, a Chicago-based philanthropic group that usually bestows awards on the likes of composers and scientists. Randi was honored as an educator, a doctor on the committee having said that he had saved more lives by opposing alternative medicine than most doctors had. Randi was overwhelmed by the recognition the award bestowed. "It's so wonderful," he enthused in one radio interview. "No one can take it away from you. You don't even have to continue in the same field. You can announce you are a communist, a transvestite or a child molester, and no one can take the money."

With the money banked, Randi set up a modern, headline-grabbing version of an old ruse which went back to his hero Houdini's day in the 1920s and before—the offering of a permanent ten thousand dollar prize (later a million) for anyone able to demonstrate anything paranormal. The catch was that such a demonstration had to be under his own conditions, which magicians and scientists alike point out are unattainable; Randi is, as constantly needs to be pointed out, an illusionist.

The Randi-Geller feud has continued to the present day, yet the two, as a *Los Angeles Times* article has noted, "have lived a strange symbiosis, two exceedingly colorful characters, each a foil to the other." Later, Randi split from CSICOP after his scattergun verbal attacks drew a fifteen-million-dollar libel writ from Geller. He has since set up his own think tank and propaganda unit against everything from Geller to alternative medicine—the James Randi Educational Foundation—which stands in suburban Fort Lauderdale . . . right opposite a chiropractor's clinic.

What seemed so novel about Randi's approach in 1973—a magician setting off on the track of a suspect paranormalist—had been done before. When D.D. Home was doing a contemporary Uri Geller in the court of Napoleon III in 1863, Napoleon paid a succession of conjurers to "do a Randi" on him; they failed. Another account, from the pharaohs' Egypt, suggests that sending for a magician is, quite literally, the oldest trick in the Book—in Exodus, to be precise. During the Jewish people's liberation struggle in Egypt, God told Moses and Aaron to demonstrate a number of miracles to Pharaoh as a way of wearing down his morale—but warned that initially the Egyptian leader would not be impressed:

So Moses and Aaron went to Pharaoh and did as the Lord commanded. Aaron threw his staff down in front of Pharaoh and his officials, and it became a snake.

Pharaoh then summoned the wise men and the sorcerers, and the Egyptian magicians also did the same things by their secret arts. Each one threw down his staff and it became a snake. But Aaron's staff swallowed up their staffs. Yet Pharaoh's heart became hard and he would not listen to them, just as the Lord had said.

The same thing happened with the first plague, the turning of the water in the Nile into blood. The magicians had no problem in replicating this but they failed with the plague of gnats. They even warned Pharaoh, in a momentary lapse from skepticism (shades of Carl Sagan!), "This is the finger of God." But Pharaoh, a true skeptic, ascribed to his boys abilities even they didn't claim. The plague of boils reportedly afflicted the magicians as badly as anyone, whereupon they disappeared from the account, leaving Moses to work his way unchallenged through the rest of the plagues. Later Jesus had a similar problem with His disciples, who did not quite believe in His miracles. "Do you still not see or understand? Are your hearts still hardened?" He asked them. "Do you have eyes, but fail to see, and ears, but fail to hear?"

In mid-1973 in the aftermath of the *Time* article, when Johnny Carson invited Uri on to *Tonight* he should probably have sensed an oncoming encounter with eyes that would fail to see. If he realized that Carson meant trouble, he faced it every bit as bravely as the hostile reception at *Time*; perhaps it was a measure of his self-belief that he could not imagine another such disaster, especially as he had been a huge success on a string of shows, with Mike Douglas, Merv Griffin, Barbara Walters, Jack Parr, and Tom Snyder among them. But the chance of going on the highest-rating talk show in the country was irresistible, even though Puharich, who was surprisingly well connected in TV, warned him that Carson was a serious skeptic.

The *Tonight* appearance was a watershed for Uri in the States, the twin reason, along with the *Time* article, why the *New York Times* felt obliged to insert its caveat about him in its leader the following year. Although Randi was unable to be in Los Angeles for the show, in the way he had been on hand in disguise for the *Time* encounter, he was closely and secretly involved in the *Tonight* edition's planning. He insisted that all the props be chosen by the *Tonight* production team, that Uri be allowed nowhere near any of them before the program, and—his top priority—that Shipi be kept at a distance from the backstage area. Whether all this was hokum, or whether Randi and Carson simply got lucky on the night because Uri was off-form is a matter of speculation: the odds had equally been magician-loaded against him at SRI and he had still succeeded. But whatever happened to him, the show was hideously embarrassing for him. As I mentioned at the beginning of this book, he failed in twenty-two minutes to make anything work. He had blown his biggest opportunity, and knew it.

One of the tests on *Tonight* was "ten-can Russian roulette" with which he had triumphed at SRI. Randi had guessed that his method at this was "accidentally" to bump into the table on which the canisters were placed and judge from their reaction which contained water. At NBC, where he was kept carefully away from the table, Uri shook his head sadly and said he just couldn't do it. In a station break, Carson and one of the crew later said they thought he was stamping his feet hard in time to the music, perhaps in hopes of jarring the cans. If so, it didn't work—and mysteriously failed to show up on any video tape. The incident has nevertheless become part of skeptical folklore, as one of the—for them—lamentably few occasions on which Geller had been found overtly and demonstrably cheating. It is only a shame for the skeptics that they have no evidence of the foot-stamping sequence—but, as they would doubtless agree, such phenomena are famously hard to tie down. Uri vehemently denies attempting anything so crass.

Uri is not unwilling today to discuss the Carson disaster. "They thought I was a magician, so they thought they would set me up by locking away the stuff that they were preparing for me," he said. "But it wasn't my intention to touch anything. I don't bring my pads or pens or spoons on to shows. I always tell people to prepare them. So when I was on the Carson show, I immediately felt his negativity toward me. He wanted me to fail, he didn't want it to work. Later on, they all tried to say that I was shaking the floor to see which can moved and which didn't. What's interesting is that the spoon in the actor Ricardo Montalban's hand—he was on with me—did bend slightly. They didn't talk about that. But it's so stupid trying to explain that I failed because *they* set me up. That's not true, because I failed on other shows too. But I felt that this was a huge failure because everyone told me that if you get on Johnny Carson, you have *really* made it.

"So I was really depressed. But then I slowly understood again that all publicity was good publicity, and people said if I failed on that show I must be real, because if I was a magician, it would work all the time. I went through a learning phase there, and skeptics still use that clip to try and debunk me. Me, sitting next to Johnny Carson and trying to dowse for something in a can and Johnny rolling his eyes to heaven. No, I can't pretend it was a good evening. But I think the guy was obsessed with debunking me. If I don't believe in something, I just say I don't believe in it. I have good friends who don't believe in me. But

Carson was frenzied about it. A couple of years ago, I was shooting an infommercial in Malibu, and I bent a spoon for the people who lived in the house where it was filmed. I didn't know but their neighbor was Johnny Carson, and after I'd gone they rushed round to show it to him. And they later told me he was furious with them and muttering about Randi. Shortly afterward, I was at a garden party in London given by Sir David Frost. Carson was in town, I assumed, for Wimbledon and knew David, I bumped right into him in a marquee. I shook his hand warmly and introduced myself, and said, 'Well, after all these years, we end up at the same party.' And he didn't say a single word."

For a different perspective on Uri's *Tonight* appearance, I turned to a paradoxical and interesting professor of sociology, who came from a circus family, is an expert on magicianship and mentalism, has many leading mentalists as friends, and was one of the founders of the anti-Geller group CSICOP. Marcello Truzzi, whose seat is at Eastern Michigan University at Ypsilanti, became disillusioned with what he regards as the group's intellectual dishonesty, and left it, although without abandoning his skepticism. Today he is a friend of Geller. "I don't think it was nearly as much of a fiasco as Randi asserts," Truzzi told me. "First of all, when the show aired originally, no mention was made on the air of Randi's 'controls,' and it simply looked like a failure to perform rather than a failure at a test. Carson was pleasant about it. Second, and this has been ignored by Randi, Ricardo Montalban apparently felt the metal *was* bending, though not in camera view. So, to some degree, Uri was salvaged by this. My point is that Randi constructed this appearance into a 'fiasco' by his repeated descriptions of the failure, and it was not really universally viewed that way at the time. Of course, I'm sure Uri was upset by it all, and I'm sure it was embarrassing to him, but it was not as if he had his hand caught in the till. Uri failed, but he was not 'exposed' on the show. Randi has since used the failure in his own attempts to expose, which is not the same thing at all. The important thing at the time was that Carson did not then go on to draw any conclusions from Uri's failure. Of course it was bad for Uri, but far from the devastating incident Randi claims. It was not so much the harm the show did to Uri as the fact that Uri was deprived of what might have been extremely good for him, had he succeeded on the show. I think most people forgot about the show until Randi brought it up much later on his own shows. By the way, years later Carson presented Susie Cottrell as truly psychic, and she demonstrated, apparently successfully, on his show. This infuriated Randi. I think this incident may have severed Randi's relationship with Carson, for I don't think he ever appeared on the Carson show again after that."

What really happened to Uri on the first Carson show? The obvious answer is that Randi's cunning proved conclusively that his powers relied on prop-dependent tricks. However, it may be that he was simply put off, or even made nervous and unsure of himself, by the hostility surrounding him. Over the past two years my growing impression of Uri has been of a kind of virtuoso mental athlete, whose ability to produce anomalous phenomena is unpredictable just as the performance of many athletes varies according to mood and atmosphere.

Yet what kind of "scientific effect" can these *psi* phenomena be if they are so unreliable? skeptics ask. Scientists reply that many accepted phenomena are far more fickle than *psi*. Quantum physics deals with effects that are so subtle and elusive that they make Geller phenomena look positively robust in comparison. Many elements of quantum mechanics have never been demonstrated or depend on the point of view of the observer. In chemistry, catalysts work every time, but it is not clear why. In medicine, allergies are little understood and regarded as a near-hoax by many doctors. Radioactivity is so random that Einstein reputedly refused to believe at first "that God plays at dice." "But He does," one physicist told me, "and He often loses."

It is simpler to list what the Carson episode wasn't for Uri rather than what it was. It was not the end of him. Uri says interest in him increased as a result of it, and this appears more than a vainglorious claim. There was certainly no question of him leaving the USA as a result of the embarrassment, as is alleged by many opponents—he had been in America just over a year when the show was aired, and did not leave the country permanently for another twelve years. The peak of his celebrity, as well as the zenith of his scientific acclaim (both at SRI and in Europe), occurred in the two years or so after his first appearance on *Tonight*. However, the experience also led to a series of depressions or an addiction in the mid-to-late 1970s, which caused Uri to adopt a lower profile and spend time out of the US.

Meanwhile, in Israel, the left-wing magazine *Haolam Hazeh* had published what seemed to be a serious exposé of Uri, an impressive-looking piece of journalism the magazine had been building up to since 1970, when it first attacked Geller. The article included detailed statements from Hanna, about how she, Shipi and others had assisted Uri's mind-reading from the audience. The headline over the anonymously written piece was "Uri Geller Twirls The Entire World on His Little Finger." It alleged that Geller couldn't perform unless Shipi or Hanna was in the front row, and an employee of Miki Peled, a driver called Saban, was quoted as saying that Geller had confessed to him in a heart-to-heart that his entire act was a sham. All Uri's enemies were quoted, from the magician Eytan Ayalon, to Professor Kelson, the conjuring physics professor, and Baruch Cutani, who had connived with Uri in the licence-plate-guessing scam. The *Haolam Hazeh* article was purported to reveal "the eleven basic tricks with which Geller fooled people in Israel and elsewhere." His watch effects were said to be caused by a magnet he bought from an (un-named) Tel Aviv jeweller, and concealed in his sleeve—even though he rarely wore long sleeves, and magnets can hardly start broken watches. Geller bent spoons, the magazine said, either physically, while no one was watching, or "He used a special chemical that he could smear on it after he put his fingers into his pocket." After a show in a restaurant in the town of Nahariya, the writer stated, Geller had gone for a meal with some friends who, when he bent a spoon for the waiter, noticed "the funny chemical smell from the fork."

The story seemed an incredible scoop for the magazine—except that Han-nah and Saban, among several others, swear that they were never contacted by a reporter from the magazine. Most important, the spoon-bending chemical does not exist—as even James Randi has freely admitted: if such a substance had been used, it would, of course, have burned a hole through Uri's fingers long before it damaged a spoon. But the best indication that the story was a hoax comes from the newspaper's editor-in-chief, Eli Tavor, who in 1986 wrote to Uri from his retirement home in New York State:

> Concerning certain things that were written about you throughout the years, ac-tually I have no explanation for them. But I can tell you a few things about the article which appeared in *Haolam Hazeh* number 1903, in which your wife is quoted. I cannot remember who worked at that time at *Haolam Hazeh* because there was always a high staff turnover rate. But what I can tell you is that who-ever wrote that article probably never met her at all. During these years many people worked here who were liars and frauds, who fabricated stories from their hearts.

Tavor added that he felt he had been an honest skeptic when he was run-ning the magazine's campaign against Geller, but concluded: "I have changed my mind about you. I am convinced today that you are endowed with abili-ties that allow you to perform feats which I cannot explain."

What was most remarkable about the *Haolam Hazeh* article, however, was that it had no impact; the foreign press failed to follow it up, and when I asked in Israel what damage it had done to Uri's reputation, almost no one knew of its existence. This curious lack of repercussion was noted by Randi in a book he published in 1975, *The Magic of Uri Geller* (reissued in 1982 as *The Truth About Uri Geller*), which promised to reveal "the astonishing truth" about how Geller's feats were achieved. Randi devoted an entire chapter called "He Didn't Fool Them In Israel!" to a translation of the piece, with occasional annotations by him where he disagreed with its conclusions. The book is interesting for the insight it gives into its author's raw emotions over the Geller issue. The material comprises pure polemic, spoiled by heavy overuse of clumsy irony, whole passages in capital letters and forests of exclamation marks, and gives the impression of a man so angry that he has lost sight of the very quality he is supposed to be promoting: rationality. It seems a treasure chest of revelation, yet it is so riddled with sophistry and contradiction that it loses credibility on every page. Randi is clearly obsessed with his subject, to which he has admitted. He also writes with a slightly anti-Semitic tinge, which he denies, angrily, in the repeated sneering references to "the Israeli Wonder" and "the Israeli miracle worker." The lurid cover of the first paperback edition of the book includes a caricature of Geller in which a wart was added to the end of his nose. Interestingly, Nazi caricaturists usually added warts to the noses of Jews in cartoons. An unfortunate coincidence, perhaps, for Randi.

We learn from Randi's gleeful accounts of his own hoaxes on scientists and journalists that he is an accomplished fake and liar. Why, then, should we accept his word on anything? Why, too, should there be a quantum leap from knowing that Randi can "take-off" Geller to supposing that Geller's motivation is similarly dishonest? In cricket, some bowlers enhance spin by cheating; others can achieve the same within the rules. For skeptics, the problem with James Randi is his reckless behavior in the handling of facts. Uri can be irritatingly cavalier and has been known to embroider his accounts of incidents but as the psychologist Dr. Marc Seifer of the Community College of Rhode Island points out: "Try to find a single instance of Uri Geller *lying*. I doubt if you will succeed." It was an intriguing point. Although the nature of some of Uri's accounts of intelligence work makes them impossible to verify, and some of his witnesses are dead, many more check out. And as for some of the exotic CIA and Mossad work he claims to have done, nothing should surprise us about the exploits of government employees.

Randi's *The Magic of Uri Geller* was reissued with many corrections to the first edition, and an additional list of *erratum* points was stuck in post-printing. In speaking about Geller, Randi has been even more hotheaded. Charles Panati, *Newsweek*'s retired science editor, alleged: "Randi's whole life is based on deception. I caught him in one deliberate lie in a show we did called

Panorama out of Washington, DC. They had me on for my book, *The Geller Papers*, and brought Randi on to present an opposing view. We got along very well, except Randi made a claim that *Newsweek* had done a favorable article on psychic surgeons in the Philippines. He claimed that he had a copy of the article, and I said, 'That's ridiculous, I've been there a number of years and I know we didn't do it.' After the show, the host, Maury Povich, asked to see the article because Randi said he had it with him. But Randi couldn't produce it, and there was no such article. I thought that was a very low blow. I don't like dishonesty, and he was dishonest in this case and I have had nothing to do with him since. I have no particular belief in parapsychology, and I cannot say for certain whether Uri is genuine or not. But Randi and his people are zealots. There is no other word for it. I believe that the good they do, they themselves trample upon with their zealotry."

One major omission from Randi's book was his failure to explain, as he promised, how Geller bends spoons. Randi is also inconsistent with both opinion and fact; perhaps the most reprehensible example of his deception exists in his reprinting of the *Haolam Hazeh* "eleven basic Geller tricks": in neither the original nor the corrected later edition of *The Magic of Uri Geller* does Randi intervene to reassert his own point that there is no spoon-bending chemical. The journalistic fiction is simply left for gullible skeptics to believe it has the endorsement of the master behind it—and believe, they do.

Professor Truzzi has fundamental disagreements with Geller, yet the two are friends. David Berglas, the president of the British Magic Circle, is an old intellectual enemy of Geller, yet a close personal friend. Such cross-bench harmony is one of the joys of civilization, so how has Randi become so bitter as to have likened Geller, as he did in a *Los Angeles Times* interview, to Hitler—and himself to Churchill? It would seem almost that Geller had destroyed Randi's livelihood and murdered his brother rather than having challenged his belief system. Perhaps Randi is so highly principled that he has simply been unable to back down.

Is it possible that Randi merely wanted to be part of the Geller roadshow, rather than a disgruntled customer heckling from the back row? Between February 1975, when he was coming to the end of composing *The Magic of Uri Geller*, and February 1998, he wrote Uri a series of extraordinary letters. The first was almost a fan letter: "I make no secret of the fact that I consider you to be one of the finest performers that I've ever seen. Your demeanor, your mechanical skill and your psychological handling of the most difficult situations has evoked great admiration on my part." He went on to claim that he "*really*" understood how Geller achieved his effects and pleaded for a secret meeting with him—to save Geller from certain ruination.

Uri ignored the letter, but another followed in July 1975, which he again ignored. Five years later, almost like a stalker, Randi wrote to Geller to beg for a meeting. He flattered him as engaging, clever and presentable, as a superb performer and so on, as well as a man with all the showbusiness experience, appeal, control and presence required to make him the greatest illusionist of his age. There followed eighteen years of silence, after which Uri received a thirteen-page, close-typed rant, seven thousand words of venom. It opened "Geller:" and went on to suggest strongly that Randi had been gathering intelligence not just from press cuttings but on the Geller children and Uri's financial affairs. Most of the letter, however, was sheer insult, along with the claim Randi had been making since 1975 that Uri would never amount to anything, and would end up, "miserable, alcoholic, friendless, drug-crazed and disgraced." Before signing off that he would leave Uri to his kismet, Randi warned that if Geller used the letter in any way, he would put the full text in the public domain. Uri saved his seventy-year-old foe the trouble, and sent a copy to anyone who requested it.

The letter came as a complete surprise, because the timing seemed apropos of nothing. Repeated readings suggest that it was a kind of deathbed statement, and that perhaps Randi was ill. There was none of the ambiguous love–hate–love undertow of Randi's earlier missives. There was still less ambiguity in April 1999, when Uri spotted his nemesis at an event in New York City, and things between the tempestuous duo reached a further, and pretty well final, denouement. "He was wearing this Dracula cape and looked very old and tired," Uri relates. "I suddenly felt sorry for him. So I decided to walk over and talk to him, and asked Shipi, who happened to have his video camera, to film our meeting. I stretched out my hand and said, 'Hi, Randi,' but he mumbled something and turned away. So I asked him why he wouldn't shake my hand, and he looked at me very angrily and said, 'Because I hate your guts.' It was the first time he'd ever admitted that, at least in front of other people."

What is to be made of a man who writes increasingly intemperate letters over a period of twenty-three years to the same person, ending in such a public declaration of personal loathing, is for the individual to decide. I would merely contend that James Randi is not quite the hero of dispassionate, rationalist thought that his supporters, who even today include such luminaries as Richard Dawkins, Professor for the Public Understanding of Science at Oxford University, make him out to be.

Chapter 14

Britain

"If people say Uri Geller is a magician, they have simply failed to read the published scientific evidence."

J. B. Hasted, atomic physicist, professor of experimental physics, Birkbeck College, University of London, interviewed in 1997

....

However damaging the Johnny Carson experience and the scoffers' consequent merriment had been, it did not dissuade a leading BBC television show, David Dimbleby's *Talk-In*, from giving Uri Geller a fanfare on his first "official" visit to Britain in November 1973. In a sense, it was the beginning of his journey to what would become home, and what was, in some respects, his roots. He had been brought up on stories of his father's exploits in the British Army, and had enjoyed a traditional British education in Cyprus.

At times, the live Dimbleby show looked as if it would go the way of *Tonight* a few months previously. There was an agonizing period of silence before things started to happen in the studio—and the Geller furor was unleashed in Britain. In the immediate aftermath of the show probably the most ringing endorsement of Geller came from science writer Brian Silcock of the *Sunday Times*. The following Sunday he described an encounter with Uri in a taxi "leaving this initially highly skeptical science correspondent with his mind totally blown." Uri had caused Silcock's thick office key to bend in the flat of photographer Bryan Wharton's hand, and made a paper-knife bend too. "It is utterly impossible to remain skeptical after seeing Uri Geller in action," Silcock wrote, adding, "I am convinced that Geller is a telepath too," after Uri had re-produced pictures the journalist was only thinking but had not drawn. (Over the years that followed, Silcock reversed his opinion: "I became convinced in my own mind that it was just a conjuring trick," he says today. "I have no idea how the trick was done, but I think there was a process of my natural skepti-cism reasserting itself. I tend to be of a rather skeptical, downbeat frame of mind, and I somehow got shoved out of it. I don't really understand how that happened, either.")

Perhaps the difference between failure with NBC and success with the BBC was Dimbleby who, although a skeptic—he is now one of Britain's senior po-litical commentators—had been shaken before the show to see a key he was holding bend under Uri's gaze.

Also present on the show, as its resident scientific skeptic, was John Taylor, an expert in black holes, who was professor of mathematics at King's College, London, and previously professor of physics at Rutgers University, New Jersey. Lyall Watson, author of books on anomalous science, was also on hand to ex-plain that he had wasted his first experience of Geller by looking all around him for the catch. There were, he pronounced, no tricks involved with Uri.

Uri was his usual engaging self, and said that he was convinced that his abil-ities came from some "outside power" or from people around him. He per-formed a successful telepathy test, which drew gasps from the audience; he wreaked havoc with some BBC canteen cutlery, and seemed to cause the hands on Watson's watch to bend under the glass while he was still wearing it.

Today, Dimbleby recalls the show as a huge success, and explained his view of Geller with characteristic crispness: "I saw him doing the metal bending several times with Yale keys, and I can only say what I saw. He would take a key and rub it between his first finger and thumb, then put it down and hold his hand over it, and it sort of lifted up towards his hand. I saw it lift up. Once it snapped and once it was just completely bent in half. I am very pragmatic about these things. I don't know what the rubbing consisted of and what hap-pened during that process. The conjurer who rubbished him on telly after-wards, Paul Daniels, said everyone had been conned and it was just sleight-of-hand. But it was clear to me that what wasn't sleight-of-hand was that the key was on a table or in the palm of his hand, or sometimes being held by the person who had proffered it. I certainly saw the key moving without his actually touching it two or three times. He did telepathy on the program quite impressively, and I have never seen anyone simulate properly the key-bending or forks drooping and seeming to melt in his hand. The odd thing about him is that the little things he does are quite impressive and mysterious, but ten seconds later he'll be telling you how he mislaid his camera in South America and had it flown through the air and re-form in Tel Aviv or whatever. So today I am quite cool about the whole thing, and wouldn't endorse him because a lot of the things he has done are meretricious junk."

Professor Taylor was entranced by what he saw in the BBC studio: "I believe this process. I believe that you actually broke the fork here and now," he said on the show, in a mixture of delight and bafflement. He took Uri off for testing at King's College, and became his enthusiastic supporter. One scientific colleague recalls Taylor having in his eyes the obvious gleam of someone who could see himself getting a Nobel prize for discovering the new scientific principle behind Uri Geller. Taylor wrote a popular book, *Superminds: An Enquiry into the Paranormal*, largely about Uri but also about dozens of children—known as mini-Gellers—who were discovered in Britain after the Dimbleby show to have similar metal-bending abilities. For a few years in Britain, the names Taylor and Geller were almost uttered in one breath. But then Taylor underwent a change of mind on the entire paranormal field. In 1980 he published *Science and the Supernatural*, a sort of anti-matter version of *Superminds*, in which he concluded that the evidence for paranormal spoon-bending was "suggestive but certainly not watertight."

"This is the conclusion I have come to more recently on carefully reconsidering the cases which I had investigated personally and which led me earlier to conclude that the phenomena was truly authentic," Taylor wrote, adding that when he developed a method for testing spoon-bending which Randi approved, "In spite of the very friendly atmosphere he [Geller] did not succeed at all. Nor has he returned to be tested again under these (or any other) conditions, in spite of several warm invitations to him to do so. One could suppose that his powers desert him in the presence of skeptics, but during the test at no time did I or any of my team express any form of skepticism; I do not think we even thought a harsh thought! As far as I am concerned, there endeth the saga of Uri Geller; if he is not prepared to be tested under such conditions, his powers can not be authentic."

"Taylor's case is a strange one," comments Professor Truzzi in Michigan. "He began by being quite convinced and pursued a new theoretical explanation. When he found his theory would not work, he started questioning everything that he affirmed earlier. Many of us think he got badly burned by his doubting colleagues and largely wrote this negative book to salvage his reputation. His initial description of Geller's spoon-bending would seem to preclude any fraud of the sort Randi claims." Uri shrugs over the Taylor incident and points out, as ever, that he often fails to produce any phenomena at all, and not only on tense live TV shows. The same had happened when the quantum physicist Richard Feynman came to see him in Los Angeles out of curiosity fuelled by never having witnessed an ESP experiment that worked. "I don't know what happened with John Taylor," Uri said. "He just switched off one day and decided that psychokinesis is not paranormal. You never know what happens in the minds of these scientists." As for what Professor Taylor thinks twenty years later, we cannot know. When I tried to contact him, his wife told me that he prefers not to talk about it anymore.

Far less noisily in the background, however, an experimental physicist was working intensively with Uri in his laboratory in London as well as at his home in Sunningdale, Surrey. John Hasted, who held the chair in experimental physics at Birkbeck College, London, was an unusual scientist. As well as being a world authority on his speciality, atomic collisions, he was a lifelong lover of folk song, had been deeply involved in the London skiffle scene in the fifties and sixties, and was an early anti-nuclear activist, who went on the Campaign for Nuclear Disarmament's first Aldermaston march.

Hasted now lives in St. Ives, Cornwall, in a bungalow overlooking the lighthouse Virginia Woolf wrote about in *To the Lighthouse*. Frail, but still mentally agile, he still reads voraciously—everything from new scientific papers to Martin Amis and the classics. In the 1970s, after exhaustive laboratory tests centering on his use of mechanical strain gauges to measure the bending in metal, he proclaimed Uri Geller genuine. In 1981, his book *The Metal Benders*, almost 300 pages of close-typed scientific data, speculation and anecdote, set out his experiences with Uri and some of the child spoon-benders, along with his theories on the phenomenon. Today, he still believes strongly in paranormal metal-bending, although he regards his work as a comparative failure because he never managed to work out for certain how the phenomenon occurred.

"If people say Uri Geller is a magician, they have simply failed to read the published scientific evidence," Hasted told me, as we sat down to tea on a leaden winter day. He had been introduced to Uri by Professor David Bohm, the renowned American-born theoretical physicist, who was interested, like Russell Targ, in the links between eastern mysticism and modern physics. Bohm, a member of the top-secret Manhattan Project, which developed the atomic bomb, and a friend of Einstein, was almost convinced that Uri was genuine, but Hasted, while fascinated by, as he puts it, "the nine-tenths of science which is unknown," had no experience of the paranormal or psychic phenomena. Yet he, too, soon became convinced.

"I never had to be concerned that I was imagining seeing spoons bend," he explained, "because right from the very start I insisted on instruments, quite correctly of course. Randi came to see me at Birkbeck. He was absolutely fanatical about this, but he was not very convincing. It took me about a minute before I saw how he did it, by pre-stressing the spoon. He is back in the days of bending spoons by using physical force, you see, but he has never attacked my more important experiments, the ones with instruments, because he doesn't understand instruments. I don't think he could have duplicated the first experiment in Uri's hotel when I first went with Bohm, because I brought my own key, and I had identified it by weighing it very carefully—and I didn't let Uri see it until I popped it on the table. He started to stroke it, and eventually it bent—not a lot, but it bent.

"I found these *professional* skeptics to be every bit as much a menace to scientific truth and impartial observation as the worst psychic charlatans," the professor continued. "They write that researchers in the parapsychology field are emotionally committed to finding phenomena, yet forget conveniently that they themselves are emotionally committed to finding there are no phenomena. I was often reminded of a saying: 'Them as believe nowt, will believe owt.'

"It was a slight shock seeing that key bend, but there are far worse shocks than that in science. I was just puzzled. I doubt if I would have taken it much further had not Bohm pointed out to me that if it was genuine we were on to something very important. David Bohm's main contribution to science was the insistence on what are called non-local phenomena in quantum theory, and he was one of the great experts on quantum theory throughout the world, so I took him very seriously indeed."

Hasted, like Bohm, came to believe that what was happening in the case of Geller and the genuine child metal-benders (some were shown to be attention-seeking hoaxers) was "a non-local quantum interaction." In other words, atoms in the metal were being dislocated at a distance by some instantaneously acting force. Neither man could suggest what in the human brain could cause this, but the theory was a starting point. "Of course," Professor Hasted said, "any law that connects such things as quantum theory and brain function would no doubt have to be Sod's law, and it would be Sod who would get the Nobel prize." When John Hasted brought Uri home socially to Sunningdale the "slight shock" of seeing metal bend in the laboratory was replaced by some major traumas. An extraordinary series of poltergeist-type phenomena began to occur within minutes of his arrival: Hasted and his late wife, Lynn (who was deeply dismissive of the paranormal), observed an ivory statuette that normally stood in the sitting room fall vertically from the kitchen ceiling to the floor. Then the key of an unused antique clock, which stood next to the statuette, appeared in the air. Over the next few weeks, there were countless instances of objects appearing to have travelled through solid walls or from inside containers, often when an increasingly frightened Lynn was on her own. The clock key kept making its own way to the identical spot by the back door, the statuette would be found on its side. When the clock, which had no pendulum and had not worked for thirty years, chimed, Lynn phoned Hasted at the laboratory and begged him to come home. That evening, the clock—which has now returned to its dead state but still has pride of place in Hasted's sitting room—chimed continually.

The strange occurrences culminated in a particularly disturbing incident two days before Christmas. The Hasteds had a good local butcher in Sun-ningdale, and a friend asked them if they would collect his turkey for him. Late in the evening, he came round to pick it up. When the Hasteds and their friend went into the kitchen, the turkey's liver had apparently extricated itself from inside the still-sealed plastic bag of giblets, and rematerialized outside the unbroken bag, in the middle of a plain white table.

Dozens of other bizarre physical phenomena were happening to Hasted at work, to his work colleagues and to the Hasteds' friends, but the turkey inci-dent, however, was one too many for Lynn, who threatened to leave her hus-band over it. She and he had come to suspect that somehow Geller had let loose the avalanche of psychic phenomena through her unwitting coopera-tion. "It was a remarkable series of incidents," Hasted said. "It was a hard time for my wife and myself—we nearly fell out. We really had quite serious emo-tional troubles about it."

The phenomena dried up, but Hasted began to move on from puzzling over spoon-bending to considering the wider question of teleportation. "My atti-tude on this is that when metal bends, atoms move about in the metal, and if enough atoms moved around, then the whole object *could* jump, and this would be teleportation—which I now believe to be merely another branch of metal-bending. In fact, teleportation is probably the more fundamental event, and both Uri and some of the children I studied at the time have done it for me under very good conditions indeed. Eventually, this could be a solution of the transport problem. Yes, beam me up, Scottie! I think we might get there within fifty or a hundred years—except that it will be very dangerous in that your head might come off or something like that. Teleportation from A to B is instantaneous, because it is another demonstration of quantum non-locality. Non-locality means the same thing—being in two places at once, things not moving, but just appearing, going through walls. That's been my experience. I have seen it happen."

Some while after his work with Geller, Hasted was invited to an all-men dinner at Buckingham Palace with Prince Philip and a selection of technologists and scientists. At Philip's round table, sitting next to the industrialist Basil de Ferranti, he expounded his views on metal bending. "Prince Philip was interested and, I thought, sympathetic," he recalls. "The others were all skeptical. I hoped they would appreciate what an asset Britain had in having attracted Uri from the USA, but I don't think the other guests were convinced of the reality of events." After the dinner, nevertheless, Hasted was invited by members of Prince Philip's staff to continue his description of the experiments with Geller. An invitation followed from Prince Charles, inviting Hasted to dinner at Kensington Palace. Here, the guests included the writer and philosopher Laurens van der Post, the journalist and author Brian Inglis and the comedian Michael Bentine. "The whole event was much more pleasant than the one at Buckingham Palace," Hasted says. "I think Charles was sympathetic to the phenomena." It is worth noting, nonetheless, that neither Philip nor Charles subsequently asked to see Uri Geller personally.

Before I returned to London, Hasted took me into his cluttered study, where he keeps the mementoes of his pioneering metal-bending work alongside half-disembowelled computers and other electronic gadgets. The mangled forks and spoons are carefully marked: most are the product of metal-benders other than Uri, and the grotesque distortions are greater than anything he produced. "There's no doubt," Hasted said, as I photographed him with his wrecked cutlery, "that some of the children were real mini-Gellers, and some were more powerful than Uri. I had one, whose parents were Oxford academics, who on one occasion walked through his bedroom wall in front of them. Most of these children, we found, were rather unhappy, and usually had problems with their father, and were closer to their mother—which I believe describes Uri's position. You will find, however, that in adulthood, they are almost all reluctant to talk about what they could do as children, or tell you whether they can still do it, some because they were cheating and are embarrassed, and others because it brings back this tortured time in their past. Uri was unusual in taking a different course, I think, because he wanted to impress, but also to be a good publicist for the cause. That was his whole end object."

Two interesting postscripts to my interview with John Hasted came in the week after it. First, after much international phoning and e-mailing, I tracked down two of his child metal-benders, one in Wiltshire, the other in Canada. Neither wished to be interviewed again but one said, "It was all perfectly genuine, and please give my best wishes to Professor Hasted. But I wouldn't want my friends and neighbors to know about what happened back then, and have all those accusations about attention-seeking starting again."

Second, on the Friday of the same week in which Hasted had told me that teleportation could become an established scientific effect, *Nature* published a five-page article by Professor Anton Zeilinger and other researchers at the University of Innsbruck, Austria, describing the first-ever successful verification of quantum teleportation—not quite of Scottie or of an ivory statuette or a turkey liver, but of the electrical charge on a single photon particle two meters across their laboratory. The Innsbruck team were not looking into the possibilities of mind-over-matter being a quantum effect, but suggested that theirs was the first experimental proof that quantum mechanics might soon be used to transfer information in computers infinitely faster than we can now do by electronics.

The *Nature* article happened to be published within days of press reports of another experiment in the USA, which produced the first virtually incontrovertible evidence of mind-power influencing material objects. Physicist Professor Robert Jahn's team at Princeton University documented subjects beating odds of 1,000 billion to one when willing a random number generator to produce specific sequences. A few months later, there was good and bad news for the paranormal from Japan, where the Sony Corporation announced it had proved after seven years' research that ESP exists—but it closed down its ESP research facility because there did not seem to be any way to turn the knowledge into marketable products. Neither the Princeton team nor that at Sony suggested that a quantum effect was behind their respective discoveries. But at least, for the first time, the possibility of an explanation for the Geller effect—that his brain and those of others, can cause atoms in metal, entire objects and thoughts to move around by some quantum teleportation method—began to look, however dimly, realistic.

A key event John Hasted organized to show off Geller when he was in England was an informal gathering of high-powered, interested parties in his laboratory at Birkbeck on a June Saturday in 1974. Among those who came were Val Cleaver, the chief engineer of the Rolls-Royce rocket division, Byron Janis, Uri's pianist friend, Arthur Koestler, the engineer turned science writer, who later bequeathed £1 million to found a chair of parapsychology at Edinburgh

University, Arthur C. Clarke, the science-fiction writer, and Arthur Ellison, professor of electrical engineering at City University, London, and a part-time researcher into the paranormal. The meeting became famous as the source of an ongoing argument between Arthur C. Clarke and several of the others. According to Ellison and others present, when Clarke saw his front-door key bend before his eyes, he exclaimed, "My God, it's *Childhood's End* come true." He was referring to one of his own novels, in which the alien overlord Karellan explained to the human race some centuries hence that the ancient mystics had been right, and science wrong: such phenomena as poltergeists, telepathy and precognition were real. Clarke then said to Byron Janis, "My God what is this world coming to?"

"Five or six years later," Janis related at his apartment in Manhattan, "Clarke said it hadn't happened at all, and that he had been in a hypnotic state. It pissed me off, because I remembered it so well." Indeed, Clarke had turned abruptly on Geller. Ten years later, in the foreword to a paranormal book of his own, *Arthur C. Clarke's World of Strange Powers*, he urged his readers to study Randi's work, and was scathing about Geller. He admitted that he had made the comment as reported when his key bent, but said that everyone else's memory of the bending process had been at fault, and that Geller had actually manipulated the key.

Professor Ellison remains resolute. "Clarke got out a Yale key and he put it on top of Hasted's secretary's typewriter," Ellison recalls. "We were standing around the desk in the outer office. Clarke put his finger on the key, which was all alone on that flat surface, and said to Geller, 'See what you can do with that.' I was to one side within a foot of it, Arthur Koestler was a foot away elsewhere, and Geller came up between us and stroked it on the flat back of the typewriter. All of us were watching that key like a hawk, and the end curled up in about a minute. You could rock it to and fro. Our attention was not distracted, we weren't born yesterday, we were all aware of magicians' tricks, and there was nothing else that happened that I haven't mentioned, so there's not the slightest doubt in my mind. If I have seen something I will say so. I will not be short of the courage of admitting if I see things that most scientists think are impossible. Clarke was amazed at the time, so I was surprised when I saw him on a TV program that he was very noncommittal about Geller. I think he probably feels that if he admits to seeing a paranormal phenomenon, everyone will assume he's going round the bend and will cease taking him seriously."

Ellison, who is now retired, lives in Beckenham, outside London. The son of a tailor from Birmingham, he began in heavy electrical engineering but went on to become both a world-renowned scientist and a leader in psychical research. He is also prominent in the Scientific and Medical Network, an international group of nearly two thousand doctors and scientists with an interest in spiritual and paranormal matters.

"My rule has always been," Ellison explained, "that if ever I talk about anything paranormal in the university common room, then I make jolly sure that the evidence for its truth is about an order of magnitude stronger than for anything else in normal science. The standard and the quality of the research in parapsychology is a great deal higher than it is in most subjects. I have had several sharp rows on the radio about the paranormal with people like Richard Dawkins, who is the Oxford professor for the public understanding of science, and Lewis Wolpert at the Middlesex School of Medicine. I have discovered the way to deal with Lewis now is to talk about quantum mechanics, the fact that a great many distinguished physicists think that what's out there depends on our consciousness for its meaning in reality. Nobody would say that the fathers of quantum mechanics, like Niels Bohr and the other distinguished members of the Copenhagen group of physicists, were idiots. Even Lewis wouldn't say that. Life just isn't as simple as people like these, who I call naïve materialists, love to believe.

"As for Geller," Professor Ellison continued, "I think he is important in that he shows how certain things that some normal scientists consider impossible are not impossible, but as they have been conditioned by their education and training to 'normal' reality, they just dismiss it all as conjuring, so that it is not as important to them as it ought to be. If they had the truly open mind of a real scientist they would be very interested in things that don't appear to be obeying what they consider to be the normal laws of nature.

"Now Randi, of course," Ellison added, with obvious irony, "has the benefit of already *knowing* that all this is impossible, so when he finds some way of imitating it by conjuring, he knows that's the way it must have been done. What is unfortunate is when scientists are half blind too, and don't see things, don't do the right experiments, don't do any experiments, because they already know it's impossible."

Remarkably, for a man who is listed in *Who's Who* as a visiting professor at the Massachusetts Institute of Technology and who is the author of many papers and books on matters such as the problems of noise and vibration in electrical machines, Professor Ellison goes beyond even quantum theory to explain Uri Geller. "I don't actually think it is Geller who bends the metal," he said. "You will no doubt be what I call a naïve realist. You think there is no doubt that all these objects are around us, and you have in your mind a model of the physical world, which usually works all right, and so do I much of the time. But I actually think there are not real objects around us, and that is the result of my own experience of the paranormal. I have been to every kind of seance you can imagine, I have had every kind of experience that there is within the paranormal. My boggle threshold is at infinity, I think. I have seen an apport arrive in the middle of a seance in a good light, an object that wasn't there before, a rose, a living rose, slowly materializing. I have seen objects floating in the air in a good light. I was once in a seance when the control personality, through the medium in trance, while the light was still on, said, 'Hold my hand,' so I linked fingers and there was a luminous trumpet kind of painted on the carpet in the middle of a big circle of spiritualists. And I held my hands out, and this trumpet floated up in the air, went round and round my linked hands half a dozen times, before it floated back down onto the carpet again. I have seen and made notes on some thirty full-scale materializations, so you'll understand that I didn't turn a hair at seeing a key bend."

Psychism, Ellison added, occurs at an unconscious level, over which people have no control, and cannot be switched on like a tap. He considers that it sometimes occurs in people who do not expect it when they experience what some psychiatrists term a "temporary suspension of disbelief."

Arthur Ellison is often sharp about Uri Geller, and is far from an acolyte, yet still supports his claims. He had wanted to study Uri in 1973, but was beaten to it by Hasted and Taylor. "Geller did invite me out to his house, once, when, I think, he really wanted this legal document to help him, an affidavit about the Arthur C. Clarke business. He promised to invite the family to see a bit of metal-bending, but he never did. He is most unreliable. I slightly suspect he sometimes tells stories that aren't quite accurate, and occasionally makes promises that he can't keep. I also can't swear that he doesn't at some times use stage magicianship. If anyone is paid as much as he is and it doesn't work one evening, I imagine it's a terrible temptation to fake it a bit, if not for the self-respect, then at least for your money, to give them what they paid for. That showmanship thing has done quite a lot to damage the subject. But the great thing with Uri is that he can get members of the audience, with no extra grind, to bend their own keys. Now that's fantastic, and I applaud Uri for it, because it's not Uri doing it. They are doing it themselves. It's that temporary suspension of disbelief."

Uri's 1973 and 1974 trips to Britain were focussed on striving for scientific acceptance and it is easy to forget that in fact he was principally concerned with maintaining a rock-star existence. In the midst of the scientific controversy, he found time to make and promote his first record, called *Uri Geller*, for which he wrote and voiced the words, Byron Janis wrote the music, and an arranger who had worked with the Beatles set the finishing touches. The record was a success, and he recorded it in Italian, French, German and Japanese. "It was recently rereleased in Japan," Uri told me, with considerable pride, "and has also been voted the worst cover award in Australia, and was discussed as late as 1998 on ABC TV's *Good Morning, America*, where it was mentioned as the third or fourth worst record in the world."

He also concentrated as much effort as he could muster in Britain on simply having fun—in one case with bizarre consequences: "While I was in London, I went to a casino, something I'd only done once since the time in Italy, when I did well. In the States, I went to Las Vegas with Yasha and Shipi, and it was a disaster. We lost every penny and ended up sleeping in a borrowed Lincoln Continental. But in London, I either predicted where the roulette ball would fall or made it fall onto the number that I had chosen—I don't know which—and I won seventeen thousand pounds. That was a lot of money for me, and I was sitting feeling happy with it in the back of this Daimler. But as we were driving, I heard a voice in my head, terribly loud, shouting at me and saying, 'Why did you do it?' I got so scared that I grabbed the driver. I actually broke the glass partition between us and started shaking him. He stopped the car, and the door opened as if an invisible hand had pulled it, and I felt as if I was thrown out of the car, with a massive weight on my chest and body, pressing me right into the ground. It lasted maybe fifteen seconds, and I threw out the money on the hard shoulder of the M4, seventeen thousand pounds, all bundled up in rubber bands. And it felt such a relief. I never gambled again after that.

"Maybe it was me," he speculated of this incident, the impact of which is marred only by his failure subsequently to track down the driver as a witness. (Perhaps the driver later retrieved the money?) "Maybe it was my inner conflict, telling me never to do it, and it translated it in such a way that it scared me, and it was me building an energy force around me being able to psychokinetically open the car door. I will never know those things. I never know what is going to happen to me tomorrow. The mystery to me is why am I allowed to fly in an airplane and open maps and tell big mining companies where to drill and be paid for it, but I cannot try to win the lottery or go into a casino. I don't understand it."

Chapter 15

Independence Day

"Melanie wanted my child because she believed that a child from me would be a space child. And I believed it, too."

Uri Geller on Melanie Toyofuku, his lover in the mid 1970s

....

Uri's twelve years in America fell into two uneven parts: the time he spent with Andrija Puharich in Ossining, which lasted until the end of 1973, and the period based in his own Upper East Side Manhattan apartment, with his mother in Connecticut.

The break with Puharich released Uri into his first experience of independent adult life. But it was as emotional a separation as any between parent and child. "I had a row with Andrija," Uri said. "He signed me on a contract, he owned me for seven years and all my income. I don't think it was that Andrija locked me into this contract for monetary reasons. He wanted to own me because of what I represented to this alien intelligence. I was their tool, and he wanted to own the tool. Andrija was convinced that, through me, he was dealing directly with God. I never accepted that, because I am a believer in God, so when Andrija concluded from the messages that this was God speaking directly to him, that, I guess, was the first step of me realizing that it had gone too far. Nevertheless, everyone around me was telling me how foolish I was. We were very gullible and naïve. I had no lawyers, but I threatened the publishers of the book Andrija had just finished on me, *Uri*, and the whole fight was in London in a hotel room. I wanted him to tear up the contract, otherwise I would have refused to endorse *Uri*. It was a damaging business until we made up again, but after I left him, he started gathering other people around him and he was OK. We saw him a couple of times in America, and when he came to London about eight years later for me to film him—that was just something I wanted to do for posterity—we embraced and hugged each other."

According to Hal Puthoff, the breakup with Puharich was worrying Uri at a deeper level than the financial. Puthoff's memory of his private discussions with Uri at the time suggest as powerfully as almost any other account just how sincerely Uri believed in his own abilities, even if opponents felt he was enjoying a huge joke at the expense of science. "Puharich told Uri that if they broke up as a team, Uri would lose his powers," Puthoff explained. "Uri spent a lot of quiet time with us asking if we believed that, because he didn't want to lose his powers. He felt obligated to demonstrate his abilities, and he was concerned that if at any time he did the wrong thing ethically, he might lose them. What did we think he should do, did we think Puharich's involvement with him helped strengthen his powers, and so on? It wasn't a con thing. He was genuinely concerned, and he kept coming back to it."

A letter Uri wrote to Puharich on a flight just before Christmas 1973 came to light after it was sent to Uri in 1998 by Puharich's first wife. It reveals a great deal about what was in Uri's mind at this troubled time. Some of the meaning is a little obscure, but it would be difficult for the harshest critic to deny its sincerity:

> Words mean nothing if feelings don't cry. A lot we struggled for God in heaven but on the road we stopped. Never, never have I in my mind, body or soul thought but about you. For me inside, I am still proud to know you Andrija. Whatever your decision is, to stop or keep going, I will understand your human feelings. I truly care about the mission. I also care about my people, so I asked you to trust my feelings towards you and Spectra. And if you still don't want to hear me or feel my wanting you, then maybe this is how it has to come to an end, although I don't feel so. Still loyal to you. Uri

Uri's obvious regret that the relationship was breaking down is understandable. Both men feared they needed the other, and both knew it had not been a bad life for Uri, Shipi and Yasha Katz in Ossining. "I didn't have to go down to the local store to buy food," Uri said. "Andrija did it. It was a more down-to-earth, rustic kind of living than I was used to but Andrija organized everything, and it was very comfortable. So when I left Andrija, it was quite a shock for me, knowing that I had to rent my own apartment, and that to have breakfast I had to buy it. Suddenly I had no money at all, I was broke. I couldn't sell the Tel Aviv penthouse that my mother was living in. And that's when Byron Janis loaned me forty thousand dollars, which was a huge amount at that time—and he wasn't a rich man. But with the money, I could afford the apartment, the furniture, and Yasha's salary, and I never had to worry again, because almost immediately, I had TV shows all the time, I was lecturing in universities for as much as five thousand dollars a time, and was getting book advances. I did a commercial for exercise machines in Japan. And I remember getting forty thousand dollars in thousand dollar bills for a show in Tokyo. So I could quickly pay Byron back with interest, and before long, I actually had two apartments on the twelfth and seventeenth floor of the same block.

"I lived in one alone, and Shipi and the girls lived in the other downstairs. I had three girls working for me, Melanie and two sisters called Trina and Frida, who used to write me fan letters, and I gave them a job. Melanie was deeply in love with me, and she wanted my child because she believed that a child from me would be a space child. She really went on that. I believed it too. In the end, she became very disenchanted and felt betrayed, although she never showed it to me. She is very beautiful and fragile. I haven't seen her for many years. She married a Sufi; she waited for Uri Geller, the Saint, the Guru, like a lot do. Many cults have looked to me and been disappointed. That's why when I think of Melanie, I think of a sadness in her eyes. The sisters left too. They thought I was on an ego rampage, and it's true, I was. I didn't care sufficiently for those around me."

Shipi's somewhat ill-defined role in the Geller entourage had become clearer by now: "Shipi was my personal manager, but also my confidant," Uri said. "There were certain things that I couldn't tell Yasha, but I could tell Shipi. I told Shipi everything. We used to discuss how the group at Andrija's really seemed to want to turn me into a guru, a messiah. And Shipi always knew me better than even Hanna when it came to my powers, and to the business side. My problem with Shipi was that he obviously knew I was involved with his sister, but she was in Israel most of the time, and we weren't properly going out yet. She used to come and see me. I was too busy to go and see her in Israel, so I would just send her tickets all the time, and then there were times when she would stay for months with me, and then go back. So, as regards women I was seeing, I had to tell Shipi, 'Look, you'd better be on my side because this is me, this is what I am.' There are certain times when I felt he wanted to protect Hanna but, of course, by the end of the 1970s, it happened naturally anyway. Hanna came over and we were together for good. What was great with Hanna was that she understood that I was out to make it myself and I had no time for other people, really, and that it was all a totally egocentric fame-and-fortune type of thing at that time. It was important because I learned so much from it. I had to go through that phase in order to develop further. But I was always aware that it was quite difficult at times for Shipi."

Uri's new life in New York, at 357 East 57th Street on the corner of First Avenue, was a celebrity whirl. At a party given by Elton John, he met John Lennon, and the two immediately clicked. They arranged to meet again in the coffee-shop of the Sherry Netherland Hotel on Fifth Avenue, and made this a regular date. They talked about the paranormal, spiritual matters, Sai Baba, a popular Indian guru in whom Lennon was interested—and who performs materializations of objects for pilgrims who come to see him from around the world—and UFOs.

A few weeks before he was killed, and the last time Uri and he met, Lennon told Uri an amazing story. He had been lying in bed in the Dakota Building where he lived in Manhattan when he saw an exceptionally bright light seeping under the bedroom door. He told Uri that he thought someone had aimed up at his apartment an outdoor floodlight of the kind used at film premieres. He got out of bed, opened the door and saw that the source of the light was in the next room. He felt something touching the back of his knees and his elbows, and urging him into the light. "I asked him obviously whether he was drunk or on drugs," Uri said, "but he insisted he was perfectly awake and aware and had not taken any drugs. In the middle of the light, he said, he saw a hand stretched out. He described it as, 'a typical alien hand,' like the ones you see in science-fiction books, and it held something. He knew intuitively that the hand wanted to put something into his, and he held out his hand. Then the light went off, the room was clear. And he found himself standing there with this smooth, almost egg-shaped, brass-type lump of metal in his hand. And then John put his hand in his pocket and said, 'Uri, I want you to have this.' It was as if he felt he was going to be killed and wanted someone to have this thing who would know where it came from and would believe him and look after it."

Uri keeps the smooth metal object today in the hands of a sixteenth-century Tibetan brass statue in his house. The little piece of solid metal is heavier than its size suggests, but Uri said, "I don't want to have it analyzed because I don't want to be disappointed. I don't want someone to come up with a story that it's made in Korea. I'd rather leave it mystical."

Another icon who became friendly with Uri was Muhammad Ali. Uri was taken to meet him at his training camp in New Jersey by a journalist. "Ali was fascinated by what I did. I learned that he loved magic and did all kinds of sleight-of-hand tricks. He realized that what he was seeing was real. Then we became friendlier when he was interested in me teaching him how to concentrate and look in the eyes of opponents in the ring to help overcome them."

He was also befriended by the surrealist painter, Salvador Dali—an amusing choice of companion, some will feel, as Dali too is regarded by many as a charlatan in the art world. "I was introduced to Dali by this incredibly beautiful woman called Amanda who, it was rumored, used to be a man, and who was hanging out with Dali at the time. She wrote a book in which she mentioned me. I used to meet Dali at the St. Regis Hotel in New York. I showed him my doodles and paintings, and I think he was quite impressed. He wanted to know why I drew the doodles the way I did and the meaning of each. He actually inspired me to try some surrealist painting myself, which I still sometimes do. Then I stayed with him at the Ritz in Barcelona for a couple of days. It was while I was there that I bent a gold fork in his hand and he was so shocked and scared that he took himself off to a room in his house and locked himself in there for hours. He finally emerged holding this beautiful rock crystal sphere—I don't know whether he made it or found it somewhere. Dali gave me several sculptures, which I have all over the house." The sphere now takes pride of place as the hood mascot of Uri's old Cadillac, now kept in his garage outside Reading, which is covered in riveted-on bent cutlery. Uri once planned to drive it to Baghdad on a peace mission to Saddam Hussein, but was discouraged from doing so by friends who suggested that the dictator might know of his connections with the Mossad and fail to take the gesture in the spirit in which it was intended. Uri continues to insist that one day he will drive his Cadillac to Baghdad.

At the beginning of this social mountaineering came the single most dramatic and, if we are to believe him, traumatic psychic event of Uri's life. Whether it really happened or whether Uri felt the need to contrive the whole thing, or even if he invented it, the following is revealing of the tension between himself and Puharich.

On a freezing Friday evening in November 1973, Uri went round to Byron and Maria Janis's apartment. There, he made a couple of phone calls, one to Puharich in Ossining, which is thirty-six miles north of New York City. Byron recalled that Uri said then that he had to go down to Bloomingdale's to buy something, and had some other things to do. "He was very excited," Byron said. "I assumed it was to do with a woman. He liked women very much." At five thirty, Maria said, referring to notes she made later that night, Uri left. At a jog, as Uri did it, Bloomingdale's was eight-minutes away and his apartment five minutes in the opposite direction. The round-trip to the store, into the camera department (where he bought a pair of binoculars), and home would thus have taken twenty minutes or so. Maria knows this because she has paced out the journey in an effort to explain what then happened. Twenty-five minutes after Uri left, the phone rang. Maria answered it, and Byron picked up the extension. It was Andrija Puharich, calling from Ossining. "There's someone here who wants to talk to you," he said gravely.

"Then," Byron said, "Uri came on the line. He said, 'Maria, I'm here.' He was obviously in shock. She said, 'Uri, what are you doing there?' I thought it was a joke. But it was obvious that, somehow, Uri had got to Ossining, and it was clear that he was a complete wreck. He went through the story on the phone. He said that as he got to the canopy in front of his building, 'I felt this sudden pull backwards and up.' Those were his exact words. 'And the next thing I knew, I was falling through the screen door in Ossining.'" It seemed unlikely to the Janises that this could have been a stunt, even if they thought Uri capable of pulling one, or that he felt the need to impress them, of all people, who were his devoted supporters. Yet they considered everything: a train or car journey to Ossining was impossible in twenty-five minutes, especially during a busy winter rush hour. Even a helicopter operation would have taken longer, because of the time needed to get to a helipad in central Manhattan.

In an unpublished account found by his children after his death, Puharich confirmed the Janises' chronology. In his meticulous style, he recounted having been watching the six o'clock TV news while lying on his bed—the main story was of Henry Kissinger's shuttle diplomacy between Israel and Egypt—when he felt a shudder with a simultaneous crash from a conservatory he used in the summer as a dining room. He also heard Uri calling his name. When he found Uri, he appeared to have crashed through the roof of the conservatory, rather than the screen door. He had landed on a round wooden coffee table, whose glass top had shattered. He was unhurt, but clearly confused and dazed. And he was carrying a Bloomingdale's bag.

Uri's own account is compelling. "The sidewalk wasn't crowded at the time," he said. "The first recollection I have is of me looking at the pavement and seeing myself a few inches above it. The next thing I can remember is like someone had cut out a split-second piece of my life, like a piece of film taken out with scissors. I remember the lifting off, then I recollect there being a screen in front of me, and putting my arms up to protect my face, as my instinct told me that I was about to crash through something. Then my palms were slicing through the screen, but ever so gently, then there was falling on the round table, and a glass on the table slipping from under my hands, and breaking on the floor, and me falling on the table, and onto the floor. I didn't know where I was. I didn't recognize it as Andrija's porch at first, until I got my bearings. I had had many breakfasts there in that round porch in summer."

Uri, like the Janises and Puharich, spent many months trying to puzzle out what happened that evening. "It's beyond my understanding and comprehension to believe that my body was disintegrated molecule by molecule and reconstructed itself thirty-six miles out of New York. My explanation is that people, animals and objects can fall into a time warp, like a whirlpool of time, space and matter. You are sucked into some kind of void, a vacuum, an emptiness that could move you in space and time and replant you elsewhere. I could have gone back into the past or the future, I have no doubt. Hundreds of people go missing each year without a trace, and no one knows where they disappear to. Probably what is happening is that there are velocities and speeds in the universe and in our bodies and in our minds and, most likely, everything is happening right now. The past is now, the present is now and the future is now, and somehow we are just stuck in it. It is like a mixture of speeds we don't understand, so what happened to me is that because my mind, my subconscious, or even deeper than that, was so concerned about my relationship with Andrija and how I wanted to tear away from him at that time that it just flung me into this vortex and I teleported there. Perhaps it was him wanting me to be back there. There were times, you know, when I began to doubt whether Andrija was human."

If Uri was a hoaxer and practical joker, much of what had been happening at SRI, at the Lawrence Livermore Laboratory and in New York suggested he must have been a workaholic practical joker. Yasha Katz, another who needed no convincing of Uri's powers, was also experiencing a string of strange incidents at this turbulent time. Katz became disaffected with Geller over money, went back to Israel, and gave James Randi, who was making a TV film about Uri, a damning interview in which he claimed he had colluded in his former employer's cheating.

He could have stayed with the story, but he now says he was paid by the TV team to lie, and went along with Randi to make mischief—although after being convinced by Randi that Uri had duped him. "I was a little bit disappointed with Uri because he asked me to leave him, and after so many years of devotion I felt that I deserved a little bit more," he explained at his Johannesburg office, where, aged sixty-five, he now sells life insurance. "Randi came and he talked me into believing that all of it was a hoax, but I regretted it at the same time as doing it. I lowered myself to the minimum and made myself very, very small. Because when I've thought about it, and I still do think about it, it is very easy to show all the things that Uri does by sleight-of-hand at a show. But we all *lived* together, and we saw things that happened without him having control. When you put one and one together, it's obvious that something was happening.

"One Sunday morning in our apartment in New York, a whole series of things occurred in quick succession. I went to get a newspaper, and when I came back, I saw my plant-holder, which was a very, very heavy glass thing, which one person could not lift, in front of the elevator door. I thought maybe Uri played a joke on me, and I went into the apartment and he wasn't in. He was in the other apartment, so I phoned him, and he came down, said he didn't do anything. We both had to lift it and put it back in my bedroom, and as we came out from the bedroom, the lamp that was in the lounge started rattling and moving. I had a little marble frog in my bedroom, and all of a sudden, it fell through the wall from my bedroom into the main room. It actually went through the wall. I saw it do so. Then a chair that was in the lounge turned around and fell in front of us, and Uri was a little concerned. He said, 'Yasha, I have to write this down. Can you get me a Coke?' And I went into the fridge and, as we opened it, a pencil came out of the can.

"Another time, we went to a gala opening on Broadway called *Galactica*—it flopped. We were sitting there, and Shipi, myself and another Israeli friend of ours were next to Uri. I noticed that there was no arm between our two chairs, and Uri didn't feel very comfortable, so I put my jacket down, and he put his arm on it. We went out and it was pouring with rain and our car was parked in a garage. While I got it, they went into a telephone booth to keep out of the rain. On the way to collect the car, I saw something floating in the air—floating, not falling. It slowly dropped down. I picked it up and I saw it was the arm of the theater chair. I still have it. The funny thing was that, although it landed in a puddle, it was completely dry."

Katz also told of how a large round film-reel box—it had contained Zev Pressman's SRI movie on Uri—apparently teleported from Zürich, where Katz had left it, to New York, where Uri was annoyed about not having it to hand. "We heard a boom," Katz says, "and looked behind us and saw the box appearing from the ceiling and falling into our lounge. We phoned the guy I left it with in Switzerland straight away and asked him where this box was, and he said it's in the cupboard. So we asked him to go and have a look, and he did, and came back and said it's not there.

"When Randi came to Israel to convince me to repudiate Uri, he stayed for hours and he was quite persuasive," Katz concluded. "But I think it was only greed on my part. And then, I only got something like five hundred dollars for this interview, and I was very, very sorry. Later Uri and I were reconciled, and we became friends again and I am strongly behind him. Whatever he thought of me, it took a big man to forgive something like that, and he did. Then, in 1994, I had cancer of the colon and had to go for an operation. Uri obviously didn't know about it, but one day my secretary phoned me just as I was going to the hospital and said, 'Uri Geller phoned you at half past eight.' He hadn't phoned me for at least a year. My wife spoke to him and he said he just felt that something was wrong. I think he phoned about ten times to wish me well."

In the late 1970s, Uri, too, had had health problems, but no one other than he knew about them. It all started, he says, with a call from the impresario Robert Stigwood. "Robert is a multimillionaire. He was the manager of the Bee Gees, he did *Evita, Jesus Christ Superstar* and *Saturday Night Fever.* He first read about me on a plane, in *Time,* when they did their negative story on me. He had a burn on his finger, and he saw my picture, placed his finger on my face, and it healed by the time his flight landed. He called me out of the blue over to his apartment overlooking Central Park. He said, 'Uri, I want your story,' and offered a quarter of a million pounds to sign me on a deal. So he bought the rights to make a major motion picture based on my life. But then one day he said to me, 'You know, Uri, I want you to lose weight if you are going to be in the film.' Now, I was chubby because I loved eating, and I thought about this and said, 'I am not going to give up food. What I will do is when I eat, I'll just vomit it.'

"It was as if I had invented bulimia. I had no idea it already existed. And I didn't know that it would mean me losing minerals and vitamins. So it was a great way for me to continue indulging in the excess of wealth. I was getting rid of guilt, stress, anxiety—and getting myself looking good. I vomited everywhere. When a plane landed, I used to stay on in the first-class compartment until every one got off, and then I would take the sick-bags out. I collected sick-bags from all the airlines. The stewardesses didn't see what I was doing, but at one point, I was asked by a male steward and I said that I collect airline symbols. To tell someone that I collect vomit-bags would have been crazy.

These bags were solely for use in cars, so when I ate a lot of food and we had to drive back home or wherever, I used to sit alone in the back of the limousine, pull out the bag and force myself to vomit in the back of the car. I always managed to do it somehow without anyone noticing. I was really killing myself, slowly but surely.

"I hid it from everyone. It was private. It is hard for me to tell you in words how I camouflaged it, how I hid it, the maneuvers that I used to do, the showers that I turned on, the taps that I let water run in the bath from, the toilets I'd flush, bidets I'd sprinkle, tissues I'd stuff under the doors to muffle the noise of my throwing up. Of course, it was taboo. Compulsion is an understatement, it was an addiction, a total addiction. Hanna noticed I was getting thin, but she thought it was because I was running around the reservoir in Central Park five times. That was my excuse. I'd say, 'I exercise a lot,' and I did. I ran three hours a day. I was already obsessed by money and on an ego-trip where I wanted everything. Now I could walk into a restaurant and order ten desserts and devour everything and still look nice and trim thanks to my excusing myself to go to the toilet, sticking my finger down my throat and vomiting. It was perfect for a control freak like I was."

Eventually Uri saw a doctor because his bulimia was accompanied by panic attacks, when he thought his heart was about to explode. He did not mention the vomiting, so the doctor said there was nothing wrong with him, although he was too thin, and prescribed Valium.

It was in Israel more than in the USA that people noticed his weight loss. "They used to say, 'How thin you are, you're a skeleton, what happened to you?' I used to say, 'Oh, I'm exercising, I couldn't be fitter.' I didn't see the Auschwitz figure staring back at me from the mirror. I saw someone really good-looking, thin. Scales were another obsession of mine. In the morning, I would get up and be on the scale; after breakfast, I would get on the scale, before I went to sleep, I would check. I used to weigh the glasses of water I drank, just to check how many pounds they would add to my weight. And I wrote all these weights down—with shoes, without shoes, with clothes, without clothes. I was so satisfied when my weight was low.

"When I realized that I would kill myself in this vicious cycle I had to stop it. I was being driven back to my apartment from somewhere in the Cadillac, the one I have the spoons on now. I was in the back, and I opened the door, but was so weak I couldn't get myself out of the car. I had to grab the roof and pull myself out. I was losing protein, I was losing fats, I was losing energy. And I remember that I was walking very slowly towards the apartment and I said,

'Wait a minute,' and it all flashed in a few seconds in my mind. I said to my-self, 'OK, Uri, if you don't stop this you'll be dead. Now is the time to stop it.' And in the middle of the street, in the middle of the day, a few feet from the canopy, where that weird teleportation had happened, I shouted, 'ONE, TWO, THREE, STOP!' People looked at me. But who cares? I got into the house, said hello to the doorman, went into the elevator, got out in the apartment and never vomited again. I just stopped.

"After that, I gradually went back to my ordinary weight and even today I imagine I weigh what I was when I was nineteen or twenty. But I don't even know what that is—I don't get on scales anymore. The funny thing was that Robert Stigwood kept paying me lots of money and made me a very wealthy man, but he got busy with his other big movies and never made that film. The rights reverted back to me and I was quite happy. I still speak to him. There's nothing not to be friendly with him about. On the contrary I have to thank him for putting me on a firm financial footing. My bulimia wasn't his fault at all—it was my obsessive personality, I guess. It was vanity, and the obsession that no one tells me what to do. It was not wanting to lose the power of being able to create phenomena around me. And the physical weakness didn't seem to affect my powers."

It was in the midst of his bulimia that Uri became involved in another odd episode. Between 1976 and early 1978, he lived in Mexico City as a sort of psychic court pet to Carmen Romano de Lopez Portillo, known as Muncy, the glamorous wife of the country's president, Jose Lopez Portillo. He was brought to Mexico originally by a TV station. Muncy saw him, was fascinated and introduced him to her husband's predecessor, Luis Echeverria, who had a hunch that Uri could help to locate Mexico's oil reserves. Lopez Portillo put this to the test after he became president in January 1977.

Uri's ability to dowse had been discovered in England by the chairman of the British mining company, Rio Tinto Zinc, Sir Val Duncan, who had met him at a party in London. Duncan advised Uri that there was more money in finding metal than in bending it, took Uri to his villa in Majorca, and told him of his knowledge of dowsing, the ancient art of psychically seeking out hidden precious substances. Then he experimented with Uri, who did well enough for his new patron to try, unsuccessfully, to persuade the RTZ board to take him on as an official dowser. Anglo-Vaal, a South African mining company, as reported by *Newsweek*, employed Uri, with some success, to locate coal deposits in Zimbabwe, but generally, large companies, as Uri later discovered, tended not to want their board and stockholders to know that they were using psychic help. Now he is mainly employed by smaller oil and mineral companies, who hire him under conditions of great secrecy. They certainly seem happy with what they get, Uri said, although he would not tell me who used his services. "I'd love to be able to tell you," he said, "even though only one of the oil companies is a household name. But I don't want to blow my living away, because total non-disclosure is part of my contract in every case. But let me put it this way, this house alone costs £140,000 a year to run, which is quite a lot from taxed income. We travel by helicopter to most places, we live quite well, we give to various charities. I still do some paid entertaining, I write books and columns, but you can't compare that to oil and gold. So you have to ask yourself where my wealth comes from. You have probably gathered that drugs and crime aren't quite my thing. So you may draw the conclusion that someone somewhere has paid me for legitimate work. The price is usually a million dollars, payable in advance, whether the search is successful or not. So I can't complain. Although his dowsing work is an area on which Uri is frustratingly unforthcoming, I got several indications that he does very little anymore, and is probably living on the proceeds of massive successes of some years ago.

An article in the May 1987 edition of the magazine *International Mining* provided some clues as to the specifics of Uri's prospecting work. In 1983, it seems, he was given a contract by an unnamed Japanese corporation to look for gold in Brazil. Over a six-year period he earned two million dollars, a million payable before starting work, a further million on satisfactory completion of the assignment. In 1985, Peter Sterling, the then chairman of an Australian minerals and exploration company, Zanex, hired Uri to prospect for gold and diamonds in the Solomon Islands, in the South Pacific.

Zanex took the unusual step of announcing to its stockholders in an October 1985 statement that as a result of Uri Geller's advice, exploration had been extended to an uninhabited island in the Solomons group, Malaita. A sample taken from a site identified by Geller from an aircraft had been examined by a geologist at Melbourne University, whose report suggested that the presence of Kimberlite meant there could well be diamonds on the site. What Zanex then did with the information was never released; today, the company denies it found anything as a result of Uri Geller's advice, but Peter Sterling, who is no longer with Zanex, was certainly happy to issue an open testimonial to Uri's powers, and told the *Financial Times* on 18 January 1986 that he was "well pleased" with his investment in Geller.

"Our company had been successful with alluvial gold in the Solomon Islands but we were also interested in ore bodies," Sterling told the newspaper.

"We sent Uri some topographical maps and he rang us back and said 'You should be looking for diamonds on Malaita." No one had thought of looking for diamonds on that island—we weren't sure the Solomons were geologically old enough for diamonds—and we were skeptical but he insisted."

Sterling confirmed there had been much opposition from his board to using Uri. "I'm an engineer—I have no idea how it works, though I think that in twenty to thirty years time science will know, and will be building machines to do the same thing. But now—well the reaction is a bit like witchhunters in the dark ages, or flat earthers. There are a lot of flat earthers around." Of the eleven projects Geller had undertaken in the past ten years, the *FT* reported, Geller claimed four as big successes, where the royalties went way beyond his original £1m advance; three or four had been "total failures," and the rest partially successful.

In Mexico in 1976, with a growing foreign-debt nightmare, they were less fastidious than in the developed world about employing a psychic to find oil. When President Elect Portillo invited Uri to Los Piños, the Mexican White House, he brought along a man called Serrano, the director-general of Pemex, the state oil company, who was later jailed for corruption. Uri was put through an informal test in which he was to search Los Piños for a hidden liqueur glass of olive oil. He located it in a flower-pot, which Serrano had rather cleverly buried the glass in, so that the oil was by now part of a lump of greasy dirt. The gathered Mexican elite was delighted, and soon Uri was in a private helicopter with two Pemex geologists, on his way to dowse for oil. Afterward he was told only, by Serrano, that his dowsing had been "very precise." He believes the Mexicans located oil in massive quantities at his suggested site.

He was not paid in money for this work, but instead received the munificent patronage of Muncy, who saw to it that Uri Geller became Mexico's number one citizen, whisked around Mexico City with armed outriders, given all the best seats in the best restaurants, and photographed daily by the press with the First Lady. Uri insists, and he is not one to deny such things, that he was not sleeping with the wife of the Mexican president, and the rather gray, ageing Lopez Portillo does seem to have been very trusting of a handsome thirty-year-old who had once seriously considered being a gigolo as a career. The president presented him with a gold- and silver-plated Colt semi-automatic. He was given a card entitling him to free first-class travel anywhere in the world on Aeromexico, and another identifying him as an agent of the National Treasury, and thus able to carry the gun, even into the US, should he so wish, on his free flights—a hint, perhaps, that even as a Mexican presidential favorite, you couldn't be too careful. He was also given full Mexican citizenship for life, with naturalization certificate number 00001, signed by the president. Shipi was made naturalized Mexican number 00002. Both men also received lifetime Mexican passports, on which they still travel, Uri under his official name in Mexico, Uri Geller-Freud.

Unlikely as the idea sounds of Uri Geller being appointed a gun-carrying agent of the National Treasury of Mexico, impeccable independent corroboration of the story comes from a retired senior special agent of the US Customs Service, Charles S. Koszcka. Koszcka, who is 62, lives in the Bronx and works voluntarily for various churches, remembers being asked one day in 1976 to sort out an unusual situation which had arisen at JFK airport. Geller, whom he had only vaguely heard of at the time, had been stopped by Customs as he entered the US and had a gun seized. He was, Koszcka learned, telling a rather strange story of having top-level Mexican government connections; as a law enforcement officer of a country contiguous with the US, Geller would indeed have a right to carry a firearm. Uri was becoming agitated at the airport and demanding to make calls to Mexico City, but noody quite believed a man famous for being an Israeli spoon-bender might also be a Mexican Treasury agent.

Koszcka, who once studied for the priesthood and majored in philosophy, and whose specialties were art fraud and child obscenity, was put on the case because he had just returned from an art-related assignment in Mexico. "I learned that Geller had made a call to the Mexican government and they had contacted the American embassy in Mexico City, who in turn contacted the State Department, who contacted the head of Customs, who contacted the special agent in charge of New York City, and it was he who was saying, 'Charlie, find out what the big problem is, because the Mexicans are all upset about this.' It was clear the guy had good connections, so he was permitted to leave, but they took his gun away. I visited him at his apartment in Manhattan, and he showed me his credentials and he knew the law. I had to admit, I was impressed by his credentials. They were metallically engraved in gold so that they were more tamper-proof than the ones I carry. So I went out to the airport and got his gun back to him. It was a very nice .45 automatic, an attractive piece of metal, although as one who carried a .357 Magnum on the streets of New York City but am proud of never once needing to fire it, I am not a great devotee of guns."

Even from Mexico, Uri continued making social inroads in the USA, specifically into politics. At a dinner for Henry Kissinger and the wife of the US

President-elect, Rosalynn Carter, Geller bent a silver spoon in Mrs. Carter's hand. He then maneuvered himself next to Kissinger, and promised to read his mind. He recalls that Kissinger recoiled, looked worried and pleaded, "No, no. I don't want you to read my mind. I know too many secrets." Uri said he wanted only to do his telepathy-with-drawings party piece, which went so well that Kissinger asked sharply, "What else did you get from my mind?" Uri replied, jokingly, "I'd better not talk about that here," and Kissinger became quite agitated. An awkward silence followed, until Uri explained he'd been kidding. Nevertheless Kissinger ended the encounter looking thoughtful, Uri said.

Kissinger may have appeared to be ambushed by Geller, but it appears now that this had been orchestrated by a CIA agent, known as Mike, who obviously thought Uri was close enough to the Los Piños regime, yet provenly loyal to the USA, to be useful again. Mexico represented a major security problem to the US: far more than Cuba, it was a huge KGB spying station. Not only was Uri an intimate of the Lopez Portillo circle, which meant he might be able to help influence the Mexicans to reduce Soviet presence in their country, he was also concerned about his and Shipi's visa arrangements back in the USA. Mike worked out that Uri would be happy to help Uncle Sam if Uncle Sam helped him. And although he might not have been representing CIA policy exactly, Mike was interested in the possibilities of psychic spying, and of Uri doing a little work from the outside looking in at the KGB's building in Mexico City. All in all, he seems to have concluded, Uri Geller was a useful asset to the CIA. Not only that, but Mike was fascinated by the fact that Jimmy Carter, who was due to move into the White House in January, appeared to be a fan of the paranormal. Could Uri be used to help bring about funding for an official paranormal program at the CIA? Mike thought and hoped so, and it was he, Uri said, who asked him to approach Kissinger and Mrs. Carter at that Mexico City reception.

Thus began Uri's brief career as an unpaid, voluntary super-spy, or technically as a double agent. Under Mike's direction, he snooped into the business of KGB officers, their local agents and arrangements. It was Mike who introduced the question of whether Uri could stop a man's heart, with special reference to Yuri Andropov, then head of the KGB. "I was used," Uri said, "to erase floppy disks on Aeromexico flights when KGB agents were flying with diplomatic pouches to the West. I did that a few times, because the agents went home via Aeromexico to Paris, and then from Paris took Aeroflot to Russia. I would sit there and concentrate on these pouches chained to their wrists.

I must have been successful, I guess, because the CIA guys kept asking me for more and more. I told them about dropouts and drop-ins in the Russian embassy, and they also took me out to the desert to test if I could move a drone, a spy model airplane, with the power of my mind. I managed to do that too. I just loved it because there were by now two agents in charge of me, and it was so James Bond-y. It brought back the memory of Yoav Shacham's plans for me to become a secret agent."

Mike had now decided, Uri said, to try to get him into the Oval Office, to establish a direct line of communication over his pet psychic-spies project with President Carter. Rosalynn was receptive, Kissinger had apparently been impressed. Mike promised Uri would be in the White House for Carter's inauguration in January at which he wanted him to beam a psychic message into the President's brain to give funds to a paranormal program.

It sounds like an indeterminate mixture of a maverick, anonymous CIA field agent's fantasy and Uri Geller's famously over-the-top imaginative capacity—but for one thing. On 20 January 1977, when Jimmy Carter was inaugurated as the thirty-ninth president of the United States, Uri Geller was at the White House. Apparently Rosalynn Carter said, "Jimmy, this is Uri Geller, you remember, the young Israeli I told you so much about." Uri beamed his psychic message at the President, while shaking his hand. The President asked, "Are you going to solve the energy crisis for us?" Uri says he cannot remember what he answered to this unexpected question.

Seven years later, a report in the *New York Times* claimed that in 1977 Carter ordered a high-level review of Soviet psychic research, and called in Uri Geller to discuss what the Americans could do in response. Uri, never normally reticent, still refuses "to confirm or deny" the *Times* report. I am confident, however, that a half-hour meeting with the President happened exactly as described by the newspaper.

Charlie Kosczka, Uri's new Customs agent friend, similarly tells how, while Uri was still based in Mexico, he endeavored to keep busy—and keep up his profile—in America too. During the 1976–77 "Son of Sam" murders of five young women and a man and the wounding of seven others in the Bronx, Queens and Brooklyn, Kosczka wondered if Uri Geller might be able to help where the police and FBI were getting nowhere. "It was obviously not a US customs matter," Kosczka says, "but I knew a police detective and told him Uri was keen to help. I explained that Uri needed to handle something that belonged to the killer, like his note to a journalist. So the detective asked if the letter could be made available. Uri didn't want to read the contents, but just to get what I would call vibrations. But some lieutenant said, no, we are not going to let this happen, which was frustrating. So as plan two, Uri said could we go to some of the crime scenes. So one Thursday, we went to Forest Hills, and then another area on the way to JFK, between Brooklyn and Queens. Uri walked through these parks and got what I would say was a reaction. He said, 'Charlie, do you have a map of New York City?' I got one of those free ones you could get from gas stations back then, and Uri called me on the Sunday morning and said, 'I think the person who is responsible for these killings lives not in the five Boros, but adjoining them in Yonkers.' I called my detective contact and said for what it is worth this is what he has told me. Then, that Wednesday, David Berowitz was arrested in Yonkers, New York."

Uri and Shipi's sojourn in Mexico, however, came to an abrupt halt. Uri's social progress around Mexico City with Muncy set tongues wagging, not just among the Mexican elite but as far away as Fleet Street, London, where in February 1978 the *Daily Express* gossip column ran a tiny piece headlined "Bending the Rules for Uri." It suggested that observers in Mexico City were speculating that Uri's "warm friendship" with the president's wife was thought to be on the point of precipitating a Mexican Watergate, and talked of the pair "behaving intimately" at a shared holiday in Cancun. The text was telexed to Lopez Portillo by some brave soul in the Mexican embassy in London for him to read over breakfast. Within minutes the president's son, Pepito, was on the phone to Uri to say that his father was in a rage about the *Express* piece, and advising Uri and Shipi to "Get out of Mexico—quickly." They were on a plane to New York—first class Aeromexico, of course—by mid-morning.

Chapter 16

The Magicians

"The fact that I can paint a picture like Picasso doesn't mean that I mean that I am Picasso, or that I could originate something which has the value of a Picasso."

James Randi, in an interview, April 1998

....

Events that I shall call paranormal, although I would still be happy to accept a rational explanation for any or all of them, continued to occur as my research proceeded on this book. These singularly undramatic, unfrightening micro-happenings were new to me. Although I had been aware at various times in my life of a clustering of minor coincidences, and had even read a little Jung and Arthur Koestler on the subject of coincidence, I would not have classed myself as someone who collected suspect paranormal events as if they were stamps. Apart from one occasion in 1972, when my elder brother knocked over a wineglass, which broke in a most unusual way, at what turned out to be the moment at which our father died unexpectedly, I would be hard pressed to think of anything I had witnessed that hinted at the supernatural.

Now, though, since I had begun meeting Uri Geller regularly, I was experiencing such incidents on something like a monthly basis. They continued to follow a couple of patterns, one of which was that they never occurred when I was expecting them. Household machinery functioned normally, our cutlery at home remained stubbornly straight. Then, when it was furthest from my mind, some tiny thing would happen of a Gelleresque nature. Frequently, I noted with interest, this would be when my belief in Uri's powers had taken a dip, which often happened after I had met a magician or was reading the works of Randi, or when my son David underwent a period of doubt, often as a result of seeing some skilled magician on TV. This tendency reinforced in me my growing central belief that the Geller effect involves a subtle interplay between him, or the thought of him, our own subconscious, the material world—and possibly, *just* possibly, some peripheral "outside force" of the type Uri is convinced is behind it.

Another pattern I came to expect, if the paradox of expecting the unexpected can be permitted, was that people's reactions to my peculiar little happenings varied wildly. Something I thought was astonishing would leave others cold; a little oddity I regarded barely worthy of mention would cause friends and colleagues to gasp. My skeptical journalist office mate and research assistant on this book, Gabrielle Morris, often laughed at me when I was amazed by something, but was taken aback by something else I mentioned only as a joke.

One Sunday morning, on the road to Uri's house, I passed an old Peugeot 404 and remarked to myself that it must have been decades since I had seen one. Half an hour later, Uri mentioned that the first luxury car he owned in Israel had been a Peugeot 404. On another Sunday, I had met the whole Geller family in London and they were giving me a lift home. I had invited them in for coffee. As Shipi, who always drives the family, was searching for a parking space, Uri asked me, "Do you have a Labrador dog?" We were all laughing about something, so I felt my pockets and said, "Not on me, no." Then I explained that as we lived in a fifth-floor apartment we couldn't keep a dog, but anyway, we preferred cats. When we arrived my eight-year-old daughter, Ellie, answered the door. She was wearing a T-shirt I had never seen before, with a large photo of a Labrador on the front.

One morning in March 1998, I was in the Geller conservatory when I mentioned that I was thinking of replacing my aging Radio Shack microcassette recorder with a MiniDisc machine. Uri jumped over to a pile of things behind me and extracted from it a new Sony MiniDisc he had just bought. My tape machine was on a table behind me as we admired the Sony. When I turned back to the table, I noticed that part of its metal casing had warped most oddly, and looked as if it had tried to peel itself off. The next day, its motor failed. The following day it started working again. A week later, I happened to pass the same branch of Radio Shack on Market Street, San Francisco, where I had bought it five years earlier. On impulse having decided against buying a MiniDisc, I went in and bought a replacement machine. An hour later, when I opened the box, I found a similar but smaller warp in the new recorder's casing.

One Saturday in our local high street, I went into an optician's to get replacement lenses for David's sunglasses, whose frames were made of nitinol, Eldon Byrd's "memory metal," now commercially available in unbreakable spectacle frames. You can sit on nitinol frames, twist them or even bend the arms over double and they will spring back to their original shape. The optician was looking up the price of new lenses, as I was saying to David that I had to hurry: I was going over to Uri and I was late. As I spoke, one of the arms of the glasses snapped in two between my fingers—a sheer break in metal so tough you could tie a knot in it. The time of the break, incidentally, was 11:11 a.m.—a number Uri believes is so powerful that he has incorporated it in one of his phone numbers.

In June 1998, as I mentioned in Chapter 9, Uri came to see me in my office, which is round the corner from our flat. He sat on Gabrielle's chair. After he left, the electric clock, which has hung above the chair for some five years, went wrong. After testing the batteries, we threw it away. When I got home, Sue, my wife, who did not know that Uri had been over, showed me something odd that had happened during the afternoon—when Uri had been at the office. She had been replacing a lightbulb but when she took the new one out of the packet its entire metal base was warped at a thirty-degree angle. A coincidence, I'm sure. For twenty years, she or I have changed lightbulbs, but the first bent one cropped up on the day Uri Geller passed by . . . A couple of days later Gabrielle bought a replacement office clock. As she hung it up it fell off the wall and broke. To my surprise, she found this more remarkable than the original one failing.

A few days later, I was trying to e-mail Leon Jaroff, the retired *Time* writer in Long Island who had written the Geller story in 1973. My CompuServe software went into spasm, and the e-mail would not go. I had to reboot the computer twice before it was sent. As it went, my Psion Series 5 palmtop computer had a minor fit for the first time in its life, and needed resetting. As I was doing that, I was hit by a waft of some sweet smell so strong that I winced. Seconds later I had recognized it as the incense the Gellers often use at their house.

I went over to the Gellers another Saturday morning to take a photo of the whole family. A couple of photographers had warned me to take an extra camera if I went there, as Uri had stopped theirs working. As I arrived I checked out my Minolta. It was fine. When Uri appeared, and I tried to use it, its electronics were dead. After he had held his hands over it, it worked long enough to take a few shots, then died for good. While I had been waiting for the family to get ready, I had sat in the kitchen reading a supplement of the *Guardian*. I made a mental note to buy a copy later in the day. After I had taken the photo and had coffee with the family, I left. On the back seat of the car when I reached home, lay the *Guardian* supplement. I had not bought the paper—or stolen the Gellers' copy!

When I went to interview James Randi in Fort Lauderdale, Florida, I confess—with apologies to Randi—that I played a little stunt. It did not come off quite as I had planned. As I was driving up the freeway from Miami airport, to which I had flown in from Houston, I called Uri 3,500 miles away on my cellular phone. I told him I was about to go into Randi's office—why didn't he try to make something really strange happen right in front of Randi's eyes? Uri sounded sheepish, as if I was asking a little too much of him. When I got to Randi's, I moved two of the heavy spoons I had brought with me from England from my suitcase into my shoulder bag. I wanted to see the great man's spoon-bending skills. I checked the spoons, which were brand-new, in tissue, with their Dickins and Jones' price labels on them. They were in good order. During the interview nothing odd happened. But when I got out the spoons, I frowned: one already had a little distortion in the middle of the handle, a ripple. Randi saw it, said, "That's faulty from the manufacturing process, you get a lot like that," and rushed on to do his—quite impressive—stuff with the other. I found myself almost hustled into agreeing with him. Later I wondered, what was I *talking* about? I had looked at the spoon with great care in the car and had established that it was perfect.

After the interview, Randi left, but two of the people in his office—a college student and a local schoolboy—asked if I wanted to go for something to eat. I thanked them, but refused: I had a long drive ahead of me. It was already 7 p.m., and I had to drive to Sarasota, on the other side of Florida, for a story I was doing for *Time*. I realized it was a little late now to phone home—it was midnight in the UK—although it was two or three days since I had spoken to my family. Still, they had my cellular number so could always reach me in an emergency. I took the wrong route and drove for longer than I had expected, six or seven hours across endless country roads. What I did not realize was that the cellular didn't work in the backwoods of central Florida. While I was still driving, my family were trying anxiously to reach me. I got to bed at 2 a.m., knowing I would almost certainly sleep through until lunchtime the next day.

At eight, however, I awoke with a violent start. I was furious, certain that even with the curtains closed to prevent the Florida sun streaming into the hotel room, I would not get back to sleep. Five minutes later, I felt the urgent, almost desperate, need to call home. My elder daughter answered, sounding shocked. "How the hell did you know?" she shouted. I could hear that there was uproar at home. It turned out that the family had been trying to track me down by phoning every Marriott Courtyard hotel in Florida, to no avail. Then they had had the idea of calling Uri. He confirmed that I had called him the previous evening, and told them to wait: he would wake me up. He concentrated hard for a few minutes. Over in Florida, I woke up with that annoying start. If I had dialled the moment I awoke, I would have been on the phone home within thirty seconds of Uri's psychic wake-up call. Back in England, a Seiko Kinetic watch Uri had given me for my birthday (he liked the similarity of its name to "psychokinetic") appeared spontaneously to wind itself forward by ten days after we had had a minor disagreement on the telephone. The date-change adjustment on this mechanical Seiko model is a fiddly one, especially when the watch is worn; for it to trip ahead accidentally is, I would judge, pretty well impossible. Another time, I called my office late at night to find my phone busy. Assuming I had merely knocked it off the hook, but concerned that perhaps the office had been burgled, I drove there. The phone was off the hook; I replaced it and drove away. Two minutes down the road, my cellular phone went. It was Uri, asking what was going on. "Nothing particular," I replied, puzzled. "So why did you leave me that bizarre message?" he demanded. "Was it just a joke?" I asked what he was talking about. He insisted he had just had a garbled phone call from me, in which I, or someone with a remarkably similar voice to me, had apparently said, "Uri, I'm locked in my office, I can't get anyone to rescue me, please help," and then hung up. He had called back, but found the office phone busy and therefore tried me on my mobile. The mysterious "rescue me" call had not registered as coming from a traceable number.

Was I going mad? I don't think so. Was I reading more into things than they deserved? Very possibly. Dr. Graham Wagstaff, the psychologist at Liverpool University, had experienced the apparently inexplicable spontaneous healing of his Ford Anglia in Newcastle without it changing his life or his belief system. I knew I had to see some stage magicians, who would surely talk some sense into me.

If, of course, I could get them to talk straight, something I was to discover many find quite difficult. The central magicians' ethic of never revealing tricks has been, it seems, a confounded nuisance in their attempts to destroy what Randi now calls "the unsinkable Geller."

The first magician I contacted was Ian Rowland, a London illusionist who specializes in replicating Geller effects as a way of promoting the skeptical view. After a lengthy e-mail correspondence Ian refused to see me, ostensibly because I would not pay him for interviewing him. I suspect, however, that the underlying reason was more fundamental: after all, in the time he took e-mailing me, I could have interviewed him twice over. "Sorry," he wrote early on, "but as I've studied Geller closely and continuously for the past 25 years, we will have to agree to differ about the value you place on my potential contribution to your book." Ian seemed to be one of those people who weigh every word less to clarify than to obfuscate. His Web site carries a prime example, for me, of this exasperating trait. "How to walk on water," announces one section. When you click on it, intrigued that he might be giving away an illusion as a free sample, you find a request from him to e-mail his Web site address to three other people who might find it interesting. "It's a big favor to ask, but if you do it, you'll walk on water in my eyes," he writes. Very droll.

David Berglas, one of the world's greatest (though now retired) illusionists, was another matter, and far more effective than Ian Rowland at deflecting me from my growing belief in Uri. After I went to Berglas's home in Cockfosters, north London one wet Sunday afternoon, I have to confess I nearly threw in the towel as far as believing Geller was concerned, as he was the first informed person I came across to challenge my original premise: that a spoon bent in front of me without Uri Geller touching it.

David, president of the British Magic Circle, has a complex connection with Geller. He was originally an enemy, who was present in the audience taking notes on the Dimbleby *Talk-In*, and later gave Randi the idea for his debunking book while the two were in a London taxi going to Fleet Street to explain to journalists how they were being fooled. He was a founder member of the British skeptics' organization but later left it because of its narrow-mindedness, which he found "unintelligent," and became a dear friend of Geller. At the age of seventy-two, he is not a convert to belief in the paranormal, yet is an advocate of the view among a remarkably high proportion of magicians that a part of what they do *does* defy rational explanation.

It sometimes seemed as we spoke that the only difference between David Berglas and Uri Geller was semantic: what Uri calls psychic, David calls intuition. "Some things in my professional career happened that I don't know how they happened," he explained. "Something would work because of extreme luck, or you'd made a lucky guess, but again and again and again. It's perfectly possible for a psychic to be a magician and a magician to be a bit psychic. I'm not a skeptic. I have an open mind, and like to investigate things. Having been part of CSI-COP, I now regard skeptics as scoffers, who are ignorant about magic.

"My definitive statement about Uri is this. If the man is a genuine psychic, has paranormal abilities, can bend metal by his mind, can duplicate a drawing that you're only thinking of, can make seeds sprout, stop and start a watch, can do all the other things that he claims, then he's a world phenomenon, because he's the only person who can do it, and must be respected. In my lifetime, nobody else has ever achieved such international fame and incredible respect. If, on the other hand, he's a charlatan, a cheat, a con man, a magician, a trickster, a crook, and he's achieved that level of notoriety, you must respect him. Whichever way you look at him, he's a phenomenon. Even magicians haven't pinpointed what he does. The public are demanding, and he's done it consistently everywhere in the world. You can't get away with doing something badly and get such acclaim."

But he was not prepared to go as far as endorsing Uri. "I'm afraid I don't accept your description of what you saw," he said, of my first Geller experience. "But I know what *could* have happened or *might* have happened. As a magician, people who say, 'I'm not going to miss this because I'm not going to take my eyes off it,' are fine. That's what I want. That's how I can fool scientists, because I know how they think. Sleight-of-hand, the hand is quicker than the eye, this is all fallacy. It's not the answer. Yes, some tricks work that way, and most magicians are interested just in moves of the hand, but there's far more to it in the psychological area."

"But," I protested, "our spoon *bent*. It flexed like a little Loch Ness monster arching its back. Surely we are agreed that to bend a piece of metal pressure has to be applied to it, aren't we?"

David Berglas smiled patiently. "No," he said quietly. "There is no one answer to that."

As I was leaving, David said: "I can hear how confusing this is to you. If I had a video of what happened I might be able to tell you more. But when we did tests with some of the mini-Gellers, the child metal-benders, back in the early 1970s, we got Customs men, trained in close observation, to watch, but not one of whom detected anything untoward. They would *swear* they had seen the spoon bend, but I saw as a magician that the children had cheated. They were very, very adept, and what made it more complicated was that a lot of them genuinely thought they *weren't* cheating. They were self-deluded. Just bear one thing in mind. Uri, whom I love very dearly as a friend, never does anything in front of me."

What was David Berglas getting at when he denied that you have to use physical pressure to bend metal, and when he said that the children believed they were metal-benders but weren't? Had what he said been patter, another example of the magicians' habit of never answering a question properly?

Even his parting shot, that Uri had never so much as bent a spoon for him, was puzzling, because his son Marvin has seen Uri do this several times. Marvin Berglas is an accomplished close-up magician, who designs tricks for his own company, Marvin's Magic, the largest of its kind in the world, with shops in Hamley's and Harrods in London, FAO Schwartz and Caesar's Palace in the USA. "I watch for any sleight-of-hand big-time, I really do," Marvin said, when I called him, "I have also seen it and studied tapes and watched it on TV. But you tend to get so wrapped up in Uri, in his personality, that you are wanting it to happen, and you are willing it to happen. It's a nice little trick, yes. It looks absolutely perfect the way it bends. I also find it fascinating that as he gets older, he seems to get exhausted by doing it. Is he a magician? I am not skeptical, but I veer on the side that there is logic behind most of these things. Personally, I think he is a mixture of things. Let's say, if he is a magician, he has got to be one of the best, if not the best, in the world."

My meeting with Randi, in contrast to the one with David Berglas, was not disturbing. Randi's position is so well known, of course, that seeing him was almost a formality. He seemed defensive, which is unusual for someone on the attack. "Do I call you Randi or James?" I asked, as we sat down. "You can call me God if you want," he replied. I established that he preferred Randi, after all.

My first question was whether he thought spoon-bending was a good trick. "God, what a dumb thing," he replied. "I think it's a pretty stupid trick and I'm talking about the tricky way, not the divine way that Mr. Geller does it. I have to be very careful about that. He says he does it with divine help from the planet Hoova and the great flying saucer in the air. I am very careful to say that if that's the way he does it, then OK, he can have his fantasy if he wants. I would simply say that when I first saw it, I thought it was a parlor trick. It's the kind of thing you do at Boy Scout Camp, but it didn't amount to much more than that. But you must admit that if the simplest sleight-of-hand trick were real, then we would have to rewrite the laws of science as we know them."

When Randi bent the spoon for me, his hands moved at extraordinary speed, like a blur of light; they do so even in ordinary conversation. He brought the spoon close to my face, then moved it back again, playing havoc with my focus and perception. He took me into a video-viewing room to show me a clip of tape from a BBC Noel Edmonds show, in which, he claimed, Geller cheated. With Randi and his two young assistants sneering at the screen and shouting excitedly, "There's the move, look at it!" I could have been persuaded, but it would be a hair's breadth judgment. And even if he had cheated, I see no logical reason why that meant, *ergo*, Uri Geller could only cheat.

As for my experience with Uri and the spoon, Randi said, "I have no idea what you saw." At this one of the boys, a striking lad of fifteen with a pony-tail and wearing a tuxedo over a black T-shirt, offered the wisdom of his experience. "What happens is, every time you repeat the story, it becomes fresher in your memory than the actual event. We are only capable of seeing so much and observing so many things." This reminded Randi of a story of a national TV presenter, whom he begged me not to name, who believed—wrongly, he says—that Geller bent a key in her hand. "She really, honestly believes that he never touched the key, because she has told the story again and again."

Why, I wondered, are scientists wrong when they support Geller but right when they support Randi? "They are not right or wrong, they are not sufficiently informed," he said. "When they become sufficiently informed, I have had a number of scientists turn right around in midstream. Look at John Taylor in England. He is a perfect example of a well-informed, educated man with a good mind, but who made the assumption that he is so intelligent and such a good observer that what he saw doesn't have any explanation. But it did have an explanation, one about which he didn't know."

Would anything ever persuade Randi that there was something in even the most routine parapsychology? "All I say is that the parapsychologists haven't come up with anything to this point. As soon as they do, I'll accept it, no question of it, and gladly, as long as there is good evidence." The older of Randi's assistants, another handsome, bright fellow, chipped in with a critique of quantum theory, a branch of science that Randi had said sounded too much like metaphysics for his liking. The young man followed his own confident view by stating: "There is no room for the phenomenon of parapsychology."

Why, I asked Randi, should we believe you if you are, as you say, a charlatan? "It is quite possible that I'm fooling you," he admitted. "I don't really have two hats. I'm an entertainer. Basically, I use trickery to produce the effect of a genuine wizard, someone who has magical powers, and that's what the David Copperfields and the Paul Danielses and all the people over the world who actually do this sort of thing accomplish. But I do highly resent people who are doing tricks and claiming that they are the real thing. That is a prostitution of my art. If David Copperfield were to come on stage and say to his audience that he is really going to cut this girl in two with a saw, you would be reasonably offended that he would ask you to believe some stupid statement like that."

So did James Randi feel he owed Uri Geller something, for having given him his vocation in life? "No, I'm not thankful for it," Randi said. "I was fighting little spiritualists and people who were selling dowsing rods in New York. Then along came Geller, and suddenly we had a major figure here who was fooling scientists in a very big think tank. But we're not concerned with Geller now. He is a fait accompli. We have done with him long ago. And if anyone is still going to believe it, in spite of the evidence we produced, then there is no hope for them." It was odd that Randi was saying that he was not concerned with Geller any more, yet two months earlier he had written him that vituperative thirteen-page letter detailing why he regards him as a fraud—and hates him so profoundly.

Randi's assertion that there is "no hope" for anyone who believes in Geller will amuse a young American magician called David Blaine. Blaine is a new cult figure in America, where he has astonished prime-time TV audiences with his brand of what he calls street magic. In many ways, Blaine is a new Uri Geller. His trademark effect is an uncanny levitation in which he stands any-where—but he prefers to do it in a public spot such as on a city sidewalk—and appears to rise slowly above the ground before sinking back again. Already, just as happened with Uri, a storm of controversy has blown up among magicians over Blaine. Many of his tricks are routine magic-shop products, but performed with terrific style. His levitation, however, has them foxed. Anguished debates are unfolding on the Internet over how he does it, and several rival videos are available, claiming to teach people to replicate the effect. Some say Blaine cannot do his levitation without specially adapted Converse sneakers. Others say that when ABC TV launched him with a lengthy David Blaine special in 1998 they enhanced their video to make the levitations look better. Some magicians even suggest that Blaine may be the "real thing," genuinely able to levitate. Blaine has a highly mystical outlook, and does not deny that he is truly para-normal. None of the furor, just as with Uri again, has done him any harm. In his early twenties, a laid-back New Yorker, handsome, and a must-have at private celebrity parties, he gets more famous by the day. His best friend is Leonardo DiCaprio—and his ultimate hero is Uri Geller.

Uri had never heard of David Blaine until, one day in the spring of 1998, Blaine phoned out of the blue from New York to ask if he could meet him. Uri agreed, and within twenty-four hours Blaine had flown over, checked himself into Brown's Hotel and had taken a train out to Reading. I went to meet the young American too, and was greeted by a fascinating scene. In his kitchen, Uri was trying to teach Blaine to move a compass by the power of his mind. So intently were the two men concentrating that I am not sure that either realized I was there. Uri was indicating a point in the center of his forehead and explaining passionately, with his fist clenched for emphasis, how the power came from HERE, HERE. Blaine had not yet managed to do it. (The center of the forehead, site of the pineal gland, is thought by many serious students of the paranormal to be the "third eye," where our sixth sense is located.) Was this all a contrivance for my benefit? Or was Uri Geller, illusionist, trying to pull the wool over the eyes of David Blaine, illusionist? I can't say for sure, but I had the strong feeling it was a powerful demonstration of Uri's deep belief in his powers.

All the Geller family, plus the crew of a Virgin helicopter that Uri had hired to take Blaine for a spin around the locale, had seen Blaine's levitation and said it was extraordinary. Blaine took me outside into the garden for a chat away from Uri. "I wanna tell you something," he said, his voice slow and deep. "I've seen some things here today. Uri bent a spoon for me. The first time he did it, you know, I thought there must be a trick. The second time I was stunned, completely, completely stunned and amazed. It just bent in my hand. I've never seen anything like it. It takes a lot to impress me. Uri Geller is for real and anyone who doesn't recognize that is either deluding himself, or is a very sad person." Was Blaine a paranormal or a regular magician, I asked. He parried the question skilfully, but made it fairly clear that he was a hybrid. He asked me if I had ever seen levitation. I had not, and he said, "OK, let's do it." He turned his back toward me, and shuffled his feet. I was interested to see him from the side, so moved round to get a different viewing angle. He turned round again so his back was to me, but he was clearly not happy. Perhaps I seemed negative. "You know, I've done this so many times today, I don't think I can get it right now," he said. "Let's go in and eat." So I never saw a levitation, other than on the ABC TV film, which he brought over with him, and we all watched over dinner. It was certainly amazing to watch—but I noticed that he always had his back to the people for whom he levitated. I left later laughing to myself. I remembered David Berglas saying that Uri had never done anything in front of him. Was I now the sort of person for whom psychics would never perform because I knew too well what to look for?

The friendship between Geller and Blaine grew apace. Blaine sprung to US and worldwide fame in April 1999, when his second, and still more amazing, TV special was aired, immediately following a public "buried alive" stunt by Blaine in Manhattan on a scale not seen since the heyday of Houdini. At a site on Donald Trump's Riverside Boulevard, Blaine had himself interred for a week in a glass coffin surrounded by tons of water, and invited the public to come and see

him a state of apparent suspended animation. It was a spectacular feat that Houdini had considered but never achieved, and alongside the hundreds of news crews
and photographers present when Blaine emerged from the coffin was Houdini's
niece, Marie Blood, Uri Geller—and James Randi. Randi had been brought along
by a TV station to check out whether Blaine, perhaps, only appeared to be in the
coffin and the public was in fact viewing a hologram. Randi seemed embarrass-
ingly to have no rational explanation for Blaine's feat—which may explain why,
when approached by a conciliatory (but possibly just plain mischievous) Uri offering a handshake of peace, Randi turned his back on him and snarled that he
hated his guts.

Another, and thankfully less confrontational, magician I ran into in my investigation was the twenty-eight-year-old Guy Bavli. Son of an ace Israeli
fighter pilot who now flies for El Al, Bavli is Israel's current answer to Uri
Geller. As I said earlier, Bavli is unstinting in his praise of Geller, although he
has never seen him other than on TV. However, he resolutely rejects the paranormal or the idea that the mind might have any unknown power. "Uri Geller
is a genius, but that doesn't mean he's supernatural," Bavli explained, and went
on to set out a view I had often heard expressed in Israel. "I think he's the most
gifted magician in the world. But I don't actually care what he really is," he
said. "In fact, I don't understand why people like you are so obsessed with
whether he's 'real' or not. If he's managed to convince the world for thirty
years that he's a psychic, for me, that's a major part of the illusion. In fact it's
better than being psychic. If you were born psychic, then so what? But what
Geller has done is a fabulous achievement."

Bavli recommended that I see the man who taught him spoon-bending,
Roni Schachnaey, the grand president of the Israeli Society for Promoting the
Art of Magic. Schachnaey was an early thorn in Uri's side, a prominent and respected magician in Israel, where he still performs regularly as the Great
Ronaldo. Two years older than Geller, Schachnaey performs, as well as high-
class conjuring, a mentalist act in which he replicates the whole of Geller's
repertoire, from spoon-bending to ESP.

A little incongruously for a leading magician in Israel, the Great Ronaldo is
based in Scarborough, in North Yorkshire, where he owns a fish-and-chip
shop with two holiday flats above it, and lives in a cozy former council house
with his English wife. In Britain, too, he performs a Geller-style act, part entertainment, part a pointed, non-paranormal dig at Geller; in Britain, he is
known as Ronaldo Wiseman, complete with mystical paraphernalia and
ponytail. The obvious contrast between Schachnaey's level of material success

and Uri Geller's could not be greater, and yet he was neither bitter nor resentful when I met him. He seems a happy man. Although he had clashed in the past with Uri in Israel, his main concern was to be reconciled with him—which I brought about by giving Uri Roni's phone number. They were soon chatting away like old friends and arranging to meet up.

And yet Roni Schachnaey is still Uri's bitter opponent, claiming that he is "more skilled at manipulating the truth" than as a performer. Schachnaey has a complicated relationship with both psychism and skepticism. He insists there is no such thing as being psychic, yet admits that mentalism is *almost* psychic, or at least "intuitive." Then again, his CompuServe address is "Psychicservices," and, while on stage in his Ronaldo Wiseman guise, he claims psychic powers, although he leaves the audience in no doubt that in reality this is not so.

Schachnaey is friendly with the professional skeptics, but accuses them of being consumed with unnecessary venom and regards James Randi as someone "who would be a nothing if it weren't for Uri Geller." He regards Uri, meanwhile, as "a great man," thanks him for giving him his livelihood, and regrets only Uri's belief in the supernatural, which is where he diverges from him. "Uri should be the rabbi of the mentalists, the successor to the great Houdini, not wasting his time doing silly things with football teams like he does today," Schachnaey said.

Leaving Roni Schachnaey and speeding home across the Yorkshire countryside, the old post-Berglas confusion crept back into my feelings about Uri. Although strictly "hands-on," Schachnaey's spoon-bending was the best I had seen from the Uri Geller clones, and was far better than Randi's. Could Schachnaey be right? Maybe Uri Geller *is* a magician who simply fell among "spiritual" people and began to believe in himself. Yet while Schachnaey derides Uri's stage work as naïve, and says he can't see why people regard his younger countryman even as charismatic, the central paradox remains: Uri Geller is a world-famous multimillionaire, while Roni Schachnaey is not; if both, as Roni insists, are merely illusionists, it would appear that Uri is the better insofar at least as he has illusioned more people out of their cash.

The Randi premise that magicians universally hate Uri Geller and consider him a fraud is faulty: Geller has gathered some impressive (and apparently straight-talking) testimonials from some in the profession. In 1974, he agreed to be examined by Leo Leslie, a leading mentalist and magician in Denmark. "The judgment of all of us who were present for what occurred was one of total endorsement of Geller's paranormal claims," Leslie wrote in a book published in Denmark on Geller. "While Geller was in Copenhagen, I did not catch him in any deceptions. Therefore I have to continue to rely on my own judgment and experience as a mentalist; they tell me that Uri Geller is genuine." Arthur Zorka, a member of the Society of American Magicians, is on record as saying, "There is no way, based on my knowledge as a magician, that any method of trickery could have been used to produce the effects under the conditions to which Geller was subjected." Ben Robinson, a coming name in magic in New York and on TV in the US, has said, "His psychic gifts are genuine and he provides a model for humanity at large to aspire to." The Reverend Roger Crosthwaite, an Anglo-Catholic priest in Worthing, Sussex, a former British Close-up Magician of the Year and the author of several books on magic, said on BBC Radio 5 in 1993, after meeting Uri and seeing him perform: "I know a little bit about sleight-of-hand, I know a little bit about the methods of revealing what a person is thinking, through body language and through other means, and I would challenge any magician to duplicate [Geller's] effect with me."

There is another possible answer to the baffling connection between Uri Geller and the traditional conjuring world, hinted at by Berglas and David Blaine but regarded as heresy by more bread-and-butter sleight-of-hand men—and which, incidentally, makes a nonsense of this book's title, *Uri Geller: Magician or Mystic?*. The theory is that magicians and mystics are not different species altogether, but are different genera of the same species. It is a startling idea, which explains a great deal about the suspicion that Uri is in possession of more conjuring skills than he cares to admit, and that some of the great mentalists, and even straightforward conjurers, seem to have something of the supernatural about them.

The idea is often mooted by out-and-out paranormalist writers like Colin Wilson and Lyall Watson, who have speculated that even men like Randi have *psi* abilities, but was also floated by a skeptic, Professor Truzzi, the Michigan sociologist, in a landmark 1996 paper, "Reflections on the Sociology and Social Psychology of Conjurors and Their Relations with Psychical Research" (It appeared in Advances in Parapsychological Research 8, by Stanley Krippner, published by McFarland & Co., 1997). Truzzi discovered that, in private, magicians *do* believe in *psi* and ESP, but cover up their belief in public because they feel it is more respectable in a scientific age not to make paranormal claims. He discovered a 1981 survey in California, in which eighty-two percent of magicians at an assembly expressed a belief in ESP; a 1980 poll of members of the German Magic Circle found that seventy-two percent thought *psi* was probably real. Truzzi took his own poll in 1979 among members of the Psychic Entertainers' Association, an international group dedicated to the simulation of *psi*—the kind of act Roni Schachnaey and Ian Rowland do. He was surprised to find that eighty-seven percent of the members believed *psi* "truly exists." In 1993, Truzzi noted, the belief seemed to have declined, with only forty-seven percent of PEA members saying they believed in ESP, twenty percent unsure, and thirty-three percent saying they did not.

What had happened between 1979 and 1993? Perhaps Randi's message had sunk in among a new generation of conjurers. But what was more likely, Truzzi thought, was that the apparent reduction in ESP belief was the result of a change in membership of the association. By 1993, far more amateurs belonged than professional performers. It seemed to Truzzi that professional magicians, with their superior skills and experience, were more inclined to believe in ESP than amateurs.

From that deduction different people will reach different conclusions, but it suggests that magicians are not the unanimous, anti-paranormal, anti-Geller front of the Amazing Randi's imagination—and that the better and more successful they are, the more likely they are to acknowledge that Uri Geller really is something extraordinary.

If James Randi pulled off the brilliant feat of making common cause between conjuring, philosophical rationalism and science, Marcello Truzzi may be likened to a complicated road intersection, where skepticism meets occultism, and merges with magicianship. He is one of the most learned men I have ever met, his book collection rivals many local libraries, with some nine thousand volumes on his specialties, conjuring, mentalism, scientific anomalies, skepticism, occultism—and Uri Geller.

Son of the greatest juggler of his generation, Truzzi's first love is magic. "There are a lot of things in the magical community which border on real magic or real psychic phenomena," he explained. "There are some things which are well understood like muscle reading, contact reading, being able to sense movements in someone, in cold-reading techniques. That's far in advance of the basic stuff that the mentalists all know. Things such as, if you're asked to choose one of five objects, people always go for the second from the left. If you're asked to think of a number between one and fifty, two digits, both odd, most people will come up with thirty-seven. Think of a vegetable, most will say carrot, a wild animal, eighty percent go for a lion."

Wonderful revelations for the uninitiated, but the principal question to ask of Truzzi was how he developed a friendship with Uri Geller without ever having believed he was a real psychic, or even seen him bend a spoon? "I was

led to believe that Uri's motives could be nefarious, that he might start a religious cult. There were lots of rumors Randi and others were spreading
about that he was bilking wealthy people, and all kinds of alleged backstage
stuff, which I was inclined to think might be true at that time. But, as time
went on, I realized that Uri fitted the mold of a lot of mentalists in the past.
I began to wonder about some of my skeptical colleagues, and whether they
were mis-estimating him. I didn't see the horror of what he was doing. As I
saw it, mentalists have always fooled scientists. Mentalists are like that. Houdini escaped from prisons, supposedly, when really there was collusion with
the wardens.

"As soon as I met Uri, here in Ann Arbor at a radio station, the first thing
he said to me was, 'I know you don't believe in me and what I do, but I don't
see why your skepticism should prohibit our friendship.' What else could I ask
for? He wasn't asking for me to commit to him. And I have no reason not to
think he's a decent human being. He's a performer. That's what he does. And
anyway, hell, he might be real. I'm still hoping something truly paranormal is
going on here. So I see no reason to be hostile to him. Over time I have found
him to be a decent man, a very charitable person, a very caring, sincere person. And at the same time I found that a lot of my fellow skeptics turned out
to be pretty unscrupulous, and were as bad as the people they were criticizing.
In my opinion, most of the people in the skeptics' movements are scoffers, and
I make a big distinction. They are like the atheists as opposed to the agnostics.
As far as a smoking gun is concerned, the closest they're going to get is the odd
videotape, which is inconclusive. You couldn't get a jury to convict him as
being guilty beyond reasonable doubt with that."

Truzzi contends, as a sociologist, that parapsychology is more tough-
minded than many other academic fields yet, paradoxically, it remains a fringe
subject. "Parapsychologists really want to play the game by the proper statisti-
cal rules," he said. "They're very staid. They thought they could convince these
skeptics but the skeptics keep moving the goalposts. It's ironic, because real
psychic researchers are very committed to doing real science, more than a lot
of people in science are. Yet they get rejected, while we can be slipshod in psychology and sociology and economics and get away with it. We're not painted
as witch doctors but they are."

Randi would have been less than delighted to know that I was going to see
Truzzi, but he was keen for me to meet Mike Hutchinson, Britain's leading
skeptic and anti-Geller campaigner, as well as the UK representative of the
CSICOP publishing offshoot, Prometheus Books.

I spent a fascinating couple of hours in Loughton, Essex, with Hutchinson. He is an intellectual version of Forrest Gump's box of chocolates: you never know what you're going to get. Although Hutchinson's hero is Houdini—who believed in reincarnation, premonitions and once claimed to have seen an apparition of his mother—and he has been Randi's friend for over twenty years, he professes not to be keen on magicians. "Because I am basically honest, I am not good at conjuring because I don't like fooling people and telling lies to people," he said. "Sometimes magicians have a superior-than-thou attitude, and all this stuff about exposure of magic and its secrets is just silly."

Hutchinson also has a clever line in lateral thinking, which I admire. "Geller getting on TV programs talking about football and claiming he can help teams win is very funny, because in my opinion if he helps a team and really has psychic powers, that would be cheating. So when Geller says he is cheating, I don't think he is, but when he says he isn't cheating, I think he is."

What did he think of my growing contention that professional skeptics are merely the modern version of Flat Earthers? "I don't think it's a good suggestion," he said calmly. "Skeptics are often called closed-minded, but they are more likely to change their minds than believers. What would convince somebody who is into astrology that astrology doesn't work? Nothing. What would convince a skeptic? A really good trial. It's the same with Geller. Hardly anything would make a believer disbelieve in him. Even if he admitted tomorrow that he was a fake, there'd still be people who wouldn't believe it."

Would he ever be prepared to believe in *psi*, considering the success people like Professor Jahn at Princeton University, in New Jersey, are now having? "I am almost prepared to say that now, although I don't think that the evidence is absolutely irrefutable. But even if there was something which was only noticeable through statistics, it still wouldn't mean the psychic or the metal-bender is able to do what they claim. It would be a very, very weak effect, which would be extremely interesting, but it would mean nothing to the man in the street.

"Did you know I caught Uri Geller bending a spoon physically?" Hutchinson asked, after showing me a clip from an ancient Oprah Winfrey show in Baltimore, *People Are Talking*, in which it looks possible, although by no means conclusive, that a spoon-bending Uri did was not quite on the level. Hutchinson claims to have spotted his "cheating" incident at Olympia in London, at a charity Telethon. "While Geller was doing his bit on stage, I was actually showing some of the people in the front of the audience how to break a spoon in two," he recalled. "I saw him bend the spoon physically, and I looked underneath his hand to see that it was already bent, and said, 'I think you've already bent that. You are hiding the bend with your fingers.' And he said, 'Shame on you. This is for charity.' After that, when he offered to auction the spoon, nobody volunteered to pay for it, and somebody at the back of the audience said, 'I'll give you ten pounds,' so he signed it, and off he and Shipi went. As they left I introduced myself. He said, 'Do you believe in God?' I said, 'No.' He said, 'Well, fuck you,' and walked away. I shouted after him, 'Well, you're not God, Uri,' and that was that. I wrote it up the same day for a skeptics' magazine." (Uri is amused by the idea of Hutchinson believing he caught him red-handed, when nobody else has, in decades. "It's wishful thinking, Mike's fantasy," he responds to Hutchinson's Olympia story. "It's possible he really believes what he says. A lot of these skeptics believe all kinds of strange things.")

So, thanks to Uri Geller, magic begat skepticism, skepticism begat Prometheus Books and Prometheus, being the mythological bringer of light, begat CSICOP. These days, however, Prometheus sheds a diffuse light from its New York state headquarters and Essex outpost in Mike Hutchinson's flat. Although it still claims a strictly rationalist ethic, rationalism has come to include libertarianism and, from there on, pretty much anything goes. Prometheus Books, rationalism's brave riposte to Uri Geller and the forces of medieval darkness, has had to diversify, a demonstration, perhaps, of the ultimate truth of Randi's assertion that the skeptical world is all done with Uri Geller. Even Randi calls some of what Prometheus publishes today "awful stuff"—so "awful" that recently Mike Hutchinson felt obliged to ask the local obscene publications squad to adjudicate over a book. It said it couldn't recommend it, an avowedly anti-pedophilia work but with some passages Hutchinson thought "were a little bit too descriptive" to be distributed in Britain.

One book on Prometheus's list is a British academic text on child abuse: *Children's Sexual Encounters With Adults*, republished in the States—with a bright red jacket on which the title is printed in bold black letters three-quarters of an inch high, for the benefit, presumably, of short-sighted researchers into child sex. The book consists of hundreds of pages of detailed case histories of adults having sex with children. Other Prometheus texts have surely still less claim to academic status: *Cannibalism: From Sacrifice to Survival*, *The Horseman: Obsessions of a Zoophile*, *Whips and Kisses: Parting the Leather Curtain*, *The Breathless Orgasm: A Lovemap Biography of Asphyxiophilia*, *Death Dealer: The Memoirs of the SS Kommandant at Auschwitz* . . . It is all some way from magicians' arguments over spoon-bending.

Chapter 17

Party Time

"Uri does not aspire to be an exclusionary icon—his is an enabling talent."

Sir David Frost, 1996

....

Before he retired, David Berglas had a routine in his shows in which he handed out metal bars as thick as a finger to members of the audience, and asked the strongest men to try to bend them, which of course they could not. He would then ask for a female volunteer, give her one of the metal bars, look straight at her, tell her not to think about anything but that she was getting very strong and the bar was getting weaker. In almost every case, the bar would bend, sometimes ending up in a fish shape. When Berglas handed it back to the audience, however, the men could never straighten the bar.

Of course, Berglas will not say how he achieved this, but there is some evidence that he may have been engendering Geller-style metal-bending power in ordinary people.

Sir David Frost describes Uri Geller as someone who is as interested in being "an enabling talent" as in gathering glory for himself. Although in a small sense it is "bad for business," Uri believes that many of us have the power of mind to bend metal. And some astonishing research over the past twenty years in south California by a fifty-nine-year-old aeronautical and astronautical engineer called Jack Houck seems to indicate that virtually all of us can do it—and, furthermore, that bending cutlery is far more than a parlor trick. It is, argues Houck, a metaphor for the power of the mind to do everything from maximize creativity, to self-cure disease, to extract rusty bolts from machinery. And Houck is not just talking about concentrating hard to maximize strength. He believes the mind can be trained truly to interact with molecules of material. Which is why, although it is not really about Uri Geller, this chapter is probably the most important in the book.

Jack Houck is as different a personality from Uri Geller as it is possible to imagine. Introverted, quietly spoken and slight, he would not allow me even to photograph him. A graduate of Michigan State University, he taught aircraft structure there before moving to work in the space industry. He is now a systems engineer for a company near his home in Huntington Beach, while his Ph.D. wife, Jean, is a dean of education at California State University in Long Beach.

Houck hit upon his discoveries on metal-bending via a roundabout route. In 1976, he became interested in Puthoff and Targ's remote-viewing program, read all their papers, and began to conduct his own research into the subject. One aspect of it fascinated him: a strange time-shift, which occasionally cropped up in remote-viewing experiments. Remote-viewers would accurately describe a spot thousands of miles away, whose bare coordinates they had been given, but would include a detail that had existed only in the past—or even, in some rare cases, would exist in the future. In one experiment Houck ran, a psychic remote-viewer adequately described a randomly selected set of coordinates in the Caribbean, but with the alarming detail of a harrowing shipwreck in which he sensed dozens of people dying. Houck discovered that nine years earlier such a passenger-boat accident had happened at this spot. He developed a theory that certain "peak emotional events" (PEEs) could transcend the boundaries of the known dimensions, that, as he puts in it his own engineering terms, "If you add an emotional vector to the space/time vectors, you have the start of the way things work." As an extension of that idea, he wondered whether a paranormal event could be created by inducing a highly emotional state in someone. In England John Hasted had, after all, long since noted the way in which child spoon-benders tended to be highly strung, and Uri Geller himself is not exactly lowly strung or the calmest individual.

Houck discussed his idea at various university parapsychology departments but it was not considered likely to work. Knowing of Uri Geller's twin abilities to view remotely and bend metal, and assuming that they were part of the same phenomenon, Houck invented what would become known as the PK (psychokinesis) party. Working with a metallurgist, he gathered twenty-one people for a Monday-evening party at his house, about half of whom were proven remote-viewers and the rest friends from his tennis club. He invited them to take part in an unspecified experiment. The surprised guests were each given either a fork or a spoon and told they were going to learn to bend them like Uri Geller by relaxing and having fun. It seemed a ridiculous idea, but its very silliness seemed to do the trick. The guests were all soon chatting and laughing, as Houck had hoped. The metallurgist then gave them instructions: they were all to "get a point of concentration in their head," make it intense and focused, then "grab it and bring it down through your neck, down through your shoulder, through your arm, through your hand, and put it into the silverware at the point you intend to bend it." Then they were to command it to bend, release the command . . . and let it happen.

For some while, nothing happened. Then a fourteen-year-old boy, in full view of the circle of guests, watched the head of his fork flop down. At this, almost everyone experienced, as Houck puts it, "an immediate belief-system change," and within minutes, cutlery was softening and flopping over in nineteen of the twenty-one guests' hands. Within a couple of hours, the plasticity of the forks and spoons seemed to exceed anything in Uri Geller's experience. People were tying knots in the prongs of the forks, and rolling up spoon bowls as if they were leaves. At subsequent parties, of which Houck has now given over three hundred, some involving more than 12,000 people, spontaneous bendings became relatively common, while on average, eighty-five percent of guests achieved some level of near-effortless bending, particularly if they were allowed to use their hands. The *Jurassic Park* author Michael Crichton, a Harvard-trained doctor, was among the astonished guests who found themselves easily contorting spoons at one of Houck's PK parties. Crichton devoted a chapter of his 1988 book *Travels* to the experience, concluding that paranormal phenomena were misnamed, not because they didn't exist, but because they were utterly normal events which humans have simply forgotten they are capable of.

The manually assisted metal bending which occurs at PK parties is not quite Gellerism in action, but still astonished those who seemed suddenly to develop the power to bend often quite heavy spoons and even thick metal rods with ease. Seven- and eight-year-old children have been among those bending such ironware. People at the parties bend so much cutlery that often they don't take it all home. Houck showed me suitcases full of grotesquely distorted spoons and forks from his parties that he can't bring himself to throw out.

Houck tried to work out what was happening, and developed a theory that the mind somehow manages to "dump" energy into dislocations and flaws naturally occurring in metal when it is forged, which softens the metal as surely as heating it to eight hundred degrees F. He even documented cases where metal was missing from spoons after they had bent. He says he borrowed from quantum theory in his theoretical thinking on the phenomenon, but was more inclined to look for straightforward engineering solutions. "The only thing I don't know is how the mind dumps this energy into the dislocations. After that, it's just engineering."

He, and other researchers who have picked up on the PK party idea, have videoed hours of these wild metal-bending parties—at which no alcohol is allowed as it seems to interfere with whatever process is occurring. "We've shown the tapes to skeptics," he says, "but they just say they won't believe it unless we have got more tape from different angles. That's how these people operate: nothing is ever enough. It you taped it successfully from different angles, they'd query the type of camera being used and so on forever. Only recently I had a stage magician at a party who went around doing his own spoon-bending trick and saying, 'See,' to everyone. He seemed to think that because he knew a trick that looked the same, it was the same. He got so angry he left."

As befits his profession, Jack Houck is a practical man, who finds unacceptable the idea of metal-bending as a stand-alone phenomenon. What, he wondered, is it *for*? "It's about allowing yourself to apply your mind to goals, whether that goal is healing, or writing better, or fixing a dent in your car," he told me. "You laugh, but I had a letter from a PK party guest in Georgia who claimed he got out a rusted-in bolt from his truck, a bolt on which he'd already broken tools, by commanding it to unscrew."

People repeatedly tell Houck and other PK party enthusiasts that they feel empowered by seeing what they are able to do. The idea is catching on at the fringes of medicine. In one trial in Colorado—where virtually everything from garbage collection to heavy engineering is done by someone adhering to New Age precepts—such mind-over-matter metaphors as wooden-board breaking and aikido (but not—yet—spoon-bending) have been taught to cancer patients as a way of encouraging them, alongside medical treatment, to overcome their illness.

But it is not only the alternative world that started duplicating Jack Houck's pioneering PK parties in the 1980s. At SRI, Russell Targ, the laser physicist and magician, was impressed. "It was at a PK party, under quite good conditions, that I saw a person, someone I trust, sitting quietly with a teaspoon in her hand with the handle protruding and her eyes closed, in a meditative state until she screamed because the spoon came alive in her hand," Targ says. "It reminded her of holding a cricket. She opened her hand and the spoon bowl had bent through 180 degrees. Seeing somebody have the bowl of a spoon gracefully roll up into a gentle curve, as though it were fluid, something that is impossible to do by manual force, is quite impressive."

In Washington, DC, John B. Alexander, a US Army colonel, became fascinated by PK parties as a phenomenon of military potential. Colonel Alexander, who retired in 1988, was originally in the Special Forces. He commanded undercover military teams in Vietnam and Thailand, and later moved into military science, working as director of the Advanced Systems Concepts Office, US Army Laboratory Command, then as chief of Advanced Human Research with INSCOM, the intelligence and security command. On retirement, he joined Los Alamos National Laboratory with a brief to develop, like Eldon Byrd, whom we met in Chapter 11, the concept of non-lethal defense, which is now his passion. With his rare Ph.D. in thanatology—the study of death—Alexander, like Byrd, has believed strongly for some time that inducing recoverable disease in an enemy's troops is preferable to blowing their bodies apart. He has written in this respect in several defense publications, and been written about in a wide range of newspapers, from the *Wall Street Journal* to *Scientific American*.

John Alexander, who now runs a privately funded science think tank in Nevada, which studies, broadly speaking, the paranormal, is a charming but slightly eerie-looking man with amazing pale eyes. With Jack Houck's help, in the early 1980s he began teaching metal-bending by the PK-party method to American forces officers "including some senior level people."

"As far as Uri Geller is concerned," Alexander told me when we met, "I originally thought it could be a trick, but I dismissed that later. We even had magicians involved in looking at Geller. The idea of him relying on sleight-of-hand is nonsense. He is, of course, extremely gregarious and an extreme extrovert, and that worked against him, although had he not been an extrovert, the chances are that nobody would have heard of him.

"The reason for teaching spoon-bending was to show people that things could happen that they did not expect, and to emphasize the importance of that, particularly from an intelligence standpoint. It was important that they ensured that when they looked at unusual data of any kind, they did not dismiss it just because they thought it couldn't be true. The overall problem with the professionally skeptical class of people is that they are very scared. If *psi* is true, their world-view is incorrect. I worked with an Army engineer once on a *psi*-related project, and he actually came out and said, 'Don't tell me something that says I have to relearn physics, because I do not want to hear it.' But most of the skeptics are not that honest. They won't say, 'I don't want to hear it.' They will just say it's not true, therefore it isn't. When all else fails, ignore the facts. Data that doesn't fit is categorically rejected.

"We stressed to folks," Alexander explained, "that bending silverware is of very limited practical value. You can make mobiles and things like that out of bent forks, but as far as something to do it doesn't make a lot of sense. What we did suggest was that it certainly impacts belief systems, and also that they could take and use similar kinds of energy for things like healing and other practical applications."

How high in the military world did word of the PK party plan spread, I wondered. "Well, I had the deputy director of the CIA at my house in Springfield, Virginia, for a PK party. But compared to potential war with the Soviet Union, it was just noise, so, no, we didn't have the President there."

The most dramatic of John Alexander's PK parties took place at a military camp for a senior group of US army commanders from intelligence, who had come in from around the world for a regular quarterly meeting: "We were using the Xerox training center outside Washington. We had a session and there was a commotion over in one area. This guy, who was a science adviser at a civilian equivalent of a two-and-a-half-star general, turned his head, and saw a lieutenant colonel's fork drop a full ninety degrees. I didn't see it, but the guy next to him did, and screamed, 'Did you see that?' I said I suspected a trick, because there were a lot of people there who would have liked to see me fail, and I was waiting for them to say, 'Ha, ha, we did it, you don't know what you are looking at.' So I was cautious, but by now people were watching. And while we were all watching, the fork went back up, back down again, and finally went about halfway and stopped. This is with all the generals and colonels watching, and the colonel just put it down and said, 'I wish that hadn't happened.' It scared the crap out of him. Fortunately we were sequestered, which means it was an isolated, live-in conference, and we had a shrink with us. But it took a couple of days to put him together. His belief system was not prepared. He was based in Europe, so he went back to his station OK. What he did tell someone later was that he tried it once again at home by himself and it happened again, but by now he was able to deal with it."

Jack Houck is a man with a mission, but not a glory-seeker: he seems to have been happy just to help the cause of parapsychology with his PK parties.

Five years ago, he taught spoon-bending to delegates at a convention of the American Board of Hypnotherapy. Among the participants was a therapist called Gary Sinclair, who was in his forties and originally from Maine. Sinclair had a special interest in the power of mind over matter. When he was thirty-six, and eighty percent incapacitated by multiple sclerosis and a lifetime lung condition, his doctor broke it to him that soon he would have to start using a wheelchair. Sinclair decided to heal himself by will-power, and believes he did so. Five years later, the former restaurant manager was no longer taking medication for the MS and was, he says, winning ice-skating championships. Now he is a remarkably youthful and fit fifty-three-year-old, and has reinvented himself as the ultimate south Californian therapist.

The walls of his consulting room in his beautiful Solana Beach apartment, which is on the Pacific north of San Diego, are covered with qualifications in an exotic pick'n'mix of therapies. He is certified, among many other things, in Neuro-Linguistic programming, Ericksonian hypnotherapy, advanced neuro-dynamics, Time-Line Therapy, past-life therapy, transpersonal hypnotherapy, and bridging mind, body and spirit. He has gone on to combine all these into a therapy of his own invention, which he calls cyberphysiology. "I created it," he told me, "because it incorporates all of the transpersonal works together, whether it is spirit releasement or wounded child or soul retrieval or past-life regression or hypnotherapy or neuro-linguistic programming. I designed the therapy of therapies."

He has a waiting list of clients happy to pay $1,500 for an intensive "life clear-out." To his vast repertoire of therapies, Gary Sinclair has recently, thanks to PK parties, added spoon-bending as a metaphor for healing. And, he promises, you don't have to go to all the trouble of a party to learn to bend a spoon. He can teach on a one-to-one basis—and tutored me to the first, most basic level of manually assisted spoon-bending in less than half an hour. After getting me to mangle a series of progressively bigger spoons as if they were made of Plasticine, he had me coil up the handle of a huge, heavy-gauge cooking spoon into a tight corkscrew that looked as if it had taken an hour on an engineer's bench to create. People back in England still gasp at the thing, try to unbend it—which they can't—and ask me how I did it. All I can answer is that I don't know, but it seemed effortless at the time, as if the spoon were made of rubber. The following, however, is a transcript of my tape of Gary's instructions to the first part of his spoon-bending course, which may work for some people even without his highly charismatic presence. I suggest you use the instructions first with a light tea-spoon, and progress through the cutlery drawer.

First of all you have to find the energy of you on the inside. Where is your energy on the inside? How do you find the energy of you? Close your eyes, and in the process of closing your eyes, I want you to think of me walking up to you with an envelope. In this envelope is a letter, this letter tells you everything that you need to know about the rest of your life. All the questions that you wanted answered are inside this letter, and in addition to that, there is a winning ticket for the lottery for $70 million. I have to decide whether I am going to give you this letter or not. It's your letter. Is that true? Whoever wrote it absolutely wanted you to have it, because it explains all the answers to the rest of your life, and then they added in this little gift of $70 million. I want you to notice what it feels like when you have this letter coming. OK? . . . And then I want you to notice what it feels like when I stand in front of you and tear the letter up. Feel the feeling as I tear it into all these pieces. Now open your eyes. Notice that you are actually feeling something, you are feeling an energy. Where do you feel the feeling? Well, that feeling, that's you, that energy is you. You must feel the energy that is you. Find the energy inside you. Once you have the ability to feel who you are, you can simply bring that energy into your hands. It is a fireball. Take the fireball and slowly move it with your hands. That energy will go wherever you pay attention. When you pick up an object like this and you intend it to bend, and you know that where you pay attention is where the energy goes, then the energy is going to go there . . . focus between the fingers . . . you *expect* it to bend . . . make an agreement with the metal that it is going to bend . . . now go!

After I had bent a couple of small spoons, Sinclair told me, "You are now at the point where you know that it is going to bend. What you have to do next is visualize it bent, and know that what you are doing is getting that metal to bend ahead of time, as you see it in your mind, so that you know you are now transferring your energy to that metal, so that it will in fact bend." It was now that I bent the big spoon.

"You can't believe you did it," he explained, "but the reason that you did it was that, at the time, you didn't doubt that you could. You see, everyone else is still trying to make some scientific phenomenon out of it, but it isn't a scientific phenomenon, it's a fact. Once you believe you are capable of doing it, from that point on, it's possible."

Chapter 18

Meanwhile, Back in Israel . . .

"Whether Uri is the amazing phenomenon we tend to believe he is, or the greatest crook of all time, he deserves our admiration. Those grudging Israelis who won't stand for any Israeli making good abroad can get as green as a sour grape. They've lost the battle against Uri once and for all."

Novelist Ephraim Kishon, writing in *Ma'ariv*

....

Uri does not know the date on which his father died, other than it was around 1980. (It was actually in October 1979.) "I don't even know the exact year," he said. "I try to totally erase it out of my brain. It is only when I have to light a candle that Hanna looks in the diary. I don't want to know. It is totally erased. Another thing which still upsets me is that when I flew for his burial, we were all in the cemetery, and my father was all bundled up in the tallis [prayer shawl] and his wife, my stepmother wanted me to cry and I couldn't. I was almost embarrassed and ashamed that there were strangers around me weeping, and Uri, his own son, wasn't. What it was, was that I really don't believe in funerals. That's why I never go to them, I knew that his soul was out there looking at me and saying, 'I'm here,' so tears didn't come to my eyes. Eva, my stepmother, probably never forgave me for that, though she loves me very dearly and she spends time with us now in England. My father was her great love. One of my few regrets was that my father died before seeing my children.

"But my father's death was also a huge shock to me. I knew he had angina, I knew he was smoking, I knew he drank. I was in Rome with Hanna, in Villa

Borghese, when my secretary called the hotel. She said, 'There's some bad news.' I knew that my father was dead. I don't know whether that happened psychically, or just as every son or daughter would know it.

"But for years, since I was about thirteen, in Cyprus, I had a recurring nightmare of walking into an apartment. The windows are open, overlooking the Mediterranean, and I walk into the next room, and also the windows are open to the Med, and I look on the floor and I see myself lying there, dead, and then I would wake up, frightened. When my father remarried, he rented a tiny little one-bedroomed apartment overlooking the Med opposite the Sheraton Hotel in Tel Aviv. I never connected it until the day he died, because he died exactly on the same spot as I had dreamed I was lying overlooking the Mediterranean, with the windows open, the same tiles, the same color, the same window frames. And that's when the nightmare stopped. I never dreamed about it again. I said to myself, 'Why didn't I recognize it?' I'd been to the apartment dozens of times. It was only when he died and I went up there that I realized, my God, this is the place. I get goosebumps."

Such flying visits were how Uri kept his link with Israel from the 1970s to the present day. It has been a good way for him to ensure that he is still regarded in Israel—even by those who consider him a fake—as a local boy made good. Only recently the electronics company, Motorola, featured him in a big TV, radio and newspaper advertising campaign for an advanced mobile phone. By spreading himself thinly, he has maintained affection and credibility for himself in the one place, one suspects, where it really matters to him. Friends in the US believe the Gellers were happiest there, that they will return there one day, but I would be surprised to find Uri anywhere but Israel in old age.

There is something of the return to the nest in every trip Uri makes to Israel. By all accounts, he becomes ebullient, but vulnerable too, as he steps off an El Al jet at Ben Gurion Airport. "I think part of my success in Israel was that people saw some kind of savior, a man with powers to save Israel from further war, even to help people contact their beloved sons, killed in the wars," he told me once. "Maybe I chose the wrong path by becoming part entertainer, part psychic, part teacher, part science experiment, part communicator. Perhaps I should have gone into politics."

There are inevitably a million Israeli stories about Uri Geller, but the two that follow reveal much about the man as he matured. Both are from the 1980s, when Uri was approaching forty, had young children, and was between living in the States and moving to England. The magician, Roni Schachnaey told me the first.

In 1980, Roni says, after several years' absence, Uri came to do a show at the Mann Auditorium in Tel Aviv. "I think it was a mistake, because the magicians were after his blood. I brought along forty magicians to sit at the show, right at the front. I insisted that we behave properly. I would allow no disrespect for a fellow artist, but I thought the show was very poor, seventies stuff. It was like chewing-gum, stretching everything out. Then, when he was bending the spoon, something extraordinary happened. Uri threw a spoon into the aisle right next to me and said, 'Even *he* can't bend a spoon like I can.' Now what has always puzzled me was how did he know I was there? He had never met me, he didn't know me. That incident to me was proof that he plants people in the audience.

"So after the show I was leaving and his manager came across and said, 'Uri Geller wants a word with you.' I was taken into his dressing room, face to face after all these years of opposing him. He seemed very nervous. The first thing he said to me was 'You have very kind eyes.' That took me by surprise. Then he said he knew I didn't want to hurt him. I said, 'Look, I know enough about you. I don't need to hurt you. You're hurt enough.' But then he took me by the shoulder into the bathroom. He wanted somewhere quiet where we could speak.

"Then he said this. And I promise that this is the gospel truth, told completely without venom. Uri said, 'I'm going to tell you something I've not told anybody before. I swear on my mother's life I was lucky. You know, the thing with the oil. I really did get lucky and I made a lot of money. So now you know the truth, why not let me carry on working without disturbances?' Now for me, that was enough. I said, 'Well, if you want to be one of us,' and I had a little lapel badge for our association, which I took off and pinned on his shirt and told him, 'You are one of us.' As long as you wear this badge whenever you're up on stage, we won't trouble you. But he didn't, and it always made me laugh that he wrote later that I gave him a *medallion*, like it was an award, and he couldn't be sure whether I thought he was the greatest illusionist or a true psychic."

The second story came from Zvi Bentwich, a professor of medicine at the Hebrew University in Jerusalem. Dr. Bentwich, a clinical immunologist, is one of the world's leading authorities on AIDS, and is based at the AIDS center at the Kaplan hospital in Rehovot, which is affiliated to the university's medical school and the Hadassah hospital in Jerusalem. He was introduced to Uri as early as 1969 by his secretary, who happens to be Uri's old friend Leah Peleg. Because of this connection Bentwich had the distinction, nearly twenty years later, of being the last scientist anywhere to have conducted tests on Uri Geller. Uri had not been inside a laboratory for over a decade. "What I saw Uri Geller do in the laboratory," he attests, "was a truly mind-blowing experience which cannot be overlooked, and should be made common knowledge once we have established it. I have no doubt that he manifests an extreme case of some unusual power, capacity or energy, which I believe is genuine and not magician- or performer-based, and which probably represents what all human beings have in much lower intensity.

"To start with, when we were younger," Bentwich told me, "I was impressed with the regular things he can do, the telepathy he showed me at parties, the bending of spoons and the seed-sprouting. What was most impressive in my mind was that the spoon continued to bend when it was clearly out of his touch. The seed sprouting, I found intriguing, rather than disturbing. I approached him at that time and asked him to give himself to further testing within our medical school, and I was amused by his almost paranoid reaction. He was extremely anxious at my suggestion. I felt there was something problematic in his coping with his powers not being under his control, in his attraction to showbusiness, which I thought did him a big disservice.

"However, to my delight, in 1987 Uri agreed to come and be tested in my laboratory, and at the Weizmann Institute, which is nearby. My colleagues and I designed three experiments to test if he has any special effects when he concentrates and puts his hands over a culture of cancer cells. The bottom line of these experiments was that they were all negative, so there was another guy, an endocrinologist, who came in and said, 'I have some ox-sperm cells. Maybe this would affect the sperm.'"

The sperm, Bentwich explains, were in frozen vials. "They were put into a plate and were swimming around very energetically, and then we had two similar culture plates that contained sperm in more or less the same amount as a control. Uri put his hand over one and without touching it, concentrated. It was hot, in summer, so he wasn't wearing long sleeves or anything, and we checked out his hands for anything hidden. And, lo and behold, the sperm cells stopped moving. Most of them became either very slow in movement or dead. We repeated this three times. It was very impressive, so we did it again and again. However, when he asked what it was we were doing and we told him, he was extremely upset. He really thought he had a destructive power. This was a dramatic result, but he wasn't happy with it, and at that point he said he didn't want to do anything more.

"After seeing such results, I told him, 'Look, we should continue testing. It is so interesting and amazing.' But he didn't like the idea at all. At a later stage, I suggested that if he was concerned about negative forces, maybe we could try out some healing effects. He said that he liked that much more, but I didn't insist beyond a certain point, and we did nothing more, which I think is very regretful.

"I think Uri is a very fine person. I like him personally but, in a way, I always considered him an immature personality with an exceptional power that somehow he doesn't know how to cope with. He is attracted too much to showbiz and to performance, and not to more important things. Eleven more years have now gone by, and nobody has been studying him on any similar things, which is ridiculous. There was too little to go on, but what we had already seen was probably the most significant piece of evidence ever in terms of biological effect of what he is capable of, yet he refrained and said, 'Forget about me, try it with somebody else.' He is far from being systematic. He is chaotic, so he didn't make the connection with AIDS and cancer, or even think about it. It was like he was missing the main point while looking round for nonsense."

Chapter 19

Home, Home on the Thames

"I seem only like a boy, playing on the seashore and diverting myself in finding a smoother pebble or a prettier shell than ordinary, whilst the great oceans of truth lay undiscovered before me."

Sir Isaac Newton, father of modern science—and practicing occultist

....

There were many reasons why Uri Geller effectively retired in his early thirties as there were methods that conjurers had invented to bend spoons by sleight-of-hand. His principle mission was accomplished: the accumulation of enough cash to keep him happy, settle down with Hanna, perhaps have some kids. His mother was in Connecticut, in a house that skeptical investigators—an example of how obsessive they were becoming—claimed to belong technically to the wife of the president of Mexico. A check at the local city hall would have confirmed Margaret Geller was, in fact, the owner.

Also, Uri had achieved as much respectability as was ever likely to come his way—the *Nature* article, recognition by dozens of serious scientists, show-business stars, maverick elements within the CIA and Mossad, the briefing he unquestionably gave President Carter. On one occasion, in 1986, Uri was phoned at home by William Casey, a newly appointed head of the CIA. Casey did an impromptu ESP test with Uri, whereupon the director pronounced, 'I'll be darned,' thanked Uri for his time and was not heard from—directly, that is—again. All this had happened, but still he was doubted by a few skeptics and called a fraud. He became aware that with some people he would never win. There was also the question that with age his powers might fade. Most children grow out of their psychic abilities; they become embarrassed by them, stop practicing, the poltergeists move on. Uri seems to maintain his powers by remaining, in many ways, a teenager. But performing psychically, even at small-scale charity events, began increasingly to make him physically tired, which has impressed many people as the crowning proof that he is no fake. And while there is no evidence that the public had become bored with Uri Geller I am also certain that a further element contributed to his winding down. It was as impossible for someone in his position not to know a few magicians' tricks for emergency use as it is for a professional athlete, a cook, a comedian, a lawyer or an actor not to know a few ways to keep the public happy on an off day, and to keep ahead of the game. But, I believe, Uri hated trickery, and barely, if ever, resorted to it.

"There definitely was a phase of semi-retirement," he said. "It was my choice. I just got fed up with airports, with hotel rooms and the stress of appearing in front of thousands of people. I was fed up with driving to colleges and being interviewed by newspapers. And when you are famous in every country, someone can live in, say, England and for three years not hear about Uri Geller, but meanwhile I'm in every newspaper and magazine in South Africa or in Norway. When I was not on American television I was probably on Danish or Swedish TV. Every country had its heyday. There came a point where I almost broke down, when I had had enough. I was in hotel rooms where suddenly there was no meaning to my life anymore. I woke up and there was an emptiness, a slight depression, but there were still people standing downstairs in the lobby waiting for my signature. I was ever so famous. I was a celebrity, I was a super-psychic. I was unique. You have got a Mick Jagger, an Elton John, a Peter Gabriel, but only one Uri Geller. I didn't see a way out of fame and fortune. I was like, So what else is there? I've got the Cadillac, the two apartments, a magnificent house in Connecticut. I had to break that pattern. That's when a major change happened in my life and I became a vegetarian, I started exercising and I started reading books about philosophy, health and well-being." Uri even set about relinquishing all his possessions; today, technically, he owns nothing—everything is held in a trust. He says he finds this liberating.

In the USA from the late 1970s to the mid-to-late 1980s, Uri busied himself with banging on the doors and windows of government, power, influence—and pursuing legal cases. The teenage drive and energy, combined with a childlike desire for justice and a wealthy adult's bank account, made him a law junkie who brought a multitude of law suits, even though, to the present day, he has never been in a courtroom, most cases either being settled to his satisfaction out of court, or fizzling out.

His power games were more important and interesting than the legal side-shows. He is anxious to play down his White House connection, which may indicate there was more—or less—to it than meets the eye, but regards two specific episodes as the summit of his years of what might be called political influence. In February 1987, he was attending a reception given by the US Mission to the Geneva arms negotiations with the Soviets; a fortnight later, he was briefing a gathering of senior senators and congressmen, plus forty Capitol staffers, Defense Department and Pentagon aides in a room in the Capitol Building sealed and screened electronically from possible Soviet eavesdropping. He was at the Geneva reception because he had been invited by Senator Claiborne Pell, then chairman of the Senate Foreign Relations Committee, in the hope that he could telepathically influence the Soviet negotiating team, especially its head, Yuli Vorontsov, into making some serious concessions to the West, preferably, as a first step, reducing Russian missiles in Europe. Pell had been introduced to Uri, who now lived in Britain, by Princess Michael of Kent. So impressed was he, that a few days before the Geneva meeting, he arranged a three-way meeting at the Cavendish Hotel in London with Uri, himself and Max Kampelman, the chief US negotiator. According to a full-page report in *Newsweek*, the day after the reception, Mikhail Gorbachev made an unexpected new offer: the removal within five years of all medium-range nuclear missiles based in Europe. Uri was quoted as saying that he was convinced that, having received his ESP message, Vorontsov had called Gorbachev straight after the reception.

It all sounded, even with the *Newsweek* story, like a tale that would fall apart a decade later under investigation. Apart from anything else, the *Newsweek* photo appeared to show, next to his now friend Al Gore, Uri Geller in a suit and tie, a near impossibility for an Israeli. I took a train out to Rhode Island, therefore, to see Claiborne Pell, a retired six-term senator. His simple, elegant home, on the ocean in Newport, is the fulfilment of every romantic vision of those brought up on images of John F. Kennedy's Camelot—a black-and-white picture of Pell with his friend JFK, another with Lyndon B. Johnson, another with Queen Elizabeth II. In a corner stands a chair from the investiture of the Prince of Wales. Pell had not been well and on the coffee table lay a letter from President Bill Clinton, wishing his senior Democrat colleague well, and adding Hillary's best wishes to Nuala, Pell's wife. Had JFK ever been here, in this house? I wondered, as we sipped tea from fine china. The elderly senator looked shocked. "Oh, no . . . I mean not often. He might stop his boat out there and drop by, but not formally, no. Only at our home in Washington." It was time to get down to business. I asked if the Uri Geller story was true. "Well, yes, actually. I was interested in parapsychology, telepathy and life after death. I had no ability or experience in this area, but I believed in it, and I would love to have had the experience. So I thought it would be fun for Uri to bring his dog and pony show to some of the American and Russian delegates at a cocktail party. I was interested in seeing what impression Uri might be able to make on the Russians, and I think they were mystified. I'll never forget the Russian ambassador, Vorontsov, now the ambassador to Washington. Uri bent his spoon. Then he put the spoon into the ambassador's hand, and the spoon continued to move in his hand. Everybody saw that. It was a key moment for me." Whether Uri influenced Vorontsov, Pell reasonably says he can't know, and that it would be highly unlikely for Vorontsov to know, either.

Nuala Pell remembers Vorontsov refusing to give Uri his watch. "What I remember was Uri putting the grass seeds in the palm of his hand, and they grew. He did it in front of us all. We just couldn't believe it. Everybody was floored. I truly believe in Uri, and I think everyone did. The Russians just looked stunned. They didn't know whether to believe or not to believe. I know Claiborne's colleagues in the Senate who were on that trip never got over that. They couldn't believe that Claiborne got him there, and then he performed, and they were so impressed. It was the talk of the Senate for some time. Claiborne was very determined; he believed in Uri and was determined that other people should have the chance to see him too.

"I'd seen that kind of thing before," the senator explained, "and thought it might be a conjurer's trick. I talked with that guy Randi once, and he said it was a trick, and he could do it too. There's a great depth of feeling there against Uri, you know. It's almost vicious. But Uri was far more impressive as a person. I think Uri is a very likeable, decent sort. I never felt he was dubious. I respect him. I think he has good ideas, and is genuine. I also remember how unless he was in full vigor, he couldn't make things happen, which I found most interesting."

It was Pell who arranged the meeting at the Capitol, for which the official agenda, for the benefit of any Soviet spies, was to talk about the plight of Soviet Jews. The meeting was held in the Capitol's only SCIF—a superior compartmentalized intelligence facility. Colonel John Alexander was in attendance. "He talked about the stuff the Soviets were doing psychically,"

Alexander recalled, "but everyone wanted him to bend something. There wasn't a spoon around, so someone went outside and found one in the guard's coffee cup.

"I was in the front row watching very closely. I had been trained by magicians by now, and I had watched Randi do it frame by frame and I could catch him at it. Uri took the spoon, stroked it lightly, and the thing bent up quite noticeably. He put it down on the top of this chair and he continued talking, and I watched this spoon continue to bend until it fell off the chair. There was never a time when Uri could have applied force. And even if the touch were strong it would have bent down, not bent *upwards.*" Although Pell says he did not think the meeting was a huge success, at least one senator disagreed with him, according to *Newsweek.* Representative Dante Fascell, chairman of the House Foreign Affairs Committee, rushed directly to the library to read up on Uri Geller.

"I saw Uri do that several more times after that," John Alexander added. "I introduced him to Steven Seagal, and we did it there in Seagal's house, the inner sanctum of his bedroom, with all these old ancient Tibetan tapestries on the wall. [Seagal, the macho actor, has been described by the Dalai Lama as "a sacred vessel."] I don't think Steven has any doubt. His belief system is that these things can happen, although it goes without saying that this is not totally unique to Uri Geller."

"Even from England, Uri assiduously kept his up his American contacts and friendships. I suppose in a spirit of gratitude for having got his gun back when it was confiscated at JFK," recalls US Customs agent Charlie Kosczka."Uri invited me and my wife to his apartment and we started a friendship which has lasted through the years. I visited Uri in England and stayed there close to a week when I was flying undercover in the terrorist years in the 1970s. I saw him do some amazing things. I had a ring of keys on me, one of which was the key to my parents' home and Uri bent it by gently putting his hand on it. I had to put it in a vise to try and get it back in my parents' lock. On other occasions when I visited Uri, I found keys bent in my pocket when I was sitting on a soft cushion. There is no way that you could sit on a soft cushion and a key would bend. His detractors say that Geller is basically a magician, he had a bent key in his hand and he switches. I can say categorically that did not happen. There is no way he removed the key and had it duplicated. In law enforcement, you have a tendency to be hypercritical, almost cynical about people, and you fight this because you don't want to think ill of your fellow man. Most people are honest, but law enforcement people just don't run into them. So I always assumed that with psychics, it was a case of the hand being quicker than the eye. But I believe he is gifted with abilities which I don't fully understand—and I have never known him to use them in an improper way.

Accordingly, perhaps Uri began from the late Seventies to rely on legal muscle rather than any psychic power to pursue his fervent desire not to be, as he saw it, cheated or defamed. He even became something of a law junkie. Through an ever expanding file of legal cases against his perceived enemies, he gathered a team of committed lawyers in the US and Britain, who understand him and have become wise counsel to him in both the legal and the personal sense. In the USA, Richard Winelander, a Baltimore attorney, took over the Geller file by accident when an ex-colleague, Don Katz, was disbarred. "I'm a criminal attorney," said Winelander. "I don't even believe witnesses. But I believe strongly in Uri. He's a genius, and he's my buddy. He managed to stop me smoking fifty a day, and the spoon-bending is real. It is totally unbelievable."

In New York, Uri has Ruth Liebesman, who was on the defense team for the Mafia godfather, John Gotti. Liebesman was born in England, where her father was a US Air Force doctor, and is a tough, big-time attorney, with a difference: Liebesman is convinced she has been seeing UFOs since she was sixteen, and has been abducted by them. The most dramatic incident, she told me, when we met in a New York coffee shop, occurred when she was staying in the Gellers' guest cottage outside Reading, on the night, interestingly enough, that Andrija Puharich died. She awoke from what she thought was a nightmare with a row of painful blisters on her stomach. Two days later, back in New York, she took the scarring to her doctor, Jack Aylward. "He said to me, 'All I can see is your laparoscopy scars, which are at least three weeks old.' I said, 'Jack, I've never had a laparoscopy. Never when I signed a consent form, anyway.'"

In New York, Uri also retains the services of Bob Fogelnest, a leading defense lawyer who lectures on courtroom skills with the nationally famous Wyoming trial lawyer, Gerry Spence. Another close Geller adviser is a retired Federal Judge in Santa Barbara, California, Lee Holden who, like a lot of lawyers, was highly skeptical of Uri when he first met him, but now credits him with being "one hundred percent real"—and says his life changed dramatically by adopting Uri's positive thinking techniques. It is perhaps unsurprising, given such a range of family friends in the law and a father so fascinated by law, that Daniel Geller, at just 17 and a prefect at his private school near Reading, currently hopes to make his career as a European commercial lawyer.

The important thing about Uri's cases as far as "the big picture" is concerned is that none has involved proof or disproof of the paranormal, and almost all have involved James Randi's excitable turn of phrase. In 1990, he sued Randi and a Japanese publisher for Randi's claim in a Japanese magazine that Dr. Wilbur Franklin of Kent State University committed suicide because he was so ashamed when Randi discredited Geller. In fact, Franklin had died of natural causes. Randi was ordered by the court in Tokyo to pay half a million yen (£2,500) for the insult while the Japanese publisher settled out of court with a high six-figure sum—in dollars, not yen. Geller successfully sued a newspaper in Hungary, in which Randi had been quoted accusing him and Shipi of being swindlers. Uri explained that he was bringing the case because he was embarrassed that his Hungarian relatives might have read the comments. The newspaper had to publish a retraction and pay damages and costs. Uri sued Randi and CSICOP for a comment in the *International Herald Tribune* that his "tricks" were "the kind of thing that used to be on the back of cereal boxes when I was a kid." In the US, he sued Timex for featuring a metal-bending performer in an advertisement, claiming this effect was his trademark. In London, Florida and Hawaii, he sued Victor Stenger, a skeptical scientist living in Hawaii, and Prometheus Books for writing falsely that he had been arrested in Israel for misrepresenting himself as a psychic. Uri only regretted not suing Randi in the 1970s for inventing the story of Uri being convicted of a crime.

The Timex case failed. In the Prometheus case, over the alleged arrest in Israel, Uri gained a written apology and acknowledgment of error from both the American and British branches of CSICOP. In the States, the *Herald Tribune* case had to be dropped when his then lawyer Don Katz failed to file on time, while the argument that Randi was an agent of CSICOP was rejected. This led Uri, ironically since he was the plaintiff, into having to pay CSICOP $82,000 as part of a global settlement of all the cases, although in the long run, both CSICOP and Randi seem to have been more damaged than Uri by the six-year legal morass. Randi continues to maintain that he won all the cases Uri brought. A lot of Uri's mismanagement of cases was clearly the fault of Katz, his original Baltimore attorney, who seems to have been almost psychotically stressed out when he made an error on an unrelated case for which he was briefly disbarred. Katz's co-counsels' insurers repaid Uri most of what he lost over the case.

A case not directly involving Uri, but which would not have happened without him, came to court in 1993. Five years earlier, Randi had referred in an interview to Eldon Byrd being "in jail as a convicted child molester." Byrd sued in Baltimore, with Winelander as his attorney. At the 1993 trial Randi accused Geller in passing of blackmailing him with a transcript and a tape that appeared to be of Randi having intimate sexual conversations with teenage boys. Randi said in explanation that he had been working alongside the telephone company in its attempt to track down a minor who had been making obscene calls to his home. After a discursive trial, the jury found Randi guilty of libel with malice, but awarded no money to Byrd, having discovered that Byrd had a past conviction for possession of pornography. Randi has since repeatedly claimed he won this case too.

If Uri Geller's "semi-retirement" in the USA looks more like a whirl of activity, it has taken a somewhat hyperactive form in Britain too, where he lives in a state of permanent reinvention. He came to Britain when crime and shootings in the USA had made him and Hanna doubt that it was where they wanted to bring up Daniel and Natalie. On an airplane he met Clement Freud, a distant relative on his mother's side, then a British MP, who suggested he settle in England. The Gellers needed little persuading.

Bizarre, exciting events continued to punctuate Uri's life even after he had moved to the more tranquil atmosphere of Britain. In 1985, for example, he was approached in London by a member of a Saudi Arabian family whose construction company was tendering for a $2 billion contract in Mecca. Smoking a hubble-bubble pipe in his Bayswater house, the Saudi watched Uri perform a few effects, and then shook on a deal with him. If he could, by using the power of his mind, persuade the Saudi king to award the contract to his family, Uri would receive £15 million in cash, paid wherever he wanted. They were given a number in Jeddah and a code name—Mr. Davis—to call the Saudi if the ruse worked. Uri and Shipi remember skipping with joy across Hyde Park on their way back to the Kensington apartment they were renting. They obtained a photo of the king, had it blown up and placed it all over their living room. Uri started concentrating on it daily for 30 minutes at a time. He hired a private jet to fly as close to Saudi airspace as an Israeli dare do, just to concentrate his thoughts more intently still on the king. Some months later, an Israeli contact who knew of the deal sent Uri a cutting from an English-language newspaper in Saudi reporting that the contract had been awarded their man's company. Uri promptly phoned the Jeddah number as "Mr. Davis," but he refused to come to the phone. The Saudi continued to reject all approaches; Uri was furious and was determined to sue. He spoke to a friend who had worked for an American bank in Saudi—and was advised to drop immediately any thought of suing. "Can you imagine what would happen to you and all concerned if the Saudis discovered a Jew had been hired to psychically influence the king?" the friend said, implying heavily that Uri might well end up being killed by either Saudi agents or the construction family's hit men. For once, Uri Geller, who had after all come to England to avoid danger, swallowed his pride and conceded defeat.

Although, such adventures aside, Uri gives the impression that over the past fifteen years he has been quiescent, his own account of his activity—prompted, as ever, by Randi and his claims that "Geller is finished"—belies the idea of retirement. "In the past ten years," he said, "I've written ten books, which have been translated into dozens of languages in thirty-three countries. I am working on five more books. I write eight different columns for magazines and newspapers, including *The Times*. My Web site has received as many as 400,000 hits in one day. A full-length motion picture about me by Ken Russell and distributed by Disney was sold to sixty countries in three days at the American Film Market. I have starred in countless TV specials and commercials, been written up in recent months in *Newsweek* and *Sports Illustrated*. And the latest Nieman Marcus catalogue in the States uses my name—without having asked me—to advertise a new range of silver cutlery. *Matrix*, the blockbuster movie starring Keanu Reeves, contains a spoon-bending scene inspired by me. I don't mean to brag, but it's a damned funny kind of 'finished.' Poor old 'Amazing' Randi continues to imagine things."

It's true that he is rarely out of the media. Since he came to Britain there have been several major TV documentaries on him. One of the first, a BBC *QED* program, was unfortunate for Uri, especially as the director, Tony Edwards, who believed in him, had to fight hard to get the slot and admits he would have loved the film to be more positive toward its subject. Part of it was made in Madison, Wisconsin, at a psychic event at which Uri was lecturing. The problem for the scrupulously ethical Edwards, who also made a brilliant series for the BBC on "heretical" scientists, was in inviting Randi to the Madison event in disguise, in a high-risk attempt to provide some balance to the documentary. If Randi had admitted he was stumped, then *QED* would have aided Geller hugely and given Edwards a remarkable documentary. But naturally, Randi insisted that Uri's spoon-bending was fraudulent. A spoon he broke at Madison was taken to a metallurgist at Leeds University, who reported on film that, as far as he could see, it had been a routine fracture by physical bending. "It was a shame," Tony Edwards says today. "Even though Randi was in an excellent disguise, and I don't think had even arrived yet, Uri was in an elevator with me at the hotel, and said, 'I can *smell* Randi.' I do think Uri has some special powers, but they didn't work for us in the film."

A 1997 British documentary, in Channel 4's Equinox series, *Secrets of the Psychics*, was a standard, unsurprising trot through the usual skeptical routine, with a clearly tendentious agenda, and soundbites from Richard Dawkins, John Taylor, Ray Hyman, Randi, Mike Hutchinson, Susan Blackmore, George Lawrence, Ian Rowland and Professor David Marks, a New Zealander who holds the chair in psychology at the University of Middlesex, in Enfield. Marks, who has written books on conjuring, said on the film: "As far as I am aware, from my observation, Geller has no psychic ability whatsoever. However, he's a very clever, well-practiced magician." (David Berglas, President of the Magic Circle, who agrees on the psychic question, nevertheless disputes Marks's knowledge of magicianship.) Also in the documentary were Marcello Truzzi and Russell Targ. His clips, Truzzi says, were clearly selected to maintain the editorial slant of the show. Failing to appreciate the show was more polemic than investigation, Uri complained to the Broadcasting Standards Commission about *Secrets of the Psychics*. His complaint was rejected.

Although today he undergoes no laboratory testing, Uri still meets scientists and doctors in more gentle settings, and is keen to garner their support. He recently spent some time demonstrating his abilities to Brian Josephson, professor of physics at Cambridge and winner of the 1973 Nobel prize for physics. He and Josephson sat cross-legged on the floor at a conference to talk. A few months later when I asked him for his view on Uri, Josephson was enigmatic: "I think Uri is a magician, but I don't particularly believe that he is using trickery in his demonstrations," he said. "I believe there are psychic abilities. They don't accord with any science we have at the moment, but maybe some future science will back them up with theories."

Uri also met, by chance, a London consultant psychiatrist, Dr. Lawrence Ratna, who reported favorably on him. "I am a psychiatrist with thirty years' clinical experience, a conjurer with a wide knowledge of magic and someone who has investigated paranormal phenomena and found them wanting in the past," Ratna said. "Uri Geller gave me a demonstration of spoon-bending. I could find no evidence of trickery nor the use of gimmicks. The fact that the spoon continued bending after he had handed it to me, for my mind, puts the event beyond rational explanation, be it scientific or a feat of conjuring. He also demonstrated two examples of thought transference, first accurately reproducing a geometric figure I had drawn, and second, perhaps more significantly, transmitting to me a figure and a color. As a lifelong skeptic I must record my total astonishment at these feats."

Uri remains a magnet for strange, dissonant individuals, which means that sometimes, even the positive media coverage the fiftysomething Uri attracts in Britain needs to be examined as carefully as the negative stories. In 1996, the *Sunday Telegraph* carried the large and startling headline, "*Uri Geller Vindicated as Historic Sub is Found.*" The story told of how a skeptical radio producer, William Scanlan-Murphy, had wasted a million pounds over eight years in his search off the Scottish coast for a sunken submarine, only to find that it was lying at a spot Geller had marked for him on a map. The submarine, it turned out, was not all that was lying. Over a year later, Scanlan-Murphy wrote to Uri from his home in the Peak District saying he had made up the entire story, and that, owing to a "financial reversal," he was planning to sell the story of his "hoax" to the press. "I shall not do anything with the story before Wednesday," he concluded. Whatever he hoped to sell, which was not at all clear, did not find a market. Uri passed the letter to the police, and nothing appeared.

Every post brings letters from people who regard Uri as a guru. A woman in San Francisco changed her name to Uria; another writes to him as "Golden Uri." A Swedish woman blames him for making her pregnant by bending her IUD; a former agent of Uri in Germany was jailed for tax fraud, and called him in New York, demanding Uri teleport him out of prison; an English fan named his daughter Ella after Uri's 1998 novel of that name. "Can you imagine, if I wanted to pursue the idea of being a guru, how much money I could have made then?" Uri says. "I could have been like the Bhagwan. But I've never even been tempted. I'm an entertainer, a catalyst, an enabler, but not a guru."

As such, he still keeps a steady stream of celebrities and politicians flowing through his house. The Israeli defense minister, Yitzhak Mordechai, who has visited, represents one extreme, perhaps, the Duchess of York the other. "She came over to my house with a policewoman one morning, and she really poured out her heart to me. She is very intuitive. I bent a spoon for her and Prince Andrew for their wedding at their request. But, then, I really can't talk about other royalty I have met because it would be a breach of confidence. Fergie wouldn't mind me saying this because she is very much into being positive. She writes down positive phrases. She spent a few hours with me, and she met Natalie and Hanna. We stay in touch via the telephone. I call her occasionally, and try to give her confidence to continue and to shut out all the negative abuse that is thrown at her.

As if to emphasize his commitment to being a strictly earthbound non-guru, Uri has developed a passion for football, but even that gets him into trouble. His support for his local team, Reading, ended in October 1997 in a dispute with the club chairman, who decided to stop giving free tickets to the Geller family in return for their support. In the subsequent season, Reading, who had done quite well in the English First Division during their years of Geller support, even making the play-offs for the premiership, were relegated. Sports commentators continued to laugh at Reading's decline, citing it as a Geller failure, unaware that he had abandoned the club at the start of their disaster season. Uri's reasonable point that it was minor vindication of his powers was somehow never reported. Neither has the fact that the family now supports still more lowly Exeter City, on the basis that Uri believes Daniel Geller had a past life in Exeter.

The strange Glenn Hoddle affair was less of a joke. Hoddle, the England manager, until he was fired in February 1999, is currently suing the *News of the World* newspaper over a claim by Uri that the enigmatic Hoddle visited him two years before the 1998 World Cup, and took part, along with his friend and faith healer, Eileen Drewery, in an exorcism of Uri's "problems" by laying hands on him. Even in the frantic midst of the Cup preparations, Hoddle issued a writ against the newspaper, which is still outstanding. One of the mysteries of the case is that Hoddle said at a widely reported press conference that he had met Geller only once, four years earlier, and had not seen him or had any association with him since. The week after that, the *News of the World* published itemized phone bills, which Shipi had found in the cellar and which seemed to show several calls, including one of thirteen minutes, from Uri's house to Hoddle's. When the libel writ arrived, it did not contest that Hoddle had been to the Geller home, only that he had *taken part* in an exorcism. Hoddle's writ still lay at the time of writing, but had not been pursued in several months.

In matters of health, the Gellers have been lucky to steer clear of tragedy, apart from in one sad instance: the death of what would have been their third child. "We were going to name him Gadi," Uri said, "but he died two months before he should have been born. We let Daniel and Natalie hold him at the hospital because they so wanted a brother. It is interesting. That is something that I totally want to shut away in my mind, not only place it in a box and close the lid, but I also took this box out of my head to send it into space. I don't want to remember, it is just too painful. We have an ultrasound picture of the baby, but we keep it behind a frame. I never thought Hanna and I would grieve so deeply for such a long time. I'm sure Gadi is with my little brothers and sisters, who also weren't born."

The Gellers' is an unusual household, as might be expected. Hanna, as Uri said, "doesn't really want to involve herself with the paranormal world. She prays to God. She wants to keep it very holy, very spiritual, very religious, whereas sometimes, paranormal or psychic phenomena don't go hand in hand with religion. So most of my everyday life and work activities, Shipi knows more about than Hanna."

Although it is possible that Natalie will be as powerful a psychic one day as Uri Geller, many eyes are fixed on Daniel to take after his father. Will he or won't he inherit his father's powers? "He has a very powerful telepathic link with me," Uri told me. When Daniel was six or seven, he developed the odd ability, which he no longer has, to be able to put a day of the week to any date in the future. Daniel says, "When I'm with my father, I feel I may have the power in very small amounts, but if I try to do something alone, it doesn't really work. It's a bit disappointing, but there is an extraordinary connection between us. I think the most amazing thing he ever did was to stop Big Ben. He went out to his gazebo one morning, where he prays, and concentrated very hard, willing it to stop. Later that day, Mum ran screaming from the house. She'd heard on the news that it had stopped, but no one could work out why. Unfortunately, he couldn't prove he'd done it, but I knew because I saw it.

"I never tell people my name straight away because they immediately form an opinion," Daniel continued. "I'd rather just be myself, but it's difficult because my name is Geller and either they're going to say, 'Can you bend something?' or they are going to start rebutting my dad. I was teased at school at first because a lot of the kids thought what my dad did on TV was a trick. It made it harder for me to make friends because there would be a chain reaction. One person would start saying, 'He's a fraud,' and the rest would follow. I found it very hurtful because I couldn't understand why they didn't believe in him. I try to explain, but if they won't listen I just choose to ignore it.

"My father has an incredible aura, a presence that I still find amazing. No matter what anyone says, I get to see the happenings and phenomena and it's fun. I'm never embarrassed by him. When I have exams, he goes out to his gazebo and concentrates very hard and I can usually tell he is helping me. I've always felt different, and sometimes I wouldn't mind being ordinary. I'd quite like to live in a medium-sized house, but my friends love coming over here because we have a tennis court and a swimming pool. They're always asking him to bend spoons. I don't mind, but he can't do too many because it drains his powers."

At the time of writing, Daniel Geller, who is 17, is studying French, German and Biology at A-level, with a view to taking a European Law course at University. He is something of a star pupil at school, and, although he often has to be persuaded to relax and be more self-confident, is marked out by teachers as being extremely bright and diligent—and a particularly outstanding linguist. His sister Natalie, who is 16, has clearly inherited the more flamboyant Geller gene. She is currently in her GCSE year at a theater school in Maidenhead, and is planning to take Theater Studies, Drama and French at A-level. Neither child has any vestige, or so it appears, of their father's psychokinetic ability; Daniel says he has tried but failed to bend spoons—a matter of some relief to him I suspect.

Even after two years of my being close to the family, Hanna Geller remains an enigma. Intensely shy and self-contained, she has never given an interview to the press, or even commented on Uri publicly. The couple finally married in 1991. They felt the children would become increasingly subject to social pressures if their parents remained unmarried. Uri was also keen to marry before his mother and his Hungarian relatives, still in Budapest, became too old. The ceremony was held in Budapest, at the civil register office—which he was delighted to find was on Uri Street. Uri and Hanna wanted to marry in the synagogue where his parents married, but found it was closed for repairs. After the ceremony, with Daniel and Natalie in attendance, the happy couple celebrated in unique style—by going for a run together along the River Danube; Hanna is as keen a fitness fanatic as her husband, and like him looks far younger than her age. After their post-nuptial jog, Uri, Hanna, Daniel, Natalie, Shipi and Margaret joined twenty Hungarian family members at a restaurant in the old city of Pest for dinner, and then returned to Reading to carry on exactly where they left off.

It is evident that Hanna is exceptionally houseproud. She refuses to employ staff to look after their large house, built 40 years ago. Consequently, Hanna is one of the few multimillionaires to be found on her hands and knees doing housework, and cooking magnificent and complicated vegetarian dishes for the family plus a continual stream of visitors. In private, however, one gets the impression that she is the linchpin of the family, and is by no means prepared to tag along with her husband's often eccentric ideas. As Uri's candid, not to say show-off, account makes clear, Hanna went through a lot during Uri's "rock star" years, and there seems to be an implicit understanding that almost as a *quid pro quo*, she is now the single most important person in his life.

Not that this stops Uri at least *having* some fairly original ideas for the family's future. In the summer of 1998, he put the house and its seven riverside acres discreetly up for sale for £7.5 million. "It is the longest I have ever lived anywhere," he explained, "and we all think it's time to move somewhere a little less ostentatious. This has been a phase, and we've done it now. We have talked for a long while about La Jolla, near San Diego, California, which is a very beautiful place. But while the children are still being educated, I think we will stay on the River Thames. Although Daniel and Natalie have American passports, they have been brought up in England and are really English kids." It would seem that Uri's daily, muddy walks along the river with his five dogs are also a factor in his inclination to stay in England. After following this routine since he was in his late thirties, I think Uri finds it hard to imagine himself doing the same on a south California beach with Chico the Chihuahua, Destiny and Medina the Dobermans, and Joker the eighty percent blind wire-haired fox terrier, who is Uri's fifth dog of the same name since he was a boy, and Jon-Jon, the greyhound.

For the family's new, simpler lifestyle, Uri said, he is thinking of buying a plot of land and building a house on it. "There's a company in France which makes revolving houses," he said. "I am talking to them about building us a revolving house that will look like a UFO." An interesting plan, but I suspect Hanna may have a thing or two to say about it on grounds of practicality, as might the trusty Shipi, whose quiet, wry input into the family chemistry can never be underestimated.

Daniel and Natalie's uncle lives in his own house on the estate and, like his sister Hanna, is as private as Uri is public. In his twenties, he was briefly married (to Eldon Byrd's ex-wife, June). He has girlfriends now, but no plans to marry again. "If he does, and decides to start his own business or whatever, I will certainly miss him because he has a great way of protecting me," Uri said. "Remember, it's a family thing. We've been together, and our families have been friends, for over thirty years. It happens a lot in Israel to be united like that. It's the same as in Arabic and oriental cultures, where the family is one unit and you would rather have your family run your business affairs than a stranger. If you let someone else deal with your life, you are bound to fall out."

What Uri would do without Shipi confounds most friends of the family. It had occurred to me that, as Puharich had believed, Shipi was a powerful part of the Geller effect. I asked Uri whether he could perform without Shipi. He was adamant that he could, and subsequent enquiries in Israel confirmed that he had bent metal and read minds for years without Shipi, while he was still a schoolboy. But could he, I asked, bend metal when he was entirely on his own?

Uri blushed for the only time since I had met him. "I am not often on my own," he said, after some thought. "I have built this thing psychologically that I can't act alone. I'm sure I must have bent a spoon on my own once, but I can't think of a moment when I would have had the opportunity, partly it is because I refuse to touch money. I don't have a wallet, I don't carry credit cards. I don't think I've written a check in the past twenty-five years. If I buy something, Hanna pays for it, or Shipi. I have driving licences for everything, even a tank. But I don't drive. Come to think of it, you know, I am exactly like the Queen—except she does drive sometimes."

Chapter 20

Conclusive Proof?

"It still astonishes me after all these years. I'm amazed and transfixed and excited by all these phenomena. I should have got used to it and become blasé, but it grabs me and astounds and puzzles me, although I've done it thousands of times."

Uri Geller

....

At the start of this book I promised that I had come to a conclusion about Uri Geller, and so I have, but I readily admit that, in doing so, I have borrowed some ideas from the people I have interviewed or read along the way. Sometimes, I have appropriated an entire theme; at others, a mere nuance seemed to me to box above its weight.

As a big theme, I loved the analysis at which William A. Tiller, professor emeritus of physics at Stanford University, arrived after seeing an especially on-form Uri at a conference in Seattle. Tiller believes Uri is a "coherer" who "absorbs energy unconsciously given by others, and transforms it into the form needed to produce such spectacular psychoenergetic displays." Tiller became convinced that this explained why Uri was consistently less successful with negative audiences, because with such people Uri is "unable to tap their collective energy fields." Throughout history, Tiller adds, charismatic individuals have been coherers and had a great effect on crowds of people.

A small point made by the Los Angeles criminal attorney Bob Brooks, who was at school in Cyprus with Uri but has only come to take his powers seriously in adulthood, also swayed my thinking. Brooks said he had been thinking of not telling me about it, in case I took it as a damning point but trusted that I would understand its importance, as well as its lack of importance. "Uri was very good with his hands," Brooks said. "He once took me round the school field and picked pockets. He would tap the boy on the shoulder and say, 'You just dropped that.' I think it was just a phase, like so many little boys go through. It may have been for a week, or just a single afternoon. I most certainly don't think it's a big, dark, indicting secret that explains everything but, on the other hand, he was darned good at it." Brooks's point was a molecule rather than a whole chromosome, yet it persuaded me that Uri was not as innocent of the manual dexterity required to be capable of sleight-of-hand as he has sometimes suggested. Did he for a few silly moments, aged eleven, harness some of that highly developed, feral psychic power that I believe criminals use for malevolent ends? I have always marvelled at the kind of sixth sense that must be needed for many non-violent, "intelligent" crimes.

The third interviewee who influenced my thinking was Roger Crosthwaite, the Anglo-Catholic priest and recent award-winning close-up magician in Worthing, on the south coast of England. "I know Uri well and I think he is a very fine man," he said. "I don't go so far as to endorse his paranormal abilities, although I am very interested in quantum theory. I also do not dismiss the idea of miracles—and I think there are definitely some strange, unanswered questions about Uri. I was at his house once, and I looked him straight in the eye and asked him if he ever used trickery, even to enhance his effects. He said he had never, ever used trickery in the laboratory or in scientific testing, and I believe he is telling the truth." I do too. Like a lot of Jews, Uri is rather fond of Catholics—the more so, in his case, thanks to the admiration he had for many of the priests at Terra Santa College in Cyprus; he is too superstitious, I believe, to lie to a priest. As for the implication in what Uri told Crosthwaite that he might have cheated *outside* the laboratory, I return to one of my own central themes: that all sorts of professionals have a few tricks of the trade for bad days, and that Diego Maradona really could play football despite the odd handball into goal. Why would Uri never admit to this ability to manipulate things to look more psychic than they are? For the same reason that most of us have probably stolen something but wouldn't admit to it. You can probe too deeply into someone's soul. The point is that Uri Geller is no swindler; everything points to the fundamental truth that he can do what he says he can, and that is what matters.

Another point that swayed me was made over lunch by Matthew Manning, the prominent British psychic healer. As a teenager Manning, forty-three, was one of the Geller-influenced young metal-benders. At home in Cambridge, he saw Uri on TV, and discovered he could do the same—with ease. He was also the victim of a powerful poltergeist, which nearly succeeded in getting him expelled from his boarding school. "I believe whatever Uri and I have has nothing to do with little green men from outer space, but originates from way back, when we were in caves and needed psychic powers for survival," Matthew said. I had often thought Uri is simply a more highly evolved being than most of us; it had never previously struck me that he could be a genetic throwback. Matthew felt sad that Uri would be remembered principally for bending spoons, and that he should have developed his healing powers, as Manning has. On the other hand, he had an interesting answer to one of the most pervasive criticisms of Geller: his fixation on tabloid publicity.

Many times over the past two years Uri has gravely presented me with a cutting from some American supermarket tabloid as if it were a shard of parchment from the Dead Sea Scrolls. He seems to have no idea that middle-class people are more influenced, on the whole, by more elevated journalism. Uri's flashiness is one of the bases of what I see as New Age criticism of him: he can't be real because he's not spiritual enough; if he has accidentally been given spiritual powers, he is abusing them by using them for self-enrichment. Manning has concentrated his publicity fire on the broadsheet press, and works as a healer. Yet it was he who made the point that, in doing so, he is acting in accord with his own middle-class origins. He credits Uri with having, as a result of his working-class background, made it his mission—perhaps subconsciously—to help regular, working people, tabloid readers if you like, to develop a spiritual awareness, to be aware that there is more out there than working, sleeping and eating. It may be that Uri uses only one implement out of the psychic kitchen but, in doing so, he has propagandized on behalf of the spiritual life much more effectively than the more exclusive New Agers, whom tabloid readers would no doubt scoff at. It should never be forgotten that a lot of the antipathy to Uri Geller has stemmed from pure snobbery, some even tinged with a touch of anti-Semitism, I suspect. It is an irony not lost on Matthew Manning, who has also made a fine living from psychic gifts, that because he is the public-school-educated son of an architect, because he instinctively knows the ways of the British middle class, he is mostly immune from criticism. Oddly enough, he dresses more flashily than Uri—yet attracts no opprobrium for doing so.

Finally Guy Bavli made a point, which impressed me and was later repeated by other Israelis, including the novelist Ephraim Kishon. His argument was that in Europe and America people were obsessed with whether or not Uri Geller had genuinely paranormal abilities when perhaps it would be far more exciting if he was really a magician. There is no doubt that a con on such a scale *would* be the "crime" of the century. And a book of how he did his tricks, with step-by-step instructions for fooling the world, would surely be one of the best sellers of all time. Yet Uri continues to insist he is psychic.

As far as my view on magicians in general and their take on Uri Geller is concerned, I have come to believe that conjuring makes people a little arrogant, from the moment they realize the power of tricks over others. I have seen for myself, by learning some tricks from books and trying a couple of the basic mentalist ruses Marcello Truzzi told me about, the awestruck looks when something "impossible" is achieved by deceit. It is no wonder to me that women, who have less propensity to arrogance than men, are almost never interested in magic or magicianship. I suspect the magicianly cockiness makes conjurers a little like doctors, who are often susceptible to disease but simultaneously not remotely self-aware. I have a feeling that magicians, by virtue of spending their lives creating illusions, become incapable of believing that they too can labor under one. They feel invulnerable in their knowledge of sleight-of-hand. Of late, Uri has become increasingly friendly with magicians. I wonder if this is because he no longer cares how he is regarded. Because of the doubt over what he is, he exists in a no man's land, halfway between mystic and magician. It suits him to be neither, since then he has no responsibility to be anything. The only thing which would require him to "confess" would be if *everything* was fake, and always had been. And what a confession that would be!

Scientists have surprised me throughout this project by being far more open-minded and, if you like, spiritual, than I had imagined. I gained the impression that, as a profession, they have come on a little since Hermann von Helmholtz, the nineteenth-century physicist, announced: "Neither the testimony of all the Fellows of the Royal Society, nor even the evidence of my own senses, would lead me to believe in the transmission of thought from one person to another independently of the recognized channels of sense." I have found that many are open to accepting the existence of untestable hypotheses. In 1998, *Newsweek* Magazine noted this trend too, in a wide-ranging cover story on how more and more scientists were turning away from empiricism and toward more supernatural explanations for the meaning of life. Medical doctors, too, are not all like the scoffers who, in years past, laughed at people like Joseph Lister. In 1865, Lister, professor of surgery at Glasgow, pioneered the use of carbolic acid as an antiseptic against the microbes in the air which

Louis Pasteur had identified. The concept was met with derision and hostility by doctors and nurses. Until then, it was assumed that inflammation produced microbes, not the other way round. According to a contemporary account, a surgeon at St. Bartholomew's Hospital could always raise a laugh by telling anyone who came into the operating room to shut the door swiftly "in case one of Mr. Lister's microbes should come in." It was almost impossible to convince highly educated doctors that tiny objects 0.001mm in diameter and floating in the air could cause septicemia. The idea was too absurd.

The professional skeptics have seemed to me more dogmatic than the bulk of scientists. I suspect that a hundred years from now, the skeptics will seem in retrospect like superstitious primitives who missed the big picture, rather than Prometheus-like bringers of light in an age of gathering paranormal darkness. How will Uri Geller seem a hundred years hence? Perhaps like Mesmer, who accidentally discovered something and slightly misattributed the reasons for it. I do not think he will be seen as a guru. In his dark 1998 novel, *Ella*, Uri gave a hint of how, with the freedom of a novel, he sees himself. Although it concerned a female psychic in Bristol, the novel echoes Uri's own life closely. Ella, having spent her life being alternately celebrated, manipulated and damned because of her powers, finally walks up Mount Sinai on her birthday and jumps off, apparently to fly like an angel. It is left to the reader's imagination to extrapolate that she has turned into a celestial being. If it should turn out in the future that Uri was, indeed, a Jesus figure, I should be a little surprised, but delighted. It will have meant, for one thing, that I have accidentally written the New Testament.

At the end of *Ella*, the angelic transformation that accompanies her death is captured for the first time on video. This gives a measure of Uri's preoccupation with the single most striking weakness in his entire case for being a real psychic: the fact that the phenomenon of metal bending *on its own*, the extraordinary phenomenon which I witnessed with my children at the start of this adventure—and to which hundreds of others of the highest standing swear—has never been filmed.

There are many possible reasons for this, from the obvious—that all of us are deluded—to the far out, as represented by one of Uri's own theories. He believes it is proof that his powers are controlled by some outside force or intelligence, and that this power does not yet wish the human race to know for sure that something as improbable as metal-bending on its own can occur. There is little doubt that if the effect were videoed, it would merely cause a new outbreak of controversy over whether the video was fake. It is hard to believe that if he had succeeded spectacularly on the Johnny Carson show in 1973, Uri Geller would have been accepted unanimously as real. So perhaps there is some grand design involved in keeping the phenomenon happening only when there is no camera rolling; I only wonder if the design is located in Uri's head, and that it is he who subconsciously controls who gets to see metal bending and who does not. There is another point: Uri has an uncanny effect on cameras. John Randall, a professional cameraman and sound recordist in London, was among many in the same job who attest to Uri sending cameras into spasm. (In 1998 after Randall had filmed Uri for a TV appearance, he told me that "We were packing up the Transit, and the producer came down and said, 'Hey, look at this. Uri has done this spoon.' We saw there was a little kink in it, but on the way back, heading down the A40, the spoon was on the front seat of the van and it literally went to about forty degrees. That was, well, spooky. It was by itself, sitting on the front seat of the van. No one was touching it. We actually saw it moving.")

In the end you have to ask if it is *really* plausible that Uri Geller could have faked it for nearly fifty years—repeating the same simple effect thousands of times, in front of children, teachers, his own family, his wife's family, his best friend and business partner of thirty years' standing, magicians, secret agents, girlfriends, soldiers, scientists, conjurers, journalists, airline pilots, lawyers, agents, sportsmen, politicians, diplomats, in front of TV cameras on live shows, at parties, in restaurants, again and again. And if he *had* faked the whole thing, there is another major factor to take into account: the great illusionists and illusionist-query-psychics of the past, the Houdinis, the D. D. Homes, were performing in dimly lit Victorian parlors and theaters, in front of tiny audiences. Uri does it in the jet age, in front of hundreds of thousands more people, all over the world and under the scrutiny of TV cameras, which must surely be dozens of times more revealing than gaslight.

For two years I have considered the possibilities for what I saw when my spoon bent in my son's hand, and am still sure that it happened. The evidence for Uri Geller, I submit, is utterly compelling, if not completely conclusive. To be pedantic for a moment, I would have to argue that, in the absence of any proof of psychic powers from, say The Royal Society, Uri Geller has to go down as the greatest magician of all time. Plenty of highly qualified people certainly believe so. On the other hand, for me, Occam's Razor, the much hallowed belief that, all things being equal, the simplest explanation is always the most likely, suggests that rather than being the most brilliant illusionist ever, Uri Geller may merely be paranormal.

Index

Margolis, Jonathan.
Uri Geller.

$24.95